THE
SINEWS
OF
POWER

THE
SINEWS
OF
POWER

War, Money and the English State,
1688 – 1783

JOHN BREWER

HARVARD UNIVERSITY PRESS
CAMBRIDGE, MASSACHUSETTS

First Harvard University Press paperback edition, 1990

This edition is published by arrangement
with Alfred A. Knopf, Inc.

Library of Congress Cataloging-in-Publication Data
Brewer, John, 1947–
The sinews of power: war, money, and the English state, 1688–1783
John Brewer.—1st Harvard University pbk. ed.
p.   cm.
Originally published: London: Century Hutchinson, 1988.
Includes bibliographical references.
ISBN 0–674–80930–0
1. Great Britain—Politics and government—18th century.
2. Great Britain—Politics and government—1689–1702.
3. Great Britain—History, Military—18th century.
4. Great Britain—Economic conditions—18th century.   I. Title.
DA480.B74   1990
941.07–dc20   90–4414
CIP

'The sinews of War are infinite money.'
Cicero, *Orationes Philippicae*

'By our constitution the crown [is] . . . the steward
of all the Publick Money.'
The Present State of the National Debt (1740)

'All taxes of what nature soever, are paid in every kingdom with a bad grace.'
Thomas Mortimer, *The Elements of Politics, Commerce and Finances* (1772)

'The Security of our Liberties are [*sic*] not in the Laws but by the Purse
being in the Hands of the People.'
Carteret, BL Add. Mss 35875 f. 169

CONTENTS

LIST OF TABLES

LIST OF FIGURES

PREFACE

'Nothing is certain in this life, except death and taxes.'
Benjamin Franklin.

This book is about the growing powers of central government in a period more famous for its praise of liberty. It is a study of the most important changes in British government between the reforms of the Tudors and the major administrative reconstruction of the first half of the nineteenth century. But, unlike those administrative innovations, the changes of the late seventeenth and eighteenth centuries were concerned not with domestic regulation but with enhancing the government's ability to wage war. My subject is not, however, war as such. I am first and foremost interested in investigating the effects – on government, politics and society – of Britain's transformation into a major international power.

Much of this book is therefore concerned with such technical matters as military and civilian administration, taxation and public finances. These are topics with which readers are often unfamiliar and which, despite some outstanding detailed studies, are rarely incorporated into histories of the Stuarts and Hanoverians. My aim is to remedy this omission: to put finance, administration and war at the centre stage of the drama – where they rightly belong – without elbowing other performers into the wings. I have tried to write about these complex and sometimes arcane matters in as accessible a manner as possible, and I trust the account is not obscure, for this book is primarily intended not for those administrative, military and financial historians who will already be familiar with many of the particularities of the argument which follows – though I hope they will find matter of interest to them – but for readers who, while I am sure they can certainly tell a whig from a tory may not have studied the distinction between a customs duty and an excise.

I have had to rely heavily on the work of a large number of scholars whose researches into the fields of finance, military affairs and administration have delved much deeper than my own. I would especially like to thank Peter Dickson and Daniel Baugh, not merely for their brilliant and inspiring published work, but for their kindness in reading part of this manuscript. Their criticism and painstaking help on matters of finance and the navy have proved invaluable. Many other friends and colleagues – Bernard Bailyn, John Beattie, Bob Brenner, Linda Colley, Robert Culpin (the only bureaucrat to read the manuscript), Vivien Dietz, John Dinwiddy, Tom Ertman, John A. Hall, Peter Hall, Joanna Innes, Margaret Levi, Wallace MacCaffrey, Roy Porter, Nick Rogers, Simon Schama, Lawrence Stone, John Styles, Kathleen Wilson – read and commented on earlier drafts of some or all of the chapters. I have also benefited from the guidance and comments of David Bien, Mike Collinge, Geoff Eley, Geoffrey Holmes, Eckhart Hellmuth, Clyve Jones, Charles Maier, Patrick O'Brien, David Sacks, Theda Skocpol and Charles Tilly. The staff at the History of Parliament Trust, notably Eveline Cruickshanks and David Hayton have, as always, been extremely kind – offering not only their exceptional expertise on eighteenth-century politics, but access to their files and transcripts. Graham Smith, at the Customs and Excise Library at King's Beam House, provided aid and advice as well as excise lore. Tim Wales acted as research assistant on some of the more difficult excise material. Nancy Koehn played a vital role in the completion of this work, acting as researcher, editor and exceptional organizer of someone whose absence of system and good order she bore with unflagging good cheer. Jan Albers, Lee Davison, Marcia Wagner Levinson and Paul Monod all provided me with useful references. Claire L'Enfant proved that editors can be friends even when an author's tardiness requires the patience of Job. The contribution of Stella Tillyard is beyond even my hyperbolic powers of description.

One of the pleasures of scholarship is cooperation with colleagues, and one of its necessities is funding. I have been fortunate to have received support for this project from the National Endowment of the Humanities, who funded a year's research in England in 1983-4, from Harvard University, the American Philosophical Society and from the University of California in Los Angeles.

This book is dedicated to three historians and friends. Simon Schama, who, more than anyone else, made my years at Harvard a pleasure I shall never forget; and Joanna Innes and John Styles, whose kindness, support and example have brought me back to England year after year.

INTRODUCTION

'The hand that signed the paper felled a city;
Five sovereign fingers taxed the breath,
Doubled the globe of dead and halved a country;
These five kings did a King to death.'

Dylan Thomas, *Collected Poems, 1934–1952*

From its modest beginnings as a peripheral power – a minor, infrequent almost inconsequential participant in the great wars that ravaged sixteenth and seventeenth-century Europe – Britain emerged in the late seventeenth and early eighteenth centuries as the military *Wunderkind* of the age. Dutch admirals learnt to fear and then admire its navies, French generals reluctantly conferred respect on its officers and men, and Spanish governors trembled for the safety of their colonies and the sanctity of their trade. European armies, most notably those of Austria, Prussia and the minor German states, marched if not to the beat of British drums then to the colour of English money. Under the early Stuarts England had cut a puny military figure; by the reign of George III Britain had become one of the heaviest weights in the balance of power in Europe. She had also acquired an empire of ample proportions and prodigious wealth. New England merchants, Southern planters, Caribbean slaves and Indian sepoys were subject to her authority. No sea was safe from British traders; even the Pacific and the Orient were beginning to feel the British presence. Thornhill's Painted Hall at the Naval Hospital at Greenwich (1717–25), with its extravagant depiction of Britain's military power, contained its share of wish fulfilment, but the allegorical presence of the four continents was not misleading: Britain was on the threshold of becoming a transcontinental power.

The extent of this transformation depends, of course, on the extent of the period one chooses. The change from the 1660s to the 1760s seems greater than those either from the 1650s to the 1750s or from the 1680s to the 1780s. The loss of the first British empire was even swifter than its acquisition. But we need to think not in decades but in larger epochs. The transformation of Britain into a major power in two or three generations is all the more striking when compared to the strategic and military history of the previous two hundred years. Ponder the question of how many English victories over continental powers you can name between the battles of Agincourt (1415) and

Blenheim (1704). The most famous English soldier in the era between Henry
v and Cromwell, Sir Philip Sidney, died at Zutphen (1586) in a futile action
during a disastrous campaign. Nor will the obvious naval victories compensate
for the poor showing of the nation's armies. Before the late seventeenth
century spectacular naval victories never amounted to control of the oceans.
Drake may have singed the King of Spain's beard, but he was incapable of
cutting his throat. Aptly enough the *Sovereign of the Seas*, the pride of the
seventeenth-century royal navy, had to be reduced in size because her three
decks made her so unmanageable. Her effectiveness could not equal her preten-
sions. Only in 1763 did Britannia truly rule the waves, and by then she also
controlled a lot more land.

There are several ways in which to explain this remarkable achievement.
The most popular is implicitly patriotic and explicitly military, emphasizing
the collective qualities of British redcoats and Jack Tars and the individual
heroism of their leaders. To the former are normally ascribed those saturnine
and English qualities of doggedness, tight-lipped determination and obduracy
(though for some reason sailors are usually depicted as much less grim than
soldiers), while to their officers are reserved those mercurial qualities of quick-
wittedness, imagination and energy. Both, in their due proportion, are deemed
valiant and brave. Seen in this light the history of Britain's military and
strategic prowess resembles a gallery of eighteenth-century portraits in which
the subjects, successful army and naval officers dressed in military regalia and
touting swords, telescopes, maps and charts, occupy the foreground, while
in the distance we observe some violent action fought by undifferentiated
humankind. Marlborough, Cobham, Cumberland, Wolfe, Hawke, Anson,
Vernon, Hervey and Rodney provide an exhibition of heroes, many of whom
command more admiration today than they did in their own lifetimes.

Such an approach is not without its merits. For, though its rhetoric sometimes smacks of the *Boys' Own Paper* and tales of derring-do, it usually attends
to the details of warfare – tactics and the conduct of battles – which, together
with those quirks of fate which fascinated Tolstoy and infuriated Clausewitz,
make up the substance of war and so often determine its outcome. Yet such
accounts often lack a larger context. They are seen as part of the history of
'battles', or, in a more expansive version, of strategy, but remain disconcert-
ingly separate from the overall history of a particular era.

A second interpretation of Britain's rise to power rejects the sanguinary
glamour of battles and tactics, preferring to emphasize the economic and
commercial roots of Britain's strategic advantage. There are at least two
versions of the argument that Britain's aggrandizement was impelled by the
powerful forces of commercial capitalism, the desire to increase profits and
accumulate wealth. One is discreetly celebratory, the other overtly critical.
The former points to Britain's commercial prowess and economic growth: the
increase in output, the strength of her agricultural base, the abilities of overseas
traders, the skills of her merchant marine and the wealth of her people. The

latter draws our attention to the victims of British expansion: the costs incurred
by the slaves, indentured servants and native peoples whose fate was inextricably bound up with the acquisition of new lands and the development of
commodity markets.

At their worst these histories invoke 'the invisible hand' of the market as
the explanation for all forms of behaviour, neglecting the complexities of
culture and power. In their pessimistic version they can also reduce economic
relations to an unmediated account of oppression and resistance. But the
insights they offer are salutary. They remind us of the global context of
Britain's newly acquired status and of the vital part – epitomized by the
privatized imperialism of the East India Company – played by private initiative
in the growth of wealth and empire. They underline the importance of economic and social resources – capital and labour, wealth and manpower – in
enabling nations to become great powers. And some of this literature,
especially the most eloquent and passionate writings, point to the stark contrast
between the view from the metropolis and from its periphery. Englishmen
may have prided themselves on their liberties and the rule of law, and praised
the growth of commerce as a civilizing process, but authority was exercised
very differently – often brutally and barbarously – in those distant lands
and over those subject peoples which occupied the frontiers of commercial
development.

Military heroics, economic growth and the global expansion of British
enterprise all contributed to the changing international status of Britain. But
to a very large degree they were accompanied by and depended upon a number
of altogether less dramatic developments. Victory in battle relied in the first
instance upon an adequate supply of men and munitions, which, in turn,
depended upon sufficient money and proper organization – what modern
military men call 'logistics' and sociologists dub 'infrastructure'. As seventeenth and eighteenth-century commentators knew, no amount of commercial
skill, merchant shipping or national prosperity could secure the domination
of trade routes or the protection of bases and colonies. These required troops
and a navy, which in turn, required money and proper organization. Otherwise Britain might have fallen victim of what was recognized in the eighteenth
century as the Dutch disease, a malady that prevented a nation enjoying
unequalled individual prosperity and extraordinary commercial sophistication
from remaining a state of great influence and power.[1] Substantial economic
resources were necessary to acquire the status of a major power; they were
not, however, enough. Great states required both the economic wherewithal
and the organizational means to deploy resources in the cause of national
aggrandizement.

To illuminate the accomplishment of generals and admirals and cast light
on the economy and commerce is, perhaps, to obscure or put unnecessarily
into the shade those changes in government which made Britain's success
possible. It is the aim of the following chapters to expose the hidden sinews

which animated the British body politic, rendering it capable of those feats of strength which so impressed its allies and enemies. Though my account is very much concerned with war, it deals with bookkeeping not battles, with ink-stained fingers rather than bloody arms. Its focus is upon administration, on logistics and, above all, on the raising of money. Its heroes, if any there are, are clerks in offices. And its perspective is neither global nor from the periphery, but from Whitehall and Westminster, very much at the centre of the core.

Administrations thrive on routine. They abhor the stock in trade of the dramatist and the historian – change, disruption, violent action – aspiring to a ubiquity of sameness. Theirs is not only the quotidian: each day should be the same. But every administration creates friction in its attempt to impose order and structure on the entropic enterprise of collaborative human endeavour. It is precisely this tension between the desire for order and routine and the actualities of public conduct that creates the drama and conflict administrations are so eager to contain. The struggle for power and control may not have been fought out in the bright, sanguinary colours of battle nor on the large canvas of several continents but, no matter how contained or muted it might appear, its effects were far-reaching. The ability of government administrators to establish the routine by which revenues were collected, money raised and supply requisitioned could make the difference between victory and humiliation.

At the seat of dullness were the clerks. These pale and shadowy figures have never received their due. The eighteenth century saw an unprecedented expansion in the number of transcribers, copyists and record-keepers. A quick glance at the business accounts, financial records and government documents of this period attests to the prodigies of penmanship performed by men and women unaided by any mechanical means of duplication. Yet these clerks have no history. No group can ever have written so much and yet remained so anonymous. This is partly attributable to the difficulties of reconstructing their lives, but it is also the consequence of snobbery. The English revere the ownership of land and the tasks of manual labour; they have little time for pen-pushers, either clerical or intellectual.

What the clerks transcribed in the service of government – tax accounts, inventories of supplies, financial statutes, tables of revenue and trade, rules governing the borrowing of money and the purchase of equipment and supplies – is also not immediately accessible, for it requires a certain amount of technical knowledge. Modern readers, living in the era of the small investor and of media ever-attendant to the fate of stock-markets and rates of exchange, may have a better grasp of public and private finance than those eighteenth-century back-bench MPs who seemed incapable of understanding any money matter which could not be compared to the running of a landed estate. But they nevertheless confront a system, if such it can be called, whose technical complexities were considerable and whose practices, though superficially similar to those of today, had their own distinctive logic.

Yet, for all these difficulties of tedium and technicalities (problems I hope to dispel), the chief reason why financiers and administrators have not received their fair share of attention, except in the most technical of scholarship, is because their importance does not accord with the conventional wisdom about the English/British state. It has long been a source of self-congratulation to the British liberal tradition that Britain was wise and politic enough to avoid the enormities of a 'strong state'. This view could scarcely be more fashionable in the present political climate, which seems intent on repudiating the political objectives and dismantling the administrative apparatus of the post-1945 era. Seen from the liberal perspective, the state intervention that was typical of British politics between 1945 and 1979 looks like a temporary diversion from the mainstream of the British political tradition. The eighteenth century, on the other hand, exemplifies the weakness of central government. It is portrayed as a period when the powers of central government were devolved on the localities and diluted by a spoils system which provided income and office for the scions of the landed classes.

But there is another picture we can paint of the same era, the one depicted in this book. The late seventeenth and eighteenth centuries saw an astonishing transformation in British government, one which put muscle on the bones of the British body politic, increasing its endurance, strength and reach. Britain was able to shoulder an ever-more ponderous burden of military commitments thanks to a radical increase in taxation, the development of public deficit finance (a national debt) on an unprecedented scale, and the growth of a sizable public adminstration devoted to organizing the fiscal and military activities of the state. As a result the state cut a substantial figure, becoming the largest single actor in the economy. This was no minor adjustment in the scope and priorities of government; it was a major commitment of resources. Taxes rose to levels as high as any of those in Europe, matching those of many modern, underdeveloped states. Borrowing reached such heights that if eighteenth-century Britain had gone to the modern International Monetary Fund for a loan it would certainly have been shown the door. The creation of what I call 'the fiscal–military state' was the most important transformation in English government between the domestic reforms of the Tudors and the major administrative changes in the first half of the nineteenth century.

How are we to reconcile this view of an exceptionally active state with the liberal interpretation? Or are the two positions entirely incompatible? We should first notice that we are discussing two rather different aspects of government. States are Janus-faced: they look in, to the societies they rule, and out, to those other states with which they are so often locked in conflict. In the former instance the business of the state is usually that of maintaining public order and exercising public justice ('law and order'); government also probably takes responsibility for various forms of economic and social regulation. In the latter case, states compete with each other, employing either the peaceful means of diplomacy or the violent means of war. The liberal focus on the British state has resolutely concentrated its gaze on relations with the domestic polity. I want to draw attention to the state's international role, to its actions as a military and diplomatic power.

Perhaps, then, this is the answer to our conundrum. The British government was able to act effectively against its international enemies but was weak in its dealings with its own subjects. This dichotomy is neat, but raises more questions than it answers.

Political commentators in early modern Europe were haunted by the fear that changes in the character of warfare, particularly the emergence of large standing armies controlled by rulers, would enable monarchs and autocrats not only to subjugate their foes but to enslave their subjects. Liberty, and the institutions which guaranteed such freedoms, notably parliaments and estates, could be swept away by brute force. Clearly seventeenth-century analysts – rather like twentieth-century sociologists – were sceptical of the view that a state's international standing and activities could be sharply separated from its power over civil society. They were right to be sceptical. Admittedly, before the mid-seventeenth century the chief beneficiaries of the growth of standing armies were not rulers but private entrepreneurs: money-lending and tax-gathering syndicates, military enterprisers who specialized in raising and leading troops. It was also possible to wage war by using conquest and tribute rather than domestic resources to fund hostilities. But by the mid-seventeenth century rulers were gaining control of the forces that marched in their name, and self-sustaining warfare – the technique used by the Swedes in the seventeenth century and the Prussians in the eighteenth – was increasingly recognized as a hazardous, short-term solution because it could brook no check or set-back. In the last resort states had to depend on domestic resources, in the form of money and men, and these were increasing under the direct control of monarchs and rulers.

The British were no exception. Indeed, judged by the criteria of the ability to take pounds out of people's pockets and to put soldiers in the field and sailors on the high seas, Britain was one of Europe's most powerful states, one which had acquired prodigious powers over its subjects. Whatever the situation when it came to the administration of law and order, in the fiscal-military sphere the state gained a hold as never before. This grip did not, however, become the stranglehold of autocracy, which raises, of course, the question of why Britain was able to enjoy the fruits of military prowess without the misfortunes of a *dirigiste* or despotic regime.

Before being seduced into that orgy of self-congratulation to which British historians are prone, we need to enter at least one qualification to the view that the British regime, for all its military effectiveness, was characterized by lightness of touch. The heavy-handedness of British rule increased the farther it extended beyond the metropolis. This may seem paradoxical, for British authority was much weaker outside England than within it. But it was for precisely this reason that the formal powers of British rule were so much greater farther afield. Coercive powers were required where tacit compliance was less assured. Subjects' rights were not the same on the banks of the Ohio, in Spanish Town or Dublin Castle as they were in London.

Yet, even in the metropolis, it was felt that liberties were under threat. Though the liberal view characterizes the eighteenth-century British state as conspicuous for its absence, this was not what most eighteenth-century commentators believed. They were obsessed by its growing presence. This anxiety is easy to understand. In the aftermath of the Glorious Revolution of 1688 the balance of political forces shifted decisively against those who had opposed or sought to limit Britain's role in international conflict. Britain plunged into a major, protracted struggle with Louis XIV's France.

The proponents of small government and limited warfare did not, however, surrender without a fight. On the contrary, they dug themselves in for a long struggle and, protected by the well-built fortifications of English constitutionalism, were able to conduct an effective war of containment. They fought to restrict the domestic effects of the fiscal–military state. And, although theirs was necessarily only a rearguard action, they enjoyed some success. The powers of the army over the civilian population were severely restricted, efforts to use civilian officers as a general 'police' rather than as tax gatherers were checked, and the bureaucracy's growth limited to those circumstances necessary for its successful operation.

The intensity of the struggle over the British state – about how it should be structured and what it should be allowed to do – is the most eloquent testimony that government had indeed undergone a radical transformation. But the protestations of those who opposed standing armies and big government were more than the mere symptoms of an important change; they became an integral part of Britain's institutional transformation. The war against the state helped to shape the changing contours of government: limited its scope, restricted its ambit and, through parliamentary scrutiny, rendered its institutions both more public and accountable.

Yet, paradoxically, this success made the fiscal–military state stronger rather than weaker, more effective rather than more impotent. Public scrutiny reduced peculation, parliamentary consent lent greater legitimacy to government action. Limited in scope, the state's powers were nevertheless exercised with telling effect.

This irony can best be understood if we reflect on what tend to be our rather naive and uncritical assumptions about what is meant by a 'strong' or 'weak' state. Too often strength is equated with size. But a large state apparatus is no necessary indication of a government's ability to perform such tasks as the collection of revenue or the maintenance of public order. Indeed, the opposite may prove true. In the hive that was the early modern European state there were often as many drones as workers; frequently as many sinecures as efficient offices. In short, big government is not always effective government.

A second solecism is that which fails to distinguish between what a state is entitled to do and what it can actually accomplish. To use the terminology of one distinguished social scientist, a regime may be strong in 'despotic power', entitled to dispense with its subjects' goods and liberties without legal restraint, but it may be weak in 'infrastructural power', lacking the organization to put its despotic power into effect. Conversely, a state may be weak in 'despotic power' with strict limits on what it is entitled to do, but it may be strong on 'infrastructural power' capable of performing its limited tasks to telling effect.[2]

To this distinction we need to add a consideration of the question of authority. The effective exercise of power is never merely a matter of logistics, a question of whether or not a state has the requisite bureaucracy or military cadres. States are not just centres of power; they are also sources of authority whose effectiveness depends on the degree of legitimacy that both regimes and their actions are able to command. Broadly speaking the less legitimacy, the greater the 'friction' produced by the conduct of the state and the more resources it has to devote to achieve the same effect.

The British fiscal–military state, as it emerged from the political and military battles that marked the struggle with Louis XIV, lacked many of the features we normally associate with a 'strong state', yet therein lay its effectiveness. The constraints on power meant that when it was exercised, it was exercised fully. As long as the fiscal–military state did not cross the bulwarks erected to protect civil society from militarization it was given its due. Yet it was watched with perpetual vigilance by those who, no matter how much they lauded its effectiveness against foreign foes, were deeply afraid of its intrusion into civil society.

The desire to restrict the political and military effects of war on the English polity, together with the almost total absence of hostilities on English soil, can give the impression that eighteenth-century wars were of little domestic consequence. Military action, after all, occurred far away, beyond the horizon: in continental Europe (where foreign soldiers fought and died on Britain's behalf), in the colonies and on the quarterdecks of British battleships. Most of the military action was out of sight. It was not, however, out of mind. For the effects of war were never purely strategic, nor were they confined to the scene of battle. They were felt on the home front, particularly on the economy.

War was an economic as well as military activity: its causes, conduct and consequences as much a matter of money as martial prowess. Nowhere in eighteenth-century Europe was this better understood than in Britain. As Casanova, visiting London shortly after the Seven Years War, discovered in his conversations with Augustus Hervey, the captor of Havana, the British viewed war as far more than a matter of honour. It was also a question of property and profit. The progress of hostilities was followed by many members of the public with an assiduity worthy of Tristram Shandy's Uncle Toby, but their interest was not in tactics or siege warfare but in the economic repercussions of war.

These were difficult to measure then and remain so today. Nevertheless most eighteenth-century commentators were sure that fluctuations in the fortunes of war and the conduct of peace affected the everyday conduct of economic life. Similarly, they argued that the longer-term changes in the nature of government – the emergence of the fiscal–military state – had altered the balance of social forces in Britain by penalizing the landed classes, creating a new class of financier and laying a heavy burden of taxes on the ordinary consumer. For more than a generation the state was seen as one of the major agents of social and economic change.

These developments were not watched idly by interested parties. Changes in government produced new organizations in society at large. Special interest groups were formed. These new organisms, the offspring of a new environment created by an expanding state, sought to flourish, in evolutionary fashion, at the expense of other new species. Lobbies, trade organizations, groups of merchants and financiers fought or combined with one another to take advantage of the protection afforded by the greatest of economic creatures, the state. They struggled for access to the corridors of power, for information that would enable them to thwart, create or affect policy, and for the support of those parliamentarians who could hold the fiscal juggernaut in check. As their tactics grew more sophisticated they learned to transcend their sectionalism and to appeal beyond their self-interested ranks to the public at large. By the second half of the eighteenth century some of them had learned the value of parasitism, making the state, as Adam Smith pointed out, their host if not their hostage.

In this, narrowly defined commercial and trading interests were following a pattern that can be observed throughout the eighteenth century. When the fiscal–military state first emerged it enjoyed considerable autonomy and excited much hostility and confusion. But gradually a variety of social groups and interests reached an accommodation with it. Some, notably the 'landed interest', were much more successful than others in taking advantage of new circumstances, but none could afford the luxury of ignoring the remarkable changes in the British state which were the early eighteenth century's most distinctive feature.

The account that follows is divided into five sections. The first examines the English/British state prior to 1688.[3] Part II anatomizes the sinews of power after the Glorious Revolution, examining military organization, money-raising and administration. In Part III I examine the political crisis that gave birth to the fiscal–military state. Part IV looks at the effect of the state on both the material circumstances and attitudes of its subjects. And in the final section, Part V, I assess the nature of some of the responses to the changing character of government. Taken as a whole, this analysis offers one (but by no means the only) framework within which the late Stuart and Georgian polity can be understood.

I

BEFORE THE REVOLUTION:
THE ENGLISH STATE IN THE MEDIEVAL AND EARLY MODERN ERAS

To understand the particular form that the fiscal–military state assumed in England after the Glorious Revolution we need to examine not only the proximate circumstances of 1688 but also the long-term evolution of the English state before its transformation under William and Mary. Though the fiscal–military state emerged as a result of a particular political crisis, it had to exploit and accommodate itself to existing institutions. These, in turn, owed their distinctive configuration to three earlier developments in the English state: its centralization in the period between the tenth and thirteenth centuries; its escape from involvement in the major international conflicts that occurred in Europe between the mid-fifteenth and late seventeenth centuries; and its success in avoiding the development of a substantial administration populated by venal office-holders.

Early Centralization

Though commentators on the early modern English state have often emphasized its weakness, medieval historians have long regarded the English case as exemplifying a state well equipped with strong, uniform and centralized institutions. State-building, moreover, began at an early date – some would say before the Norman Conquest – and had gone far to create a united and coherently administered polity by the end of the twelfth century. Nowhere else in Europe was the monarch so successful in harnessing feudal overlordship and transforming it into an effective system of royal administration.

The strength of England's emergent national institutions was partly attributable to the weakness of regionalism and particularism. The early date of political consolidation, at a time when local privilege, law and custom enjoyed only a precarious existence, meant that there were few obstacles to the growth of a national system of law and governance. The local unit of the county, into which England was divided during the Anglo-Saxon period, proved too small to sustain a local assembly or produce powerful regional loyalties.[1] Nor were provincial magnates and local lords a major threat to centralized power.

Successive conquests and invasions – by Danes and Normans – had undermined or eroded their authority. The Norman and Angevin monarchs, moreover, adopted a deliberate policy of undercutting regional loyalties by employing notables to manage the local workings of a national scheme of justice, a 'common' law. The overall effect of these developments was to create a single layer of governance which embodied (even if it did not always reconcile) national and local interests. As Alexis Tocqueville remarked with pardonable exaggeration on his journey to England in 1835, 'the English . . . [were] the first people who ever thought of centralising the administration of justice'.[2] This enduring structure was to remain the form of English regional government and national administration until the nineteenth century. The administrative hierarchy may have changed with the rise of justices of the peace and the appointment of lord lieutenants and have been replaced during the civil conflicts of the seventeenth century by a bureaucratic and military regime, but the units of government were astonishingly resilient until the great reforms of the industrial era.[3]

As early as the thirteenth century feudal suzerainty in England had come to resemble royal sovereignty. The royal courts handled almost all important legal cases, the royal writ ran throughout the land, the monarch had established one of the most sophisticated financial systems in Europe centred on the royal exchequer, and the crown exacted taxes from the entire realm.[4] The king could claim with some justice to be a public figure, the head of a community whose interests he undertook to guard, the ruler of a realm whose safety he had sworn to protect. An emergent national identity became associated with a single, powerful ruler. Authority was concentrated and public; particularism harnessed or eclipsed.

The emergence of a powerful, centralized monarchy was accompanied by the development of a strong national parliament. Monarchs like Edward I wanted an effective parliament whose members had full authority (*plena potestas*) to bind their constituents to whatever they agreed with the king. Parliament, in this sense, was an adjunct of royal power. But it also provided an institutional focus for opposition to the crown. As a result, the institution became a place for negotiation between the monarch and his subjects. By the fourteenth century parliament had begun to transcend (though it never entirely lost) its original judicial functions and was becoming a *political* body. Not only did it provide a forum for the expression of competing interests but it also claimed the sole right to approve the levying of taxes and full power to speak for the entire 'community of the realm'. The fiscal requirements of the crown during the Hundred Years War – between the reigns of Edward I and Edward III royal revenue doubled in real terms – only served to enhance the estates' bargaining power.[5] The monarch's dependence on taxes – notably those on wool – which affected both landowners and merchants, together with the presence of knights and squires in the same assembly as burgesses, helped create a politically unified body. Parliament, of course, was always at risk from the crown. It could be dispensed with and had no title to perpetuity,[6] but it also had certain recognized powers that the monarch could ignore only at his peril, and no regional or local estates challenged its *national* authority.

This double concentration of power in king and parliament meant that from a very early date political conflict in England was highly centralized. Serious rebellions, though they might be regional in origin, were not separatist in intent. They were designed either to seize control of a national institution or to secure redress of grievances by a central authority. Control of the main institutions of government conferred great powers because their legitimacy was acknowledged throughout the land. Regionalism was not absent but it lacked any institutional focus to challenge the authority of the central state.

Seen, therefore, from an *English* point of view the state was extremely powerful; viewed from a *British* perspective it was rather less so. In neither Scotland, Wales nor Ireland was overlordship transformed into full sovereignty. Scottish kings may have held English estates, paid homage to English kings and attempted to copy aspects of their administration, but they and their subjects retained much autonomy. Edward I might enforce his lordship through brutal conquest, but only at the expense of provoking rebellion and resistance which continued for more than a century. The Scots kept the English at arm's length, never allowing them total control, though rarely able to deny some degree of subordination or to prevent English military superiority on the borders. The forms of fealty were there but not the substance. Scottish integrity remained intact.

The same could be said of Ireland. Henry II established Norman lordship of the country, but conquest was never translated into effective control. The conquered land lacked any kind of central apparatus which could be used to develop strong feudal suzereignty, which was also hampered by the presence of numerous independent warlords and grandees. Particularism was never defeated, a fact recognized by the contraction of effective English monarchical authority to an area known as 'the English land' or 'the English Pale'.

Only Wales was subject to any significant incorporation within the English state apparatus. Edward I's conquest, his garrisons and castles and the Statute of Rhuddlan (1284), which brought the Welsh English law, have all been seen as the end of any Welsh independence. Yet even here much autonomy remained. Welsh law was not entirely abolished and Welsh abhorrence of the English regime was amply demonstrated in the decade-long struggle against English rule led by Owain Glyn Dwr, who called the first and only parliaments of Wales.

There was certainly an English medieval state, made from a Norman template, but not a British one. Though English interests, both monarchical and baronial, penetrated much of Britain, just as they penetrated much of France, they lacked the permanence, legitimacy and institutional structure necessary to secure a durable or unified polity. Nevertheless the English core of what was eventually to become the British state was both geographically larger and better administered than its French equivalent in the Île de France across the Channel. In consequence powers peripheral or adjacent to England were weaker than those which abutted the French domain.

The comparison between England and France, between the two greatest rivals in medieval western Europe, emphasizes the remarkable degree of institutional uniformity and centralization achieved by the island kingdom. The French state developed somewhat later than its English counterpart and its emergence was more gradual. As late as the end of the twelfth century the effective power of French royal institutions did not extend beyond the royal domain of the Île de France. Not until the late fifteenth century did the bulk of France come under the control of the Valois monarchy. As the state expanded it was confronted by a highly developed and intractable regionalism institutionalized in the form of local law and regional assemblies and sustained by powerful local notables. It could only *superimpose* its control on a number of entrenched and thriving institutions. This was achieved both by manning local forms of authority with royal officials loyal to the central state and by creating further administrative layers to supervise local government. Notables from Normandy or Poitou were not to be trusted, because their attachment to the regional practices, law and custom from which they derived their authority was likely to override their allegiance to the central government. This compromise between regional and state power produced a many-layered administration linking disparate provincial practices to a national system of government. Particularism was built into the French state apparatus. This 'mosaic state', to use Strayer's phrase,[7] was therefore much less centralized but much more administratively encumbered than its counterpart across the Channel. From its inception, and even before the proliferation of offices through their sale by the crown, the French state was heavily populated with administrators and bureaucrats.

If the French reached a *modus vivendi* with regionalism and local law, a national French representative – the estates-general – was unable to transcend particularism. First called in 1302, the estates-general never overcame the entrenched regional powers of such provincial estates as those of Languedoc, Normandy and Champagne. In consequence, it failed to establish a plausible claim to speak, like the English parliament, for the entire 'community of the realm', nor was it able to establish a monopoly of approval for taxes.

The estates-general also failed to become an effective arm of royal government. The growth of the *parlements*, the development of an independent system of royal finance and the refusal of local assemblies and communities to be bound by its decisions made the estates-general a weak instrument of royal authority. Squeezed between a national ruler and powerful regional institutions the estates-general was eclipsed by the crown as the institution which gave the nation its emergent identity, and brushed aside in the negotiations for revenue the monarch conducted with numerous local bodies and provincial interests. The parlous position of the estates-general is epitomized by the emergence in the late fifteenth century of the distinction between the *pays d'états* and the *pays d'élections*. In the former provinces – Burgundy, Dauphiné, Provence, Languedoc, Guyenne and Normandy – taxes were negotiated with the regional estates; in the latter, in the heart of the realm, they were collected directly by royal officers. The estates-general was redundant. Politics became a struggle between a national administrative apparatus presided over by the king and the well-entrenched forces of particularism. In consequence domestic conflict revealed the French state's inherently fissiparous tendencies.

On the Margin

If the first important feature of the English state was its early centralization, the second was its decline as a European military force in the sixteenth and seventeenth centuries. In the fourteenth and fifteenth centuries England was one of the most effective states in Europe, with a much-feared army and the military capability to command a sizable 'empire' on the Continent. But from the mid-fifteenth century, when the artillery of Charles vii won the decisive victory of Castillon and drove the English out of almost all of France, to the year 1558, when England lost her last continental foothold at Calais, British military might underwent a marked decline. Between the end of the Hundred Years War (1453) and the outbreak of hostilities with Louis xiv in 1689, England ceased to be a major military power in Europe. With the exception of Henry viii's delusions of grandeur at the beginning and end of his reign, English military activity for a period of more than two hundred years consisted largely of naval warfare, civil war and the occasional (all-too-often unsuccessful) expedition to the aid of a friendly continental power. Elizabeth's succour to the Netherlands, James i's support for Count Mansfeld's disastrous expedition of 1625, Buckingham's catastrophic attempt to relieve La Rochelle, the Protectorate's altogether more successful contribution to the capture of Dunkirk in 1658 and Charles ii's regiments raised for French service during the Third Dutch War are typical of the military activities of what can only be described as a marginal power in the great European struggles of the sixteenth and seventeenth centuries. In a period of ferocious and continuous warfare, England was remarkable for its lack of participation in international conflict and for its many years of peace. England, in other words, was not a major participant in the so-called 'Military Revolution' of sixteenth and seventeenth-century Europe.[8] Only after 1688, when she embarked on the second Hundred Years War with France, did she again become a major force.

Historians have argued that the 'military revolution' changed the character of warfare in the sixteenth and seventeenth centuries. New tactics, involving greater manoeuvrability and linear formations on the one hand, and less mobile siege warfare on the other, were developed by Maurice of Nassau, Gustavus

Adolphus, Baron von Coehoorn and Sébastien de Vauban. Campaigns became more complex and protracted. The emphasis on drill and co-ordinated movement required well trained and properly disciplined troops. In consequence more and more states acquired standing armies. English military men were not ignorant of these changes. They could read about them in any of a number of military manuals which were circulated throughout Europe and translated into several languages. The new tactics were even put into practice by Cromwell's armies. But when it came to the most important change in European warfare – its increased scale – English forces lagged behind those on the Continent.

The essence of the military revolution was the astonishing increase in the size of national armies and in the number of troops deployed on the field of battle. In the space of some two hundred years these increased tenfold. By the last quarter of the seventeenth century the Spanish army consisted of 70,000 troops, the Dutch of an astonishing 110,000, the French 120,000, the Swedish 63,000 and the Russian army of 130,000. In contrast the British army had only 15,000; it was smaller than it had been in 1475.[9] For most of the period before the Glorious Revolution, the English army boasted fewer troops than it had during the Hundred Years War. The numbers exceeded 30,000 only during the Commonwealth and Protectorate, when civil conflict and an exchequer filled with revenues from sequestered royalist lands made a large army both politically necessary and financially possible, and during the last years of James II's reign.

For much of the period between the late fifteenth and late seventeenth centuries England lacked a standing army. While other European nations acquired such forces, the English state relied increasingly for domestic defence on a militia or trained bands. Only foreign expeditions – the militia could not legally serve abroad – were manned with professional soldiers, drawn from bodies either of paid retainers or of foreign mercenaries.

The militia and trained bands, though they came to be better trained, were hardly the stuff of which great armies are made. But the men who might have made up a powerful English army – and had indeed done so in the fourteenth century – were deliberately kept in check by the Tudor monarchy. During the Hundred Years War English monarchs, unable to oblige their subjects to serve abroad, had manned their forces through contract armies, raised for hire by magnates and landowners, who brought with them a retinue of their own retainers. No longer employed by the second half of the fifteenth century in campaigning in France, these aristocratic English *condottieri*, with their large retinues of client gentry, liveried servants and tenants were a serious threat both to royal power and to public order.

Though all Tudor monarchs had in emergencies to depend on such trained and able military men, they did their best to circumscribe the powers of these armed grandees. Between the succession of Henry VII and that of Charles I the English aristocracy was gradually but effectively demilitarized. The attack by successive monarchs on the practices of 'bastard feudalism' and gratuitous aristocratic violence, the persecution, attainder and execution of many of the grandees, and changing conceptions of gentility and virtue amongst the landowning classes themselves all contributed to the demise of the armigerous over-mighty subject. The evidence of this decline was there for all to see: dilapidated and ill-maintained castles now replaced by the 'prodigy houses' of courtiers and royal servants; rusty weapons in depleted noble armories; the diminishing size of aristocratic households; the decline of violence and the rise of litigation; the switch from military service to political clientage; and the growing lack of experience in military matters evinced by the aristocracy.[10] As Stone has pointed out, three-quarters of the peerage fought in Henry VIII's wars of the 1540s. A hundred years later, before the outbreak of the Civil War, four out of five aristocrats had no military experience at all.[11] No other ruling class of a major power in seventeenth-century Europe was so ill-equipped to go to war.

This situation, of course, changed radically during the course of the Civil War. The Commonwealth boasted a standing army of 70,000 troops, many of whom were experienced campaigners. But at the Restoration the standing army was once again drastically reduced and was only to achieve significant numbers in the 1680s. The aspiring British soldier, like the young John Churchill or the Earl of Ossory, had to serve a foreign monarch to learn the skills of his trade.

If the Tudor monarchs had opposed a standing army because it was likely to enhance aristocratic power, in the seventeenth century successive parliaments opposed a standing army because it was likely to enhance the power of the executive. In either case such opposition could be effective only as long as the state was not under direct military threat. Provided no foreign foe was able to invade the kingdom and that no domestic power challenged the state's monopoly of legitimate violence – a matter for the politicians – England could remain the least militarized of European powers. Her military commitment could be confined to a navy, a domestic militia fit only for defensive warfare and to the occasional body of professionals paid to fight abroad.

This pattern of military development, which contrasts with the emergence of standing armies among the major continental powers, is often ascribed to England's peculiar strategic position. As Namier put it, 'a great deal of what is peculiar in English history is due to the obvious fact that Great Britain is an island'.[12] The argument, one to which Hintze subscribed, is that England's insularity, together with her prowess as a naval power, provided adequate protection against foreign invasion. A standing army was not therefore a necessity in England but a matter of choice. The path to absolutism, which was paved by the standing army, could be avoided. According to this view naval power may have been England's greatest military asset, but it was also one of the most important means by which the nation avoided extensive militarization. We can see why many seventeenth-century politicians thought that navies and parliaments complemented one another.

The most powerful argument in early modern Europe for a large and expanding standing army was 'state necessity'. Such emergencies as an imminent threat of invasion or the presence of the enemy on native soil enabled executive authorities to sweep aside the opposition of political groups hostile to military expansion. The fiscal and political scruples of estates and representative assemblies received short shrift when the enemy was at the door. And when the danger receded, the armies tended to remain. Greater military power could then be used by rulers to suppress domestic opponents and to dispense with parliaments and estates. England's insular defences, then, made her the exception to the European rule.

But the view that England's security, the consequence of her insular geography and naval strength, enabled her to avoid both a standing army and absolutism is both an inadequate and incomplete explanation of the peculiar course of English history. It tends, in the first instance, to read back into an earlier era the naval hegemony and naval tactics of the mid and late seventeenth centuries. In the Hundred Years War English naval vessels were unable to stop Castilian and French fleets from seizing and sacking a succession of English ports, including Plymouth, Southampton, Portsmouth, Lewes, Hastings, Winchelsea, Rye, Gravesend and Harwich.[13] Henry VIII, for all his expenditure on a prestigious navy of great ships, was not able to vanquish the French.

But even if the early Tudors had managed to establish naval hegemony, this would not have meant the establishment of an impenetrable line of defence. Naval warfare was still not an autonomous enterprise, a separate kind of fighting, but a water-borne adjunct to battles between soldiers. Naval vessels were infantry transports rather than mobile artillery emplacements. They were neither designed nor equipped to act as floating fortresses, as wooden walls for the nation's protection.

The navy, of course, helped to defeat the Spanish Armada. Nevertheless its importance as England's first line of defence should not be exaggerated. Elizabeth I and William Burghley were certainly not so confident of their naval superiority as to be sure that the Spanish could be stopped by the navy alone. Some 26,000 troops were kept in readiness to repel the invaders when they landed on England's shores. Not until the late seventeenth century was England able to shelter with confidence behind her 'wooden walls'.[14]

Indeed, England's naval achievements – even in the heroic age of Drake and Hawkins – need to be kept in perspective. Naval warfare in the sixteenth century was a peculiar amalgam of private enterprise and state policy, lacking the coherence of an overall naval strategy. In addition to the expeditions of English pirates, privateers and gentry proprietors bent on plunder, operations undertaken with the royal imprimatur were heavily dependent on private support. Only 34 of the 197 vessels which sailed in 1588 to stop the Armada were crown ships; armed merchantmen outnumbered ships built by the royal navy. Elizabeth supplied only two of the twenty-five vessels for Drake's West Indies raid of 1585 and his fleets of 1587, 1589 and 1595 were similarly mixed bodies bent not only on fulfilling a strategic role but on private profit and plunder.[15]

Such arrangements were not conducive to the sort of coherent and planned naval strategy which might have secured naval hegemony. Indeed, we should not confuse the occasional remarkable achievement, such as Drake's circumnavigation of the globe, or a few spectacular instances of pillage and plunder with the establishment of English naval dominance. The likes of Drake and Hawkins may have harboured plans for English control of the oceans, but the crown lacked the necessary resources. Besides, monarchs like Elizabeth were concerned that such ambitions should not detract from the navy's main task of commanding the home straits and keeping the enemy at bay.

The prospect of naval dominance remained illusory in the sixteenth century and retreated even further in the early seventeenth when James I neglected the senior service. Though the tonnage of merchant marine more than doubled between 1550 and 1630, and though, in retrospect, we can see the beginnings of what was to become the first British empire, these developments were not accompanied by a parallel increase in the power of the navy as an instrument of war.[16] Neither the Spanish nor Portuguese, the imperial powers, nor the mercantile Dutch, though they all recognized England as a formidable maritime rival, were ready to cede her the seas.

This situation began to change in the second half of the seventeenth century. The navy not only grew in size, but also became an instrument of a national policy of commercial aggrandizement. The Navigation Acts (1651, 1662) and the three naval wars against the Dutch (1652–4, 1665–6, 1672–4) all signalled the English state's recognition that, in Paul Kennedy's words, sea-power was

desirable not only to ensure 'the Defence of the Kingdom', but also because [of] the benefits it brought in terms of trade, colonial acquisitions, and embarrassment to the foe . . . whereas the Tudor fleet was basically a water-borne home defence squadron, the navy under the later Stuarts saw nothing unusual in escorting convoys through the Mediterranean, or in destroying distant privateer bases: it was simply the military corollary of the Navigation Acts.[17]

The notion that the navy should be the sharp instrument of commercial policy – that power should serve profit – was hardly novel amongst a seafaring people who knew the value of naval plunder and the worth (not purely financial) of the fledgling colonies in North America and the Caribbean. But only after 1650 did the government have both the desire and the capacity to pursue a bellicose policy of commercial development. Under Oliver Cromwell the navy grew as at no time since the reign of Henry VIII. Between 1646 and 1659 217 vessels were added to the fleet: 111 were captured and 106 more were newly built. After the Restoration this substantial increase in smaller ships of the line was supplemented by the construction of twenty-five battleships of the first, second and third rates. Naval administration improved, officers were required to be examined, a statutory code of naval discipline was introduced, and successive *Fighting Instructions* advocated line-of-battle tactics to maximize naval fire-power. The royal navy emerged as a professional force, clearly distinguishable from the merchant marine.[18]

Formidable the royal navy might be, invincible it was not. Only the first of the three Dutch wars was a naval triumph; the second ended in the ignominious raid on the Medway and the bottling up of a beleaguered fleet; the third in another Dutch victory off the Texel. Despite English efforts, the Dutch still dominated world shipping: their commercial fleet was greater than that of the combined French and English marine. Only after the Glorious Revolution was English naval power able to fulfil its earlier promise. And only after the Dutch had been ground down by the protracted wars with Louis XIV was British merchant shipping able to rival the fleets of the United Provinces. English naval dominance was therefore slow to emerge and only gradually established.

England's naval operations undoubtedly represented her greatest international military achievements in the sixteenth and seventeenth centuries. They also marked an important shift in priorities, a move away from the continental military expeditions of the late middle ages towards a foreign policy directed at commercial expansion and national prosperity. But, as we have seen, we should be sceptical about the role of the navy, for all of its successes in preventing the emergence of a standing army. For most of the Tudor age the navy was not viewed as the virtually impregnable bulwark against foreign invasion that it was to become. As for its role in preventing absolutism, it is worth remembering that the greatest naval build-ups of the sixteenth and seventeenth centuries occurred under the most autocratic regimes – those of Henry VIII and Cromwell.

If we play down the importance of the navy in keeping her enemies out of England, we nevertheless have to explain why the nation remained comparatively immune from the attentions of warring European powers. Much can be attributed to changes in the character of warfare. The increased size of armies meant that a full-scale cross-Channel invasion of England was both a costly and complicated operation. As the Spanish discovered at the end of Elizabeth's reign, solving the logistical problems of mounting such an attack and of landing a vast army on Albion's shore was beyond the capacity of even the most powerful sixteenth-century state. England was sheltered not just by her insular position but by the scale of war in early modern Europe.

Those who point to geography and naval power as the major constraints on the emergence of a standing army assume, of course, that the pressure for such a body would come from without the nation rather than within. They do not, therefore, explain why it was that English monarchs who might wish to do so failed to create a standing army or to play a major part in European military affairs. Why, in other words, did the English not revert to their old role as predator and scourge of France?

Here again strategic and military developments were vitally important, rendering English invasion of the Continent a matter of exceptional difficulty. The vulnerability of garrisons and the growing size of armies made small-scale fast-moving expeditionary forces sallying forth from fortified bases – the tactics of Henry v – both nugatory and ineffectual. If it were to be invaded, France, especially the more powerful France of the Valois, had to be occupied by a large army. This, as Henry viii discovered when he invaded France with an army of 40,000 in 1543, was both costly and of little strategic value. The same strategic factors which restrained a continental invasion of England checked an English invasion of Europe.

Other circumstances helped to isolate England. English monarchs, because they felt either domestically and dynastically threatened or financially constrained by lack of resources, were, on the whole, happy to be left in none-too-splendid isolation. Some rulers, notably Elizabeth and James i, were temperamentally ill-disposed to war. And most English monarchs, more knowledgeable than their subjects about the vast resources of the great powers of Europe, and more conscious of the frailties of royal finance, were reluctant to embark on European ventures. In this respect Henry viii's invasions of France were very much the exception. Yet even he was aware of the value of studied neutrality. As a result most of England's interventions in Europe tended to be defensive and reactive in character; intent, above all, on preserving the security of England. They were acts befitting a nation which was dwarfed by the might of the Habsburgs and Valois.

But if England remained a comparatively minor military actor on the continental scene, this was not true in a British context. Indeed, between the mid fifteenth and early eighteenth century, the English state went far towards transforming itself, by a process of conquest, annexation, assimilation and union, into a British political entity. The pace at which this incorporation was achieved varied considerably and was, at times, thrown into reverse. And peaceable means, it must be emphasized, were as important as military action in bringing separate nations into a single body.

The major English initiatives against their Celtic neighbours came in the reigns of Henry viii, in the 1630s and under Cromwell. Henry made good his claim to the Irish kingdom, incorporated Wales, defeated the Scots (Flodden 1513; Solway Moss 1542) and pillaged their land. Under Charles I, Thomas Wentworth, appointed governor in 1633, pursued a relentless policy of centralization in Ireland, increasing revenues and building up a substantial army; in Scotland taxes reached unprecedented heights and national sensibilities were overridden by the imposition of an English form of prayer. Yet such intrusion was mild when compared with the accomplishments of Cromwell. Scotland was fully conquered for the first time since the fourteenth century, Ireland was brutally brought into subjugation. For the first time both nations were incorporated within a unitary British state. By the Instrument of Government (1653) they were represented in the legislature at Westminster.

Each of these major initiatives was accompanied by centralizing initiatives within England itself – Henry VIII's abolition of special jurisdictions, Charles' aptly named policy of 'Thorough', Cromwell's replacement of civilian by military rule – and provoked considerable resistance. Rebellion in Ireland, war with Scotland or Scottish rebellion against the united English and Scottish crown, civil war and the assertion of English localism (albeit based on a defence of earlier national institutions) – all attest both to the intrusiveness of central government and to the limits of its success.

The imposition of institutional uniformity failed, not least because there were forces in England which feared that a unitary British state would place too much power in the hands of its ruler(s). The process of conquest created wounds, especially in Ireland, which proved impossible to heal. Particularism at the periphery was not eliminated: the Irish parliament returned with the Restoration (though it was not able to assert fully its independence of the English legislature until 1782); not even the union of the English and Scottish legislatures in 1707 prevented a thriving, distinctive body of Scottish law.

But from a strategic point of view English gains were considerable. After 1691 there was no major insurrection in Ireland for more than a century; north of the Border only the Highlands remained beyond the sphere of English influence. The Jacobite risings of 1715 and 1745 were not separatist in intent, though one of the Jacobite aims in 1745 was to dissolve the Anglo-Scottish legislative union. They did not deny the boundaries of Britain but claimed the Stuarts as their rightful ruler. Indeed, from the late seventeenth century particularist claims from the Irish and Scots were balanced by demands that they share more of the economic rewards and political privileges enjoyed by the English. The desire for a truly British state – an idea that undercut the subordination that the English would undoubtedly have liked to maintain – emanated as much from the periphery as from the metropolis.

English authority, of course, was increasingly diluted as it seeped into the nether regions of Britain. And in the eighteenth century there was little attempt, apart from the brutal pacification of the Highlands after 1745, to strengthen this either by force of arms or by institutional change. Rather a mix of political management, culture and, most notably, commerce helped knit together the British provinces.

The Limits of Venality

England's limited engagement in European military matters before the end of the seventeenth century had several consequences. One of the most important was the light fiscal load she had to bear when compared with the extraordinary administrative and fiscal pressures faced by the major belligerents in the sixteenth-century struggle between the Habsburgs and Valois and during the

Thirty Years War. This, in turn, helps explain a further distinctive feature of the English state, namely the absence of a sprawling, tentacular state apparatus made up of venal office-holders.

If we compare the form and size of the English state with that of its European counterparts of the time, we cannot but be impressed by the small size of England's institutional apparatus. Though it is extremely difficult to reconstruct accurate estimates of the size of early modern European states, the surviving figures, no matter how crude and conjectural, clearly indicate that English society bore a much lighter burden of government officials than its continental neighbours. MacCaffrey has estimated that there were some 1200 crown servants in Elizabethan England, or one officer for every 4000 inhabitants. The comparable French figures are 40,000 *officiers*, or one for every 400 Frenchmen and women. A single French province such as Normandy was administered by more officials than worked for the entire English government.[19] France, of course, was a far larger and more populous country than England. In 1600 there were 19 million French subjects, occupying a land mass more than four times greater than that inhabited by the 4.4 million English and Welsh. But it is the density of French officialdom, more than the total number of officers, which matters. Even if we include justices of the peace, who performed many tasks similar to those executed by French officers, English officials were much thinner on the ground. English office-holders were a tiny minority; French *officiers* were a large part of the fabric of public life.

The disparity between the size of the two states grew progressively greater. From the late fifteenth century onwards the French administrative apparatus, already larger than that of late medieval England, grew at a far greater rate than its neighbours. Some of this growth was to meet the burgeoning administrative needs of one of the largest states in Europe. But most of it was attributable to the practice – also to be found in Spain – of the systematic sale of public offices. The increase in the number of office-holders in France was therefore not so much a response to the bureaucratic demands of government as a means to satisfy the financial demands of the crown. The sale of offices – and this was as true in Philip II's Spain as in the France of Francis I – was a financial device to raise money.[20] It was, in effect, a way of raising a loan. The purchaser of an office advanced cash to the monarch who 'repaid' the debt in the form of a salary or annuity.

Despite considerable opposition to such venality, the practice of selling offices became a fine art in France. Francis I bureaucratized the trade by establishing the *Bureau des parties casuelles* as the official vendor of royal posts. Subsequent monarchs not only created new offices, but divided existing ones, conferring a single post on as many as three men – the *ancien*, the *alternatif* and the *triennal* – who executed the office in rotation. After 1604, with the establishment of the *paulette*, the monarch obtained a regular income from office-holders by charging an annual fee to *officiers* who wanted the right to bequeath their offices to their heirs and successors. Every opportunity was taken to enhance the profits of this venal system.[21]

The overall effect of these policies was threefold. First, it spawned an enormous administration – Loyseau claimed (no doubt with some hyberbole) that no fewer than 50,000 offices were created in the second half of the sixteenth century – which, because its rewards took the form of *douceurs* and *commissions* in the case of judicial office-holders and *droits et taxations* in the case of financial officials, placed an enormous economic burden on other members of civil society.

Secondly, the sale of offices provided the monarch with an important source of revenue. Throughout the first half of the seventeenth century revenues from the *parties casuelles* varied between 8 and 39 per cent of royal income. In the 1620s and 1630s they never fell below 25 per cent of the king's moneys, and rose to as much as 35 million livres in a single year.[22] These figures should be seen, however, in the context of the fiscal liability that the French monarchy incurred. As Mousnier pointed out long ago, revenue from the *parties casuelles* assumed a disproportionate importance in the French budget during periods of crisis.[23] In a fiscal crunch, the monarch could usually raise large sums with great rapidity by creating and selling more offices and by increasing the charges levied on existing office-holders. But this had the effect of increasing the crown's long-term liability to pay the interest on 'the loan' from office-holders in the form of *gages* (salaries) and *rentes* (bonds or annuities). In the long run the *officiers* got a better deal than the King. As Cardinal Richelieu discovered when he surveyed French finances in 1639, the crown's annual obligations to office-holders easily exceeded the receipts from the *parties casuelles*.[24] The sale of offices did not produce sound government finance; it simply incarcerated the French monarchs in a fiscal prison of their own making.

Finally, venality of office created an important vested interest. The rewards of office, it is important to emphasize, were both considerable and of more than one sort. Not only did office bring pecuniary rewards from the crown and the right to exact payment from the public, it also conferred honour, status and title upon the holder. Moreover *officiers* enjoyed fiscal exemption and were not obliged to pay the *taille*. Even though these advantages had to be weighed against the countervailing tendency of the crown to exploit office-holders in time of crisis by exacting money from them and by reducing the value of offices by increasing their number, they represented a remarkable *concentration* of privilege. And, as Louis XIV's ministers were to discover during the *Fronde*, *officiers*, though created by the monarch and beholden to him, were prepared to resist the crown when its aims clashed with their interests.

The situation in England was both similar and different: analogous in that venality was a marked feature, and divergent in its concentration and extent – in its overall importance in government. For, though many English practices mirrored those of France, there was no wholesale creation of offices for royal profit (though titles and honours grew prodigiously), nor did office-holding offer such a variety of benefits to royal functionaries.

Venality practised by the crown – as opposed to that perpetrated by its subjects – had three main features: the sale of offices, the sale of honours, and the sale of lucrative special privileges which included the right to collect taxes, control trade, monopolize an industrial product's manufacture or rent crown lands at preferential rates. The crown was not the sole vendor of offices but stood at the pinnacle of venality: subordinate offices were frequently sold by higher officials, one of whose chief perquisites was the sale of such positions. Incumbent office-holders were also able to sell their positions.[25]

This trade in offices was accompanied by the familiar features of venality: the practice of pluralism and the employment of deputies to perform an officer's duties; the extraction of moneys from the public in the form of fees, gifts and *douceurs*; and a growing concern among officers to secure the rewards of office through the claim that offices were freehold property, and by such devices as the multiplication of life tenures and the purchase of reversions – the right to future tenure of an office – often with the object of making posts hereditary. Though in some periods such venality was more conspicuous than others – the 1540s, 1590s, 1620s and after the Restoration – the sale of offices was a persistent feature – the white noise – of English administration, a sound which stopped only briefly during the Interregnum.[26]

The system of venality was less well controlled by English monarchs than by their counterparts in France. No royal institution extracted the profits of venality from office-holders, and there were legal constraints – admittedly honoured in the breach as well as the observance – both on the sale of offices and, more importantly, on the creation of new offices for sale. The establishment at common law of property rights in offices – especially in the lucrative posts of the main law courts – well before the 'new monarchy' of the sixteenth and seventeenth centuries meant that, as Cavendish's Case of 1587 showed, incumbent officials were able to prevent the crown creating new sinecures on the grounds that they infringed existing property rights.[27] Venality, then, was as much the perquisite of an office-holding elite as of the monarch.

Office in England did not automatically entitle the holder to ennoblement. Titles and honours remained a separate (albeit related) form of reward. Their sale was unusual in the sixteenth century but became common in the seventeenth. Some of the 'inflation of honours' under James I can be justified as compensation for the niggardliness of Queen Elizabeth and explained by James's impetuous desire to gratify his followers and friends. But the fuel that fired the inflation was pecuniary – the monarch's need for money. James and Charles (or, more often than not, their favourite, the Duke of Buckingham) sold knighthoods, baronetcies (newly created in 1610) and peerages. A baronetcy cost £1095, a peerage in the region of £10,000. All told the first two Stuarts raised at least £620,000 through the sale of honours between 1603 and

1629. Not surprisingly the years of greatest sale were also those of greatest
financial crisis.[28]

The fiscal demands of the crown also prompted the sale of trade privileges
and monopolies. Joel Hurstfield has described this as 'putting up for auction
the machinery of government itself'.[29] Begun by Elizabeth and rapidly
expanded during the Spanish War in the 1580s and 1590s, the practice reached
a peak in the 1630s when the monopolies on starch, coal, salt and soap raised
£80,000 a year for the crown, and between £200,000 and £300,000 for the
monopolists.[30]

Though it is less hard to compute the profits of venality to individual office-
holders, it is much more difficult to place a precise value on the system of
venality to the English crown. The absence of a specific government office
which institutionalized venality, of an institution comparable to the French
parties casuelles with its records of sales and receipts, makes it virtually impossible to reconstruct aggregate figures for the sale of offices. Gerald Aylmer,
however, has argued that, though the sale of offices helped redistribute wealth
upward – towards a small oligarchy of the rich and powerful – it was not an
important source of royal revenue.[31] His findings are borne out by Stone's
figures on the sale of honours. These indicate that over a twenty-five year
period the trade in titles probably constituted about 5 per cent per annum of
royal income; in some individual years the percentage would have been
higher.[32] This gave the early Stuarts a much-welcome annual fiscal bonus, but
it was hardly sufficient to become a major component in government finance.
In short, the sale of office and honours never assumed the fiscal importance
that it did in France.

Venality did, however, help subsidize the costs of government. Aylmer
estimates that in the 1630s the public paid between £250,000 and £400,000 per
annum in fees and gratuities to government officials.[33] If these are seen as
transfer payments, in which the costs of government were shifted from the
monarch to the public, then they were a considerable windfall for the crown
– perhaps as much as 30 per cent of the government's total revenue. But, just
as the French crown's profits from venality were offset by large disbursements
to *officiers*, so Charles I paid out between £350,000 and £360,000 per annum
to his officials in the mid-1630s.[34] Venality was less extensive than in France
and probably less of a drain on royal resources, but on neither side of the
Channel was it a very profitable fiscal expedient.

Why, despite the presence of a number of venal practices, did British office-
holding never escalate to the chronic disproportions of the French bureaucracy? It is tempting to the English historian, steeped in the parliamentary
tradition, to attribute the sylph-like shape of the English state to the ability
of the commons to constrain the powers of the crown. Certainly the commons
opposed the sale of offices and, in the 1620s, were eager for tougher legislation
to curb the traffic in places. They also wished to end monopolies and to reduce
office-holders' fees. Conversely, there is no doubt that the sale of offices,

honours and privileges was seen by the early Stuarts as one of several means to provide the crown with revenue without recourse to parliament. There is even some evidence that, in the final years of personal rule, some of Charles I's servants contemplated raising money by creating a substantial officer class, complete with special rights and exemptions. Such a move would have had the advantage of making office more attractive by concentrating privilege in the French manner. It would also have bound office-holders more closely to the crown.[35]

Though there was undoubtedly a struggle over office-holding and finance before the civil war, parliamentary opposition to venality does not seem to me a sufficient explanation of the failure of the English state to expand. To accept this view is to presume that without the civil war England would have become a monarchical state enjoying the full amplitude of French absolutism. This, in turn, presupposes that the crown *wanted* to create a large officer class, or saw venality as the way to achieve fiscal independence. This is not, however, warranted by the evidence. When Charles I achieved a degree of financial autonomy from the commons in the 1630s, he attempted not administrative expansion but retrenchment and reform. The purchase of office declined, the tenure of offices was shortened.[36] Why did the crown not expand its administrative apparatus at a time when parliament was no longer an obstruction to growth? Part of the answer, no doubt, is that existing office-holders were reluctant to accept a dilution of the rewards and privileges they enjoyed and they were able to oppose the crown using the common law. But at bottom the crown did not encourage venality because the extensive sale of offices was a draining financial liability which was justified only as a fiscal expedient of last resort. In the 1630s Charles and his advisers tried every available fiscal trick – forced loans, ship money, the sale of crown lands, the raising of customs rates – before they even considered venality. Even then it was never implemented.

It can, of course, be argued that, if the massive sale of honours and offices had been implemented, it would have foundered on the opposition of the House of Commons, the common lawyers and the classes they represented. It can also be argued that knowledge of such potential opposition constrained the crown.[37] Plausible as this argument might be, we need to see the reluctance of Charles I to pursue venality in a larger context. Almost every minister and monarch of any acuity in the sixteenth and seventeenth centuries condemned the trade in offices or attempted to retrench the bureaucracy. Sully, Richelieu, Mazarin and Colbert in France, Phillip II and Olivares in Spain all had their reforming phases, and all were conscious of the acute financial problems venality caused. But they all also presided over the extensive sale of offices. None of these men was a fool (though some were hypocrites). Why then did they engage in a practice they themselves were quick to criticize?

The answer is a simple one: the spread of venality was a direct response to the financial pressures created by war. As Swart points out,

In France the sale of offices was introduced during the wars in Italy [in the late fifteenth century], and was practiced on the largest scale during the wars of the seventeenth century. In Spain, sale of offices was embarked upon during the war against the Moors and was most frequently resorted to during the many wars against France.[38]

The reforming schemes of Richelieu and Olivares failed in the face of the catastrophic costs of the struggle between France and Spain. Similarly, with the outbreak of war with the Dutch, Colbert's schemes of retrenchment fell victim to what John Elliott has recently described as 'the definitive sacrifice of reform to war'.[39] The sale of offices, an increase in venality, was one of the most rapid and administratively least cumbersome ways of raising large sums of money when the state was in danger. In a crisis, the fiscal prudence of rulers was thrown to the winds, the long-term liability of venality overlooked in the headlong rush for immediate funds.

In England, too, the periods of greatest venality were also years of war. Henry VIII's conflicts with France in the 1540s, the heroic Elizabethan struggle against Spain in the 1580s and 1590s, and the end of King James's peace in the 1620s, when England was at war with both France and Spain, were all periods remarkable for their political 'corruption'. As Conrad Russell has pointed out, in the late sixteenth and early seventeenth centuries England shared with France and Spain the financial pressures and political conflicts engendered by the costs of war.[40]

This comparison should not, however, be strained. As we have seen, English military operations were on a diminutive scale when judged against those of the great powers of Europe. And their occurrence was remarkably infrequent when compared with the protracted military struggles in which France and Spain were engaged. The expenditures of the French state, which were primarily for military purposes, far outstripped those of the English government. As a result the fiscal burden of taxes and other appropriations borne by French society also far exceeded that across the Channel. One estimate places their *per capita* incidence at three or four times the English level, and their proportion of the national income as five times greater.[41] Indeed, in the 1620s, Louis XIII's revenues from the sole province of Normandy were equivalent to the entire ordinary revenue of Charles I.[42] One recent analyst of English taxation in the sixteenth and early seventeenth centuries has concluded that 'taxation, even in the very widest sense, did not play a very important part in English economic life, and for the most part the evolution of economic activity and social structure was not distorted by fiscal pressures'.[43] Such a statement about France in the same period could only be dismissed as risible.

The contrast between the extent of French venality and its limited ambit in England, though attributable to the greater financial straits of the French monarchy, was not a consequence of a comparative inadequacy of French financial institutions. On the contrary the French state showed itself to be more skilled than the English, at least before the mid-seventeenth century, in extracting taxes and raising loans. The English monarch certainly enjoyed some important fiscal advantages, notably. an ordinary income adequately provided through customs duties on trade and the accession of wealth, thanks to the sale of monastic lands, which funded the wars of the 1540s. But the crown neither collected nor spent a fraction of the moneys that funded the military activities of the French state.

England's greatest advantage was that it was never put to the sort of gruelling fiscal–military test that year after year drained the nation of its resources and the Treasury of its wealth. 'The only true, the only real Oeconomy is *Peace*,'[44] wrote the Earl of Stair at the end of the eighteenth century. His aphorism was as true in the seventeenth century as it was at the end of the American War. And if the commons did really play a part in restricting royal venality, they did so not by inhibiting the (largely imaginary) desire of the monarch to expand the administrative apparatus but by limiting his capacity to wage war through their control of extraordinary revenue. In this way they checked the growth of royal venality but at one remove. For the proliferation and sale of offices was not, as one might suppose, an intrinsic feature of the absolutist state. Rather it was the necessary price that the absolutist ruler paid for waging major wars. venality

What, then, is the significance of those three features of the English state I have chosen to emphasize? I want to argue that all three – early centralization, limited participation in European war and the absence of venality – were important in providing the British fiscal–military state with advantages over its rivals when it finally did emerge in the late seventeenth century.

Consider centralization. The presence of national institutions which enjoyed considerable legitimacy meant that whoever controlled them had the opportunity to exercise strong and effective governance. Of course the potentialities inherent in the state apparatus were obscured during the bitter conflicts of the seventeenth century. For more than a generation it seemed neither that the state was capable of unity, nor that its individual institutions were able to command widespread legitimacy. But, ironically, the turbulence and political experimentation of the seventeenth century revealed the durability of England's political institutions and the potency of an ideology that urged their collaboration. The Civil War, Commonwealth and Protectorate, together with the autocratic follies of James II, showed just how difficult it was for the monarch – or any head of the executive – to dispense with parliament; for parliament to dispense with monarchy (individual monarchs, however, were more disposable), and for anybody to dispense with both.

If the conflicts of the seventeenth century finally legitimized the potent combination of monarch and parliament, they also demonstrated the strength of a national system of provincial governance which relied for its implementation on local dignitaries. National centralized institutions were tolerable provided they were neither military nor administrative but judicial in character; they were not only acceptable but desirable if activated by the approval of the 'natural rulers' (i.e. landed proprietors) of the nation. Central authority in the British Isles as a whole was more circumscribed, though firmly fixed to the advantage of England's leaders.

We can see the sixteenth and seventeenth centuries as an era during which the constraints on political power at both the centre and the periphery were defined. On at least three occasions – under Henry VIII, in the 1630s and with Cromwell – and on possibly a fourth, in James II's reign – the British faced the possibility of an enduring autocratic regime. The failure of these initiatives, and the memory of their attempt, created the context within which English politics developed in the eighteenth century. After 1688 it quickly became a cardinal principle that the polity had to be ruled by king and parliament, or, to be more precise, by king *in* parliament. The unpalatable alternatives – a (radical Protestant) republic, military autarky or a putative (Catholic) absolutism – all lacked the legitimacy a mixed form of government commanded. Though the precise origins and nature of this legitimacy were long to remain a matter for dispute, and though there were radical differences over who was the rightful monarch and why, politicians of every stripe saw mixed government as the best *form* of rule. This was as true of *iure divino* Jacobites as it was of those whigs who endorsed a radical interpretation of the events of 1688.

This acceptance of the institutions of central government (even if it did not necessarily entail support for some of the individuals who manned it) meant that when king, lords and commons acted in unison, they were an overwhelming force. As we shall see, two of the most remarkable features of the powerfully extractive fiscal system that emerged after the Glorious Revolution were its extreme centralization and the extraordinary lack of resistance in the nation as a whole to such a high level of fiscal imposition. A comparatively uniform and centralized administration of public monies through the Treasury and Exchequer was possible because of the existence of national institutions and the absence of institutionalized regionalism. The lack of resistance is attributable to the universal (if tacit) consent to taxes obtained through the approval of parliament and unchallenged by regional estates.

The comparison with France brings home the point. There was no equivalent in the eighteenth-century English fiscal system to the province of Brittany with its local estates and its exemption from the *taille*. Tax rates in England were not only high but national and uniform, even if tax assessments were not. If there was an equivalent to Brittany, the most plausible candidate lay not in the English counties but in such outliers of the British realm as Virginia or Massachusetts. These had their own regional assemblies and were, of course, to prove as adept as any French province in resisting fiscal impositions. Somewhat closer to home, resistance to taxation in Scotland outlasted the political union with England in 1707, which saw the demise of the Scottish parliament.

But this is explained in large part by the widespread belief in Scotland that tax levels in the northern kingdom had been fixed at the Act of Union and that any subsequent tax increase was therefore illegitimate.

If the absence of particularism and the presence of national institutions meant that when a fully fledged English fiscal system emerged it would be capable of high rates of extraction and excite comparatively little hostility, the long period of military inactivity also conferred many benefits on the English state. First and foremost it meant that when England returned to the international military arena, she could draw on a considerable store of husbanded resources. The civil wars had, of course, taken their toll. For a short while some parts of Britain had been subject to the misfortunes – death, disease and plunder – that travelling armies bring to local civilian populations. But, as usual, it was the Scots and, especially, the Irish who suffered most. Taxes also rose. They were three times higher than those levied in the 1630s and remained at a high level throughout the 1650s. No part of Britain, however, suffered the wholesale devastation that accompanied European armies during the Thirty Years War, and taxes, though they increased, were still not onerous by European standards.

When the historian is struck by the resources and wealth that Britain mobilized between 1688 and 1714 in the wars against Louis xiv – by what looks like a great deal of slack in the British economy – he should also remember how small an impediment war had been on the nation's earlier economic growth. While the French and Spanish endured exorbitant exactions, while the Dutch drained their resources into wars of national defence (compensated, it is true, by their maritime plunder), and while large parts of Europe experienced the cruelty and devastation which inspired the shocking etchings of Callot's *Les Malheurs et les Misères de la Guerre*, England suffered less than any other major European power.[45] The English therefore enjoyed the double advantage that they were not exhausted by protracted conflict nor burdened with debt, while their major rivals – France, Holland and Spain – were encumbered by the costs of earlier wars.

The limited extent of venality, itself a consequence of England's low profile as a military power, was also a major benefit to the English state. Given that venality was first and foremost a fiscal device and that its extent was a sign of a state's indebtedness, its inconspicuousness in England was a symptom of the state's healthy finances. This does not mean that English monarchs, especially those who were improvident or who found themselves at war, never ran up debts or faced fiscal crises. But they never had to carry the chronic burden of long-term debt that weighed down the great military powers. Rarely during the sixteenth and seventeenth centuries did the English debt exceed the equivalent of one year's ordinary revenue. In contrast the Spanish debt at the accession of Philip iv (1623) amounted to ten years of royal receipts. Both the Spanish and French monarchies were driven in this period to repudiate or unilaterally reorganize their debts. Frequent decrees forcibly rescheduled royal liabilities issued by the monarch in sixteenth-century Spain, while the French monarch went bankrupt in 1598, 1648 and again in 1661. Only the Dutch, with their sophisticated banking system, were able to borrow heavily without insolvency.

England also lacked the large debt concealed in the practice of selling offices. One of the worst aspects of this type of debt was that it was difficult to retrench and impossible to redeem. As Richard Bonney has pointed out,[46] the cost of buying back offices would have been far in excess of the original sums paid by office-holders to the crown. The amount was palpably beyond the means of a state which could not even afford to pay the full annual dues to its vast *officier* class. Burke's remark of 1779, that 'no revenue is large enough to provide both for the meritorious and undeserving; to provide for service which is, and service which is not, incurred'[47] serves well as an epitaph for the early modern French state.

No doubt, if England had been an active belligerent during the sixteenth and early seventeenth centuries, the English state would have acquired its share of debts and have been colonized by a parasitic officer class. In this sense the *timing* of the emergence of the English fiscal–military state is crucial. When its mobilization occurred, it happened under the auspices of a regime which not only exploited the techniques of Dutch finance but also, through parliamentary scrutiny, placed a rein on the more egregious instances of venality. In consequence, it came to follow a pattern closer to that of the Dutch than that of France.

As we shall see in the next section, the eighteenth-century English fiscal–military state was no paragon of administrative purity, but it was more efficient than its rivals. This can be attributed, in part, to the strength of England's economy and to the character of English society. But, as eighteenth-century commentators were aware, international aggrandizement and success on the battlefield depended not merely on national wealth, economic opportunity and prosperity; they relied on the state's ability – political, fiscal and administrative – to harness and mobilize these resources. As an MP remarked in 1734-5, 'We all know, that what now makes a Nation formidable, is not the Number nor riches of its Inhabitants, but the number of Ships of War provided with able Seaman, and the number of regular and well disciplined Troops they have at their command.'[48]

 II

The Fall of James II in 1688 inaugurated the longest period of British warfare since the middle ages. Britain was at war with France, and allies of France, in 1689–97, 1702–13, 1739–63 and 1775–83. Sometimes referred to as the 'Second Hundred Years War', this belligerent era culminated in the twenty-year struggle with post-Revolutionary France which ended with Wellington and Blücher's victory at Waterloo. Though the wars in the century before 1789 were not on the scale of the titanic conflict which engulfed Europe after 1792, they marked the coming of age for the British as a major military force. Before the Glorious Revolution England had shown she was a naval power to be reckoned with, and the New Model Army had demonstrated that English troops could be as proficient and ruthless as any in Europe. But military action had been sporadic. The army and navy had occasionally and for brief periods achieved manning levels comparable to those of other major European powers. Such mobilizations were infrequent, however, and were not supported by the elaborate military infrastructure – barracks, fortifications, state armament factories – other powers developed in order to ensure the regular deployment of large armies and a permanent state of military readiness.[1]

After 1688 the scope of British military involvement changed radically. Britain was at war more frequently and for longer periods of time, deploying armies and navies of unprecedented size. Protracted warfare posed logistical problems of exceptional magnitude. Wars were now conducted on a greater scale than earlier military operations. They also dwarfed eighteenth-century civilian enterprise. The state's military role made it the most important single factor in the domestic economy: the largest borrower and spender, as well as the largest single employer. Public spending, fuelled by military costs, rose by leaps and bounds. The civilian administration supporting the military effort burgeoned; taxes and debts increased. Britain acquired a standing army and navy. She became, like her main rivals, a fiscal–military state, one dominated by the task of waging war.

2

PATTERNS OF MILITARY EFFORT

Table 2.1 sketches in barest outline the extent of Britain's military commitment during the major wars in the century after the Glorious Revolution. The overall pattern revealed by these figures is one of Britain's progressive military involvement, briefly punctuated by a levelling off in military activity in the second quarter of the century. Put in its simplest terms, between 1680 and 1780 the British army and navy trebled in size. During these years Britain fought five major wars: the Nine Years War, sometimes known as King William's War or the War of English Succession (1688–97), the War of Spanish Succession (1702–13), the Wars of Jenkins's Ear and Austrian Succession (1739–48), the Seven Years War (1756–63) and the American War of Independence (1775–83). There were other conflicts of briefer duration – such as those with Spain which began in 1718 and 1726 – and the armed forces were sometimes partially mobilized – as in 1770–1 when the Spaniards seized the Falkland Islands. But these were minor affairs when compared with wars which involved army and naval operations over several years and in more than one continent.

The frequency of hostilities and the ever-present possibility of renewed warfare meant that even the periods of peace were not properly pacific. Minor skirmishing between the subjects of the great powers was an almost constant feature on the borders of colonial possessions and in areas of trans-oceanic trade. In Europe itself one of the main peacetime activities of the major states was the fiscal consolidation and administrative reform whose chief motive was not so much a desire for financial probity and good governance as a need to be prepared once hostilities renewed. In peacetime it was presumed that war was imminent or, at the very least, that government should act as if it were so.

Though it expanded enormously, Britain's military activity after the Glorious Revolution retained much of the pattern it had assumed before 1688. The sizable peacetime standing army was certainly new, but England continued to rely on the militia as a means of national defence. The practice of hiring

Table 2.1 *The logistics of war, 1689–1784*

War	Average annual personnel			Average annual expenditure	Average annual tax revenue	Debt	
	Navy	Army	Total			Begin	End
1689–97 Nine Years War	40,262	76,404	116,666	5,456,555	3,640,000	—	16,700,000
1702–13 War of Spanish Succession	42,938	92,708	135,646	7,063,923	5,355,583	14,100,000	36,200,000
1739–48 War of Austrian Succession	50,313	62,373	112,686	8,778,900	6,422,800	46,900,000	76,100,000
1756–63 Seven Years War	74,800	92,676	167,476	18,036,142	8,641,125	74,600,000	132,600,000
1775–84 American War	82,022	108,484	190,506	20,272,700	12,154,200	127,300,000	242,900,000

SOURCE: *British Parliamentary Papers*, vol. 35 (1868–9); B. R. Mitchell and Phyllis Deane, *Abstract of British Historical Statistics* (Cambridge, 1962), pp. 401–2.

foreign troops to fight in Europe also persisted, though the sums spent on foreign regiments and armies was far greater than ever before. Both these tactics helped circumscribe the scope of the standing army.

They also enabled the state to give higher priority to its naval forces. Though the navy was consistently smaller than the army, naval spending occasionally exceeded and never lagged far behind the army expenditure. The *per capita* cost of a wartime sailor was double that of a soldier in the army, mostly because of the navy's higher maintenance costs. But it also reflects Britain's determination to sink money into the navy so as to develop its support services and infrastructure. The great military buildings of eighteenth-century England were not barracks and forts but the dry-docks, stores, roperies and building yards of the royal navy. And when we compare the distribution of military spending with that of other European powers, the priority given to the navy is obvious. With the exception of the Dutch, and the French during the American War of Independence, no other major state devoted such a high proportion of its expenditure to a floating force.

The figures for the armed forces provided in Table 2.1 have to be treated with some caution. The army numbers show men voted by parliament, not a tabulation of soldiers in the field. It is certain that these are overestimates of the actual number of combatants. The high rates of desertion common to all European armies in this period and the proclivity of regimental officers to overestimate the strength of their forces in order to pocket the pay allowances of nonexistent men, a practice that had institutional approval in many states, meant that armies were never at their full complement. On the other hand the parliamentary figures do not include troops on the Irish establishment (12,000 men in all), nor the number of militiamen mustered during the Seven Years and American Wars. They are, in any case, the only continuous series over time, apart from the unreliable estimates inserted in the preamble to the Mutiny Acts. For all their weakness, they provide a good general indication of the British army's commitment during wars of several years' duration. The naval figures, which are of men borne by the navy, including naval marines, are more accurate: they are totals of men actually listed as serving rather than of men for whom money had been set aside.

For all the problems with such statistics, it is difficult to challenge their broad trajectory, which is indisputably upward. On the basis of these estimates, the army, having doubled in size during the Nine Years War, when it reached a peak of 87,500, grew yet again in the struggle over the Spanish Succession. Between 1702 and 1713 it averaged nearly 93,000 men. In the final year of the war there were 144,650 under British arms. Compared with these earlier conflicts, the War of Austrian Succession saw, for the first and last time during the century, a reduction in the size of the wartime army. Only in 1746 did it exceed a total of 70,000 men. Whereas in 1702 an establishment of 28 battalions had been increased to 80, during the 1740s the total rose to a mere 67. But the Seven Years War saw the renewal of the upward trend. Between 1756 and

1763 the number of battalions reached 120 and the size of the army exceeded 90,000 men, an augmentation continued during the American War when, for the first time, the army averaged over 100,000.

Britain's peacetime forces were, of course, much smaller than her wartime armies. No eighteenth-century power, no matter how rich or well administered, could afford to sustain the expense of continuous fulltime mobilization. The peacetime army numbered about 35,000 in the first half of the century and 45,000 after the Seven Years War. After each of the major conflicts of the period it increased.

The reduced peacetime regiments were stationed in mainland Britain, in those outposts of the empire such as Gibraltar, which required constant protection and, above all, in Ireland. This had the advantage, from the point of view of the ministers at Westminster, that a large proportion of the peacetime force was kept on the Irish establishment, funded by the Irish taxpayer and kept out of view of the English parliament. But they could be transferred quickly to England if the need arose. In short, after 1688, England, like the other great powers of Europe, had a standing army – a body of professional 'effectives' which was in a constant state of readiness and which provided the core around which a wartime army was built. Indeed, it could be argued that this peacetime body, small as it was, was a more effective base on which to build a wartime army than was to be found elsewhere in Europe. For British 'effectives' were required to serve throughout the year. They were not dismissed at harvest time – a common practice in Prussia – nor were they granted long peacetime leaves of absence.

The size of the eighteenth-century British army is by no means the sole indicator of the nation's commitment to landed military operations. In all the major wars of the eighteenth century the government spent substantial sums subsidizing other troops to fight on its behalf. During the War of Spanish Succession over £7 million or nearly 25 per cent of all money voted for expenditure on the army was assigned to foreign subsidies. Similarly, between the outbreak of the War of Jenkins's Ear (1739) and the end of the Seven Years War (1763) some £17.5 million or 21 per cent of the sums voted the army went on foreign soldiers. Between 1702 and 1763 the British government spent over £24.5 million in this fashion.[2] Sometimes these monies were paid to small corps of foreign troops who fought in allied armies alongside the British; occasionally, as during the Seven Years War, they subsidized an entire army like the 40,000 enlisted with the Duke of Brunswick.

The standing army and foreign troops for hire were supplemented by the English militia. Before the Militia Act of 1757 this was a largely ineffectual force which was rarely embodied and which therefore lacked military experience and expertise. The Jacobite rebellion of 1745–6 and the threat of French invasion during the Seven Years War led to the reorganization and, eventually, to the regular embodiment of a national militia force. After 1762 the county militias were required to drill for twenty-eight days a year and militiamen were subject to martial law while on active service. At the end of the Seven Years War nearly 28,000 militiamen were under arms; in 1778–9, years when a French invasion threatened, nearly 40,000 were mustered.[3]

The military proficiency of the militia improved during the second half of the eighteenth century. It was not, however, tested in battle against regular troops. Confined by law to its native land, it was primarily a (somewhat flimsy) bulwark against foreign invasion. As such, it was the least important component of Britain's military effort but it did serve to familiarize many more Englishmen with the use of arms and the character of military life. Not every militiaman, especially the humble men in the ranks, gained the insights that enabled Edward Gibbon to understand the military prowess of Rome: 'The discipline and evolutions of a modern battle gave me a clearer notion of the Phalanx and the Legion, and the Captain of the Hampshire grenadiers (the reader may smile) has not been useless to the historian of the Roman Empire.'[4] But most learnt how to drill and the rudiments necessary to help defend the nation.

But it was not the militia alone that prevented the foreign invasion of Britain's shores. Rather it was the combination of the militia with the major branch of the nation's military might, the royal navy. In the century between the reign of Charles II and the end of the American War the senior service grew at an even greater rate than the army. During the wars against Louis XIV it numbered some 40,000 men. By the time of the American War, the navy had more than doubled, and briefly deployed more than 100,000 men. The increase in manpower was matched by a growth of naval tonnage, which doubled between 1714 and 1760. As in the case of the army, the navy's peacetime establishment also grew. Between the peace of Utrecht (1713) and the war of Jenkins's Ear, the number of men voted rarely exceeded 10,000, but after the Seven Years War, numbers were higher.

The scope and extent of Britain's military effort was, of course, paralleled by the major military powers of eighteenth-century Europe. But the distinctive feature of the British state's military expansion was its set of priorities. Most continental powers devoted the bulk of their resources to a standing army. Few devoted a large part of their military budget to the subsidization of foreign troops. Even fewer placed such a high priority on the navy. Even in those states whose proportion of total military expenditure on the navy was sometimes very high – the United Provinces at the beginning of this period and France at the end – found it difficult to sustain this commitment. While in England the importance of naval power was a virtually incontestable shibboleth, in both France and the United Provinces the navy was something of a political football, likely to be kicked by its adversaries out of play. Such a role was reserved in England for the army. Less populous and prosperous states like Sweden and Denmark also found it difficult to sustain a commitment to the navy, for there was no easy way of foisting its high cost on other nations. Unlike an army it could not be billeted on occupied territory. In

short, the priority that Britain gave to its navies was unique; it was also
singularly appropriate for a state which governed a commercial society with
such a substantial commitment to overseas trade.[5]

The Case of the Navy

As British armies advanced and fleets set sail, enhancing Britain's power
abroad, so state activity grew on the domestic front, advancing into civil
society. Putting large armies into the field; clothing, feeding and arming troops
in different theatres of war; supplying and servicing the huge floating force of
the British navy: all of these tasks placed an ever-more onerous burden on the
fiscal resources and organizational powers of the state. The aggregate numbers
of those who served in the army, navy and militia are therefore just the tip of
the fiscal–military iceberg. Supporting the soldier in the field and the sailor
on the high seas were a growing number of tax officials, government administrators, victuallers and contractors, dockyard workers, armament manufacturers, commissaries and paymasters.

As an organization, the fiscal–military state dwarfed any civilian enterprise.
The capital investment it demanded, the running costs it incurred, its labour
requirements and the logistical problems that it posed were all of a different
order of magnitude from even the very largest eighteenth-century private
business.

The capital assets of a large business in the early eighteenth century rarely
exceeded £10,000. Ambrose Crowley's iron works, regarded as the wonder
of their age, had a fixed capital of £12,000.[6] A substantial multi-storey cotton
spinning mill built at the end of the century cost a mere £5,000.[7] By comparison
naval vessels cost a small fortune. In the late seventeenth century the navy
spent between £33,000 and £39,000 to build a first-rate ship, between £24,000
and £27,000 to build a second-rate, and between £15,000 and £17,000 to
construct a third-rate vessel.[8] By the second half of the eighteenth century the
cost of constructing the largest ships had nearly doubled. In 1765 the 100-gun
first-rate *Victory* cost £63,174 to build.[9] Even the smaller royal naval vessels
were more expensive than most industrial plant.

The total fixed capital required to form a large navy was therefore enormous.
In the first half of the eighteenth century the British navy boasted twenty
ships of the first and second rates, approximately forty vessels of the third
rate, as well as an additional 120 smaller vessels of the fourth, fifth and sixth
rates.[10] If we assume that the costs of ship construction had not risen since
the late seventeenth century, then the entire fleet amounted to a capital investment of nearly £2.25 million whose replacement cost was approximately 4 per
cent of national income.[11] This can be compared with the total fixed capital
in the 243 mills in the West Riding woollen industry in 1800, which has been
estimated at £402,651 with an average of £1657 per textile mill.[12] The fixed
capital in one of the largest sectors of the nation's most important industry

was therefore a mere 18 per cent of the fixed capital required to launch the British navy.

This comparison is, of course, of *fixed* capitals rather than the total amounts of capital invested. And certainly, if we compare total investment and not just fixed assets, then the naval figures seem less disproportionate. Jacob Price estimates that total capital in the Atlantic trade may have been in the region of £4.5 million in the 1770s, and some of the very largest merchant capitals exceeded £100,000. Nevertheless the median range of capital of firms in the tobacco trade before the 1770s was only between £10,000 and £20,000.[13] The average business entailed less capital than a major battleship.

No nation, of course, purchases or builds a navy of this size outright. The presence on the high seas of a fully manned and well-equipped fleet was the culmination of years of unremitting effort. The effects of everyday wear and tear, not to mention the damage sustained in battle, meant that the maintenance costs of a fleet were very high. The navy spent £13,000 every six months simply to keep a first-rate battleship shipshape and seaworthy. The expense incurred to ensure that the entire mid-century fleet did not deteriorate – never mind improve its performance – was more than a half a million pounds per annum.

The maintenance of the navy depended upon adequate facilities to service, supply and repair the fleet. Though the number of naval vessels, as well as their tonnage, had increased substantially in the second half of the seventeenth century, this expansion had not been accompanied by a comparable improvement in dockyard facilities.[14] After 1688, however, old yards were expanded and new yards built. Two new dry docks and two new basins were added to the Portsmouth dockyard and an entire new yard with a basin and dry dock was opened at Plymouth. These two naval stations – the former guarding the Channel, the latter protecting England's westerly approaches – were, together with the dockyards at Sheerness, the three main yards used to service the operational fleet. These were complemented by the Thames yards – at Deptford, Woolwich and Chatham – which became centres of naval supply, shipbuilding and routine maintenance. In sum, throughout the century the dockyards were expanded, improved and updated. The two most important Atlantic dockyards – Portsmouth and Plymouth – received the most attention. After the Seven Years War nearly £680,000 was spent on their improvement.[15]

As the scope of naval operations expanded, so the senior service acquired overseas bases. In the Mediterranean, Gibraltar and Port Mahon in Minorca enabled the navy to blockade the coast of Spain and France; in the Caribbean, Port Royal on Jamaica and English Harbour in Antigua were the centres of naval operations, while in North America, Boston, and then Halifax, Nova Scotia, were Britain's bases in the western Atlantic. By the end of the Seven Years War the navy had a network of bases which greatly facilitated provisioning and repair in distant waters.[16]

Naval dockyards were, by the standards of the day, immense enterprises.

They were the largest industrial units in the country, dwarfing their nearest rivals, the breweries and the mines. During the War of Austrian Succession, for example, the Portsmouth dockyard employed a workforce of over 2000. By the 1770s the total labour force in naval dockyards had reached over 8000, with half of these men working at Portsmouth and Plymouth.[17] The navy was thus one of the largest single employers of civilian labour in eighteenth-century England.[18] Naval ships and shipbuilding operated on a scale quite unlike that of civilian industry and commerce. Capital and labour were deployed in a manner that was beyond the resources of the merchant or manufacturer. Only the state could undertake enterprises on such a scale.

One of the hardest tasks that naval administrators faced was the victualling and feeding of naval personnel. For much of this period, supplying a navy was more difficult than providing for land-based forces. Until the American War, when the British army in North America was forced by the rebellious colonists to depend on supplies brought three thousand miles from Europe, British troops in foreign theatres relied for food and fodder on supplies purchased in places through which they marched and fought. This created remittance problems – transferring large sums of money from London to the Continent in order to purchase foreign foodstuffs could be very expensive and might have an adverse effect on the exchange rate of the pound – but it avoided the difficulties of long-distance provisioning, especially those of preserving and packaging food. As van Crefeld has pointed out, as long as an eighteenth-century army kept steadily on the move, it could live off the land.[19] Provisioning crises occurred only when an army was stationary (for example when engaged in a siege), or when troops had to retrace their steps over territory already stripped bare.[20]

If the eighteenth-century army was like a caterpillar, consuming steadily on the march, the eighteenth-century navy was like a boa constrictor, swallowing up one vast supply to sustain it on its long and frugal voyages.[21] The navy could not live off the sea as armies lived off the land. Nevertheless fleets did not have to carry their entire provisions. Commanding officers were able to purchase goods at ports of call, and both private contractors' agents and official agent victuallers, working from naval bases, supplied victuals abroad.

Adequate victualling was essential to the navy's effectiveness as a fighting force. The quantity and quality of supply determined how long the navy could stay at sea, how long they could blockade an enemy fleet or harbour and how well sailors fought in battle. Perished or tainted food, or low and inadequate rations meant, in the first instance, a sick and weak crew. The failure of supply could eventually force a captain to return to port.

Naval provisioning, which absorbed about one-quarter of the naval budget, required organization on a prodigious scale. As Daniel Baugh has pointed out,[22] in the mid-eighteenth century the navy's *shipboard* population in time of war – more than 40,000 men – was greater than that of any British city except for London. There were therefore more men serving on the high seas than residents in either Bristol or Norwich, the two largest provincial towns, and their seaborne station made them far more difficult to feed.

The peculiar logistical requirements of the navy meant that victuals and supplies had to be assembled, packed and preserved at key distribution points. The most important of these was the victualling office at East Smithfield in London which extended over five acres. It is a traditional assumption that naval provisions provided sailors with a tedious diet of poor not to say perished or rotten food. But, if the food was never a feast like the repast served at a gentleman's seat, it compared well with the diet of the classes from which the ordinary seamen were drawn. Meat was served on four days a week. As Rodger points out, 'the seaman who had a hot dinner daily with beef and beer and cheese, and sometimes vegetables and fruit, was eating well by his standards'.[23] Only cheese (before 1758), butter and stockfish were sources of complaint. Otherwise ordinary seamen seem to have been satisfied with their victuals.

The navy required extraordinary large quantities of foodstuffs. In 1703, for instance, an expedition of 40,000 men needed 130,000 lb of brisket, 60,666 hogheads of beer, 2,080,000 lb of beef, 2,080,000 lb of pork, 65,000 bushels of pease, 77,500 bushels of oatmeal, 780,000 lb of butter, and 1,560,000 lb of cheese.[24] Such demands for a single expedition were only a part of total annual consumption. In 1760, at the height of the Seven Years War, the Navy Board purchased 481,600 lb of hops, 3,819,200 lb of flour, 4,636,800 lb of biscuits, 10,830,400 lb of beef, 3,628,800 lb of pork, 2,486,400 lb of cheese and 1,064,000 lb of butter.[25] What impact such requirements had on civilian prices, or what effect the navy's demand for such foodstuffs had on their production and marketing is still a little-understood but undoubtedly important subject.[26]

Its demand for the assembly of vast quantities of provisions, its deployment of large labour forces both on land, in the navy dockyards, and at sea – nowhere else but in a ship of the first rate could you find a coordinated labour force of 900 in mid-eighteenth-century England – as well as its fixed capital requirements and running costs made the navy a business on a massive scale. If we are interested in the history of organizations, and not merely in the history of production, then it is to military rather than civilian enterprise that we should turn.

Military Effort in Comparative Perspective

How does Britain's military effort compare with that of the other powers of eighteenth-century Europe? Before we can answer this question in any detail it is worth bearing in mind a number of assumptions that often underpin discussions of military effort, militarization and militarism. The first is the tendency, understandable among continental scholars, to equate military effort with the size of the standing army. Though size is undoubtedly one important measure of effort, it is not the only one. Adherence to this single standard immediately downplays the military effort of powers like Britain which devoted so much of their resources to their navies. Indeed, there is no reason why naval strength should not feature in any overall assessment of military activity. The English, Dutch, French and Spanish fleets, after all, were each considerably larger and more expensive than the armies of minor states. Equally, we should find some way to include in our calculations soldiers who were not members of a national standing army: bodies of militiamen such as those mustered in France, Spain, England, Denmark, Sweden and several German states; separate bodies of foreign troops subsidized to fight on behalf of a particular nation.

A second assumption that needs to be questioned is that 'militarized' states, those whose civilian apparatus had been either militarized or made subordinate to military control, were thereby more capable exponents of military effort in the arena of international conflict. This is to confuse the type of domestic regime and its capacity for domestic repression with its ability to wage war on other states. An 'unmilitarized' state, as the Dutch and English cases show, was well capable of distinguished 'military effort'. Indeed, as we shall see, there are good reasons to suppose that states that provided their subjects with certain civil freedoms were thereby better able to mobilize their resources for war.

Regardless of the type of regime, those who waged war needed two vital resources, money and men. Eighteenth-century warfare, greater in scale than ever before, required both in great quantities. The effects of Britain's military activities on public spending, outlined in Figure 2.1, show a clear pattern: peaks of expenditure during years of war, troughs in years of peace. The overall trend is upward. Before 1688 total public expenditure rarely exceeded £2 million per annum. By the War of Spanish Succession it had more than tripled to over £7 million each year. A generation later, during the American War annual spending reached a total of almost £30 million. Between the 1680s and 1780s annual expenditure increased almost fifteen-fold; between the Nine Years War and the American War it increased by a factor of six.

These figures do not allow, it it true, for the effect of price inflation; nor do they consider population changes in order to calculate public expenditure *per capita*. But neither inflation nor population growth has any major effect on the data. Little of the growth in public spending can be explained by inflation. Prices were relatively stable between the late seventeenth century and the accession of George III. Only after 1760 was there a discernible price increase, so that by the 1780s prices were some 25 per cent higher than twenty years earlier.[27] The population of England and Wales, according to Wrigley and Schofield,[28] increased by 46 per cent between the Glorious Revolution and the end of the American War. In the same period expenditure increased by 600 per cent in constant prices. The *per capita* increase in public expenditure was therefore very little offset by population growth.

As Figure 2.1 also makes clear, eighteenth-century English governments

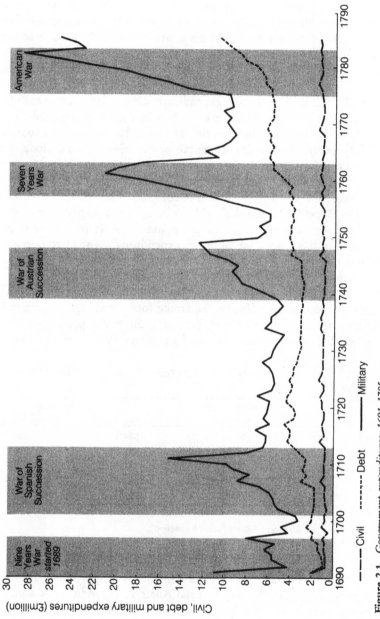

Figure 2.1 *Government expenditures, 1691–1785*
SOURCE: *British Parliamentary Papers*, vol. 35 (1868–9)

spent very little on civilian affairs. Civil expenditure – which effectively meant the domestic expenses of the monarch and his court, the so-called civil list – remained remarkably stable throughout this period, rising slowly from an average of just under £1 million per annum to just less than £1.5 million by the 1780s. For all the complaints of back-bench parliamentarians about the extravagances of the monarch and his court, the civil list accounted for only a small percentage (usually less than 15 per cent) of total government costs.

The real expenses lay elsewhere. Eighteenth-century English governments, like most European powers, spent their money waging war. Between 75 per cent and 85 per cent of annual expenditure went either on current spending on the army, navy and ordnance or to service the debts incurred to pay for earlier wars. These figures indicate that Britain had as substantial a commitment to military expenditure as any European power. Even if we exclude spending to service the debt, then current military expenditure accounted for between 61 per cent and 74 per cent of public spending during the major wars of the period (see Table 2.2). This does not compare with Russian disbursements during the Great Northern War with Sweden, when 90 per cent of Peter the Great's revenue was spent on his army and navy. It is, however, roughly comparable to the proportion of public expenditure spent on the armed forces in Prussia during the second half of the century and outstrips the 25 per cent spent by the French during the last years of the *ancien regime*.[29]

Such a comparison is, however, slightly invidious. Though the proportion of Britain's total public spending on the armed forces was high by contemporary standards (as was their expenditure per man), the outlay probably represented a much smaller percentage of national resources than in many other states.

Table 2.2 *Military spending as a percentage of total government expenditure, 1688–1783*

War	Total spending (£000)	Military spending (£000)	%
1689–1697	49109	36270	74
1702–13	98207	64718	66
1739–48	87789	55814	64
1756–63	116664	82727	71
1775–83	178482	109368	61

SOURCE: *British Parliamentary Papers*, vol. 35 (1868–9).

Britain's military spending during major wars absorbed between 10 and 15 per cent of national income (see Table 2.3). This is roughly comparable to the figure given by Peter Dickson for total Austrian expenditure as a percentage of national income in 1780.[30] But it is probable that a state like Prussia, with a smaller population, a less developed commercial economy and an extremely large army, spent a far greater proportion of its wealth on military affairs.

Unfortunately the absence of national income figures for most continental states prevents us from putting this expenditure on 'military effort' in comparative perspective.

Table 2.3 *Military expenditure as a percentage of national income, 1710–80*

Year	National income (£m)	Military spending (£m)	%
1710	59.8	5.4	9.0
1740	55.2	5.5	10.0
1760	69.4	9.9	14.0
1780	97.7	12.2	12.5

SOURCE: *British Parliamentary Papers*, vol. 35 (1868–9).

If a comparative assessment of government spending on war is hampered by inadequate economic statistics, a comparison of manpower commitment founders on the question of what manpower figures mean. Aggregate numbers of the size of European armies are an extremely crude indicator.[31] Their value as a measure of the effect of military recruitment on the civilian labour market is largely vitiated by the presence of a large (and varying) proportion of foreigners in almost all of the large armies of Europe. The French army, for example, contained many foreign units, including bodies of Germans, Italians, Swiss and Irishmen. According to André Corvisier, three-quarters of the wartime French army might consist of foreign troops.[32] A similar foreign presence was to be found in the Prussian and Spanish armies. At mid-century about 38 per cent of the Prussian troops were not Prussian subjects; by the last quarter of the century the proportion had risen to over a half. In Spain in 1751 28 of the army's 133 battalions were manned by troops who were not Spanish. British armies were equally dependent upon foreign manpower. During the campaign in Ireland in 1690, two British monarchs, James II and William III, fought each other with troops from France (both Huguenot and Catholic), the United Provinces, Denmark, Sweden and Prussia. The pattern persisted throughout the century. During the American War over 32,000 Germans fought for the British against the colonists. Drawing on the resources of those small German states which specialized in renting troops to other powers, the British hired regiments from Hesse-Cassel, Hesse-Hanau, Brunswick, Ansbach-Bayreuth, Waldeck and Anhalt-Zerbst.[33]

We face further difficulties if we ask how many subjects in a given state aquired military experience as a result of their nation's engagement in war. In order to answer this question we need to know more about an army than its size. The frequency and length of wars (which, in turn, affected the size of the armies deployed) and the turnover in army personnel also have to be taken into account. Death and desertion meant that the composition of armies changed rapidly. During the Seven Years War the French army lost about one-fifth of its men every year. Losses in the Prussian army under Frederick William I ran at a similar rate.[34] It is therefore possible that in the course of five years the composition of both armies could have changed totally.

The difficulties of using army statistics as indicators of military commitment become apparent if we compare two different estimates of English military effort during the War of Spanish Succession. Corvisier puts the number of British 'effectives' in 1710 at 75,000 or one for every 147 British civilians.[35] This figure, when compared with similar calculations for other European states, places Britain far down in his table measuring military effort. But he conflates the notion of military effort with the size of national armies. In 1710, in addition to its national army (whose correct number was nearly 139,000)[36], 105,000 foreign troops were in British pay and 48,000 men were in the royal navy and marines. In all nearly 300,000 were on the British military payroll. If we include these added numbers and even if we accept Corvisier's population figure for Great Britain and Ireland (which is almost certainly an overestimate of more than one million), the calculation of the ratio of effectives to population drops to one in thirty-six, a level akin to that he gives for Prussia or Sweden and greater than that for Austria, France, Russia and Spain.

It should be clear from this example that calculations of this sort are fraught with difficulty. The population figures and army statistics are, of course, subject to a wide margin of error. But, more to the point, crude population – army ratios seem to be of limited value. Fluctuations in army size, lack of knowledge of the precise rate of troop turnover, variations in the number of foreigners serving in national armies – all of these factors render any calculations about army manpower and its impact on the supply of civilian labour extremely conjectural.

We can, of course, change our criteria and examine the total number of armed forces – army, navy, militia, foreign troops – mobilized by a given state. This shows us that, despite quite a small population, Britain was nevertheless able to put a great many men in the field and on the high seas. And this, in turn, reminds us of the universal truth of Cicero's maxim that monies are the sinews of war. For, as we shall see in Chapter 4, it was England's ability to mobilize her wealth that explains how she was able to sustain such a powerful military effort. And the ease with which substantial sums were raised is attributable to three circumstances: the existence of a powerful representative with undisputed powers of national taxation; the presence of a commercialized economy whose structure made it comparatively simple to tax; and the deployment of fiscal expertise that made borrowing against tax income an easy task.

Civilian Government and Military Might

It is conventional to identify two different consequences of the emergence in the seventeenth century of professional standing armies led neither by a feudal warrior class nor by military contractors but officered by servants of the state. On the one hand, Western Europe – notably France and England – saw 'the isolation of the army from the populace'. On the other, parts of Eastern Europe – above all Prussia – were characterized by 'the subordination of civilians to the military authorities'.[37] As a result 'eastern and central European societies tended to become more "military" [while] in western Europe we find military social groups within but distinct from society as a whole'.[38] Though, as we shall see, there are problems with this distinction, there can also be no doubt that the British state fell into the category of those states in which the power of the armed forces remained politically and socially restricted. Eighteenth-century Britain was a society in which military might remained both subordinate to and separate from civilian government. It was also a society in which great efforts were made to circumscribe and dilute military power within England itself.

Most European armies were direct adjuncts of royal power. They were paid for and led by monarchs. Trans-national in composition, these troops were less the armies of nations than the forces of states whose diplomatic and military objectives were defined by the dynastic and territorial interests of their rulers. Most British visitors to Frederick the Great's Prussia were struck by the remarkable degree of *personal* control that the king exercised over his army and administration.[39] Their surprise underlines the extent to which British military effort was thought of as national rather than dynastic. This is not to say that British monarchs were cyphers, nor to deny that they had a vital say in diplomacy, strategy and the workings, both tactical and internal, of the armed forces. But much of the debate about war and diplomacy in eighteenth-century Britain was about reconciling the dynastic and personal interests of the monarch – William III's concern with the balance of power in Europe, the first two Hanoverians' desire to protect their beloved Electorate – with a broadly defined public interest. Such a debate only occurred because the national representative, as well as the crown, exercised some control over Britain's armed forces.

Apart from the Dutch Republic, England was the only major eighteenth-century power in which the strength and funding of the army and navy were determined by 'the estates'. After the Glorious Revolution military power was hedged about with a number of constraints, designed both to prevent the army's deployment as a tool of monarchical absolutism and to restrict military activity within Britain itself. Parliament established control of military funding and determined both the size of the army and the nature of its military law. A standing army could be raised in peacetime only with parliamentary consent. (Indeed, even military men who defended the peacetime standing army as 'necessary' conceded that it was 'unconstitutional' and required annual indemnification through a vote of the House of Commons.)[40] Foreign troops could also not be brought into England without the permission of parliament. Thus, though 'the Government, Command and Disposition of the Army' was one of the prerogatives of the crown, it could only be exercised effectively with parliamentary approval.

The structure of command both over and within the army also worked against the concentration of military power. Though the monarch was the supreme commander, he had no single military authority or board through which his wishes could be expressed. The Secretary of War, the king's military representative in the government, was a minor civilian official who did not normally sit in the Cabinet and whose views rarely affected policy. His department did not administer the ordnance and engineers, troops on the Irish establishment (who made up a large part of the peacetime standing army) nor forces in the colonies.[41] Though the monarch sometimes appointed a single military figure as captain-general – a post held by Marlborough and by George II's son, the Duke of Cumberland – commanders in the different theatres of war retained great autonomy. And even if the captain-general was able to exercise overall control of the army and, like the Duke of Cumberland, affect its *internal* organization, he was rarely capable of affecting the broader lines of policy. Only in the case of the Duke of Marlborough was the post of captain-general combined with the power to affect government diplomacy and grand strategy. Soldiers were the tools of the civilian powers, not vice versa.

This is not to say that military men never held posts with important civic and political responsibilities. At the local level, many army officers were magistrates (though they were not allowed to exercise their civilian powers in cases which dealt with the army), while nationally both army and naval officers sat in parliament. Throughout this period the military presence in both the commons and the lords was substantial. Army and navy officers comprised between 10 and 15 per cent of the total membership of the lower house (see Table 2.4). They were the largest professional group in the commons, exceeding the number of practising lawyers. Their total was almost exactly that of the merchants, bankers and industrialists who joined them at Westminster. In the lords sat such illustrious military figures as Argyll, Marlborough, Cadogan, Cumberland, Cobham, Ligonier, Amherst, Sackville, Torrington, Anson, Hawke, Keppel, Howe and Rodney. Between 1714 and 1763 thirty-nine colonels of British regiments sat in the upper house either as hereditary members of the English aristocracy or as Scottish elected peers.[42]

But in neither house did military men act as a concerted interest, except in those matters internal to the armed forces such as terms of pay and conditions of employment. They defended their own service, offered knowledgeable commentary on strategy, and could usually be relied upon to vote with the government. But, for all the apprehensions of some back-benchers, there is no evidence that they had a design to increase military power in the government at large.

Ironically, the presence of military men in parliament was a sign not of the militarization of government but of the permeation of the military by civilian politics. Army commissions were bought and sold – the so-called purchase

Table 2.4 *Percentage of military men in the commons, 1715–90*

Parliament	Total MPs	Soldiers	Sailors	Percentage military men
1715–22	739	58	11	9.3
1722–7	673	53	14	9.6
1727–34	684	53	11	9.4
1734–41	690	55	14	10.0
1741–7	685	65	19	12.3
1747–54	671	68	21	13.3
1754–90	1964	208	79	14.7

SOURCES: Romney Sedgwick (ed.), *The History of Parliament*: vol. 1, *The House of Commons, 1715–1754* (2 vols., HMSO, London, 1970); Sir Lewis Namier and John Brooke (eds.), *The History of Parliament*: vol. 3, *The House of Commons, 1754–1790* (3 vols., HMSO, 1964).

system – and their traffic was determined by a mixture of market forces and political clientage.[43] Commerce in naval commissions was forbidden and promotion limited by seniority, but at higher levels the choice commands and stations were likely to go, especially in peacetime, to those in political favour. A seat in the commons or more precisely a vote in the lower house could therefore affect a military career. As the future major-general James Mure Campbell was advised in the 1770s, 'If your inclinations are to push forward in the army, undoubtedly being in parliament is the only way.'[44]

Historians, mindful of royal control of military appointments, have been sceptical about the value of parliamentary seats to military men, but the officers themselves had no doubt about their importance. This is why 152 of the 374 colonels of regiments between 1714 and 1763 sat in the House of Commons.[45] They needed to develop 'an interest' both with the crown and with powerful political patrons if they were to achieve promotion. Faithful (not to say slavish) adherence to the administration's line could help secure a better billet and swifter advancement; conversely, political opposition, like that of Admiral Vernon in the 1740s or of General Conway in the 1760s, could lead to removal from the list of flag officers or the loss of a regimental command. As distinguished military men like John Fane, Earl of Westmorland, came to realize, opposition, especially when it touched upon matters close to the monarch himself, could provoke swift and harsh retaliation.[46] Military advancement was never merely a matter of military merit. Politics touched every aspect of English life, and neither the army nor the navy was exempt from its clutches.

In Britain, then, military power had little or no autonomous existence; it was subordinate to those civilians who wielded political authority. The organization and command of the army (the navy was less of a concern because it was deemed no great threat to civil liberty) was deliberately constructed to preclude a monopoly of military force. But this did not prevent the armed forces from acting effectively against Britain's foreign enemies and from impinging upon English society.

Military Power and the People

There were four main ways in which eighteenth-century civilian populations came into contact with armed forces. The first was the most to be feared: confrontation with a foreign army or navy which might at best exact tribute and ransom and at worst perpetrate the atrocities of murder, rape and pillage. Somewhat more palatable, but not at all desirable, was contact with the operational forces of your own country. They were likely to demand food and lodging, possibly pay for them, and probably cause less mayhem and damage than the enemy. Thirdly, most civilians were likely to face members of the armed forces bent on recruiting them, sometimes by fair means, more often by foul, into the ranks of armies and navies. And finally, armies also acted as domestic policemen, maintaining public order and pursuing those accused of crime.

It is fair to say that during the eighteenth century the British populace remained, by the standards of their fellow Europeans, remarkably free from contact with armed forces, whether hostile or friendly. Undoubtedly the single most important circumstance affecting this situation was the virtual absence of hostilities within Britain. Except during the Irish campaign of 1689-92, and in Scotland and northern England during the Jacobite rebellions of 1715 and 1745, Britons had little contact with war on their own soil. Though the struggle between James and William in Ireland involved a substantial number of troops – about 40,000 on each side – the battles during the Jacobite rebellions never involved more than 10,000 men on either side. No vast armies left their scabrous trail of disease and spoliation across the British countryside. On the whole, invading armies, because they were British, behaved with tolerable order and decency. The Jacobite literature on the rebellions of 1715 and 1745 boasts proudly, and with some justification, of the good behaviour of those enlisted under the Pretenders. The rebel armies did not engage in indiscriminate plunder but paid for their supplies with public monies, chiefly excise taxes, which they collected as they marched south.[47] Civilian casualties during these British campaigns were light, except at the sieges of Londonderry and Athlone during the Irish campaign, at the dreadful massacre of the Macdonalds at Glencoe in 1692, and after the battle of Culloden in 1746, when the Duke of Cumberland's army embarked on a campaign of terror designed to break Highland sympathy for the Jacobite cause.

The treatment of the Scots by the English was brutal and degrading, but it never matched the levels of death and destruction inflicted by continental armies. Though there were parts of Europe which were rarely troubled by troops – either hostile or friendly – large areas were repeatedly traversed and fought over. Flanders, the Rhineland, Northern Italy, central and northern Germany, Bohemia, Brandenburg and East Prussia, Poland, Moldavia and the Ukraine all suffered devastation and plunder. During the Nine Years War the Palatinate, Rhineland and Württemberg were systematically devastated by the

French. Between 1693 and 1697 the population of Württemberg fell from 450,000 to 300,000; the area sustained over 8 million gilders worth of damage. The French returned during the War of Spanish Succession. They also devastated Catalonia during the Spanish campaign. Marlborough and Eugene, on behalf of the allies, plundered Bavaria. Similar civilian devastation occurred during the Seven Years War. It is estimated that between 1756 and 1763 70,000 Pomeranian non-combatants lost their lives; a quarter of the population of the New Mark of Brandenburg was either killed or fled the province.[48]

We tend to think of eighteenth-century wars, fought after the sectarian horrors of the Thirty Years War and before the mobilization of vast national forces during the French revolutionary era, as decorous and limited affairs fought by professional soldiers who shared a common military culture separate from civilian life. But we should not be misled by the development of codes governing the conduct of rival bodies of troops, by the etiquette of an international officer class, and still less by the emergence of clearly identifiable (because uniformed) soldiery into assuming that non-combatants were protected from the horrors of war. There was probably less random pillaging and looting in the eighteenth century because officers were able to exercise greater discipline and control over their troops. But this did not prevent commanders of armies exacting crippling tribute from occupied civilian populations, nor did it preclude the deliberate devastation of lands – like the scorched earth tactics adopted by the Russians against the Swedes during the Great Northern War – as one weapon in the military armory.

Every European commander was aware that even a friendly army was a heavy burden to be borne by the civilian populace. Hence the practice of wintering troops abroad, preferably on enemy territory. Louis XIV used Flanders and Frederick the Great employed Saxony in this way. Neither wished to impose on their own subjects the cost of provender and supply when they could be extorted from another power. In Britain the number of soldiers needing quarters and supply rarely reached continental proportions. In peacetime there were usually about 10,000 to 15,000 troops in mainland Britain. The wartime figures are more difficult to calculate because so many regiments were on the move. When there was a threat of invasion the numbers were considerable. In 1756–7, for instance, the establishment in south Britain was 39,000 men, and there were also 20 battalions of Germans camped in southern England.[49]

Even on those occasions when troop numbers in England were high, civilians were reassured by the knowledge that they were protected from military excesses by the letter of the law. Where the private citizen and the armed forces came into contact, civilian law overrode military jurisdiction. Any act perpetrated by a member or members of the armed forces on the public was liable to adjudication under common or statute law in the civilian courts. This applied as much to official actions executed under orders from a military superior as it did to acts performed by individuals while in the King's service. As one eighteenth-century military manual put it, 'officers and soldiers guilty of any capital crime, or of any violence or offence against the person, estate or property of any subject, which is punishable by law, [are] to be delivered over to the Civilian magistrate'.[50] Wearing the King's uniform provided no immunity from the law of the land.[51] This meant that the lieutenant who planned to hand over his brother officer to the local justice of the peace for assaulting the eponymous hero of Henry Fielding's *Tom Jones* was acting within the strict letter of the law. It also ensured that soldiers who helped impress recruits or disperse rioters could be sued, if they failed to conform to the civil law, for such crimes as assault or even murder. Military discipline, enshrined in the Mutiny Acts, applied strictly and exclusively to army matters.

Eighteenth-century legal commentators formally conceded that in the direst circumstances (by which they meant during a foreign invasion and/or domestic insurrection) martial law could override the normal laws of the land. But on only three occasions in the period – during the Jacobite rebellions of 1715 and 1745 and the Gordon riots of 1780 – was the authority of the civilian power partially suspended. And at no point did this lead to the wholesale replacement of civilian by martial law. Indeed, when it was rumoured in 1780 that those arrested during the Gordon riots were to be tried under martial law, the government issued a swift and explicit denial.[52] No doubt the absence of martial law is partly attributable to the concern for Englishmen's liberties, but it was also a consequence of the comparative tranquillity of the nation. Only in 1715 did the government feel so insecure as to call on *all* its subjects to act against the Jacobites, promising full indemnity for any action taken against the rebels.

Not only did military law normally give way to civilian jurisdiction, but common and statute law also governed such military activities as the billeting and movement of troops within mainland Britain. Very few soldiers were stationed in garrisons, forts and barracks in England; only in Scotland and Ireland were troops so quartered. Though most military commentators were advocates of barracks, the bulk of political opinion was implacably opposed to them. In the often quoted words of General Wade, 'the people of this kingdom have been taught to associate the idea of Barracks and Slavery so closely together that, like darkness and the Devil, though there is no manner of connection between them, yet they cannot separate them'.[53] Keeping troops in the public eye and mingling them with a liberty-loving populace, it was argued, would prevent the spread of autocratic ideas within the ranks, rendering the army less likely to act as the tool of tyranny.

This did not mean, however, that troops were quartered in private residences. After 1688 this was illegal except with pre-payment and the permission of the owner. Instead troops were billeted in public houses. Such arrangements had, however, to be made with the knowledge and concurrence of local justices of the peace. Only the civil power could require landlords to provide troops with food and shelter. This contained, though it did not eliminate the damage inflicted by troops. As one lieutenant-colonel wrote after marching across southern England from Canterbury to Devizes, 'We have ruined half the public houses upon the march; because they have quartered us in villages too poor to feed us without destruction to themselves.'[54]

Troop movement as well as billeting was constrained by law. Troops were prohibited from towns where an election or assize was being held, except with the express permission of the local authorities. Within England the army was not allowed to provide transport or to impress vehicles to move goods and supplies. These had to be carried by civilians at rates and in circumstances determined by JPs. Few local carriers were willing to move army supplies over long distances. As a result, when forces needed to move rapidly within Britain, as during the Jacobite rebellion of 1745, they were hampered both by the need to find suitable transport and by the frequency with which baggage had to be removed from one carrier to another.[55]

The object of these billeting and transport arrangements, which almost all commentators recognized as making little military sense, was, as Lord Kenyon, the Lord Chancellor, made clear, 'to preserve, as much as possible from the nature of the thing, control of the Civil over the Military power'.[56] The intent of legislation was to ensure that the armed forces in England caused as little inconvenience and inflicted as little damage as possible upon the civilian population. It was more important to curb military power in England than to ensure military efficiency. ▶

If Englishmen regarded the billeting of the standing army on private citizens as one sign of tyranny, another was coercive conscription into the armed forces. For most of the eighteenth century the British army relied for its recruits on volunteers who were paid a bounty in return for enrolling in the service of the crown. Patriotically minded groups sometimes helped supplement this state recruitment by raising 'bounty' money by public subscription. In 1759, for example, several large towns, including London and Newcastle, raised money to encourage new recruits.[57] Individuals, especially those desirous of a command, also helped raise regiments. But for the ordinary soldier, as opposed to the officer, the hard and hazardous life of the army offered few attractions.

Strict discipline, great personal hazard and poor and irregular pay meant that in wartime the demand for men usually exceeded the supply, so that the government was forced to adopt the unpopular practice of impressment. In every major eighteenth-century war the government used conscription to swell the army's ranks: between 1702 and 1712, 1745–6, 1756–7 and 1778–9 volunteers were reinforced by unwilling conscripts. Recruitment into the army was closely monitored by the civilian authorities. For most of the period enlisted men had to appear before JPs to attest to their voluntary enrolment in the ranks.[58] The system of impressment similarly worked under civilian aegis. Impressment was legally confined to 'such able-bodied men as had not any lawful calling or employment'. Men were pressed by both soldiers and parish officials who brought them before press commissioners who were JPs or, after 1709, commissioners of the land tax. The poor, the friendless and the 'undesirable' (however defined) were all drawn into the commissioners' net.

The powers conferred on the commissioners were considerable and open to abuse. In Halifax in the 1740s, for example, the Methodist preacher John Nelson was impressed despite being a tradesman in good repute. Local gentry hostile to his preaching wanted him out of the way. Only several months later was Nelson able to secure a discharge. A less determined man would have been forced to remain in the ranks.[59]

But not everyone who was brought before the commissioners ended up in the army. Two out of three men were discharged as ineligible or unsuitable, and those who disputed the decision of the commissioners that they were fit to serve could appeal either to higher courts or to the Secretary of War. The real constraint on the system of recruiting was, however, the reluctance of the civilian authorities, especially the constables, to enforce the press with any rigour. They were partly deterred by the prospect of being sued for wrongful arrest or assault, but they also disliked a system of conscription that was so palpably coercive.[60]

The notoriously unpopular practice of naval impressment was even more frequent than army conscription, normally lasting the entire duration of a war. The naval press gang is usually viewed as the inevitable consequence of an entirely rational desire on the part of the public to avoid the dreadful conditions that accompanied naval service. It is as if not only historians but potential recruits had been listening to Dr Samuel Johnson when, in his no nonsense fashion, he had described the fate of the sailor: 'No man will be a sailor who has contrivance enough to get himself into jail; for being in a ship is being in a jail with the chance of being drowned . . . A man in jail has more room, better food and commonly better company'.[61] Authoritative as it sounds, this remark is palpably incorrect. Volunteers, as Rodger has shown, were vital to naval manning and, at least in the Seven Years War, came forward, seamen and landsmen both, in considerable numbers.[62] Impressment was necessary not because naval service was especially odious – it compared well with employment in the merchant marine – but because the combined requirements of the royal navy and the merchant marine outstripped the available supply of skilled sailors.

As in their dealings with army officers engaged in conscription, civil authorities were reluctant to help naval press gangs in their drive to secure seafaring men. Though the navy called on justices and constables to aid their search for sailors, the response of the local authorities was more likely to be obstructive than helpful. The organization of the naval press appeared more arbitrary than that of the army because there was no requirement that the press gangs bring their victims before a body of civilians to determine the eligibility for service of those who had been seized. It therefore appeared as if there were no civil restraint on military action. But press gang victims and their allies were not reluctant to go to law or to appeal (sometimes successfully) to higher naval authority.

The actions of the press gangs were confined to the high seas – where sailors were impressed from merchantmen – and to the major ports. Recent research indicates that the overwhelming majority of those impressed were the seafaring men the royal navy so desperately required. Inexperienced, not to say unfit landlubbers, like those conscripts often offered by magistrates eager to empty the gaols, were not the sort of men the navy was willing to employ.

Naval impressment was hazardous both for the merchant sailor and for the naval ratings in the press gang. Confrontations between the two were often bloody and underlined the coercive character of impressment. Yet, for all the opposition it provoked, impressment was invariably deemed legal by the higher courts. The argument was that of 'state necessity', the usual legal ground for extraordinary conduct in time of war. This interpretation was open to challenge, but the cumbersome, crude and expensive practice of impressment remained, not least because of the political hostility to a more overtly bureaucratic system of naval recruiting.

During the major wars of the eighteenth century the English populace was affected by the army's need for billets and by a manpower requirement the armed forces could not possibly meet by the recruitment of volunteers. In peacetime the public was more likely to confront the army acting as a domestic police force. The peacetime standing force in mainland Britain of 10–15,000 men belonged mostly to horse regiments, which were widely dispersed throughout the mainland. They were scattered not only because of a constitutional desire to have them mix with civilians, but because their distribution enabled them to perform their peacetime duties more efficiently. The task of the army was threefold: to enforce the navigation and fiscal laws – in other words to suppress smuggling; to maintain and restore public order, which meant the suppression of all forms of riot; and to crush domestic insurrection, which, in this period, took the form of the Jacobite risings of 1715 and 1745. To these ends, troops were deployed by the War Office in the main smuggling areas – Cornwall, Devonshire, Dorset and south Wiltshire, Sussex, Kent, East Anglia, the Lancashire coast and the Scottish borders – in places such as Bristol and the Wiltshire clothing towns where industrial disorders were likely to occur, and in the Lowlands of Scotland.

Government supporters argued explicitly in favour of a sizable peacetime standing army because of its value 'in keeping of restless spirits in awe'.[63] The threat of military action, government officials maintained, would secure loyalty and prevent civil disturbance. As Henry Pelham put it, 'when ever there was a small number of men [in the army], rebellions are hatched'.[64] Similar assumptions informed a government speaker's remark in the summer of 1736 that, 'with regard to mobs and tumults, we find by Experience that regular troops are of great use, not only for preventing any such happening, but for

quelling and dispersing them after they have happened'.[65] Successive administrations saw the army as an important means of securing a stable social order.

Suppressing the extensive and illegal practice of smuggling was one of the
main tasks of the peacetime standing army. As customs and excise duties grew
more widespread and more onerous, the incentive to evade them increased.
In many coastal areas extensive smuggling networks, linking small and large
traders who far outnumbered the officers of revenue, brought in spirits, tea
and tobacco without paying duty. To prevent this illicit trade small numbers
of troops were dispersed among large numbers of coastal settlements. Thus in
1739 263 men and officers were stationed in forty-two towns and villages on
the East Anglian coast. Similarly, some quarter of a century later, 150 of
the 2nd Dragoons were deployed in nineteen different towns and villages in
Hampshire and Sussex to help revenue officers apprehend smugglers.[66] Much
of the army's work involved direct and often dangerous confrontations with
groups of smugglers who were heavily armed. In December 1740, for example,
a band of smugglers shot and killed a customs official, wounded two dragoons,
including one corporal who 'received eleven bullets or slugs in his head,
shoulder, elbow and right side of his back', and seized the contraband the
soldiers had impounded.[67] When smugglers were attacked carrying large
amounts of contraband they stood their ground, for they were unwilling to
surrender their haul. Some smuggling operations therefore ended in pitched
battles between the army and smugglers. But army action was sometimes much
more covert. Soldiers disguised themselves as traders to catch the sellers of
smuggled goods and spent long hours tracing smugglers in order to win the
financial rewards offered for their apprehension.[68]

The detection and suppression of smuggling, the so-called 'coastal duty',
was very much a part of the routine of the peacetime standing army. Less
frequently, troops were called upon to suppress riot and restore public order.
The full catalogue of eighteenth-century crowd action is by now well known:
grain, bread and price riots, industrial collective bargaining by riot, enclosure
and turnpike riots, riots against government legislation and in favour of
political and religious causes. Against these, at the request of the civil magistrate, and under orders from the Secretary of State and the Secretary of War,
troops were often called upon to control or disperse a crowd. During the
militia, enclosure and price riots in 1757, for example, no fewer than twenty
regiments were employed in support of the civil power. Nine years later,
when the worst and most extensive price riots occurred prior to the French
Revolution, troops were deployed in sixty-eight towns in twenty different
counties. And during the Gordon Riots of 1780, between 10,000 and 12,000
troops were stationed in and around the metropolis.[69]

The suppression of riot by armed force often led to civilian injuries and
death. As one historian, though sympathetic to the army's task, has remarked,
'the mid-eighteenth-century was remarkable for the number of riots which
ended fatally for several of the participants'.[70] Twenty-one civilians were killed

at the Hexham militia riot of 1759, twelve died near the King's Bench Prison at the St George's Fields massacre of 1768, and there were an estimated 285 fatalities during the Gordon Riots.[71]

Riot duty was unpopular with the army. Even the Secretary of War, Lord Barrington, described the task as 'a most Odious Service which nothing but Necessity can justify'.[72] Some officers, including the young Colonel Wolfe, despised such dishonourable duty and felt some sympathy for the crowds they confronted. But much of the unease about riot control stemmed from the confused and ambiguous legal position surrounding the use of troops to secure public order. It was widely believed that army officers could not act against a crowd without the sanction of a JP. It was also, after the passage of the Riot Act of 1716, commonly assumed that no action could be taken to break up a gathering until one hour after the reading of a proclamation ordering the crowd to disperse. Neither of these assumptions was strictly correct. Under common law soldiers, like civilians, were not only entitled but obliged to act against a crowd once it pursued any illegal action (such as an attack on property) with force or violence. Yet the apprehension – sometimes realized – that officers and their men might be sued in the courts for their actions served to restrain the military. There are numerous instances in the eighteenth century of troops standing by, awaiting the instructions of a JP or the passage of an hour after the proclamation, while crowds acted with impunity.

Nevertheless, the military was an important means of maintaining public order and one to which the civil authorities, for all their soul searching, had frequent recourse. Indeed by the last quarter of the eighteenth century, rioters in England were more likely than those in France to be confronted by armed soldiers. As the continental power armed the *maréchaussé* and town watchers, so troops were left to guard the nation's border or to aid the construction of such public works as canals and roads. Though England's peacetime force performed such duties – the canal in St James's Park was built using army labour – they were far more likely to be hunting smugglers or dispersing rioters. As Houlding, the author of the most thorough account of the standing army, has written, 'the army, which if small was nevertheless omnipresent, played a police role simply by maintaining a presence ... a study of the disposition that units assumed upon their arrival in duty areas indicates that policing was clearly a major consideration when marching orders were drawn'.[73]

On occasion the line between riots and rebellion was thinly drawn. Frightened men of property regarded the Gordon Riots of 1780 as an 'insurrection', and the numerous pro-Jacobite riots, especially those of 1715–16, were similarly described. But these have to be distinguished from the occasions in 1715, 1719 and 1745 when the armed and (sometimes) uniformed troops of the Pretender challenged the Hanoverian state.

When attempting to suppress rebellion, the British army's performance proved barely adequate. Indeed, during all three Jacobite risings it was thought necessary to reinforce English regiments with Dutch troops, and Hessians were also employed in 1745. Preparations against the risings of 1715–16 were adequate, but in both England and Scotland the government's forces were able to secure military victory by the narrowest of margins. Overall, fifteen regiments of horse and eleven of foot were deployed against the Jacobites and, by 1716, Scotland was occupied by 12,000 troops of whom about half were Dutch.[74] In addition large numbers of troops were quartered in those English towns that were believed to be sympathetic to the Pretender. Soldiers clashed with anti-Hanoverian civilians in Oxford, Ashbourne in Derbyshire, Leicester, Manchester, Uttoxeter and Bridgwater.[75] Four years later three regiments of foot quashed the pathetic Jacobite rising at Glenshiel.

The events of 1745-6 reflect less well on the British army. Defeated on every occasion except the final battle of Culloden, the army was ill-prepared and its morale seriously undermined by the (overinflated) reputation of the Pretender's Highland troops. Preparations against the invasion were inadequate and coordination among the different forces of the crown was woefully lacking. Eventually 13,000 English soldiers were deployed against the young Pretender, as well as sixteen battalions of Dutch and Hessian troops. The ferocity with which the Highlands were 'pacified' after the rising is partly attributable to the desire of Cumberland and his officers to compensate for the strategic and military vulnerability that Prince Charles's supporters exposed.

The army's three main domestic tasks of policing the revenue, maintaining public order and preventing insurrection were intimately connected with each other for most of the first half of the eighteenth century. The government's greatest apprehension about smuggling was not the loss of revenue[76] – officials recognized that with high duties evasion was inevitable – but a fear that smuggling encouraged disrespect for the law, defiance of authority and public disorder.[77] This anxiety was compounded in the early Hanoverian era by smugglers' willingness to declare their allegiance for the Stuart Pretender and to aid Jacobites travelling secretly between France and the coast of southern England.[78] Indeed the Walpolean whigs – in many instances with good justification – were inclined to see all forms of public disorder as fomented either by Jacobites or by those with Jacobite sympathies.[79]

It was for this reason that they set such store by a peacetime standing army. They, at least, had no doubt of the importance of force in sustaining their regime. As Walpole himself put it with characteristic bluntness in 1737, 'whatever other impracticable notions some gentlemen may entertain, I believe that there is no maxim more true than that force is necessary for the support of government'.[80] Such views were much criticized and never commanded universal acceptance. For many critics of government, the standing army was part of an oppressive order, incapable of commanding support without coercion. As Bath put it in 1749, 'The Army causes Taxes, the Taxes cause Discontents, & the Discontents are Alledged to make an Army necessary. Thus you go in a circle'.[81] When the army helped sustain both the Hanoverian monarchy and the whig regime, its actions had the effect, as we shall see, of politicizing army affairs to a degree that was never true of the navy, colouring to an even deeper hue the already jaundiced views in English society about the proper use of troops.

Professionalism, Politics and the Public

Between the late seventeenth and late eighteenth centuries the British army and navy acquired a degree of professionalism they had never before enjoyed. Sustained commitment to both, made possible by the fiscal capacity of the state, created a standing army and permanent navy. The armed forces became a reputable calling for genteel members of society; military careers and dynasties were formed amongst the officer class. Such professionalism came first in the navy but was developed in the army by the end of the Seven Years War. But in one vital respect the history of landed and water-borne forces diverged. This difference is sometimes seen as that between the popularity of the navy and hostility towards the army. But the distinction we should draw is less simple: one between a navy whose political function commanded unanimous and widespread support even when its tactics were criticized and an army whose political role was always a matter of dispute even when its military actions excited general approval.

Whatever the public attitude towards their conduct, British army and navy officers had as much in common with fellow commanders of the forces of other belligerent powers in Europe as with the civilian population from which they emanated. They belonged to an international fraternity, both united and divided by the profession of violence. Service in more than one navy was comparatively unusual, though British naval officers sometimes served with the Russian navy.[82] But top rank army officers frequently served in armies other than those of their native states. Frederick von Schomberg served with the French, Portuguese, Prussians, Dutch and English. The two most successful French generals in the War of Austrian Succession were Maurice de Saxe, a German, and Ulrich von Lowerdahl, a Dane.

The life of the professional army officer, which was both peculiarly cosmopolitan and singularly inbred, is well illustrated by the career of Field Marshal John Ligonier, one of Britain's most successful generals. A French Huguenot who rose to be commander-in-chief of the British army during the Seven Years War, Ligonier was also elevated to both the Irish and the English peerage. He was born in 1680 in Castres in the south of France. Educated in his native country and in Switzerland, he fled to Dublin in 1697, distinguished himself in the British army during the War of Spanish Succession, and became famous as a soldier of astonishing intrepidity who lavished exceptional care on his men. Two of his brothers served as officers in the British army, while his nephew rose to the rank of lieutenant-general. It is possible that he faced a third brother, who fought in the French cavalry, on the field of battle.

Captured in July 1747 at the battle of Val, after fighting a brilliant rearguard action to save the Duke of Cumberland's army, he was presented to Louis XV as a military hero by his great adversary and admirer, the Marshal de Saxe.

Ligonier's career may appear at first sight to be uncharacteristic of those of his brother officers in the British army. Was he not a Huguenot and brilliant to boot? And did he not belong to one of those categories of displaced persons (Jacobites and Irish Catholics were others) who were to be found leading soldiers all over Europe? Ligonier *was* exceptional, but not as exceptional as all that. Like their Protestant *confrères*, the Scots, Huguenot officers were common in the British army. About one in ten colonels serving between 1713 and 1763 were of Huguenot origin, and they were still better represented in the lower ranks of officer.[83] Indeed, the Huguenot officer was a sufficiently familiar character to be parodied by Henry Fielding in *Tom Jones* as the soldier who had forgotten his native tongue but had also failed to acquire English.

But, more to the point, Ligonier was but one member (albeit a distinguished one) of a growing body of professional army officers. In Ligonier's lifetime, which almost spanned the century between the reign of Charles II and the outbreak of the American War (he was ninety when he died in 1770), the British army acquired a solid core of career army officers. Two factors were crucial in this development. The first was the twenty-five-year period of almost continuous warfare with the French, which helped create a core of battle-seasoned and militarily experienced officers. As one pamphleteer put it, with pardonable exaggeration, the wars against Louis XIV succeeded in 'teaching us The Military Art to perfection'.[84] Secondly, the provision after 1714 of half-pay for officers not on active duty meant that, despite the peacetime contraction in the size of the army, holders of the king's commission could remain professional soldiers. By mid-century long service had become the norm. Over 90 per cent of British army colonels serving between 1740 and 1763 had been in the army for more than fifteen years; 58 per cent had been commissioned for more than a quarter of a century. Most captains had fifteen or more years' service behind them, and even a lieutenant would expect to have served for several years as a cornet or ensign before his promotion.[85] Ligonier's long career was quite typical.

So, too, was Ligonier's membership of a military family. Though amongst the gentry and aristocracy as a whole, the conventional practice was to send *one* younger son into the armed forces, by the mid-eighteenth century there were families with numerous siblings enrolled in the ranks of the military. Sir James Agnew of Lochnaw gave all eight of his sons to the army. Three sons of the first Earl of St Albans' entered the army, two more served in the navy. Military service came to run in families, and families became associated with particular regiments. Nine Gores, for instance, served in the 33rd Regiment over a period of two centuries.[86] This trend was reinforced by the practice adopted by many colonels of employing relatives as junior officers in their regiments.

It is often said that the British officer corps was less professional than its European counterparts because it lacked formal military education and because the trade in commissions – the purchase system – obstructed promotion on the basis of merit. Certainly there was no institution in England to match the military schools in France, Austria, Prussia and Russia. Though a naval academy was founded at Portsmouth in 1733, and engineers and artillery officers were educated at Woolwich after 1741, Britain had to wait until 1799, with the founding of Sandhurst, to boast an academy for soldiers like the *École Militaire*, the Austrian academy at Wiener Neustadt, or the cadet schools of Prussia and Russia.[87] But, as John Childs has emphasized, we should not place too much store by the presence or absence of these institutions. In most European armies – even the Prussian – many officers had no formal training before they saw active service. But then little was probably needed. Warfare was neither so technical nor so complex that the absence of a formal education was a handicap. Much of the requisite knowledge was available in drill books and manuals which made up most eighteenth-century military literature. And, at bottom, what counted was experience – not just on the parade ground but in battle. There is no evidence that British officers were noticeably less practised in the martial arts than the leaders of the European troops they opposed.[88]

The impact of the purchase system on the professional competence of British officers can also be exaggerated. The notorious examples of aristocratic and well-heeled youths reaching high rank before puberty were few and far between. The majority of officers rose up the promotional ladder at a steady pace (always accelerated in time of war) which, first and foremost, reflected their military experience but which was also an index of their martial competence. Like all good German princes, the first two Georges, neither of whom liked the purchase system, tried and were largely successful in ensuring the advancement of their most capable officers. They were able to do so because a third of army vacancies were filled without purchase, because they could penalize a regiment in which flagrant jobbery occurred and because the system lent itself to formal regulation by the crown and informal control by the officers themselves. This is not to say that the rich and well-connected did not enjoy advantages in promotion. The purchase system was unjust, but it was not necessarily inefficient. The achievement of high rank required competence as well as influence.

If the British officer corps was both competent and experienced, it was also allowed much less autonomy than the equivalent body in many other European armies. The cumulative effect of a series of reforms, many of them initiated or strongly supported by the first two Georges, was largely to eliminate proprietary soldiering, the practice by which officers managed public funds for private advantage, at both troop and company levels. As Alan Guy, whose study meticulously charts these changes, puts it, 'strictly limited allowances were substituted for hitherto flexible dividends enjoyed by proprietary captains, without any compensating increase in their personal pay'.[89] The result of these reforms was to reduce 'the heterodox regimental economies of the early eighteenth century to a degree of uniformity, and, in so doing [to reduce] opportunities for officers to speculate with their troop or company funds'.[90] Though these reforms were far from comprehensive – they did not include the regulation of colonels' emoluments, nor did they affect some regiments of guards – they nevertheless sharply restricted the proprietary rights of many officers, preventing the sort of profiteering to be found in other European armies, especially that of Prussia.[91]

Parallel with the emergence of a body of professional army officers was the growth of a professional corps of commissioned sea officers. In the seventeenth century officers entered the royal navy under an apprenticeship scheme in which they served as captain's servants. Many of these recruits, whether or not of genteel background, were men of little education and rough manners. They were mariners rather than gentlemen. In the reigns of Charles II and James II, when the monarchs' interest in the navy made it more socially acceptable to become an officer, young gentlemen volunteers were also assigned to particular captains and ships. Regardless of their social origin or means of entry, midshipmen desiring promotion to the rank of lieutenant had to pass a written examination and were required to have served at sea for three years. A system of half-pay, first introduced on a limited basis in 1668, was extended to all officers by 1714. In the 1690s, seniority became the chief (though not sole) criterion for promotion to the ranks of captain and higher.

These changes, introduced gradually over a number of years, ensured that men of quality entered the service, that all officers, regardless of social background, were competent sailors, and that an officer could look forward to a lifelong naval career with good prospects of promotion. As Daniel Baugh has pointed out, the shaping of an officer corps was achieved in two ways – by making gentlemen into seamen and seamen into gentlemen.[92] The success of the Admiralty in creating an officer class with excellent *esprit de corps* is borne out by the pattern of officer recruitment at the end of the century. A quarter of naval officers had fathers who had served in the navy. Many more came from families with other naval relatives.[93]

Both naval and army officers were proud of their status and accomplishments. With a little good fortune – the capture of a prize, a battle in which they distinguished themselves – they could gain both honour and riches. At worst they had an income which put them on a par with a modest gentleman. They wore their uniforms (which became standard in the 1740s) with pride. If they did not appear at court in military regalia, they certainly wore them in public. It is clear from contemporary descriptions of half-pay officers that, even if they were not formally attired, they sported military dress which made them a visually identifiable group at social gatherings. The portraits of army and naval officers show them flaunting their uniforms, surrounded with military impedimenta, and against a background which depicted their military triumphs. These achievements were not only limned on canvas but perpetuated on tombs and memorials. The monument erected in 1725 to Captain Samuel Skynner in the parish church at Ledbury in Gloucestershire is festooned with swords, cannons and naval regalia and honours him as 'no mean proficient in Maritime Affairs'. Officers flaunted their bellicosity: they were known for their keen sense of honour and their willingness to fight duels (they were more likely than civilians to wear a sword). Though military men did not have the status they were to acquire in the era of Jane Austen and the Napoleonic Wars, they nevertheless held themselves in high esteem.

But how were they regarded by the public? Here attitudes towards the army and navy diverged. The navy commanded broad-based approval as an instrument of policy. There is no more telling evidence of this than the fact that, although manpower costs in the navy were twice as high as the army, complaints about the cost of the army were frequent, while those about naval expense were not. The English taxpayer believed that the navy gave value for money in a way he felt the army failed to do. If the former offered plunder, trade and commercial prosperity, the latter's benefits were much less tangible: at best an aid to domestic security, at worst the dangerous plaything of bellicose and autocratic kings.

The discrepancy between public attitudes towards the army and navy is in part attributable to the view, current in the late seventeenth century and after, that Britain's strategic interests were best served by a 'blue water' policy in which the army played a subordinate role to the senior service.[94] But it also reflects the prevalence of a deep-seated anxiety about standing armies as the potential tools of absolutism. The New Model Army, the rule of the Major Generals and James II's Catholic-officered peacetime force were, to most eighteenth-century political commentators, a potent reminder of the incompatibility of standing armies and political liberty. The violence of the debates about the standing army between 1697 and 1701 and the sharp reaction to the sometimes bombastic militarism of the Duke of Marlborough attest to the continuation of that fear, even when parliament had a large measure of control over the army's activities.

This situation was compounded by the Hanoverian Succession. Both George I and George II prided themselves on being military men. George I had served under William III; George II distinguished himself at the battle of Oudenarde (1708) and was the last British monarch to lead his troops into battle, at Dettingen in 1743, though, to judge from the colours that he was wearing, George thought he was leading not a British but a Hanoverian army.[95] Both played an active, and largely beneficial part, in army affairs. But as Germans, as proponents of the standing army, and as monarchs whose strategic aims were both very European and deeply affected by their concern for the Electorate of Hanover, they were viewed with deep suspicion not only by opponents of the dynasty but by those who feared standing armies and looked to a 'blue water' policy for Britain.

The use of the army for domestic policing, the purging of Jacobite officers after 1715, and the advocacy, by Walpole and his minions, of a strong standing army to support the Hanoverian dynasty and the whig regime only served to politicize the question of the standing army even further. As the government's opponents were fond of pointing out, the justification of the standing army as an intimidatory force designed to secure good order and proper allegiance was presumptive evidence of the government's unpopularity and of its inability to lead the nation by moral example. Seen in this light the standing army was a symbol of the illegitimacy of whig oligarchy.

Attitudes towards the army began to change at mid-century. Two circumstances contributed to this shift. First, Britain's remarkable series of victories during the Seven Years War, many of which were the result of amphibious operations involving cooperation between the army and navy, enhanced the public standing of the army. Its role in 'blue water' policies was no longer confined to spoiling operations on the continent of Europe. Second, the accession in 1760 of a monarch opposed to involvement in expensive continental warfare, though it revived the debate over the policy, temporarily cut the link between the British army and the proprietary interests of the Elector of Hanover. The army could be as 'British' as the navy.

The triumphs of the Seven Years War marked an apogee of patriotic bellicosity. The English had long been known in Europe for their contempt for all things foreign. Their recent successes, followed avidly in the press, and the emergence of a panoply of military heroes all fuelled a British chauvinism that was novel only in its intensity. Indeed, for a nation with a reputation for anti-militarism and hostility to a standing army, Britain was remarkably well stocked with martial heros. Marlborough, Granby, Wolfe, Vernon, Anson and Rodney – even George II himself – were celebrated as personifications of Britain's prowess, bravery and skill. Some, like Marlborough and Anson, were publicly rewarded, a few gave their names to inns, taverns and public hostelries and many were the subject of laudatory songs and ballads, of popular prints and engravings.[96]

Attitudes towards military matters in general and towards the army in particular therefore not only varied over time but always contained a measure of ambivalence. Martial prowess and national aggrandizement were to be celebrated in good chauvinist fashion. But, whereas the only sin of a sailor, as Admiral Byng discovered to his cost in 1757, was the failure to press the enemy too hard, soldiers were always suspected of harbouring wicked designs against public and constitution. It is as if the English, even though they had embarked on a titanic struggle with France and had committed themselves to involvement in Europe, were reluctant to admit that they had done so. They wanted military glory without what they saw as European militarism. And to a very large extent they got it.

Britain experienced her military revolution a century after most other European powers. How then does her experience compare with that of the continental states? Certainly there were important differences between civilian-military relations in Britain and elsewhere in Europe. But even if we take the archetypal militarized state – namely Prussia – we can see some important similarities as well as many significant differences.

Prussia had many features of a highly militarized state. Conscription, if not universal, was nationwide: after 1732–3 every canton had to provide a quota of men for the army. (This system was, of course, precisely that employed to man the Swedish army that had occupied Prussia during the Thirty Years War.) Service in the officer corps was *de rigueur* for most of the nobility. As Corvisier points out, 'at the end of the eighteenth century the military nobility represented 68 per cent of aristocratic families in the [Prussian] electoral provinces and 60 per cent of those in Eastern Prussia'.[97] The majority of minor Prussian functionaries and bureaucrats had also spent some time in the armed forces.[98] With the establishment in 1723 of the General Directory of War and Finance it appeared as if a central administrative body had succeeded in subordinating all the major tasks of government – including taxation, the management of the economy and the administration of the royal domains – to the imperious command of a military regime.

We should not, however, exaggerate the degree of militarization of eighteenth-century Prussia, nor the extent to which the state was uniquely centralized. In practice the canton system meant that the burden of military obligation rested firmly on the shoulders of the peasantry. Artisans, traders and merchants, as well as those employed in public service, normally enjoyed exemptions. Even the peasantry were required to be on active service in peacetime for only two months a year.[99] The system, in other words, was analogous to that employed to recruit and embody the English militia after it had been reformed by the parliamentary legislation of 1756 and 1758. The sole but important difference was that conscripts into the English militia served in units which remained separate from the regular army and which could not be sent abroad.

The overwhelmingly aristocratic class of Prussian officers developed a singular *esprit de corps*, but they failed to take over or militarize civilian government or society. The peacetime powers of land-holding officers over their men, many of whom were their serfs, were derived not from their military authority but from the quasi-feudal powers they enjoyed in local courts. Only on active service did the Junkers enjoy military powers over their serfs. This distinction between civil and military power was also observed in the Prussian bureaucracy. Though former military men served in the civilian government, they did not do so *qua* army officers. Cooperation between the military and civilian administrations was close, but was understood to be a collaboration between clearly distinguishable branches of government. Thus Frederick the Great divided his *Political Testament* of 1752 into two parts, the first covering civilian government, the second dealing with the army. By the mid-eighteenth century the civilian bureaucracy, encouraged by Frederick William I and Frederick II, had established a high degree of autonomy. Promotions from within were far more important in administrative recruitment than the incorporation of former army personnel.[100] The ambience of the Prussian civil service in the later eighteenth century was not that of the barracks and the officers' mess but of the salon and the university. Its texts were not drill manuals but learned treatises devoted to *Polizeiwissenschaft*.

The General Directory of War and Finance, though its powers made inroads into those of local jurisdictions, was never an all-powerful central body organized on functional lines. Three of its major departments were regionally based, and its powers stopped short of those of the *Landrat*, the local aristocratic official whose functions resembled those of the English justice of the peace. After the invasion of Silesia in 1740, the development of new administrative bodies and Frederick II's employment of foreign bureaucratic entrepreneurs meant that the Prussian bureaucracy became more rather than less devolved.[101] The General Directory never exercised the degree of centralized control of policy and patronage enjoyed for most of the eighteenth century by the British Treasury Board.

Though there can be no question that the Prussian state was more *dirigiste* than that of England, Prussian absolutism had to reach an understanding with the forces of particularism. The tight control the state was able to exercise over its subjects was achieved not by the wholesale destruction of existing social relationships but by reinforcing them – adding to and building upon the feudal powers of the Prussian aristocracy over their peasants by embodying that power in military form, and by drawing a clearer distinction between tradesmen and artisans on the one hand and peasants on the other.

The contours of the Prussian state were peculiarly consonant with the outlines of power within the Prussian social order. In consequence the benefits the Prussian nobility collectively derived from the military branch of the state were out of all proportion to those gained by the British or French nobilities in their respective countries. It was in this respect that Prussia was a military state. But this was not a case, as Corvisier puts it, of 'the subordination of civilians to military authorities'.[102] On the contrary, it was an instance of the amplification of civilian power by military means.

This produces a marked contrast with England, where one of the major concerns was to *neutralize* the effect of armed forces on the balance of social and political forces in civil society. The great fear of the landed classes was that the creation of a fiscal–military state would produce special interests or powers inimical to what they regarded as the public good. In particular it was feared that new political forms would alter the character of authority, whose effectiveness depended neither on *overt* force nor on quasi-feudal forms of servitude but on the rule of law. Tocqueville described the English ruling class as one which 'submitted that it might command',[103] which accepted constraints on its power in order to exercise that power more effectively. This meant that armed force was of very limited value in enforcing authority in England. In an autocracy, the power to deploy troops to suppress domestic dissent is seen as a sign of strength. But, as we have seen, Walpole's willingness to concede that he needed a peacetime force to secure the regime was viewed – and not just by his enemies[104] – as a sign of weakness.

⚜ 3 ⚜

CIVIL ADMINISTRATION:
The Central Offices of
Government

Britain's military achievements of the eighteenth century would not have been possible without adequate resources in manpower and money. At bottom this meant that without the requisite wealth Britain would not have been able to become a major diplomatic and military power. National resources were the necessary condition of military might but, as most eighteenth-century commentators recognized, they were not sufficient. There was always the possibility that the nation might contract the Dutch disease which, in the words of Lord Sheffield, would leave the British 'rich perhaps, as individuals; but weak, as a State'.[1] Resources had to be mobilized before they could contribute to martial prowess and that required, above all, some sort of systematic administration.

Before the mid-seventeenth century most European states lacked such organization and relied on private entrepreneurs to manage their war efforts, using military 'Enterprisers' to raise and command troops and calling on financial middlemen to raise loans and collect taxes. But from the mid-seventeenth century states began to exercise an unprecedented control over the business of war, largely because they succeeded in improving their administrative capability. Britain was no exception. A growing number of office-holders, organized on departmental lines and run by committees, came to dominate the fiscal and administrative operations of government. This body was not a modern bureaucracy, but neither was it a quasi-feudal special interest, wedded to corporate privilege and individual gain. Much of it was 'efficient', in the sense that it was active. This is hardly surprising. For this body came into being and was nurtured as the means by which civil society was put in harness to the juggernaut of state power.

The Growth of the Administration

Before the late seventeenth century the number of employees of central government in England was small by European standards. This was true even during the Interregnum, when taxes, public expenditure on the armed forces and the costs of civilian government all rose to unprecedented levels. Gerald Aylmer, in his comprehensive study of the Interregnum government service, was able to identify only about 1200 officials of state serving in the eleven years between 1649 and 1660.[2] This figure, of course, underestimates the total number of employees, for it does not include many minor and therefore nameless functionaries in the lower echelons of administration. But the overall picture is clear: the central administrative apparatus was tiny. Despite the putative centralization and rule by committee that developed during the Civil War and its aftermath, the business of ruling England remained overwhelmingly in the hands of unpaid local men.

This situation began to change under Charles II and James II when the state assumed control of large areas of revenue collection previously managed by private consortia of tax farmers. This meant that the government had to employ numerous officials (over 2500 by 1688: see Table 3.2) to collect taxes previously gathered by the agents and employees of private financiers.

This administrative growth had an important political dimension. After the Restoration monarchy triumphed over the whigs in 1681, Charles and James (or, at least, their ministers) embarked on aggressive schemes of administrative reform designed both to tighten the crown's hold on the growing body of royal officials and to enhance royal revenue by increasing the yield of existing taxes. These tactics, inspired by Louis XIV's example across the Channel, were intended to increase the crown's independence of parliament; they may, indeed, have been designed to dispense with parliament altogether.[3]

The Revolution of 1688 thwarted James but it did not stop the expansion of central government. On the contrary, it was responsible for raising its pace. The Glorious Revolution embroiled England in the struggle with Louis XIV and inaugurated a quarter of a century of war with France. There was no more powerful stimulus to administrative growth. Indeed, in this period, as both Plumb and Holmes have emphasized,[4] Britain's state apparatus grew as never before. The fiscal and military departments burgeoned and new offices were established administered by committees or 'boards'.

Geoffrey Holmes estimates that by 1714 114 commissioners sat on eighteen different government boards, and that by the 1720s approximately 12,000 permanent employees were in government service.[5] Between the 1680s and the Peace of Utrecht, successive administrations, whether whig or tory, built an administrative edifice whose structure survived largely unaltered until the early nineteenth century. When Joseph Massie produced his calculations of English social structure in the 1760s, he estimated that 16,000 families were headed by civilian officers of state.[6]

The one notable exception to this expansion was in the size of the personal retinue of the crown. Though the court grew under the later Stuarts, it was cut back under the Hanoverians. The royal household under George was smaller than that of Charles II.[7] When placed next to the growth in the effective administrative departments, this development meant that an ever-diminishing number of state employees were courtiers or the personal retainers of the monarch. If and how this changed the attitude of government officials to their task is a matter to which we will return later in this chapter.

Tables 3.1 and 3.2 collate some of the available data on administrative

Table 3.1 *Employees in administrative departments, 1692–1755*

	1692	1708	1716	1726	1741	1745	1748	1755
State	11	35	29	25	40	46	42	43
Clerks	4+	16	12	7	20	19	21	23
Trade	—	30	65	73	109	120	115	122
Clerks (head office)	3	6	7	7	8	8	8	6
Clerks total	—	6	—	8	16	18	10	16
Total in the field	—	—	37	51	87	98	93	100
Office of the Lord High Admiral	8	12	11	16	20	18	37	32
Clerks	—	1	1	7	7	6	20	13
Navy Board	54	18	13	17	59	63	64	200
Clerks (head office)	16	1	1	2	3	3	3	68
Clerks total	16	1	1	2	14	15	15	101
Total employees in field	30	5	3	3	42	43	37	106
Treasurer of the Navy office	—	—	—	—	26	28	29	29
Clerks	—	—	—	—	17	19	20	20
Commissioners for victualling the navy	5	8	24	10	16	16	15	56
Clerks	—	1	7	0	3	3	3	36

SOURCES: Edward/John Chamberlayne, *Angliae Notitia; or, the Present State of England*, 17th edn (1692), 22nd edn (1708); 24th edn (1716); 27th edn (1726); 34th edn (1741); 37th edn (1748); 38th edn (1755).

Table 3.2 *Full-time employees in the fiscal bureaucracy, 1690–1782/3*

	1690	1708	1716	1726	1741	1748	1755	1763	1770	1782/3
Customs	1313	1839	1750	1911	1925	1939	1832	2290	2244	2205
Excise	1211	2247	2778	3466	3745	3360	3294	3973	4066	4908
Salt		298	404	465	473	484	468	[410]	[410]	364 (1779)
Stamps		73	84	112	119	115	117	[110]	[110]	[120]
Post Office		158	231	232	155+	162+	253	[200]	[200]	[200]
Treasury and Exchequer		124	180	109	137	234	220	[200]	[200]	[200]
Wines etc.		41	29	47	56	56	55	[50]	[50]	[50]
Other			491 (hides)	155	155	245	245	245	245	245
Total	2524	4780	5947	6497	6765	6595	6484	7478	7525	8292

SOURCES: Edward/John Chamberlayne, *Angliae Notitia; or, the Present State of Britain*, 17th edn (1692); 22nd edn (1708); 24th edn (1716); 27th edn (1726); 34th edn (1741); 37th edn (1748); 38th edn (1755); British Library Harleian Mss 7431, Add. Mss 10404, Add. Mss 37838; PRO Customs 48/18 ff. 120–5; PRO Treasury 44/38, 48/23; Cambridge University Library, Add. Mss 5224, 5227, 5239.

NOTE: [ ] = estimates

growth in this period. Though Table 3.1 is far from comprehensive in its coverage of departments, its general trend is unmistakable.[8] The Navy Board, the Board of Trade and the Secretary of State's Office all grew fourfold. Contemporary comment and fragmentary qualitative evidence from other departments indicate that the growth of these offices was not exceptional. Almost every branch of government expanded in response to the exigencies of war and the administrative demands of empire.

Table 3.3   *Growth in fiscal bureaucracy, 1690–1782/3 (1690 = 100)*

	1690	1708	1716	1726	1741	1748	1755	1763	1770	1782
All depts.	100	181	223	246	256	249	245	286	285	295
Excise	100	186	229	286	309	277	272	328	336	405

SOURCES: See Table 3.2.

Though some departments had more rapid rates of growth, the greatest increase in the total number of employees occurred in the departments of revenue. These were the solid core around which subsequent expansion was built. As Tables 3.2 and 3.3 indicate, between 1690 and 1782/3 the overall number of revenue officers increased threefold, reaching a total of nearly 8300 by the end of the American War.[9]

The pace at which the fiscal departments expanded was not, however, constant. The most rapid increases occurred during the wars against Louis XIV, when revenue employment more than doubled to a total of nearly 6000. This expansion in fiscal administration was largely responsible for the swiftness with which government as a whole grew between 1688 and 1714. During the next twenty-five years, and despite the longest period of peace in the eighteenth century, the fiscal bureaucracy continued to grow, albeit at a much slower rate. Walpole was either unable or unwilling to take the opportunity conferred by the absence of a major war to retrench the fiscal administration.

This failure makes the achievement of Walpole's successor, Henry Pelham, all the more impressive. During Pelham's years in office (1742-54) the number of fiscal employees actually fell. His policy of 'economy, as far as it is consistent with . . . service'[10] had the astonishing result of checking the growth in fiscal administration, even though the nation was fighting wars both in Europe and in the colonies. Such retrenchment fell victim, however, to the financial demands of the Seven Years War. This conflict, fought on an unprecedented scale and at unprecedented expense, produced the most rapid growth in administration since the Treaty of Utrecht.

If the revenue departments were the largest employers of state servants, the Excise was by far the most important of the fiscal offices, and the one which underwent the greatest expansion. Between 1690 and 1782 it grew more than fourfold, and from the 1720s more men worked for the Excise than for all the other revenue departments taken together (Tables 3.3, 3.4). By the end of the

Table 3.4 *Excise employees as a percentage of revenue administration,*
1690–1782/3

1690	1708	1716	1726	1741	1748	1755	1763	1770	1782/3
46	47	47	53	55	51	51	53	54	63

SOURCE: See Table 3.2.

American War the Excise establishment was almost twice as large as the entire fiscal administration employed at the time of the Glorious Revolution. The excise was an indirect commodity tax on domestically produced goods, levied either at their point of production or distribution. Beginning as a tax whose chief source was duties on alcohol – notably beer and spirits – it was rapidly imposed on a wide variety of goods: such items of everyday life as salt, soap, coal, leather and candles, as well as fine paper and parchment, the gold and silver wire which embroidered aristocratic fashions, and the carriages of the rich. Excises became the largest category of taxes, excisemen the biggest body of officials, and the Excise Office a byword for administrative efficiency. Dependent upon a complex system of measurement and bookkeeping, organized as a rigorous hierarchy based on experience and ability, and subject to strict discipline from its central office, the English Excise more closely approximated to Max Weber's idea of bureaucracy than any other government agency in eighteenth-century Europe.

The numbers in Tables 3.1 and 3.2 are conservative estimates of those who made their living in government service. They do not include those engaged in part-time, seasonal or casual service. The two largest revenue departments, Customs and Excise, both drew on a large pool of temporary employees. In the early eighteenth century, for example, the Customs service in the port of London gave employment to a casual labour force of approximately 1000.[11] The growing volume of trade passing through the metropolitan port makes it unlikely that this number shrank during the course of the century. The Excise, when it collected duties on such commodities as hops and cider whose trade was seasonal, recruited large numbers of temporary officers to help handle a sharp short-term increase in business. In 1765, for example, 962 officers were hired for the duration of the harvest to help collect the cider duty.[12] Similarly, every summer a substantial number of officers were employed to assess and collect the hop duties.

Temporary and casual employment was not confined to officers in the field. Most of the central offices of the different branches of the revenue drew on the services of casual clerical labour which was paid at piece rates. These men (and, occasionally women)[13] were neither as fortunate nor as well remunerated as the full-time clerks in the government's offices. Many were hacks leading the dreary life of the copyist. They eked out a meagre living by working for a variety of employers, transcribing briefs for lawyers, entering accounts for merchants, and making fair copies of government documents.

These precursors of Melville's Bartleby and Dickens's Cratchet have not received the recognition they deserve. In an era which saw a remarkable proliferation of accounts, memoranda and correspondence, the scribe, clerk and copyist contributed both to the growth of commerce and the development of government. Their neglect by historians is only partially explained by the unglamorous nature of their work. For those who wrote so much, remarkably little about them survives. Occasionally, as in a report on the crowded conditions in the Excise Office, we catch a glimpse of them, busily transcribing reports at makeshift desks placed in windowless attics and on the office stairs.[14] Only rarely do we have an indication of their numbers. A survey of excise employees of 1779, however, reveals the scope of their employment. Most lists of officials in the second half of the eighteenth century put the number of men (and women) in the central Excise Office at between 200 and 300. But the account of 1779, which includes all clerks and is unusually comprehensive, puts the total at 1484.[15]

The Character of Administration

The expanding state apparatus that emerged after 1688 was the product of a number of political forces which affected not only its size but also its character and organization. The boards and departments that were either established or revamped in the late seventeenth century were almost all marked by some features which we would describe as 'bureaucratic'. They rewarded full-time employees with salaries rather than fees and offered a career ladder of graded appointments with progressively higher remuneration which culminated in a government pension. They also expected administrative loyalty and sought to encourage an ethos of public duty and private probity. Standards were set either by the examination of entrants into government service or by schemes of training analogous to apprenticeship. They were maintained by internal monitoring and by systems of punishment and reward.

This 'new' administration did not replace but was added on to existing institutions. Its rules and practices were not accompanied by wholesale reform of older departments, many of which contained sinecurists, pluralists and officers whose chief source of income took the form of fees. Rather administrative innovation in Britain, as elsewhere in Europe, either worked around existing office-holders and their interests or reached an accommodation with them by combining the old and new to their mutual satisfaction. The fate of the cumbersome procedures and lucrative sinecures of the Exchequer was typical. Neither were abolished or reformed. Rather their impediment on swift remittance and prompt accounting was circumvented by the use of the newly created Bank of England.

Though the broad pattern of administrative change in Britain mirrored that of the continental powers, it nevertheless differed in a number of important ways from that of her greatest rival, France. First, the absence in Britain of a large officer class meant that there was much less resistance from entrenched office-holders to administrative growth and innovation. Secondly, the limited extent of venality meant that the effective departments of state had a lighter financial burden to carry. They did not have to fund a bevy of *officiers* whose chief contribution to the state was to drain its resources. This, in turn, was indicative of the small burden of debt with which England was encumbered when she embarked on the struggle with Louis XIV.

Twenty-five years of almost continuous warfare might, of course, have transformed the British state into a corpulent body resembling its French rival. But the British state, though it grew stouter, never suffered from the dropsical complaints that afflicted France. Britain avoided the most egregious instances of venality and corruption for two reasons: first, she was able to raise large sums of money without having to resort to the sale of offices; and secondly, the presence after 1688 of a standing House of Commons, eager to root out malfeasance and reluctant to disburse moneys without good reason, created a degree of public accountability that acted as a powerful constraint on administrative malpractice. The path taken by the late Stuart state, by no means the only road administrative developments might have followed, was a consequence both of the character of politics after 1688 and of a number of historical contingencies, the most important of which was undoubtedly Louis XIV's mishandling of the question of the Spanish Succession.

The administrative apparatus of eighteenth-century England, with its mixture of medieval and modern institutions, defies any general characterization. As Gerald Aylmer has remarked, 'in the eighteenth century administrative anomaly was the norm'.[16] Offices were held under a variety of tenures – for life, at pleasure, through treasury warrant or royal patent – and offered office-holders a bewildering variety of rewards. Some placemen received exiguous stipends supplemented by handsome fees; others were paid a comfortable salary but were legally prohibited from taking any additional perquisite or reward. Officers in such departments as the Navy, Admiralty and the Excise worked what were, by eighteenth-century standards, long hours, pursuing tasks that required both skill and rigorous application. As one of Walpole's excise commissioners complained, 'there's not £1000 a year in the King's gift so dearly earned'.[17] In the 1780s the Naval Clerk of the Acts claimed to work a seven-day week in wartime. His colleague in the Admiralty, the Agent to the Marines, was normally at work from nine until three and from five to eight. Excise supervisors travelled on government business six days a week, made their books up on the seventh, and often completed fifteen-hour days. But most offices worked at a more leisurely pace: clerks were usually in attendance from ten or eleven until four in the afternoon. Some of their more fortunate colleagues never appeared at work at all. They paid deputies a small part of their stipend to fulfil their official obligations or just collected fees *in absentia*. In the late eighteenth-century Stamp Office, for example, about one-quarter of all tasks were executed by deputy.[18] No wonder that Aylmer concludes that eighteenth-century administration was 'an extraordinary patchwork – of old and new, useless and efficient, corrupt and honest – mixed in together'.[19]

The verdict of some historians, and of many of the nineteenth-century reformers on whose evidence their views are based, has, however, usually been less charitable. They have pointed to the archaic practices of some departments – the persistence of venality, patrimony and pluralism – to the continued custom of fee-taking as the chief source of remuneration, and to egregious cases of individual malfeasance and peculation as characteristic of the eighteenth-century British state. They view the institutional apparatus as the victim of personal cupidity, private interest and of a political culture which subordinated administrative skill to the operation of a thriving system of clientage and graft. From this perspective the *raison d'être* of the executive was to provide outdoor relief for the political classes. All other considerations were subordinate to that of ensuring lucrative preferment at the expense of the sovereign, the taxpayer and the state.

It is not difficult, of course, to find corroborative evidence for this view. Every sort of creature – drones, parasites, sharks and harpies – could be found concealed in the labyrinth of the eighteenth-century English state. Many official nooks and crannies were especially congenial environments for the sinecurist and the corrupt or negligent official. These included small and archaic departments, such as the office of First Fruits and Tenths whose workload was light and whose slowness of remittance enabled officials to invest state moneys for their own gain. They also numbered the patent offices in the Customs, especially those of the Port of London. These were occupied by a glittering array of aristocrats, most of whom had never opened a tax ledger, and whose tasks were performed by humble deputies.[20] In the 1780s such sinecures were estimated by a reforming customs commissioner to be worth over £36,000 per annum in fees and nearly £16,000 a year in salaries.[21] But the choicest pickings were in the Exchequer. In the year 1779–80 the emoluments paid to its ineffective officers in the lower Exchequer amounted to £45,300, and the public paid a further £38,000 in fees to the deputies and clerks who actually did the work. The Clerk of Pells, Sir Edward Walpole, collected nearly £8000 in fees and over £1600 in salary.[22] No wonder that in an earlier age Sir Robert Walpole had been so eager to provide such lucrative posts for members of his family.[23]

Even those departments whose institutional arrangements seemed designed to root out rather than connive at corruption had their share of absentees, laggards and peculators. Many central offices employed 'young Esqrs'[24] who were chiefly conspicuous by their absence. In the Treasury for example, there were always a few clerks whose membership of the office was purely nominal.[25] A similar pattern of non-attendance sometimes prevailed in the field. When George Grenville set about reforming the North American customs service in 1763, many office-holders were shocked at the suggestion that they should be

earning their salaries and fees by working in Salem, Boston or Philadelphia
rather than enjoying their gains from the comfort of their London town houses
and country seats.[26]

Active officers, unlike absentee officials, were in a position to cultivate
directly their own financial interests at the expense of the state. They granted
preferential treatment to taxpayers, litigants or government suppliers in return
for extra fees, treats and bribes. Officials who handled public money – either
on its way to the Exchequer or after it had been disbursed – also had a way
of putting it to private use. As the Bristol merchant John Cary complained,
'the money grows less in every hand through which it passes.'[27] The slow pace
of remittance – it took eighteen months for land taxes collected in the north
of England to reach the Exchequer[28] – provided placemen with ample opportunity for the private investment and use of public moneys, while the tardiness
with which accounts were audited tempted many officials to engage in speculation. It was for this reason that the reforming initiatives of the late 1690s
and after the American War both concentrated, in the first instance, not on
the structure of administration but on speeding up the pace of its operations
and on sharpening its scrutiny of accounts.

Administrative archaism and individual malpractice were certainly to be
found in the operations of the eighteenth-century British state. It would,
however, be a mistake to embrace wholeheartedly the perspective of nineteenth-century political and administrative reformers, writing off the eighteenth-century executive as yet another ramshackle *ancien régime*. The object
of such critics was a partial one: to expose the worst aspects of government
to parliamentary and public scrutiny in order to secure retrenchment and
reform. It was never their intention to provide a coherent account of how
eighteenth-century administration worked. They sought not to make sense of
the chequered pattern of the executive but to condemn its failure to follow
certain rules. Their point of comparison was not, therefore, that of other
eighteenth-century European states but an ideal reformed polity.

This perspective, moreover, telescopes or compresses the changing circumstances of administration before its reform in the nineteenth century, treating
it as a monolithic and static entity, 'the *ancien régime*'. In fact it visits the sins
of the late eighteenth and early nineteenth centuries on an earlier era. 'Old
Corruption' in its fully fledged and most egregious forms was a product
of the Revolutionary and Napoleonic Wars which were conducted on an
unprecedented scale and at a previously unimaginable cost. The enormous
amounts of money meant that, even though the opportunities for corruption
were not much greater than earlier, and even though the proportion of public
money taken by office-holders in fees had not increased, the total spoils of
office reached levels that far exceeded those attained earlier.

It is, of course, extremely difficult to calculate the full costs to the public
of the pensions, sinecures, fees and pluralism that were to be found in many
government departments. Illicit practices such as the acceptance of gifts, bribes

and unofficial fees or the investment of public funds for personal gain (the greatest single perquisite of the Paymaster of the Forces) were not practices their perpetrators wished to record for posterity. In short, it will never be possible to calculate the informal rewards of office. Moreover, the extremely common practice of providing officials with sinecures as well as requiring their attendance at an efficient office created a labyrinthine system of office-holding almost impossible to unravel. The extensive investigations of the 1780s and 1790s do, however, give us some indication of the costs and scale of the system. And what they reveal is that, though the rewards to any individual might be considerable – helping pay, for example, for Horace Walpole's magnificent library at Strawberry Hill – their overall cost, as a proportion of both public income and expenditure, was really quite low.

The three main items of expense were pensions, fees and the salaries of ineffective officers. The total cost of all pensions, not just those given to officials in the central offices of government, ran at about £167,000 per annum, paid out of the Civil List.[29] Official fees paid in twelve main departments of central government amounted to *c.* £300,000 per annum in the same decade.[30] Over 50 per cent of these fees were paid to customs officers and a further 25 per cent to officials in the Exchequer. In the same period government income ranged between £12.5 million and £16.5 million and state expenditure between £15.5 million and £25.8 million. Fees therefore constituted at most 2.4 per cent of income and 1.9 per cent of expenditure. The number and value of ineffective offices within the central departments of government together with those held by central government officials elsewhere is almost impossible to determine. But to judge by the additional posts held by the efficient officers of the Treasury and Secretary of State's offices – sinecures which would have been the pick of the bunch – they were not an enormous expense because salaries were, with the exception of some court posts, generally low.

So, though there can be no doubt that a small number of individuals fed well from the public trough, the overall cost of their privileges and perquisites does not seem high by contemporary European standards. The minimum figure for such annual expenses in France was at least four times higher.[31] The reformist perspective, then, tends to anachronism. It also provides us with no answer to two central questions: why the eighteenth-century state took the shape that it did and why it was able to operate so effectively against its chief diplomatic and military rivals.

This is not to apologize for or to overlook the numerous instances of corruption that occurred. Nor is it to claim that such practices were acceptable by the standards of the day. There were well-established conventions about acceptable administrative conduct, even if they were honoured in the breach as well as in their observance.[32] Moreover, administrators and politicians throughout the period voiced grave misgivings about two developments they saw as incompatible with virtuous and proper government. Those of every political persuasion feared that state patronage would create a class of office-holders more interested in promoting their own ends than those of the public good. They also feared that the party struggles that characterized English political life would lead to partial, inexperienced and incompetent administration. The former anxiety was more usually expressed by the parliamentary opposition, the latter by government servants and functionaries. But both, despite their different perspectives, had the same end in view. As we shall see, they wished to keep administration out of politics or at least to minimize the impact of politics on administration.

This does not mean, however, that eighteenth-century critics of 'corruption' were advocates of modern bureaucracy. On the contrary, they were fully persuaded of the value of patronage and 'influence'. The surviving papers of the most scathing critics of government corruption in this period are nevertheless scattered with evidence that these upright gentlemen used their clout and connections to secure office for relatives, friends and constituents.[33] This is sometimes taken as evidence of eighteenth-century hypocrisy and cant. It is not. Every eighteenth-century political actor was fully aware of the distinction between the justifiable and illegitimate uses of 'influence', just as they were familiar with the difference between venality and patronage. Private connection and public duty were not necessarily incompatible and it behoved both patron and client to ensure they were consonant.

To judge from prevailing political practice during the course of the eighteenth century, a compromise emerged by which private and political interests were accommodated within government administration, though not normally at the expense of its daily operations. In the early stages of administrative expansion, it is true, the struggle between whigs and tories to control public appointments, especially in the newly enlarged revenue departments, obstructed the proper workings of the bureaucracy. Successive political purges were responsible for a giddy turnover in personnel. Between June 1694 and June 1695, for example, 121 excise officers – about 10 per cent of the total establishment – were discharged for political reasons.[34] Similar purges occurred in the other major departments. But in Queen Anne's reign the most flagrant instances of politically motivated dismissal all but ceased. Sidney Godolphin and Robert Harley, who together headed the Treasury between 1702 and 1714, were determined to minimize the impact of party strife on an administration whose resources were fully stretched in the struggle with Louis XIV.[35]

The period after the Hanoverian Succession saw a reversion to the politically discriminatory practices of the seventeenth century. In the Excise, for instance, 120 officers were dismissed for political offences between January 1715 and November 1717.[36] This purging of Jacobites and tories by whig treasury ministers – most notably by Sir Robert Walpole – was less extensive than in the 1690s (political offences accounted for only 10 per cent of all dismissals), but it was extremely disruptive of good government. The revenue commissioners were prepared to dismiss officers who were openly Jacobite, but they disliked Walpole's desire to purge tories. The Excise Board, which included both whig and tory commissioners, was loath to return to the confusion of the 1690s. But the effect of the political purge was to encourage disgruntled members of the public to accuse officials with whom they came into conflict of disaffection to the Hanoverian regime. Such charges, often maliciously laid, wasted valuable administrative time, as every accusation had to be investigated. It is noticeable how infrequently officials accused one another of disloyalty and how heartily they despised any fellow-officers who did so.[37] Their attitude was more usually that of the whig and Jacobite revenue officers who joked that it did not matter who was king, for whoever ruled would always require someone to collect his taxes.[38]

The purges of 1714–17 were not repeated. Neither the Jacobite plot of 1723 (the Attenbury Plot) nor the Jacobite rebellion of 1745–6 provoked a witch-hunt within the executive. The notorious 'Massacre of the Pelhamite Innocents' of 1763, when George III and his new ministers dismissed large numbers of the Duke of Newcastle's followers, never penetrated into the lowest levels of administration, and, in deciding whom to purge, the king and his followers took administrative skill and experience into account.[39] They kept competent men in office, even if their appointment had been made by a political opponent. Thus William Burton and John Orlebar, placed on the Excise Commission by Sir Robert Walpole, were spared in 1763 because 'they are both of them very active and knowing in the Business of the Excise'.[40] Conversely, the political purge was used as the occasion to remove the now doddering customs commissioner, John Evelyn. He had committed no political offence but had grown too old to act as a proficient member of the Customs Board. The 'massacre' of 1763 did not interfere with the smooth workings of the administrative machine. Rather, it removed from office men like Thomas Steele, who held a sinecure worth £2,120 a year and employed nineteen clerks. Administratively redundant as well as a political client of the Duke of Newcastle, he was quickly dismissed.[41]

The events of 1763 epitomize the compromise between political clientage and administrative efficiency that emerged in the eighteenth century.[42] On the one hand, no aspiring office-holder could obtain a place without proper political connections or an obliging relative in high places. But, on the other, the active support of a patron was not sufficient to ensure employment. This meant that, though the system of appointing office-holders was not just – the competent were excluded for lack of a patron or because of the wrong party affiliation – it did not render administration ineffectual.

The departments of government that were newly created or radically expanded in the late seventeenth century were never entirely free of sinecurism and were deeply steeped in the ways of political clientage. The Navy Office, for instance, may have been one of the most effective branches of government, but this did not prevent its clerks from having to pay a *douceur* of two or three hundred guineas in order to secure their offices.[43] But these departments worked well. The Treasury, which presided over all government income and expenditure, the Admiralty and Navy Boards, which administered Britain's greatest military asset, and the Excise, which provided the largest single source of government revenue, were all too vital to the national interest to be held hostage by the forces of graft and corruption.

We should not, however, regard these offices as antithetically opposed to such government departments as the law courts, the seal offices and the royal household, which undoubtedly embodied many more of the features usually associated with 'Old Corruption'. Just as many sinecures were sustained by revenues collected by the efficient departments, so the efficient departments used the existing administrative structure for their own purposes. In the Treasury, for example, many of the senior clerks held additional posts in other offices which they executed by deputy or which required little or no attendance. But these perquisites were rationally distributed: they were used to reward public servants of long service (usually more than twenty years) and proven probity. Thus Christopher Lowe, the clerk who transcribed the annual supply bills, and who served in the Treasury for more than thirty years, was given the additional perquisite of the post of lottery commissioner.[44] Such rewards were almost never conferred on recently appointed employees who held office as junior clerks. A similar system obtained in other departments: senior clerks in the Admiralty often held purserships on men-of-war which they executed by deputy, while appointments to Greenwich Hospital served a similar function at the Navy Board.[45]

Such a pattern of appointments makes it extremely difficult to identify a body of officers which exemplified industrious and virtuous officialdom. A hard-working, incorruptible employee in one department turns out to be a sinecurist and drone in another. Sir Philip Ryley, whom Geoffrey Holmes discusses in his study of Augustan public servants, is a case in point.[46] Holmes describes him – quite rightly, I think – as one of 'the new men of government'. Philip Ryley was the son and grandson of two minor legal functionaries to whom historians will always be indebted. Between 1620 and 1676, and despite numerous changes in regime, the William Ryleys, junior and senior, devoted themselves to the preservation of the public records kept in the Tower. Philip, the younger William's eldest son, first attained office under Charles ii. After the Glorious Revolution, and despite his tory sympathies, he was appointed an Agent for Arrears of Taxes, a post worth £200 a year which he enjoyed until 1698. His conscientiousness in securing the payment of back taxes brought him a special reward of £100. In 1699 he became an excise commissioner, serving on the Board until 1715. He was one of its most active members, contributing to the reform of the service and to the elimination of the corruption that had crept into the office during the 1690s. In 1710 parliament voted him a reward of £500 for exposing fraud and embezzlement among the brewers contracted to supply the navy's beer. When his son entered public service in 1713 he wrote, 'I shall strictly enjoine him to take the same Methods I have done in Publique Revenues above 30 years, to make Integrity and Industry his Foundation, and expect Gods blesssing for the rest.'[47]

The 'rest' was not, however, left solely in the hands of the Deity. Philip Ryley made sure of worldly as well as spiritual reward. Between 1684 and 1733, except for a brief period of four years, he held the sinecure of Serjeant at Arms to the Treasury. This gave him an extra £100 a year. The post had the added advantage that it gave Ryley access to the most powerful dispensers of patronage on the Treasury Board. He also held the posts of Surveyor General of the Woods and Ranger of Forest of Dean. The former appointment was estimated in the late eighteenth century to yield profits of approximately £2300-£2400 per annum, chiefly in the form of fees and perquisites.[48] Though probably worth less at the beginning of the century, it was nevertheless one of the more lucrative offices at the Treasury's disposal, and was certainly more financially rewarding than the salary of £800 a year Ryley received as an excise commissioner.

Ryley's offices brought him profit and honour. In 1694-5 he was prosperous enough to subscribe £500 to a government loan. He was knighted by George II in 1728. At his death he left a number of properties including a manor near Thetford and a house in Hampstead. His only misfortune was that his son did not live to inherit the family fortune.[49]

This brief look at the career of a middle-rank government functionary is not intended to deny him the title of devoted and dutiful public servant. Nor is it to imply that Ryley was really mired in 'Old Corruption'. Our examination of his years in public office, like our assessment of the fringe benefits and perquisites enjoyed by the clerks in the most efficient government offices, is designed to show how assiduous and public-spirited men operated in a political landscape whose enduring features they sometimes criticized but which they were usually willing to accept.

It is often argued that the failure to abolish sinecures and inefficient offices in eighteenth-century England is a sign of the peculiar conservatism that pervaded the political classes after the upheavals of the seventeenth century. This view would be more persuasive if it could be shown that Britain's attachment to entrenched practices and institutions was significantly greater than elsewhere in Europe. But compromises had to be made in almost every European state in which administrative innovation was attempted in the seventeenth and eighteenth centuries. This was even true in Prussia. Only conquest – as in the case of Silesia after 1741 – made it possible to develop an administration *de novo*.

The British state was never overwhelmed by the burden of a spoils system nor by the load of its redundant sinecures and offices. Two factors ensured that this dead weight never proved too ponderous: the powerful pressure exerted both in parliament and from within the administration itself to secure some degree of separation between politics and administration, and the frequently used right of the legislature to inquire into the workings of government.

Between 1688 and 1716, as the state apparatus grew by leaps and bounds, the legislature passed a series of Acts barring certain categories of office-holder from sitting in the House of Commons and requiring others to seek re-election when they took up their posts. By 1701 land tax collectors, salt tax commissioners and the commissioners for customs and excise had all been excluded from the lower house. They were joined in the following reign by a variety of officials, including the commissioners for prizes, the agents of regiments, comptrollers of the army accounts, naval commissioners in the outports and the commissioners for wine licences, for the sick and wounded and for transports. 'New' offices, at least in theory, precluded their holders from a parliamentary seat, and with the exception of a few privileged officials – chiefly the secretaries and under-secretaries in the main departments – most officials were forced to seek re-election if they wished to remain in the House.[50]

The object of these measures was not to create an apolitical civil service but to ensure that the commons remained independent of the crown. They achieved partial success. The legislation of this era, together with an additional Place Act of 1742, which excluded minor functionaries from the commons (15 GII. c. 22),[51] managed to curb but never to eradicate the executive's influence entirely. But one of the consequences of this campaign was to reduce the political value of many offices and to prevent administrators from meddling too much in parliamentary politics.

The partial separation of politics and bureaucracy was welcomed by the many officials who cared far less about party politics than they did about working for the state. Though their motives were somewhat different, they shared a desire for a much less politicized government service with the country politician and the back-bench MPs who attacked the growth of the executive. State functionaries had learnt from bitter experience that excessive politicking led to administrative confusion, low morale and uncertain prospects for future employment. The energetic departmental reformer – and there were many active in the reigns of William and Mary and Anne – disliked party politics because it interfered with the business of improving government. They endorsed Charles Davenant's view that 'while faction is suffered to continue, it is a perpetual bar to better administration; for it emboldens the bad and terrifies the good'.[52] More prosaically, many officeholders feared politics because it threatened their security of tenure.

Though office-holders and back-bench politicians concurred in their desire for a less politicized government service, they usually parted company on the issue of legislative scrutiny of administrative (mal)practice. This was not invariably the case – William III, for instance, put the investigations of the parliamentary commissioners of Public Accounts to good use – but more often than not officials used the traditional bureaucratic weapons of obfuscation and procrastination to defend their departments. But parliamentary inquiry was extremely difficult to resist. It was remarkably easy to find a disgruntled or timid office-holder who would reveal the malfeasance of his colleagues or the abuses in his office. Peculation and corruption were therefore made more hazardous by the possibility of parliamentary exposure. Such revelations helped to limit if not to prevent the most egregious sorts of official malpractice. Though parliamentary inquiries were often instigated to gain party advantage and to score points against political adversaries, and though such investigations sometimes distracted officials from their immediate duties, their overall effect was unquestionably beneficial. In short, there were strong pressures, both within and outside the executive, to keep administration comparatively free of both party politicking and rampant chicanery. By the standards of other European administrations of the period – and it has to be conceded that these were very low – the British executive was remarkably uncorrupt.

The Professional Administrator

The growth of the executive in the late seventeenth century was accompanied by the emergence of professional administrators who devoted their lives to government service. Such employment had several attractions. Though earnings do not, at first sight, appear especially large – Holmes estimates that 95 per cent of public servants earned between £40 and £80 per annum in the early eighteenth century[53] – they compared favourably with other 'white-collar' salaries. Few Anglican curates or clerks in a merchant house would have earned more.[54] Moreover, except in the crisis years of the 1690s, government service offered regular remuneration in cash, which was very much the exception in eighteenth-century England.

A further incentive to pursue a career in government service was the status and opportunities that it presented for social advancement. In the upper echelons of administration – among the commissioners who sat on the Boards – were men of mercantile and professional backgrounds for whom the fruits of office were the means of acquiring the status (and property) of a gentleman.[55] Even at the lowest level, minor office, as Colin Brooks reminds us, was coveted for the standing it brought to land tax assessors and their like in the local community.[56] State employment also acted as a social safety net. A place in the Customs saved the fortunes of the failed London apothecary William Cornish in the late seventeenth century, just as a job in the Excise rescued the dissolute gentleman, Ralph Lawton:

He was a rake and spent his fortune upon horses and sports, and then was forced to descend to the lowest step in the Excise. He had first a ride, then a footwalk, and afterwards he was an Examiner, and from thence was made Clerk of the Diaries; he is now a collector, and has been a reclaimed, sober and sedulous man these many years.

Lawton's career points to a further unusual and attractive feature of state service: the existence of a series of formal career steps offering the opportunity for promotion and increased remuneration. As they expanded, departments created their own hierarchies of experience and competence. In at least one service, the Excise, the commissioners adopted a policy of making additional salary differentials between jobs as an incentive to industry.[57] As early as 1713 more than half of government offices also offered their employees a pension scheme.

Employment in administration not only offered prospects but also came, in some departments, to offer security of tenure and promotion on the basis of seniority. Once the political purges of the late seventeenth and early eighteenth century had ended, an assiduous officer in such departments as the Treasury could look forward to an undisturbed career culminating in promotion to the post of senior clerk. (Between 1714 and 1800 only one senior clerk and four under-clerks in the Treasury were dismissed from office.[58]) Not every department was so kind to its employees – dismissal rates in the Excise ranged between 2 and 9 per cent per annum – but in many central offices the acquisition of a post meant security for life.

As a result of these developments, a succession of aspiring administrators were able to work their way up the departmental rankings. In the Navy Board, for example, seventeen officials who began their careers as ordinary clerks between 1660 and 1773 attained the rank of Principal Officer and Commissioner of the Navy.[59] One of their number, John Clevland, joined the office with the advantage that he was the son of a distinguished naval commander. Nevertheless, he began his career in 1722 as a humble clerk of storekeepers' accounts. Four years later he became chief clerk in the same office. In 1731 he was appointed Clerk of Cheque at Plymouth, and in 1743 he reached the top of the Navy Board when he was promoted to Pepys's old office, the Clerk of the Acts. After serving in this important post for three years he moved to the Admiralty, becoming its Second Secretary. At the time of his death in 1763, he held the office of First Secretary to the Admiralty.[60]

Clevland did not exaggerate, then, when he wrote in 1763 of 'a life devoted to the public'. But the public had served him well. He began his career with a salary of £50 and ended it with an office worth approximately £2000 per annum. He also enjoyed an extra £200 a year as secretary to a naval charity, a job that enabled him to invest naval funds and pocket the interest. He sat in parliament for the admiralty boroughs of Saltash and Sandwich, left £17,000 in government stock in his will and saw his son suitably ensconced in an administrative career which culminated in fifty years service in the Admiralty.[61]

The widespread adoption of the practice of internal promotion meant that high-ranking administrators had accumulated a great deal of knowledge about the departments over which they presided. The key figures in the central offices, the repositories of wisdom and the guardians of proper procedure, were the senior clerks and accountants. When the Commissioners of Accounts appointed by Lord North turned to these men in the 1780s, they faced a formidable array of accumulated expertise. The two senior accountants in the Excise had worked for that office for forty-three and forty-four years respectively. No chief clerk in the Secretary of State's office had served for less than twenty-eight years; the chief clerks in the Naval and Victualling Offices had together worked for government for a total of seventy-three years. Like John Clevland these men had not come in at the top. Goulston Bruere, for example, had followed his father into the Excise, working in almost every branch of its accounting department before becoming its First General Accountant in 1777.[62]

The Boards of Commissioners – the commanding heights of eighteenth-century administration – also included a number of men with many years of administrative experience. Not all came up from the lower ranks – some began at an intermediate level or served on smaller commissions before being promoted to the more important ones. Many of the more fortunate commissioners came into high office without any prior knowledge of their department. Once at the top, however, a sizable minority of commissioners remained at their posts for many years. 35 per cent of customs commissioners and 27 per cent excise commissioners between the 1680s and 1783 served their Boards for more than fifteen years. Two customs commissioners – John Evelyn (1721–63) and Edward Hooper (1748–93) – worked for more than forty years on the Board, three others – John Stanley (1708–44), Samuel Mead (1742–76) and Thomas Boone (1769–1805) for more than thirty. Altogether twenty commissioners sat for more than twenty years each. In the Excise James Vernon served the Board for forty-four years (1710–26, 1728–56), and five commissioners – John Wyndham Bowyer, William Burton, William Lowndes, Christopher Montagu and David Papillon junior – were employed for more than thirty.

Government service came to run in families. Between 1660 and 1800 no fewer than forty-seven families contributed three or more members to duty at the Naval Board.[63] Ten families had four or more members serve the Treasury. Though this list includes such lustrous (or notorious) dynasties as the Walpoles, Townshends and Foxes, it also numbers the humble Barnsley family, who acted as messengers and doorkeepers at the Treasury between 1722 and 1794. Different departments had their dynasties – the Papillons and Brueres in the Excise, the Todds and Frowdes in the Post Office, the Popples at the Board of Trade.[64] The presence of these family groups can be seen in any administrative roster: the names of the sons and nephews of commissioners are to be found scattered among those of the clerks and officers in the field. No family, however, could match the contribution made by the Lowndes dynasty. Between 1674 and 1798 nine Lowndes worked in the Treasury, holding posts as exalted as that of First Secretary and as humble as that of office messenger.

Security of tenure, longevity of service and departmentalism emerged only gradually. Between 1688 and 1714, the years of greatest administrative innovation, the rapid pace of change, the ferocity of the political infighting and the inexperience of many office-holders all militated against administrative continuity. Neophyte officers worked within a flexible as well as expanding state structure. Procedures both within and between departments were only just beginning to be defined; administrators moved from one office to another, bringing with them skills and techniques acquired in their former departments. This was the age of what Geoffrey Holmes has called 'the gifted all-rounder',[65] men like Sir George Downing and William Blathwayt who moved with little apparent effort from one board or office to another. Lesser fry were equally amphibious. The departments of revenue, in particular, provided varied employment for several ambitious commissioners.[66]

This fluidity was facilitated by the frequent turnover in government personnel occasioned by the political purges of the 1690s. Twenty-two of the thirty-eight customs commissioners appointed between 1688 and 1715 served for five years or less. The comparable Excise figure was twenty of thirty-seven Board members. Excise commissioners appointed before 1715 held their appointments for less than half the time of those who took office after the Hanoverian Succession.

The frequent changes in office-holding made administration highly permeable. Office-holders moved back and forth between government and civil employment. They did not identify themselves purely as servants of the crown, much less as members of a particular government department. They were more likely to see themselves primarily as the client of a leading aristocrat or politician.

Because administration was less enclosed than it was to become, officers were subject (and less often receptive) to outside advice, and government information also circulated beyond the formal channels of power. Plans to raise new revenues or increase the yield of existing taxes, schemes to organize departments or change government policy were produced not only by government administrators but by outside 'projectors' who brought their schemes to the notice of senior ministers or laid their projects before the public. There had been and always would be a public debate in England about *policy*, but many of the projects were also concerned with the means of its execution. These administrative preoccupations are not surprising among a body of men who were often either former office-holders or aspirants for government place.

Though they usually received short shrift from the incumbent officials they sought to displace, 'projectors' were nevertheless capable of producing well-informed proposals, critical of existing government practice. They were able to do so because many of them had access to departmental materials and government papers. Sometimes these were obtained through the good offices of an MP who could call for administrative documents to be laid before the House of Commons. But quite often their availability to those outside government is explained by the practice of officials who took their papers with them when they retired or were dismissed. Two of the most famous late seventeenth-century administrators, Pepys and Blathwayt, both retained large numbers of official documents long after they left office.[67] Charles Sergison, who was dismissed from his post as Clerk of the Acts in 1719 behaved in like manner. He kept over fifty years of Navy Board minutes at his house at Cuckfield in Sussex.

These papers were of great value to the departing official. They could be used to defend a maligned reputation or to blacken the name of one's successors. The former tactic was that of Pepys. He used his substantial cache of navy papers to exonerate his conduct under James II in his famous *Memoirs Relating to the State of the Royal Navy* (1690). The latter stratagem was employed by Charles Davenant whose unsurpassed knowledge of revenue accounts, most notably those of the Excise, was deployed with telling effect against William III's tax commissioners in the *Discourses on the Public Revenue and the Trade of England*, which appeared in 1698. Friends and sympathizers were also given access to government documents. Though Geoffrey Holmes has shown that Gregory King's population estimates of the 1690s were less dependent on official sources than was previously supposed, the genealogist and political arithmetician, through the good offices of Davenant, undoubtedly had access to contemporary tax assessments, though he held no office in any fiscal department.[68]

By the middle of the eighteenth century such leaks had become much less usual because administration had become more impermeable: less data leaked out, less unsolicited advice was allowed to pour in. There were fewer projectors and most, like the distinguished statistician Joseph Massie, achieved neither government office nor any effect on state policy. Legislative schemes, such as the cider tax of 1763, originated in proposals made by officials themselves. Department documents, arranged in formal series and official categories, were guarded by clerks whose task was to manage and maintain them. They never left the office without the permission of the commissioners, except at the behest of the Treasury or of parliament.

This increased separation between government and public, between state and society, was symptomatic of the growing formality of administrative departments. Late seventeenth-century government had been a much more informal and personal business. Many state servants had been firmly attached to an individual patron. This bond was undoubtedly reinforced by the common practice by which department heads paid their clerks out of their own pocket. To cite but one of many examples, when William Blathwayt was Auditor General he paid all his clerical assistants with his own money. Minor functionaries were therefore directly beholden to their patrons rather than to the department or office. They moved with their masters and joined them when they fell from grace.

The practice of putting offices into commission – of replacing a single Lord High Admiral or Lord High Treasurer by a group of several commissioners Boards – helped change departments from personal bailiwicks into offices run by committee. Placing minor officials, notably clerks, on an official establishment which paid their salaries made them less dependent on their patrons and more directly answerable to the department as a whole.

From the 1690s more and more offices drew up office rules and established a formal daily and weekly routine. In the Salt Office the chief accountant recorded the daily times of arrival and departure of the department's clerks.[69] In the Admiralty Tuesday mornings or afternoons were devoted to hearing petitions (10,049 in the year 1696), Tuesday evenings to considering applications for employment. Thursdays and Sundays were reserved as 'cabinet days', while Mondays, Wednesdays and Fridays from ten till afternoon and for two hours 'after the house riseth' were assigned to regular business. Times were also set aside to meet with the Navy Board.[70] Simultaneously office rules became increasingly exact, assigning specific tasks to individual clerks and stipulating the hours of attendance at the office. This 'division of the Business . . . for the more orderly Carrying it on in general'[71] was extended to department documents: minutes and correspondence were organized in standard sets of calf-bound records.

This orderly system did not breed administrators of great imagination or powerful vision. It produced orderly and precise men, who were industrious rather than innovative. The best that William III could say of Blathwayt was that he had 'a good method'.[72] Charles Sergison's memorial in Cuckfield church is both more forthcoming and a trifle more flattering: 'he was . . . of great capacity and penetration, exact judgment, close application to business and strict integrity'.[73] Such men were thoroughly conservative. They were attached to the minutiae of their offices and to the punctilio of their proceedings. As Edmund Burke put it a generation later, 'Men in office go on in a beaten track.'[74]

Gradually they came to identify themselves with their offices and to distinguish themselves both from their colleagues in other departments and from those outside government. Inter-departmental rivalry – between the Customs and the Excise, the Navy and the Admiralty – increased, and officials became ever more reluctant to help the public if such aid required that they deviate from departmental rules. Departments became more enclosed: they refused to reveal information to the public, clung tenaciously to 'the usual way of doing things', and opposed innovations that might require officers to change their habits. Typically, when an enterprising entrepreneur invented a liquid soap in 1718, the Excise squashed its production on the grounds that it created insuperable problems for the collectors of the soap tax.[75] Administration became settled; routine set in. The bureaucracy had arrived.

Where, then, did the attachment of these new officials lie? They were more loyal to the crown than to the king. The extreme volatility of monarchical politics in the seventeenth and early eighteenth centuries weakened attachment to individual monarchs even as it strengthened commitment to royal, mixed government. The majority of officials showed an extraordinary ability to survive the vicissitudes of dynastic politics. Only those most closely associated with a particular monarch or most conspicuously attached to a specific party were usually purged. Even fewer chose to resign.

Most officials had their patrons, some of whom were relatives. The bonds of patronage and kinship were strong, but, during the course of the eighteenth century, they came to reinforce rather than to weaken creeping departmentalism.[76] The system of clientage sat comfortably with the growth of institutional loyalty.

If we follow a series of departmental records through the century after the Glorious Revolution, the overwhelming impression they convey is one of growing institutional definition. The roles of officials are more precisely drawn, the procedures they are obliged to follow become set in tablets of stone, the public and other departments are kept at arm's length and their actions are treated as a regrettable and ill-informed intrusion upon the orderly workings of the office. Though it would be erroneous to maintain that administrators and officials developed loyalty to an abstract entity they called 'the state' – there was no statist ideology available to them – they nevertheless became attached to a distinctive administrative order as servants of the crown.

Public Service and Political Crisis After the American War

Opposition to the conduct of the American War, the eventual loss of the American Colonies, and the growing size of the tax burden and national debt all combined to create a demand for political and administrative reform. Like earlier reform initiatives, that of the 1780s had two main components: the desire of the administration's opponents to limit the power and influence of the crown, especially in parliament; and the concern of professional officials and administrators to reduce the cost and improve the workings of government. The former impulse, usually referred to as the movement for Economical Reform, produced several major pieces of legislation in 1782: Edmund Burke's Acts, which controlled the accounts of the Paymaster of the Forces, curbed the Civil List and abolished certain departments, including the Board of Trade and the Secretary of State for the Colonies; Crewe's Act, which disenfranchized revenue officers; and Clerke's Act, which disqualified government contractors from sitting in the commons.

From within the administration itself there emerged a stream of reports into finance and office-holding of which the most important were those of the Commissioners for Examining, Taking and Stating the Public Accounts (1780-7) and the Commissioners for Enquiries into Fees in Public Offices (1786-8). These reports, together with the reforms introduced in the lower Exchequer, the customs service and the Treasury by Shelburne and the younger Pitt were the government's contribution to the zeal for retrenchment in the 1780s.

It is tempting to see these developments as a radical departure, inaugurating a series of changes in government as great as any seen since the 1690s. Certainly the period after the American War was characterized both by an enthusiasm for reform and by rising expectations about what government could and should do in both the domestic and international sphere. But this change has to be kept in perspective. The crisis at the end of the American War gave long-standing advocates of administrative reform a larger and much more sympathetic audience, but the desire for reform was not new. I am thinking here not of economical reformers like Edmund Burke but of the many ministers and functionaries who had frequently advocated and sometimes been able to practise economy in government. They include Henry Pelham – its most distinguished and effective practitioner[77] – George Grenville, Lord Shelburne and the younger Pitt – as well as numerous lesser office-holders who, in their more modest way, had implemented piecemeal reforms throughout the century. Thus the reform proposals considered by ministers at the end of the Seven Years War – the restructuring of the Customs, the removal of sinecurists and the lowering of duties – all prefigured those after the American War.[78]

It is significant that the most far-reaching reform proposals of the 1780s came not from the parliamentary opponents of the ministry – for them, as Dunning conceded, 'the saving of money, is but a secondary object. The reduction of the influence of the crown is first'[79] – but from middle and high-ranking officials within administration. These included Sir Charles Middleton, the Evangelical anti-slaver and Comptroller of the Navy whose comprehensive proposals to reform the naval dockyards and to end fee-taking and the payment of premiums for appointments foundered during the Regency Crisis of 1788; Sir William Musgrave, customs commissioner between 1763 and 1785, who proposed the wholesale abolition of sinecures within his department; Stamp Brooksbank, excise commissioner from 1776 to 1792, who described his conduct as 'always . . . tinctured with a Spice of Reform'[80]; Francis Russell, Surveyor General of the Duchy of Lancaster; and William Richardson, a customs officer who developed a scheme for a comprehensive new tax structure.[81]

Such career administrators and functionaries as these, it is important to emphasize, had no good reason to support the retention of sinecures and fee-paying offices. They themselves, together with most officials outside the Exchequer and Customs, were salaried. While for the sinecurist and fee-taker more business – the usual consequence of the outbreak of war – meant more income with no added work, for the salaried officer it meant more work for no additional reward.[82] The professional administrator had just as strong a motive as the opposition back-bencher for advocating reform. The reforming initiatives of the 1780s which emanated from *within* government were therefore in part a consequence of the earlier development of professional officials with a strong sense of public duty. They were a sure indication that the public servant had become an essential part of the workings of government.

Yet neither these men nor the parliamentary advocates of economical reform succeeded in implementing extensive *structural* reform. Only the Treasury and, to a much lesser extent, the Exchequer, were affected. Customs reform, the Public Offices Regulation Bill and Admiralty reform were all defeated. Administrative procedures were improved – notably with the consolidation and reform of accounting – but the abolition of sinecures and patent offices foundered on the rock of their incumbents' property rights. Through a process of attrition – by refusing to fill vacated places – Pitt managed to abolish 104 offices in the Customs between 1784 and 1797.[83] Henry Pelham had done more to reduce the size of the fiscal bureaucracy in the 1740s and 1750s.

The reform initiative therefore achieved only small and painfully gradual success. It marked the extension of a reformist sensibility rather than a radical departure in administrative organization. But, as on earlier occasions when the administration had been subject to public scrutiny, it helped reformers within government to tighten up and improve procedures and raised expectations about administrative probity and conduct. It was not, after all, the civil administrators of the fiscal–military state who opposed reform in the 1780s; it was parliament, which, though it might want to curb the powers of the crown, was unwilling to abridge the rights of sinecurists. The compromise between effective administration and a spoils system was questioned at the end of the American War, but it was allowed to persist into the nineteenth century.

❧ 4 ❧

MONEY, MONEY, MONEY:
THE GROWTH IN DEBTS
AND TAXES

As we saw in the last chapter, between the late seventeenth and mid-eighteenth century, the English state developed a civil administration characterized by a degree of professionalism every bit as rigorous as that of any body of officers in Europe. The single most important task of this bureaucracy was to raise money. It was vital, if the state were not to be driven into bankruptcy, that the administrative apparatus successfully obtain the vast sums necessary to cover the escalating costs of war.

An eighteenth-century state could raise revenue in several ways, but not all were available to the British government. Some of the techniques which had been tried by earlier sovereigns – selling off state or crown lands, manipulating the currency or coinage, vending public offices and honours, and levying forced loans – were recognized either as economically undesirable or as politically unfeasible after the Glorious Revolution. After 1688 the government's options were limited to levying taxes and raising voluntary loans.

In recent years it has been fashionable to downplay the importance of taxes in funding the bellicose expansion of the eighteenth-century English state and to emphasize the importance of a highly sophisticated system of public borrowing. This vogue is largely explained by the brilliant work of P. G. M. Dickson, whose book, *The Financial Revolution in England*, provides the fullest and most lucid account of the chequered evolution of a market in public securities. Dickson's history of public credit establishes beyond doubt the central contribution of borrowing to the survival and subsequent expansion of the English state.

But in ascribing the evolution of public indebtedness to the weakness of the English tax system,[1] Dickson underestimates the importance of taxes to the so-called financial revolution. No matter how sophisticated the mechanism or means, the state's ability to borrow was contingent upon the belief among its creditors that it had the capacity and determination to meet its payments. The practice after 1688 of 'funding' loans through a parliamentary statute which earmarked a specific tax to service a particular debt is usually held to have ensured public confidence in government annuities and stocks. But this fruitful symbiosis would have proved a barren union if tax collection had worked erratically or incompetently. An effective tax system, providing the government with a substantial and *regular* income, was a necessary condition of the new credit mechanisms which, as we shall see, revolutionized eighteenth-century public finance.

Such a sound system took time to evolve. Indeed in the first period of public borrowing during the Nine Years War many taxes failed to produce enough revenue to repay the loans charged against them.[2] The inability of these duties to service the government's *short-term* loans played an important part in the emergence of the *long-term* public debt. But, if the weakness of the tax system in the 1690s (which was partly attributable to the absence of a coherent and effective government fiscal policy), led to the establishment of the long-term debt, its subsequent strength was one crucial component in the success of public deficit finance thereafter. Public creditors invested in government securities precisely because they were secure. Their warranty was not only the statutory pledge of king, lords and commons to honour the debt but the ability of tax collectors to service it. As Charles Davenant put it, 'Neither exorbitant premiums, nor high interest bring credit, which is only begot by certain and punctual payments.'[3]

The tax returns which underwrote Davenant's 'punctual payments' grew rapidly throughout this period. Though they never kept up with the breakneck pace at which public expenditure increased, they nevertheless advanced at unprecedented rates. Average annual tax revenue during the Nine Years War was £3.64 million, about double the state's tax income before the Glorious Revolution. Forty years later, during the War of Austrian Succession, annual revenue exceeded £6.4 million. By the time of the American War it had reached over £12.0 million per annum (see Figure 4.1). Between the reign of Charles II and the end of the American War aggregate net tax revenue had grown sixfold.

What do these figures mean? They show that between the end of the Third Dutch War and 1715 Britain's growth in total revenue far outstripped the French and the Dutch. While French revenues remained constant and Dutch tax income doubled, Britain's increased threefold.[4] This greater rate of growth is in part attributable to the lower base from which English revenue climbed. Prior to the Glorious Revolution, the nation's ordinary revenue was only one-fifth of that of France.[5] But it is estimated that by the first quarter of the eighteenth century Englishmen were paying 17.6 livres *per capita* in annual taxes, while the equivalent figure in France was only 8.1 livres.[6] By the 1780s, Morineau calculates, annual taxes cost each Englishman 46 livres to each Frenchman's 17: the discrepancy between tax incidence in the two nations was widening.

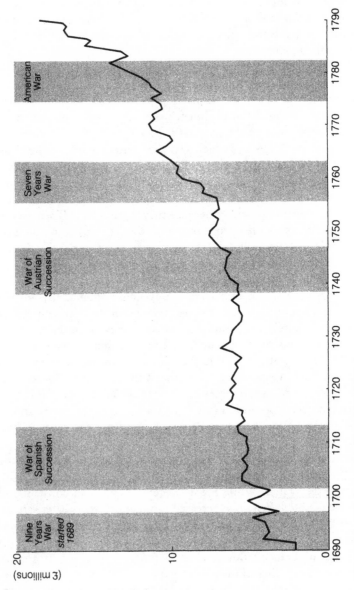

Figure 4.1 *Total net tax income, 1690–1791*
SOURCE: *British Parliamentary Papers*, vol. 35 (1868–9)

Morineau's episodic calculations are born out by the more systematic investigations of Peter Mathias and Patrick O'Brien. After making due allowance for population change and price inflation, they conclude that the traditional view that England was lightly taxed by European standards is no more than a myth. They demonstrate that the percentage of national income appropriated as taxes rose from approximately 3.5 per cent in the 1670s to over 9 per cent by the end of the War of Spanish Succession and to between 11 and 12 per cent of national income during the American War.[7] Put another way, the share of British *per capita* income appropriated as taxes rose from 16 per cent in 1716 to 20 per cent in 1760. At the end of the American War the proportion had reached 23 per cent.[8] Mathias and O'Brien's figures for taxes as a share of commodity output bear out the same secular trend: 17 per cent of output appropriated as taxes in 1715, 20 per cent in 1760, 22 per cent in 1785.[9] Though these figures do not compare with the incidence of taxation during the Napoleonic Wars, which rose to an astonishing 35 per cent of both commodity output and *per capita* income, they are nevertheless almost twice the comparable French figures for the eighteenth century. Judged both absolutely and comparatively, Britain was heavily taxed.

This was not lost on contemporaries. William Pulteney spoke for many Englishmen when he exclaimed,[10]

Let any gentleman but look into the Statute Books lying upon our Table, he will there see to what a vast Bulk, to what a Number of Volumes, our Statutes relating to Taxes have swelled since the Revolution . . . It is monstrous, it is even frightful to look into the Indexes, where for several Columns together we see nothing but Taxes, Taxes, Taxes.

Tax Collection

The effectiveness with which the British state taxed its subjects was in large part a direct consequence of a major transformation in the British fiscal system that occurred gradually between the Restoration and the mid-eighteenth century, as England moved from a fiscal system marked by heterogeneity and amateurism to a tax administration characterized by the orderly collection of public moneys by a predominantly professional body of state officials.

Tax collection after the Restoration lacked administrative coherence. The crown relied on four different bodies of men to collect its revenues: local government officials, who ranged in rank from the humble parish constable to the sheriff and JP; the employees of tax farmers who contracted for the collection of such branches of the revenue as the Customs and Excise; parliamentary commissioners, appointed not by royal authority but by members of the House of Commons, and who administered direct and poll taxes; and royal officials who were amply outnumbered by those who were not the direct appointees of the crown. This bureaucratic patchwork of authorities was not subject to uniform surveillance or direction. As a result, some taxes were

collected more proficiently than others, the same tax was collected more
effectively in one region than another. Though there was one central place of
tax receipt – all revenues went into the Exchequer – no single body monitored
both government income and expenditure, and therefore no institution was
capable of providing an overall account of government finances.

Several important reforms implemented between the Restoration and the
Glorious Revolution brought this fiscal disorder under control. The most
portentous development was the success of the Treasury Board in establishing
oversight of state revenues and disbursements. Though the precise date of this
change is a matter of dispute,[11] there is broad agreement on the character of
the Treasury's newly secured power, which was enshrined in a series of
Treasury departmental orders. These were intended, in the first instance, to
curb expenditure rather than to control income. Disbursements in the spending
departments required the specific sanction of the Treasury, which enforced its
authority by requiring that it countersign warrants issued by departmental
treasurers. Spending departments were also ordered to make weekly returns
of their accounts, so that the commissioners were fully cognizant of the state's
financial needs.

As the Treasury gained control over spending, so it acquired a monopoly
of comprehensive fiscal knowledge. In such circumstances, it is not surprising
that the Board secured the right to determine what financial business came
before the Privy Council. Probably by the late 1660s, and certainly by the
late 1670s, the Treasury had established its authority over the monarch, the
Privy Council and the spending departments, and successfully defended its
power against the expanding authority of the secretaries of state. It had also
introduced the bookkeeping procedures which were to remain standard
Treasury practice into the nineteenth century.[12] It had yet, however, to achieve
mastery of state income by winning control of the tax system.

The chief taxes on which the crown depended for its regular or 'ordinary'
income in the late seventeenth century were the customs (taxes on international
trade, chiefly imports), the excise (duties on domestically produced commodities, especially alcoholic drinks) and the hearth tax (a graduated property tax
based on the number of household hearths). The collection of all of these was
farmed out to private business interests.[13] This practice was in part forced
upon the government because of the inadequacy of its fiscal administration,
but it was also an attractive method of revenue collection because it helped
the crown to raise loans. The government sold the right to collect a particular
tax, or even part of it, in return for a substantial downpayment in cash. This
advance was in effect a loan financiers were prepared to extend to the crown
because the right to collect taxes over a number of years provided them with
collateral. In this way the roles of tax gatherer and government creditor were
combined.

Revenue farming had several advantages for a financially beleaguered
monarch. It meant plenty of cash-in-hand and a regular, predictable income

because the farmers usually paid a fixed annual rent for the tax regardless of the yield. Thus, if prices were stable or falling, the farmers absorbed the loss and the revenues remained fixed. The farming of administratively complex taxes or of those requiring cumbersome or technical means of collection was also to the monarch's advantage. Such duties had high overheads which the farmers were required to absorb. They also had to recruit and train skilled personnel. Finally, tax farming deflected the public hostility towards taxes away from the crown and towards the financial entrepreneurs engaged in fiscal collection.[14]

But tax farming also had its disadvantages. Above all, in surrendering the task of tax gathering to some of its major creditors, the government ran the risk of financial subordination to an individual or consortium controlling the two major sources of state income, namely loans and taxes. Even if the state maintained its independence by playing off one group of financiers against another, it could not take advantage of rising tax revenues if it practised fixed-fee farming, except by the cumbersome procedure of frequently renegotiating the farmers' leases. What the government gained in convenience and credit it lost in its lack of fiscal control. As a borrower, therefore, the state was in favour of farming because it facilitated credit, but as a tax gatherer the control associated with direct collection by royal servants was clearly preferable. As long as credit and taxes were linked by a class of financial middlemen there was an irresoluble tension between two conflicting fiscal needs.

Royal servants and treasury officials such as Sir George Downing were well aware of this problem and were eager, in consequence, to escape the clutches of the large financiers. By the accession of James II they had achieved their goal. In 1671 the customs farm was cancelled; the excise farm ended in 1683 and the hearth tax farm in the following year. The Treasury now controlled income as well as expenditure.

The transition from farming to direct collection occurred more gradually than might at first appear. Before the farms ended, government officials had succeeded in reducing the independent powers of the farmers by superintending the farms with increasing rigor. In the Excise, for example, fixed-fee farming had been replaced in 1677 by a scheme of 'management' in which the excise commissioners carefully monitored the farmer's receipts in order to ensure that the state shared in any increase in revenue. When direct collection replaced farming much of the apparatus and many of the personnel employed by the farmers remained in place. In 1683 three former farmers were appointed to the newly constituted Excise Commission. They were needed to help superintend a system of collection they had first developed in 1674, and which, according to Davenant, was 'the foundation . . . of that improvement which was afterwards made'.[15]

Though direct collection severed the link between the revenue farmers and the crown's creditors, it did not end the crown's practice of borrowing on the credit of such taxes as the customs and the excise. Instead of negotiating with a

otential tax farmers, the crown adopted the tactic of appointing
'cashiers' in the revenue departments. These financiers, who
bstantial funds in the private money market, were prepared
ns to the monarch in return for access to the constant flow
ted into their office. The partners in the bank at the sign of
the grasshopper, Charles Duncombe and Richard Kent, for example, advanced
the king between £150,000 and £250,000 a year in their capacities as cashiers
of the Customs and Excise.

After 1688 this system of 'undertaking', which had spread to the spending
as well as revenue departments, received a new boost. William III, desperate
for quick cash with which to fund his campaigns against James and Louis XIV,
appointed a number of financiers to the revenue boards. Men like Sir Robert
Clayton, the whig banker who was one of London's richest citizens and who
persuaded the London Common Council to lend William £200,000, helped
solve the new king's short-term financial crisis, but their appointment as
customs or excise commissioners had a deleterious effect on the collection of
taxes. The financiers had little knowledge and no experience of running an
administrative apparatus designed to levy and collect the king's revenue. Only
when the state developed new means of raising money (most notably after the
foundation of the Bank of England in 1694) was the tax collecting system
extricated from the tenacious grasp of the financiers.

For all the continuities with farming and despite the difficulties the tax offices
had in escaping the influence of the 'monied men', the state's assumption of
revenue collection was an important departure. Fiscal reform was now of
direct interest to the sovereign; it also provided him with the opportunity to
consolidate and centralize monarchical power. This was not lost on James II
who launched an aggressive campaign of administrative reform designed to
secure maximum fiscal extraction in the 1680s. He could hardly have done so
at a more auspicious moment, for a boom in industry and trade was then
enlarging the tax base for customs and excise duties.[16]

But James was unwilling to rely on prosperity alone. The link between
periphery and centre was tightened. Customs commissioners began regular
circuits of inspection, checking officers' performance in the field.[17] Similarly
the excise commissioners and subordinate officers with the titles of general
riders and general supervisors toured the countryside inspecting the work of
their gaugers. The Excise introduced standardized instruction for their
employees according to 'the Method'.[18] Officers were brought to London for
instruction and, when properly 'Methodized', were sent back to the provinces
to teach their fellow-officers the most effective means to gauge and measure
taxable goods.

By 1688, therefore, the administrative foundations of the eighteenth-century
tax system had been firmly laid. There can be no doubt that without this
achievement the fiscal apparatus of the state would have collapsed under the

ponderous encumbrance of wartime levies after the Glorious Revolution. Post-revolutionary finance was built on a pre-revolutionary model.[19]

The regime that ousted James II in 1688 did not retain the existing tax structure in its entirety. The hearth tax, which had always been unpopular and whose collection had often been resisted, was abolished by Act of Parliament as a 'badge of slavery' upon the people. But the other chief components of the tax system were essentially those of the Restoration era. The customs and excise taxes, the chief source of 'ordinary' royal income before the Glorious Revolution, continued to provide almost all indirect tax revenue for most of the eighteenth century. Not even the substantial increase in stamp taxes over the next hundred years succeeded in challenging the predominance of these two branches of the revenue. And, though the land tax proper was a development of the 1690s, it essentially embodied the principles of the two earlier direct taxes: the monthly assessment, first collected in the Interregnum, in which each county was required to raise a fixed sum which was determined by its presumed wealth and the subsidy, which charged a rate nationally both on personalty and realty.[20] These three taxes – customs, excise and land tax – were to provide approximately 90 per cent of the state's revenue in the century after the Glorious Revolution.

Patterns of Fiscal Imposition

Though the customs, excise and land taxes were the mainstay of the English fiscal system after 1688 their relative importance fluctuated in the century prior to the American War. Figures 4.2 and 4.3 outline the changing significance of the chief fiscal impositions. They indicate a decisive shift in the pattern of taxation at the end of the War of Spanish Succession. Put in its simplest terms, the fiscal history of the period between 1688 and 1714 was dominated by direct taxation in the form of the land tax; thereafter indirect taxes, most notably the excise, were overwhelmingly the most important source of state income.

Between 1688 and 1697, during the Nine Years War, the land tax provided 42 per cent of all tax revenue; during the War of Spanish Succession it provided 37 per cent. In only three years between 1688 and 1712 was the aggregate amount of land tax collected exceeded by any other source, and in the *annus mirabilis* of 1696 the tax provided 52 per cent of all receipts. But after 1713 the importance of the land tax declined sharply. The tax rarely contributed more than 30 per cent of the total revenue. Even when the aggregate return rose in the Seven Years War and the American War to the levels of the 1690s, the tax remained of secondary importance. The same sum that made up 52 per cent of King William's tax income in 1696 represented only 20 per cent of George III's receipts at the end of the American War.

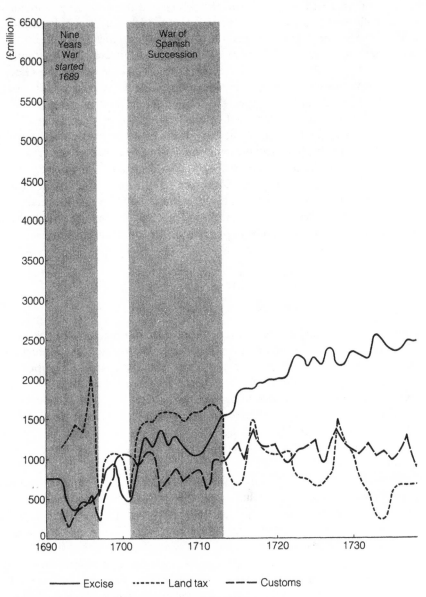

Figure 4.2 *Sources of net tax revenues, 1692–1788*
SOURCE: *British Parliamentary Papers*, vol. 35 (1868–9)

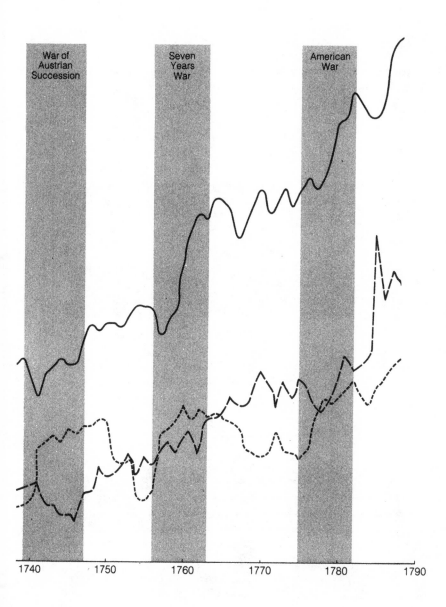

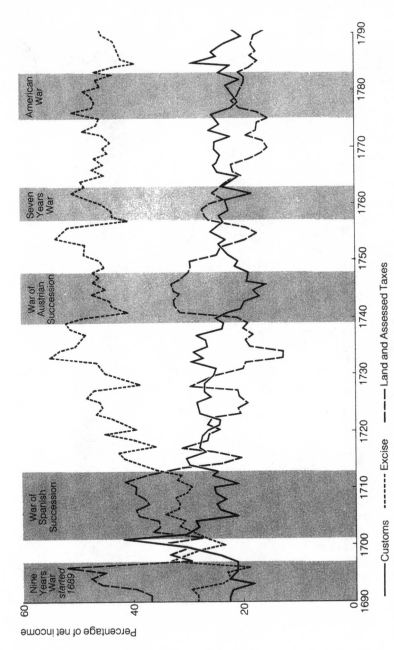

Figure 4.3 *Percentage contribution to government revenue of three principal taxes*
SOURCE: *British Parliamentary Papers*, vol. 35 (1868–9)

The history of the excise is the very reverse. In the period before 1713 the excise's performance was sometimes weak and often erratic, though it showed a gradual improvement in the last years of the War of Spanish Succession. Thereafter the revenue grew steadily, gradually outrunning all other sources of tax income. For most of the period after 1714 it constituted more than 40 per cent of all receipts. In the year of the Excise Crisis (1733), when Sir Robert Walpole's proposed reforms expanding excise jurisdiction were defeated, the tax accounted for 55 per cent of revenue. A gradual rise in receipts up to the 1750s was followed by a sharp increase during and after the Seven Years War. By 1760 excise revenue alone exceeded the total of average annual state revenue collected in the Nine Years War. The American War repeated this pattern of swift incrementation: by the end of the conflict returns had almost reached £6.5 million.

Though the customs revenues never grew as quickly as excise receipts, their aggregate return advanced steadily from the mid-century, after a period of gentle increase and mild declension. Returns in the 1780s were more than double those at mid-century and showed a marked improvement at the end of the American War. When added to the excise receipts they clearly indicate the extent to which Britain had come to rely on indirect taxes as the chief source of state income.

Within these broad trends there were many short-term fluctuations. The land tax receipts varied according to the rate, which, in turn, was determined by whether or not the nation was at war. Until the Seven Years War there was a marked discrepancy between war and peacetime rates: it was rare to have to pay more than 2 shillings in the pound in peacetime, and normal during hostilities to pay the maximum of 4 shillings. But the expense of the Seven Years War and of Britain's colonial acquisitions pushed up the peacetime rate. After 1755 the land tax was never again levied at less than 3 shillings in the pound.

Customs and excise receipts were, of course, dependent upon changing levels of economic activity. As a tax on domestically produced goods, chiefly the products of agricultural processes, the excise depended to some degree on the success of harvests; and, because it was often a tax on consumption, it was also affected by fluctuations in demand. Tight money, low demand and poor harvests – the circumstances of the 1690s and of 1741 – pushed down receipts. Similarly the customs returns usually dropped in time of war, because of the enemy's disruption of English trade. The Seven Years War was the first eighteenth-century conflict in which the customs revenue rose.

In the long-term history of English taxation, the period between 1688 and 1714 stands out as an anomaly. Before the Glorious Revolution indirect taxes provided most of the government's revenue. After the Hanoverian Succession a similar pattern obtained. Only under William and Mary and Anne did direct imposts in the form of the land tax dominate revenue collection. The land tax, despite its heavy incidence on the landed classes, was preferred by the House of Commons over other taxes because it was the most limited case of the exercise of executive power: limited because both its imposition and rate were approved annually by parliament; limited also because its collection was controlled by gentry in the localities. The land tax was administered through a system of 'self government at the King's command' and not through the deployment of a large body of centrally appointed officials. Opting for the land tax, then, was one of several parliamentary strategies designed to reduce the growth of the fiscal–military state. Though this stratagem enjoyed some short-term success, in the long run it failed. Not until the Revolutionary and Napoleonic Wars and the advent of the income tax did direct taxes assume an importance as great as they had in this earlier period.

The eclipse of the land tax was symptomatic of two developments which were of major importance to the subsequent history of the English state. The switch from direct to indirect taxation meant that the bulk of the revenue was no longer collected by a hodge-podge of amateur and local officials but by a centrally appointed body of crown employees. It also signalled the birth of the long-term national debt as more and more indirect taxes were assigned to fund government loans. In this way the preponderance of indirect taxes was inextricably linked to the growth of public credit.

How do we explain the growth of tax revenue, especially of indirect tax income? One obvious cause – the growth in the economy – needs, as Patrick O'Brien has recently argued, to be treated with caution. As he shows, between 1670 and 1810 tax receipts outstripped economic growth by a ratio of sixteen to three. Put another way, if the early administrations of George III's reign had collected the same proportion of national income in taxes as in Charles II's reign, tax receipts would have been only 30 per cent of recorded returns. Economic growth and the highly commercial character of the English economy helped increase government revenues and facilitate their collection, but they are not sufficient to explain higher tax returns. Indeed, O'Brien argues that economic growth comes a poor third to the imposition of new taxes and the introduction of higher rates on existing taxes as an explanation for greater aggregate revenues.[21]

Both new taxes and higher rates were concentrated on excise taxes. Direct taxes were handicapped by the implacable hostility towards the sorts of scrutiny necessary to assess taxes on income and by the reluctance of landowners to increase the incidence of the land tax which was based on an assessment of national land values drawn up in 1692.[22] The imposition of new or higher customs duties, after a sharp increase in such taxes under the last two Stuart monarchs, was hampered by the nature of imports (raw materials and basic foodstuffs which were not considered proper objects of taxation) and by the reluctance to inhibit British trade by taxing exports. And higher customs duties were widely recognized as counterproductive because of the way in which they increased the economic incentive for smuggling. Higher rates did not therefore promise higher returns.

The appeal of the excise, on the other hand, was that it was a comparatively discrete tax levied on a sizable but limited number of commodities – including beer, spirits, wine, cider, malt, hops, salt, leather, soap, candles, wire, paper, silk and starch – whose producers and distributors paid the tax but passed on the cost of the duties by charging consumers higher prices. It was, of course, essential to the success of excise collection that these industries were both reasonably well consolidated and capable of responding to a sustained demand for their products. But the effectiveness of the excise also depended on the skill and efficiency of its administration. And one reason why Hanoverian ministers were so eager to rely on excise taxes was because they knew that they would be collected by a body of men widely regarded as the most proficient revenue officers in government.

The Case of the Excise

Compared with the Excise, the other branches of fiscal administration posed many problems. The land tax scarcely had an administration at all. Assessment, collection and remittance were all administered by a *non-professional* force of royal subjects. Local assessors and collectors (the two tasks were often performed by the same person) were usually men of moderate means, the tradesmen and farmers who also served as headboroughs and churchwardens. They were appointed not by administrators in London but by local land tax commissioners, gentry and men of substance who oversaw the administration of the tax. And they took their moneys to the country receiver, a prosperous citizen, who remitted the revenue directly to the Exchequer in London.[23] Such an organization ensured administrative flexibility, granted considerable discretion to those in the localities and thereby reduced opposition to the tax. But it meant that, from the Treasury's point of view, the tax was the least well monitored. As a result tax remittance was extremely slow and the tax was often in arrears.

The Customs was far more bureaucratized than the land tax administration. Its officers were state employees, appointed and supervised by central government. But they laboured under many difficulties which reduced their effectiveness as collectors of revenue. The Customs, as we have seen, was densely populated with sinecurists. Its efficient officers had to perform a variety of tasks, including enforcing the navigation laws and quarantine regulations and guarding the coasts against foreign invasion, which intruded upon their tax-collecting duties. They were also, to an unusual degree, buffeted by political forces. Unlike excisemen, whose appointment in the localities was determined by the excise commissioners, custom officers' appointments were under the patronage of the Treasury who attended as much, if not more, to local political considerations as to the running of the revenue itself. Excise officers also needed a political patron to secure appointment, but the system of excise removes, by which officers were periodically transferred to new stations, not only meant that they were less likely than customs men to be complicit with local traders and smugglers but that they avoided *local* political entanglements. Moreover excisemen were subject to much closer scrutiny than their colleagues in the Customs. As Walpole reminded the commons in 1733, 'in the Customs, the officers . . . had no cheques upon one another; whereas in the excise they chequed one another, which made them not liable to be bribed'.[24] Hence the administration's desire to switch the supervision of imported goods to the excise commissioners.

Of all the new and burgeoning departments of the eighteenth century, the Excise best exemplifies new patterns of administrative practice, for bureaucratic change occurred not only in the central offices of government but out in the field. This transformation was publicly visible: not only was the Excise the biggest government department, it was also the one which had most contact with the public.

Though the excise administration had teething problems – the office was in a state of disarray during the 1690s – it quickly established itself as one of the most proficient organs of government. It was almost the only fiscal department to escape censure by the Commissioners of Public Accounts established to investigate the state of public finance at the end of the American War. Regarded by such different politicians as Lord North, the younger Pitt and Sheridan as 'the best managed branch of the public revenue' and praised for its 'regularity and vigilance' by the Select Committee on Finance in 1797, it was the model towards which all other branches of the revenue aspired.[25]

The Excise was a highly centralized system of revenue collection which embodied two chains of command, both of which led to the central Excise Office, presided over by the Board of Commissioners in London (see Figure 4.4). The provinces or 'country excise' were divided into a number of collections (36 at first, eventually 53) which came to correspond roughly with the English counties. Each of these was presided over by a collector who toured his collection eight times a year (nine before 1759), receiving money from traders according to the assessments made by his officers (usually called gaugers), and remitting it to a receiver-general in the London main office. Most collectors employed a clerk, and nearly all were also accompanied by supernumeraries, young trainee excisemen, whose job was to carry their portmanteaux and help guard the moneys. The officers who gauged excisable commodities in the countryside – beer, malt, hops, soap, salt, candles and leather – numbered between 1000 in 1690 and some 2800 in 1780. As they made their rounds – either a footwalk or a longer 'ride' – assessing and measuring goods at their point of production or distribution, they were scrutinized and monitored by their supervisors (58 in 1690, 272 in 1780) to prevent fraud or collusion with the traders.

The metropolitan organization mirrored the provincial system: London was

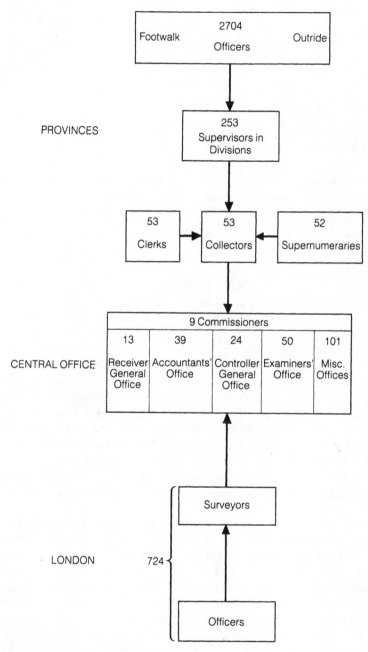

Figure 4.4 *Excise structure, 1770*
SOURCE: PRO Customs 48/18 ff. 120–5

Table 4.1 *Excise establishment, 1690–1783*

Country	1690	1694	1699	1700	1701	1701–14	1708	1714(1)
Collectors	36	39	42	42	42	42	50	52
Supervisors	58	80	91	89	86	101	140	199
Gaugers	1015	1019	1139	1090	1088	1356	1810	1994
Others	40	75	50		53	60		41
Country total	1149	1213	1322	1221	1269	1559	2000	2286
London						(1705)		
Field officers	113	120			152	147	166	
Central	51	54			36			
					(no clerks)	86	81	
London total	164	174			188	233	247	
Total	1313	1387			1457	1792	2247	

SOURCES: Edward/John Chamberlayne, *Angliae Notitia; or, the Present State of England*, 17th edn (1692); 22nd edn (1708); 24th edn (1716); 27th edn (1726); 34th edn (1741); 37th edn (1748); 38th edn (1755); British Library Harleian Mss 7429, 7431, Add. Mss. 10404, Add. Mss 37838, Portland Loan 29/283; PRO Customs 48/11 ff. 135, 269–74, 48/18 ff. 120–5, 251–6, Treasury 44/15, 44/38, 48/88 ff. 227 et seq. London University Mss 134.

a single collection with 113 field officers in 1690 and 780 in 1780. Among these were a body of surveyors – the London equivalent of the provincial supervisor – who were answerable to an inspector-general. The only difference between London and the provinces was that there was no metropolitan equivalent to the country collector who handled excise moneys. Traders paid their taxes directly to the receiver-general in the London central office.

In the central office itself the majority of its officials (51 in 1690, 309 in 1783) were engaged in one of four tasks: they received moneys from collectors and traders; they drew up current accounts; they audited accounts; or they inspected the excise officers' journals which were sent to London at the end of every collector's round. The commissioners presided over the whole operation, attending the Lords of the Treasury one day a week, taking two days to sit and hear excise cases in their capacity as the metropolitan court of summary jurisdiction and devoting the remainder of their time to routine business.

The work performed by excise officers was technical, complex and time-consuming. Entrants to the service were required to pass both a written and practical test and to complete a period of pupilage. The examination was not a formality. John Cannon of Lydford in Devon studied 'Cockers decemall Arithmetick Lightbodys art of Gauging' and hired a schoolmaster to help him with his mathematics.[26] Tom Paine, perhaps the most famous of all excise officers, studied for fourteen months before becoming a supernumerary in 1761.[27] Many trainee officers found the work too difficult and arduous and simply gave up. Those who succeeded in qualifying were undoubtedly as technically proficient as any body of revenue officers in Europe. They learnt

1714(2)	1717	1726	1735	1741	1748	1755	1763	1770	1771	1776	1779	1783
51	48	49	50	50	50	50	52	53		54	53	54
208	198	118	118	190	190	190	247	253		264	272	294
2101	1973	2700	2700	2700	2300	2300	2598	2704		2799	2794	2888
104	91	98	98	98	98	98	174	105		351	397	482
2464	2310	2965	2966	3038	2638	2638	3071	3115	3150	3468	3516	3711
173	310	476	528	547	552	503	684	724	730	647	778	883
101	158	123	131	160	170	153	218	227	230	327	1484	309
274	468	599	659	707	722	656	902	951	960	974	2262	1192
2738	2778	3564	3625	3745	3360	3294	3973	4066	4110	4442	5778	4910

how to use decimals, square roots and cube roots as well as the geometry of cones, spheres, rhomboids and cylinders. They were also instructed in bookkeeping and accounting, the use of the slide rule and the art of gauging. Excisemen were skilled and proud of the fact: they described themselves as 'artists', wrote treatises and textbooks on mathematics and measurement and offered private instruction in penmanship and arithmetic.

The work was not only skilled but arduous. A footwalk which was surveyed every day by an officer was between 12 and 16 miles in length. Outrides were much longer.[28] When the scheme of excise rounds was first developed in the 1680s, many of the outrides surveyed by officers were between 40 and 50 miles. Warminster, for example, was a 50-mile ride and required the survey of over a hundred victuallers. Marlborough was even larger – 63 miles in all.[29] But by the Hanoverian Succession most rides had been reduced to 30 miles, though additional excises meant that more premises than ever before needed inspecting.

Carrying their books, seven instruments, pen and special inkpot attached to their lapels, officers often worked long hours.[30] Their supervisors worked for even longer. In 1710, George Cowperthwaite, supervisor in the Richmond (Yorkshire) district, travelled over 290 miles in 23 days between 12 June and 5 July. On that round he visited 263 victuallers, 71 maltsters, 29 chandlers and one common brewer; in all he took 81 gauges. He visited 15 premises a day and checked the work of 9 different excisemen. Eight years later Cowperthwaite was working at the same pace in the Wakefield district. He travelled an average of more than 19 miles a day, six days a week. On a normal day he would inspect four or five premises, take a full set of gauges in at least one of them, and carefully examine the books of one or two officers. On Sundays he made up his diaries for the examiners' office in London.[31] Tom Paine, summarizing the remarks of many officers throughout the century, said of excise work that 'There is one generally allowed truth . . . that no Set of Men

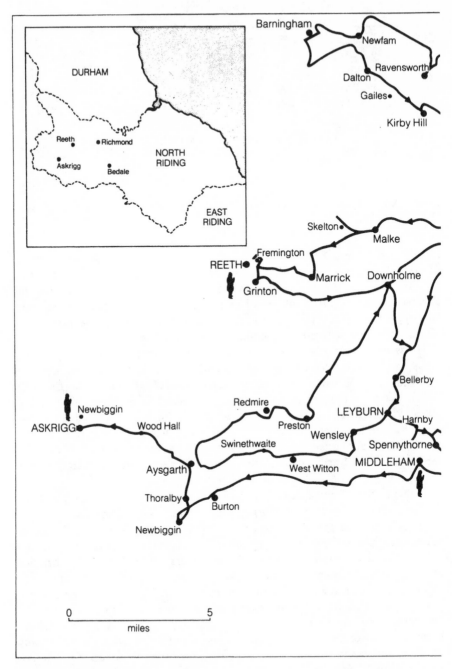

Figure 4.5 *Supervisor Cowperthwaite's excise round, 12 June to 5 July 1710, Richmond, Yorkshire*
SOURCE: BL Lansdowne Mss 910

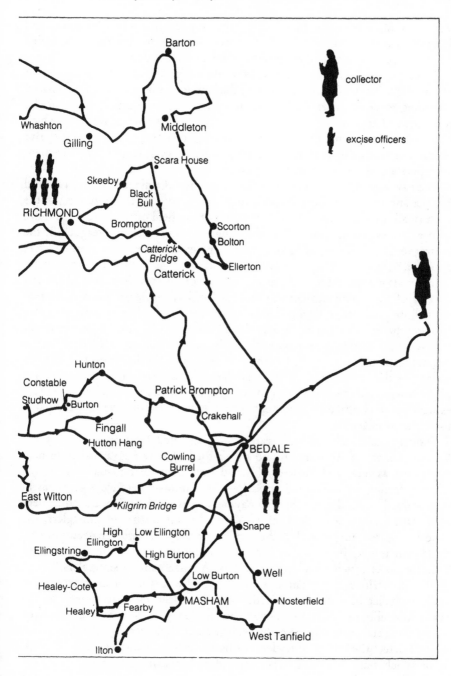

under his Majesty, earn their Salary with any Comparison of Labour and Fatigue with that of the Officers of Excise. The station may rather be called a Seat of constant work, than either a Place or an Employment.'[32]

Promotion in the Excise was not, as in some departments, purely a question of seniority. It is true that the rungs of the ladder of advancement were spaced according to years of service. An examiner in the central office, for example, was required to have nine years experience with the Excise, three of which had to have been spent in a clerical capacity and three in the field.[33] But promotion was neither routine nor automatic. At each stage of advancement an officer's career was carefully reviewed.[34]

The pay scale mirrored the ladder of promotion. Ordinary officers received £50 per annum, supervisors £90 and collectors £120.[35] At the beginning of the century all three of these salaries, even that of the field officer, provided more than a modest competency. But the gaugers, unlike their colleagues in the central office, who were given salary increases when new duties were imposed,[36] were paid a fixed income, and this was affected adversely by inflation after 1760. Moreover, as the volume of business increased in the last quarter of the eighteenth century, salaried officers suffered when compared with those state officers who depended on fees. More business meant more fees and therefore higher rewards; salaried officers, who also had more work, received no additional remuneration. Whereas an exciseman's salary at the beginning of the century had compared well with the income of a customs officer, by the 1780s it was smaller than that of his colleague in the other branch of the revenue. This context of rising costs and comparative disadvantage helps explain the field officers' discontents which culminated in 1772 in a campaign for a rise in salary.[37]

Though excise salaries were rarely supplemented by fees – in 1785 the Commissioners of Accounts found that a total of only £2652 had been paid to officers as fees, and most of this had been paid to the small number of officers dealing with exported goods[38] – the commissioners were generous in their reward of good work. Special payments – as much as £50, the equivalent of a year's salary – were paid for the detection and capture of smugglers, the exposure of corruption within the service, or the successful prosecution of a fraudulent trader. In 1752, for instance, the Norwich collector was awarded £200 for his efforts in breaking up an East Anglian gang of smugglers.[39]

The industrious exciseman was encouraged by the prospect of promotion and the chance of gaining a reward. The idle officer was discouraged by the high probability of detection and punishment. Gaugers' conduct was regulated by the same elaborate scheme of surveillance and bookkeeping they themselves used to detect the frauds of traders. Officers dealt with three types of record, all of which were supposed to correspond with one another. First, they kept a ledger or entry book in the office in which they recorded their day's intended or completed work. (Officers were encouraged to vary their daily round in order to increase the probability of detecting fraud.) Secondly, they carried with them journals or books in which they recorded their gauges. And finally they left minutes and specimen papers with the traders they had gauged, describing the state of the premises at their departure and informing the traders of the duties that they owed.[40]

Several excise rules made it difficult to juggle the figures, record fictitious gauges or alter entries without detection. There was a strict prohibition on altering journal and ledger entries: 'no officer do . . . Upon any pretense whatsoever, erase, deface, or alter any figure, letter or character in his minute-books, specimens, ledger or journal, on pain of being discharged'.[41] The West Country exciseman, John Cannon, made such an error early in his career:

which when done it did not please me therefore with my knife I endeavoured to amend it but made it much worse and yet not content still went on to right it made it still worse till at last it became shamefully bad for that by scraping so often with my knife that I made a perfect hole through the leafe. At last I took up a resolution to cover all by burning the same with a coal or Candle in such a manner as it might be took for an accident. . . . yet well know that Scratching erasing or altering any figure in stock or gauge was not only notorious but almost unpardonable. . . . And what was worse was by my so often visiting this page I had made the book so pliable that it would open itself at the very page where my folly was done as if it had vowed to be a witness against me to discharge me.

Thanks to the intervention of his supervisor, who informed the examiners in London that he was an honest but inexperienced fellow, Cannon managed to avoid dismissal and to be let off with a severe reprimand.[42]

An officer's supervisor was likely to swoop into his round at any moment, take up the exciseman's entry book and follow him on his journey, checking his gauges and ensuring that he had left specimen papers at the premises he had declared he would inspect.[43] Few officers wished to suffer the humiliation of gauger Burge who was surprised by his supervisor when taking a midday nap:[44]

jumping out of bed and regardless of any Apparel or Cloaths saving his shirt night cap and shoes he slipt down a back pair of stairs and out into the street and so round to the Traders houses like a stupid Mad Man and stamping or setting down Surveys and gages at random (there having been much business depending upon his neglect) not regarding the truth but presumed on former lengths. And so as he thus distracted ran along almost naked so a rabble followed him crying out a A Mad Man.

The supervisor himself kept a diary in which he reported on his own activities and provided a detailed commentary on the industry, care and ability of the officers he superintended.

The system was remarkably effective. Reading through one of the few surviving supervisor's diaries (most were thoughtlessly destroyed by the Inland Revenue), we quickly learn what the individual officers were like: who was skilled or slapdash, lazy or infirm, who looked for promotion or who shirked his duties. These diaries were sent every six weeks, together with the officers' books and ledgers, to the examiners in the main office,[45] who, after carefully scrutinizing the books, recommended action to the commissioners. Excisemen could be rewarded or praised, or subject to one of four finely graded types of punishment – admonition, reprimand, reduction or discharge. The importance attached to the examination of officers' books can be seen in the growth of that branch of the central office: there were sixteen examiners at the beginning of the century; fifty by 1760.[46] But the supervisor was undoubtedly the key figure in securing efficiency and probity. As a senior official remarked in the 1780s, 'If the supervisor conducts himself faithfully and judiciously it is next to impossible that either an Officer or Trader whether connected or unconnected can long carry on a fraud without discovery or detection.'[47] Any major fraud had to involve not only the suborning of officers but the bribery of their supervisor.

An integral part of the Excise Commissioners' control of their officers in the field was the practice of 'removes'. Moving officers from division to division and from rides to walks served several purposes. It provided the central office with one means of rewarding good officers and of punishing the indolent and less competent. It was also employed, both on a regular basis and in individual cases, to prevent excessive fraternization or even collusion between officers and the traders they assessed and gauged. General removes were usually implemented in the summer when business was slack before the autumn rush. But individual removes, made at the request of the collector or supervisor, could occur at any time. Thus Miles Bowerdale, a young exciseman at Askrigg in the Yorkshire division of Richmond, was removed after only three months because his supervisor recommended his transfer to another round, 'he having contracted too much acquaintance in this'.[48] The system of removes, so central to the system of excise discipline, was never popular with excise officers. Removes were disruptive, inconvenient and attended with considerable expense. Yet throughout the eighteenth century they made the Excise a highly mobile career for its officers.

Table 4.2 provides us with some indication of the Excise Commissioners' effect on officers in the field. It covers three main areas: the numbers of excisemen leaving and re-entering the service (the data is not available to reconstruct the number of new entries into the Excise over this entire period); the number of officers who moved their station, either voluntarily or at the order of the commissioners, in a given year; and the number of men who were punished. The third set of figures on punishment is undoubtedly a serious underestimate because it does not include officers who were disciplined by being removed, except when they were also demoted.

The overall picture provided by Table 4.2 is of an active but increasingly less interventionist Board of Excise Commissioners. In Queen Anne's reign they were moving a remarkable 41 per cent of their workforce in a single year and disciplining a further 13 per cent. By the 1780s mobility had been reduced considerably. It had fallen to 15 per cent and a large minority of these officers had been moved at their own request. The punishment rate had also dropped

Table 4.2 *Turnover, mobility and discipline in the Excise, 1710–80*

	1710	1720	1730	1740	1750	1760	1770	1780
Total in service	2250	2800	3500	3750	3300	3900	4066	4800
Officers leaving and returning to excise duty								
Discharge	208	203	178	106	74	82	97	114
Death	37	51	58	63	58	68	87	118
Retirement	13	12	37	14	38	39	56	25
Resignation	55	68	63	36	52	66	70	77
Total leaving service	313	334	336	219	222	255	310	334
Restoration	103	89	69	41	26	41	67	39
Orders to restore	93	85	69	32	28	35	55	45
Petition for restoration rejected						10	26	18
Appointed after reinstruction	3	1	1		2	2		5
Total returning to service	199	175	139	73	56	78	148	107
Movement of officers								
Removes	772	698	524	462	484	589	540	672
Removes by request	1	40	46	45	35	82	54	217
Removes not enforced	2				8	8	11	2
Total removes	770	698	524	462	476	581	529	670
Exchanges (mutual)	15	16	8	23	27	36	41	30
Exchanges other	137	127	83	53	49	39	22	21
Total exchanges	152	143	91	76	76	75	63	51
Total moved officers	922	841	615	538	552	656	592	721
Disciplining of officers								
Reinstruct	9	4	4	3	3	5		4
Reduction	50	28	34	17	4	13	16	5
Reduction/remove	14	12	12	13	13	7	7	17
Suspension	3		1	2		7	12	18
Discharge	208	203	178	106	74	82	97	114
Total punished	284	247	229	141	94	114	132	158

SOURCE: PRO Customs 17: Minute books of the excise commissioners.

to a mere 3.2 per cent. It is possible that the commissioners were less obtrusive in 1780 because of the complaints about salaries and the rising costs of removes which had been voiced by officers throughout the 1770s. But much earlier – in the 1730s and 1740s – the Excise had settled down to a pattern which was to obtain until the younger Pitt's reforms of the 1780s: the annual rate of attrition was between 6 and 8 per cent, the number of officers who were moved fluctuated between 14 and 17 per cent, and the number punished ranged between 2 and 4 per cent.

This decline in the activities of the commissioners lends itself to more than one interpretation. On the one hand it can be viewed as a sign of a more lax central administration; on the other, one can see it as an indication that the service was operating quite smoothly. The evidence leans towards the latter view. Though the commissioners probably did not need to be as tough with their employees once the administration settled down, the Excise Board also came to feel that too harsh a regime – especially one involving frequent compulsory 'removes' – tended to alienate the officers. Lenience was therefore a deliberate policy, not the consequence of administrative neglect.

Moreover, in most other respects the excise commissioners were as active in the second and third quarters of the century as they had been twenty-five years before. The central office sustained a steady flow of information and advice both to and from its officers in the field. New orders and regulations, as well as copies of new legislation, were disseminated from the office in London. Nor were the commissioners above asking their junior officers for help. In 1712, for example, they asked for statistical data on hops and tanners.[49] In 1758 they canvassed opinions about how to improve the administration of the malt tax before they increased the duty.[50] A year later officers were asked to carry out a survey of the nation's shops. They produced a comprehensive census, broken down by county. It is as a result of their endeavours that we know that there were 144,000 shops in the country and 22,000 in London. More general inquiries were also made: how could the Excise Board cut down on its paper work? Could supervisors suggest a more efficient way of organizing the collection of money?[51] In this way officers in the field used their expertise to affect excise policy.

The steady flow of information meant that the excise commissioners could deal quickly and effectively with inquiries from other branches of government. When the Treasury wanted statistics on candlemakers or the War Office figures on the number of innkeepers who might be pressed into billeting, the Excise could provide the requisite data promptly.[52] By the mid-century the department had become a byword for administrative competence. No detail was too small to escape the board's attention. They bought thinner paper for gauger's petty accounts when the Post Office told them that they would have to pay for their postage by weight. They carried out systematic and scientific tests on new pieces of equipment. They used competitive bidding to find the cheapest stationer. By the 1770s, displaying the departmentalism that had become endemic in government service, they had the temerity to complain to the Treasury about its inefficiency, which, they claimed, was hampering excise operations.[53]

No bureaucracy can entirely preclude embezzlement and malpractice or prevent some of its employees from failing to perform their duties properly. But the eighteenth-century Excise was remarkable for the industry it was able to elicit from its officers and for the care with which administrative abuses were anticipated and pre-empted. Its well-developed organization in the field enabled it to police a large number of premises with great frequency. By the end of the American War excise jurisdiction covered almost every aspect of commercial life. As Sergeant Rooke wrote in 1790, when examining excise litigation for the younger Pitt, 'the Excise Laws are so much extended that they now affect, not only the brewer, but the tea dealer, the Distiller, the

Wine Merchant, the Tobacconist, and all the wealthiest as well as inferior traders in the Kingdom'.[54] The records kept by the Excise Office enable us to be more precise: in 1780 the Excise was policing over 33,000 brewers and victuallers, 36,000 publicans licensed to sell spirits, 35,500 tea and coffee dealers, several thousand chandlers and smaller numbers in such trades as calico printing and paper making.[55]

By the last quarter of the century the Excise had approximately 100,000 premises under its jurisdiction. Some, like the London Brewery, were policed continuously; most – the shops, malt houses, cider makers, chandlers, soap manufacturers, distillers and calico printers – were visited less frequently.[56] Some idea of the scope of the eighteenth-century Excise can be gained by comparing the number of premises they visited with the number of modern houses licensed to sell beer and spirits. In 1970 there were 108,000 bars, pubs and clubs and 29,000 off-licensed premises.[57] Two hundred years earlier, the Georgian Excise covered almost as many shops, hostelries and breweries. No wonder contemporaries described the Excise as the monster that 'has ten thousand eyes' and condemned the exciseman as 'watchful to excess'.[58]

Excise jurisdiction was not only extensive but also provided the revenue with great powers. The statutory legislation which backed this scrutiny was far more sensitive to the fiscal needs of the state than to the rights of its subjects. The judicial cards were strongly stacked in favour of the Excise and against the putative offender. As Blackstone, who was no libertarian, put it, 'the rigour and arbitrary proceedings of excise laws seem hardly compatible with the temper of a free nation'.[59]

It is easy to see why this was such a widely held view. Nearly all cases of fraud or evasion of duty were tried before the excise commissioners in London or, if the case were heard in the provinces, by two or more JPs. As critics were quick to point out, this meant that in London the commissioners were hardly a disinterested party: they were, in effect, both plaintiff and judge. Even when the accused appeared before JPs in the countryside, he was deprived of the hallowed right of trial by jury. This was not due process in the traditional manner of English common law, but the smooth proceeding of bureaucratic autarchy.

Yet the trader, shopkeeper and retailer had little chance of escaping this excise juggernaut. Most excise legislation specifically denied the right of appeal to a higher court through the use of a writ of *certiori*. The accused was presumed guilty unless he could prove himself innocent. He could only plead 'the general issue'. In other words no mitigating circumstances were admitted by the court which dealt exclusively with the question of whether or not the offence had been committed. Even the traditional English stratagem of countersuiting officials was rendered more hazardous by the statutory provision that an unsuccessful litigant had to pay either double or treble costs.[60] It is therefore not surprising that the conviction rate in excise cases was so high: 79 per cent in London and 85 per cent in the country in 1789–90.[61]

For all its administrative strength and seeming denial of traditional English liberties, excise law was not as unpopular amongst traders as we might at first imagine. Its greatest advantage was the swiftness of its proceedings. When compared with other courts which dealt with civil litigation – Chancery, for example – it was a paragon of efficiency which meant that even the guilty trader knew that his agonies in court would be mercifully brief. But the principles which underpinned the workings of excise law understandably distressed political and legal commentators throughout the century.

The exciseman was a ubiquitous presence in eighteenth-century England, for he worked not merely in the ports and on the coast, like the customs officer, but in every small town and hamlet where beer and ale were brewed or tea sold over the counter. He was a state official, an executive rather than judicial officer, working under a system of statutory administrative law. As such, he was the symbol of a new form of government. He was also a sign of the state's determination to extract sufficient revenues from the public to ensure that England secured its place as a major international power.

Public Credit

The effectiveness of its tax system provided the British state with a regular and secure income which made borrowing both comparatively cheap and relatively simple. Public indebtedness, as every politician and political pundit of the era complained, grew at a prodigious rate during the course of the eighteenth century (see Figure 4.6). At the end of the Nine Years War the unredeemed public debt stood at £16.7 million. After almost a decade of stability, it again rose rapidly during the final years of the War of Spanish Succession. Peace brought little respite and, by the time of the financial crash of 1720 – the South Sea Bubble – public indebtedness amounted to more than £50 million. Though the debt declined slowly during the peaceful 1720s and 1730s, the War of Austrian Succession pushed it back up to £76 million by 1748. The Seven Years War and the American War had an even more dramatic effect. During both the debt almost doubled: from £74 million to £133 million between 1756 and 1763 and from £131 million in 1775 to an unprecedented £245 million by 1783. In less than a century the unredeemed debt had increased fifteenfold in current prices. This pattern of growth mirrored, in more exaggerated and distorted form, the other indices of English public finance in the eighteenth century. Every war raised the profile of public debt: each conflict produced a pattern of sharp and ever taller escarpments punctuated by the gently declining plateaux of peace.

As aggregate government borrowing increased with each successive war, so the proportion of wartime expenditure funded by borrowing rose. Credit accounted for 31 per cent of spending during the War of Spanish Succession. By the time of the American war, 40 per cent of expenditure was funded by loans.[62] The state's dependence on credit meant that a substantial proportion

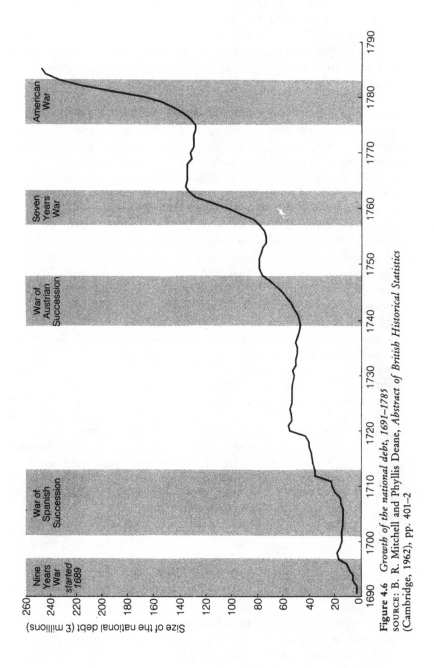

Figure 4.6 *Growth of the national debt, 1691–1785*
SOURCE: B. R. Mitchell and Phyllis Deane, *Abstract of British Historical Statistics*
(Cambridge, 1962), pp. 401–2

of tax revenue was spent on meeting interest payments on the debt (see Figure
4.7). In no year after 1707 was less than 30 per cent of state income required
to service the debt. For more than half the years between 1713 and 1785 debts
absorbed more than 40 per cent of revenues, and for sixteen years the figure
exceeded 50 per cent, reaching a peak at the end of the American War of 66
per cent of total tax revenue. As one French historian has pointed out, this
was a greater burden of debt than that which provoked the crisis of 1788–9
in France.[63]

As the debt grew so its expansion came to assume a regular pattern. By the
second decade of the eighteenth century, what had originally been a jumble
of different sorts of debt had been divided into two distinct categories of
public obligation: short-term unfunded debts and long-term funded debts.
The history of public credit is in large part the story of the interplay between
these two types of public obligation. Put at its simplest, the period saw the
transformation of short-term debts into long-term borrowing.

The short-term debt consisted of exchequer bills, navy, transport, and
victualling bills and ordnance debentures. Exchequer bills, which gradually
became the chief means of raising short-term loans, were interest-bearing bills
redeemable on demand and managed by the Bank of England. The other bills
were issued by spending departments to pay for the everyday running costs
of war. They covered the expense of supply, armaments and provender and
were paid off 'in course', i.e. sequentially in order of issue. This meant that
the more recent the issue of the bill, the longer the recipient had to wait until
he could convert it into cash.

During every eighteenth-century war the short-term debt grew rapidly (see
Figure 4.8). Sometimes, as in the case of the navy debt in the War of Spanish
Succession, its growth became unmanageable. As the size of the short-term
debt increased, so it took longer for creditors to cash their departmental bills.
It became harder or more expensive for government departments to secure
goods on credit because suppliers knew that the size of the debt lengthened
the time they would have to wait for repayment. Bills were discounted and
became less valuable, thereby making further extension of credit to the government even less attractive. In short, every war created a credit crisis, and the
longer the war went on, the more severe it became.

The solution to this problem, one that was adopted by almost all administrations towards the end of a war or shortly after the declaration of peace,
was to convert the short-term liability into a long-term funded debt. In 1763,
for example, £3,670,739 of navy and ordnance debt was converted into 4 per
cent stock.[64] The interest on such stocks was paid from specific taxes earmarked
by parliament.

New issues of government stock, whether to cover budget deficits or to
fund short-term debts, required either an increase in existing rates of taxation
or the imposition of additional taxes. These extra revenues came from indirect
taxes – customs, excise and stamp duties – not from the land tax. Fiscal policy

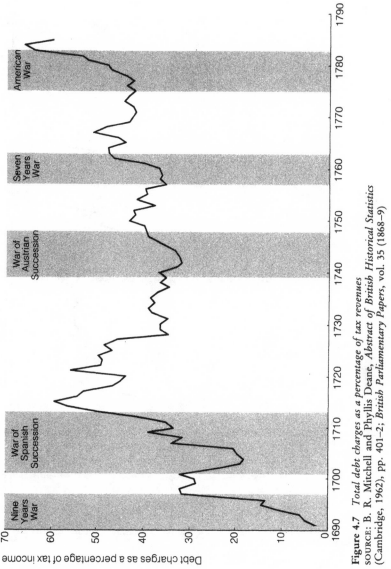

Figure 4.7 *Total debt charges as a percentage of tax revenues*
SOURCE: B. R. Mitchell and Phyllis Deane, *Abstract of British Historical Statistics* (Cambridge, 1962), pp. 401–2; *British Parliamentary Papers*, vol. 35 (1868–9)

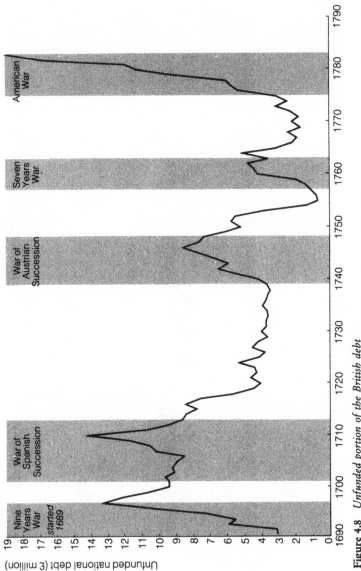

Figure 4.8 *Unfunded portion of the British debt*
SOURCE: B. R. Mitchell and Phyllis Deane, *Abstract of British Historical Statistics*
(Cambridge, 1962), pp. 401–2

during all eighteenth-century wars therefore contained two, interrelated components: long-term loans of increasing size; and an increase in indirect taxes in order to pay the interest on them. After wars were over (or in 1711 before they had ended) short-term debts were funded with new stock. Between 1711 and 1714, for instance, the Earl of Oxford introduced duties on coffee, tea, books, playing cards, calicoes, candles, coal, hackney coaches, linens, leather, paper, parchment, soap, silks and Irish salt, to raise over £8.5 million.[65] A similar pattern obtained at the end of the Seven Years War. In 1760–1 an issue of over £20 million in new government stock was underwritten by substantial increases in the malt and beer excises. The government's increased dependence on indirect taxes after 1714 was therefore directly linked to the growth of the long-term national debt.

One important consequence of this connection was that new taxes imposed to fund the debt became firmly embedded in the fiscal fabric of the state. The repeal of such a tax, thereby removing the security of a particular stock, would have been a gross breach of public confidence and a threat to the security of public credit. In these circumstances the levying of the tax could be ended in only one of three ways. The loan which it funded might be redeemed in full, thereby rendering the purposes of the tax obsolete. If the market rate of interest fell, the government could reduce the interest paid on loans and thereby reduce the annual cost of servicing the debt. This would release at least some of the tax revenue assigned to the stock. But, if neither of these options were feasible, the only alternative was to replace the existing tax with another.[66]

In its early years the debt grew rapidly and threatened to get out of control. Successive administrations struggled to raise money, adopting expedients which provided them with much-needed funds, but which created serious problems for those who were to manage the debt in the future. At first most of the debt was unfunded. As Figure 4.9 shows, over 70 per cent of the state's obligations in the Nine Years War took the form of short-term debts, and not until 1712 did the funded debt exceed unfunded obligations. This pattern differs sharply from that of subsequent wars. In no major war after 1714 did the unfunded portion of the debt exceed 20 per cent. Usually it was under 10 per cent, though it reached 14 per cent during the War of Austrian Succession. The switch from short to long-term indebtedness could hardly be clearer.[67] It is also eloquent testimony to the success of Godolphin and Robert Harley, Earl of Oxford, in putting the debt into order. Their policies may not have constrained its growth but they certainly put public borrowing on a sounder financial base.

The history of the long-term debt falls into two periods: the first, before the Hanoverian Succession, was characterized by the floating of fixed-term loans; the second, after 1713 saw the emergence of loans for which no repayment date had been set. Under William and Anne the government adopted a variety of expedients to raise money: it borrowed by self-liquidating annuities (usually for lives or for ninety-nine years), by organizing public lotteries, or by selling corporate privileges (the Bank of England (1694), the New East India Company (1709) and the South Sea Company (1711)) in return for substantial loans. After 1714, however, the state was able to take advantage of the market in government securities which had developed rapidly since the Glorious Revolution to issue large amounts of stock. As Peter Dickson points out,

the development of a market in securities in London in the period 1688 to 1756 was one of the most important aspects of the financial revolution. For unless facilities had existed to enable lenders to sell to a third party their claim on the state to annual interest, the government's system of long-term borrowing would never have got off the ground. The state would have been obliged to promise repayment in a limited number of years – and to keep this promise. This would have effectually stopped it from borrowing on the scale it needed.[68]

It could not have borrowed such amounts because the cost of paying off both principal and interest would have been beyond the means of the state's income from taxes.

The incorporated bodies of public debtors, especially the Bank of England, helped to develop the securities market. The leading figures in the chartered companies were financial and commercial capitalists of great wealth and experience. The government was able to draw on their expertise and knowledge of money markets to ease the floating of loans. And as the companies gradually assumed the management of the national debt, their administrative and book-keeping procedures, which were less antiquated and cumbersome than those of the Exchequer, made it easier for brokers and investors to deal in government securities.

But reliance on the corporations had its disadvantages. Ever since the foundation of the Bank of England in 1694 these institutions had provoked political controversy and economic resentment. Political and economic interests excluded from participating in state financing complained bitterly about the special advantages enjoyed by holders of public funds and tried to muscle their way into the action. In 1707, for example, the Sword Blade Company tried to wrest part of the debt away from the Bank of England.

The incorporated creditors also fought amongst themselves for a larger slice of the fiscal pie. In the same year that the Bank of England had to fend off the attentions of the Sword Blade Company, the East India Company orchestrated a run on the Bank to weaken its rival. And, when a large number of those who held the short-term debt were incorporated into the South Sea Company in 1711, the object of Lord Oxford's ministry was not only to restructure the debt but to create a tory – or, at least, non-whig – rival to the whig-dominated Bank of England.

The competition to hold a large part of the public debt is not difficult to explain. The acquisition of substantial public funds guaranteed their holder a

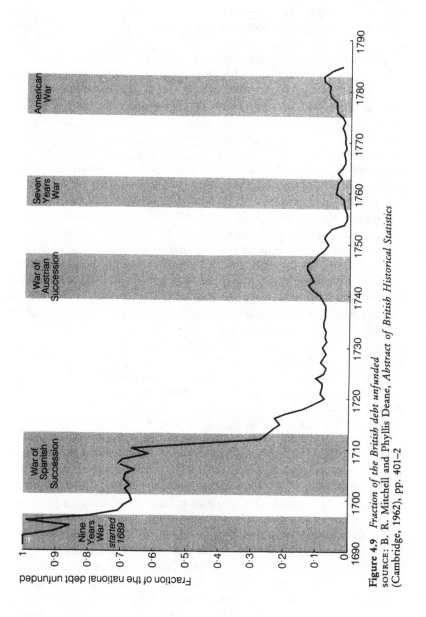

Figure 4.9 *Fraction of the British debt unfunded*
SOURCE: B. R. Mitchell and Phyllis Deane, *Abstract of British Historical Statistics*
(Cambridge, 1962), pp. 401–2

regular income in the form of tax revenues assigned to service the national debt. This security, in turn, conferred enormous power in the private money market. Backed by the large sums of money which made up public finance, an incorporated creditor could also dominate private borrowing. The prospect of financial hegemony in both the public and private spheres was the glittering prospect offered by corporate dominance of the national debt.

But by the end of the War of Spanish Succession the greatest single category of long-term debts was not that held by the great companies, but the fixed-term annuities held by individuals. In September 1714 these amounted to a total of £12,536,490 out of a total debt of £40,357,011 and cost the government over £880,000 per annum in interest payments.[69] Some of these annuities had been issued in the 1690s, but the majority had been floated by Godolphin between 1704 and 1708. Fixed term annuities were favoured because, though they were a long-term obligation, they would eventually have been paid off. Their use was symptomatic of the fear of a *perpetual* national debt.

But annuities for lives or for terms of years (often ninety-nine years in all) had the disadvantage of being irredeemable. The state had contracted to pay a certain rate of interest for a specified period of time. It could not cancel the loan by paying off the principal. If interest rates fell, the government could not borrow at a lower rate to pay off the high-interest annuities, nor could it use the threat of redemption to negotiate a lower rate of interest with the annuitants. It was locked into paying high rates (as high as 14 per cent) for the full term. The disadvantages of this inflexibility became more and more apparent as nominal and real interest rates began to fall after 1713. It was not at all obvious, however, how the government could remedy the situation without a unilateral and arbitrary rescheduling of interest, which would have shaken the confidence of creditors and made subsequent borrowing even more difficult.

The signing of the Treaty of Utrecht and the advent of peace provided the ministers of the crown with the first serious opportunity to control the enormous debt which had accumulated in the protracted struggle against France. Reducing the volume of public credit was a strategic as well as a fiscal matter. Most eighteenth-century wars ended when the protagonists neared financial exhaustion. The first power to achieve fiscal reconstruction – to pay off or reduce its former obligations – would probably wind up holding an advantage when hostilities began anew. Every attempt at debt retrenchment was made by English governments with one eye warily watching events on the other side of the Channel.[70] For it was a frequently expressed belief that the French were more skilled than the English in paying off their public debts.[71]

The situation after 1714 was exacerbated by several circumstances. The servicing of the accumulated debt, as Figure 4.7 demonstrates, was consuming an unprecedented proportion of government tax revenues. In the years 1714 to 1717 between 50 and 60 per cent of the state's income was spent on interest payments. Moreover, as we have seen, much of that debt was in the form of high interest, irredeemable annuities, which seriously limited the opportunities for fiscal reform.

Nevertheless the government had little option but to embark on retrenchment. The ministers had a limited number of tactics at their disposal. They could redeem some of the portion of the debt that was redeemable. But paying off some of the principal of the debt was obviously an extremely expensive business. They could also reduce the rate of interest paid on the debt. The former would have both reduced the size of the debt and cut its annual cost; the latter, made possible by the post-war fall in the market rate of interest, had the sole consequence of cutting its yearly expense. The policy of redemption was only mildly efficacious, but the tactic of restructuring the debt to reduce interest rates was more successful.

The first major attempt to reduce the principal of the national debt was the establishment in 1717 of the so-called Sinking Fund. This scheme, planned by Walpole but implemented by Stanhope, entailed the creation of a special fund, to be supplied by surpluses which, in turn, would be the product of the reduced cost of servicing the debt. In the 1720s and 1730s the fund and the policy of debt reduction it exemplified achieved some degree of success. In the decade after 1727 over £6.5 million in South Sea Stock and annuities were paid off, and during Walpole's more than twenty years at the Treasury he achieved a net reduction in the total national debt of £6,235,820.[72]

These measures undoubtedly increased financial confidence and eased further borrowing, but no expedient, including the Sinking Fund, could make serious inroads into the principal of the debt. As if in recognition of this, from the 1730s onwards the Sinking Fund was 'raided' for other purposes. As Hargreaves puts it, by the mid-eighteenth century the fund

had ceased to be regarded as a financial arrangement through which definite provision should be made from year to year for the redemption of the debt. It remained chiefly as a device for the coordination of the multifarious duties which were specifically raised for the purposes of meeting charges on public loans.[73]

It was no longer a means of debt reduction but an instrument in the management of the very funds it had been established to abolish. There was to be no effective fund exclusively devoted to reducing the debt until the establishment of the younger Pitt's Sinking Fund of 1786.

Walpole's willingness to use the Sinking Fund as a general means of fiscal management rather than as the source of debt liquidation reflects the changing attitude of ministers towards the question of public borrowing. Rather than worrying about the total size of the debt, Walpole and his successor, Henry Pelham, were more concerned with its annual charge. This was, of course, a tacit admission that the national debt would be a perpetual feature of public life and that the major object of fiscal policy should be the control rather than the elimination of the debt. To this end financial policy came to focus on reducing the rate of interest. New stocks were almost invariably issued on terms which enabled the government to redeem them. This was not because the state was eager to pay off the debt. Rather, the threat of redemption gave the government the leverage it needed if it were to take advantage of favourable circumstances to lower the interest rate on its outstanding obligations.

This was first achieved as part of the package of financial reforms introduced by the whigs in 1717. The lowering of interest rates in that year was accomplished with the full cooperation of the major corporate bodies holding the national debt. It was a major success. The interest rate on the redeemable debt was cut to 5 per cent and the annual charge on the total debt thereby reduced by approximately 13 per cent.[74] The next attempt at interest reduction, pushed in 1737 by the opposition MP for London, Sir John Barnard, failed in the face of hostility from the fund-holders and Walpole's refusal to support a cut in interest rates. Opinion on the efficacy of Barnard's plan was and remains divided.[75] But one lesson is clear. No change in interest rates could be achieved without the full support of the king's finance ministers, nor was it feasible unless the ground had been carefully prepared with the City of London's leading financiers.

These lessons were not lost on Henry Pelham, whose rescheduling of the redeemable debt, begun in 1749 and completed after his death, was the major fiscal achievement of mid-century. Pelham managed to reduce 88 per cent of the 4 per cent debt to 3.5 per cent in 1750 and to 3 per cent by 1757. Debt service costs were first cut by 12 per cent. If there had been no additional borrowing after this reform, by 1757 they would have been reduced by a remarkable 25 per cent.[76] Pelham's scheme aroused considerable opposition from the Bank of England, the East India Company and, above all, the South Sea Company. But, thanks to skilled political and financial management, the corporations were eventually persuaded to lend their support. As a result, Britain was able to embark upon the Seven Years War in excellent financial shape.

Pelham's scheme of 1749–57 was the last *major* reform entailing a cut in the rate of interest in the eighteenth century. Some of the debt redemption of the 1760s, it is true, was achieved by negotiating lower interest payments. Thus between 1766 and 1768 £4.9 million was borrowed at 3 per cent to pay off outstanding 4 per cents.[77] But after the Seven Years War concern about the national debt shifted back to an earlier preoccupation with its growing size. The huge absolute increase in outstanding obligations after the Seven Years War and the American War – the nominal debt grew from £74.6 million to £231 million between 1756 and 1783 – revived interest in debt redemption. After 1763 it was feared that the cost of servicing the debt had outstripped the nation's capacity to raise taxes and that a national bankruptcy might ensue. Hence the aggressive search for new sources of revenue outside England but within the British empire by the likes of George Grenville and the younger Pitt's revival of the Sinking Fund after the American War.

For much of the period before the end of the American War English government deficit financing was a great success. In the first half of the century the secular trend in interest rates was downward, and even when nominal rates rose after 1750 the government was still able to borrow more cheaply than its chief rivals. By using incentives and *douceurs* – notably lottery tickets and additional annuities – the state was able to attract investors even when credit was tight.[78] The one and only occasion on which the whole web of public finance threatened to unravel was during the South Sea Bubble of 1720.

Three major factors contributed to the explosive events of 1720. The first was the government's eagerness to reduce the cost of the national debt, an enthusiasm fuelled by rumours that the Scot, John Law, was transforming the French state into the greatest financial power in Europe. This preoccupation has to be set against two other circumstances: the growing rivalry between the Bank of England and the South Sea Company for control of the public debt, and the continued presence of a large number of irredeemable securities in the form of fixed-term annuities. The object of the scheme of 1720 was to persuade the annuitants voluntarily to exchange their securities for newly created redeemable stock in one of the big three companies. Holders of *redeemable* stock (other than company stock) were also to be able to exchange their securities. The new stock would carry only 4 per cent interest from 1727. Thus the cost of servicing the debt would be reduced and it would cease to be irredeemable. The chief obstacle to such a scheme was not the major companies, which bid against each other to take in the annuities, but the holders of the irredeemable annuities who needed to have a motive to relinquish their high return securities.

The South Sea Company not only made the largest bid for the entire operation (£4 million, with a possible increase to £7.6 million) but also provided the annuitants with a powerful incentive to sell. The South Sea Act of 1720 empowered the company to offer them cash or newly created South Sea stock. Understandably it offered the latter, which seemed, in the speculative boom of 1720, to offer unparalleled opportunities for extravagant profit. The entire scheme had one crucial requirement: that South Sea stock should keep steadily rising. Both members of the government and directors of the South Sea Company displayed great ingenuity in blowing up the South Sea 'Bubble'. Between January and July 1720 South Sea stock rose from 128 to 950.[79] The annuitants sold out to the company in droves: 85 per cent of the government's irredeemable debt was disgorged in exchange for South Sea stock, as well as a further 85 per cent of redeemable stock.[80] Most fund-holders bought South Sea paper at highly inflated prices. When the Bubble burst in the autumn of 1720 they incurred serious losses.

In the short term, the South Sea Bubble was a major disaster which shook, though it did not topple, public credit. In the long run its consequences were more beneficial. The scheme, disreputable and corrupt as it was, succeeded in its chief aim of changing the structure of the national debt. In 1717 the annual charge of terminable annuities to public expenditure was £1,870,000. Five years later it had been reduced to £212,000. The transfer of annuities into redeemable stock made possible the later consolidation of the national debt. But perhaps the most important lesson of the Bubble was, in Peter Dickson's words, 'that public faith should never again be subjected to the intrigues of politicians and company promoters'.[81]

This realization had two consequences. First, successive ministers sought to dilute the power of the incorporated companies by broadening the base of the debt. The growth in the aggregate number of stock-holders makes this clear. In 1709 there were 10,000 public creditors; in 1720, a mere decade later, their number had trebled. By the outbreak of the Seven Years War, there were 60,000 holders of public funds. These figures are an underestimate of the number of individuals who invested in the national debt. Corporate bodies such as banks, trading companies, charities and boards of trustees were counted as single investors, although they often acted as the intermediary between a substantial number of investors and the public funds. As the number of public creditors increased, so the corporations came to assume a managerial role, acting like fiscal departments of government. By mid-century the South Sea Company had ceased to engage in private trade and had become, in Dickson's phrase, a branch of the Exchequer. Its old rival, the Bank of England, though it had triumphed over the company in the aftermath of the Bubble, also became more and more of a debt manager, assuming control of first short and then long-term borrowing.

Secondly, the shock of the South Sea Bubble and of the painful financial reconstruction that followed helped secure a high level of financial probity thereafter. Dickson puts it well: 'Despite all the defects in the handling of English public finance, for the rest of the century it remained more honest, as well as more efficient, than that of any other country in Europe.'[82]

Debts and Taxes: The Comparative Dimension

The different fiscal systems developed in the seventeenth and eighteenth centuries by the major protagonists to cope with the financial exigencies of war bore a remarkable family resemblance to one another. Thus most states relied for their tax base on a combination of direct taxes, usually assessed on landed wealth, together with indirect taxes on international trade and domestic commodity production. England depended on a land tax and the customs and excise. France's chief direct tax, the *taille* (later complemented by the *vingt-ième*), matched a congeries of indirect taxes – the *gabelles, tabacs, aides* and *traites* – usually administered by tax farmers. In Prussia the *Kontribution* exacted from the land matched the *Akzise* levied on the towns. The United Provinces combined the *verponding*, a levy on real property with the *convooyen en licenten* or customs duties and the *generale middelen* on a wide variety of commodities.

The precise distribution of these taxes varied from state to state. In England, as we have seen, approximately 75 per cent of government income came from indirect taxes. Prussia and the United Provinces also placed their greatest reliance on similar imposts and duties. In the second half of the eighteenth century even France, the state usually seen as most heavily dependent upon direct taxes, derived the majority of its tax revenue from a variety of indirect impositions.[83]

Though the broad pattern of fiscal incidence in England resembled that of many other European states, there were a number of distinctive features of the English tax system. First and foremost, tax collection in England was, to an unusual degree, in the hands of *centrally appointed government officials.* The state and its minions, public appointees – not private entrepreneurs nor local government officials – controlled the bulk of the revenue. Only the (less and less important) land tax was administered by provincially appointed assessors and collectors. This was in marked contrast to the forms of tax collection practised by Britain's rivals. In France, except for the period between 1709 and 1726, most indirect taxes were under the supervision of a consortium of private *financiers*, the Farmers General. Similarly, before the tax revolts of 1747–8, the excise in the United Provinces was gathered by local tax farmers. In Prussia, supposedly the paradigm case of the well-defined state apparatus, Frederick the Great called upon a group of French tax farmers to take over the collection of the *Akzise* between 1766 and 1786.

The number of centrally appointed fiscal officials in England was large by contemporary European standards. The Prussian bureaucracy as a whole numbered little more than 3000 in mid-century, perhaps 250 of whom worked in central administration.[84] There were, of course, exceptional circumstances which explain the small size of the Prussian administration. It was not large because it did not need to be so. Tax revenues played a subordinate role in the financing of Prussian military activity.[85] The great military adventures of Frederick the Great were funded not by a system of taxes and loans but by plunder (from Silesia or Saxony), by the revenues of the royal domain and by the old-fashioned expedient of manipulating the coinage. It therefore comes as little surprise to find that the Prussian bureaucracy was about half the size of the English tax-collecting apparatus.

The United Provinces, though the most heavily taxed state in Europe, had little or no bureaucracy to speak of. At the end of the eighteenth century there were perhaps between 300 and 350 salaried officials. Even if we include the short-term, representative office-holders – the *ambtsdragers* and *regenten* – the total does not exceed 2500 at a time when the English fiscal administration numbered 8000.[86] The federal system and tax farming kept the fiscal administration to a minimum.

If English tax officials outnumbered those in other major Protestant states, at first sight they seem to be dwarfed by the number of French revenue officers. But we need to bear in mind the very different character of the French and English tax administrations. The overwhelming majority of French tax officials were not trained assessors, measurers and collectors but members of a paramilitary force whose task was to prevent smuggling and tax evasion. These men, some 23,000 in 1784, were largely illiterate and poorly paid.[87] Many were ex-soldiers performing a policing role that in England was the task of the army. If we exclude these unskilled employees, then the number of French officials is roughly the same as that in England. According to Lavoisier, 2800 fulltime officers were engaged in collecting the *gabelles*, *tabac* and *traites*, 2400 gathering *aides*, and a further 1640 administering the *entrées* and *domaines*.[88] In short, slightly fewer tax officials in France were engaged in tax collection and assessment than in England. Only the large force employed to prevent tax evasion explains the much bigger French revenue service.

The exceptionally heterogeneous and regionally varied structure of French indirect taxes made revenue policing an administrative nightmare. The problem of securing tax compliance in what was one of Europe's largest and most populous states was severely compounded by the presence of many miles of *internal* revenue boundaries. Even a large force of *milice financière* was unable to prevent smuggling on a massive scale.

In England, unlike France, there was no large paramilitary force to enforce the revenue laws. This absence is not adequately explained by the political sensibilities of a ruling class concerned to protect subjects' liberties from the power of the state. Indeed, as we have seen in Chapter 2, the army performed the same role in England that the *gardes des fermes et des gabelles* did in France.

The English revenue service did not develop a system of revenue guards for two reasons. First, England was not divided into different fiscal regions. Not only were its revenue frontiers much shorter but the boundary between land and sea posed more of an obstacle to smugglers than an inland border, so that efforts at revenue detection could be concentrated on the coast and inshore waters. Fewer men were therefore required. Secondly, the deployment of such a body did not accord with the administrative priorities of the revenue commissioners. The first concern of the revenue boards was to maximize extraction from those producers and distributors of taxable commodities who fell within the purview of the revenue service. They were determined to tap the substantial resources of the big breweries and the rich overseas merchants whose operations were on such a scale as to make outright tax evasion extremely difficult. The detection and prosecution of smugglers was necessary for the system to operate effectively, but it was of secondary importance. Revenue commissioners had a remarkably level-headed attitude to smuggling, recognizing it as the inevitable consequence of high tariffs.[89] And, as Tom Paine complained, when subordinate officers devoted their time to chasing smugglers rather than the mundane tasks of measuring and assessing, they were quickly ordered to return to the tedious tasks that the commissioners recognized as the most fiscally lucrative.[90]

If tax collecting in England focused to an unusual degree on the routines of quantification, it was also well controlled by the bookkeepers in Whitehall. The triumph of the Treasury in the late seventeenth century produced a remarkably *centralized* fiscal system in which all departments – both those of receipt and disbursement – were accountable to a single body, the Treasury Board. This enabled Britain to become the first major European state to keep full accounts of total government revenue and expenditure.

Again, this centralization was not to be found elsewhere. The federated United Provinces retained considerable regional fiscal autonomy. There was no central body of receipt and not all of the federation's moneys were accounted for by the central *Generaliteitsrekenkamer*.[91] In France, as late as 1788, the French royal treasury was receiving only half of the state's total revenues.[92] Prussian monarchs concealed their assets in several different *Kassen*, thereby preventing any adequate system of centralized accounting.[93]

England's tax system was not only exceptionally centralized, it was also uniform in its *legal* incidence. No English county or region enjoyed special fiscal privileges. Though there were regional disparities in the payment of the land tax, the north-west of England making a disproportionately small contribution, indirect taxes – customs, excise and stamp duties – which together were fiscally far more important, were levied at the same *national* rates.

The contrast with France and the United Provinces is a marked one. Unlike Brittany, which enjoyed the privilege of not paying the *gabelle*, the salt producers of Cheshire could not have secured fiscal immunity from the salt tax. Nor could an English county have declared, like the *parlement* of Aix in 1756 that, as far as the *vingtième* was concerned, Provence was a separate and distinct state.[94] Though the producers and distributors of taxable goods in England complained of different levels of enforcement of indirect duties, the problem was of little consequence when compared with the *inegaliteit* which marked the collection of the Dutch excise. Then the absence of state officialdom and the role of local regents and magistrates produced levels of compliance which varied markedly from town to town and region to region.[95] Equally, the disparities in English land tax assessment never had the economically distorting effect of the Dutch 'extraordinary' property and wealth taxes, whose collection in the eighteenth century was based on seventeenth-century assessments.[96]

English fiscal uniformity applied not only to every region but to all subjects regardless of their rank. English peers, gentlemen and clerics – unlike many of their continental counterparts – enjoyed no *legal* exemption from the payment of taxes. Legal and economic incidence may, of course, bear only a passing resemblance to one another. Certainly in numerous instances large aristocratic landowners were seriously underassessed for the land tax, and, as we shall see, there are good reasons to suppose that the English tax system as a whole penalized the middling sort more severely than the rich. But the important point is that the English system *looked* fairer than many other tax systems because it did not have inequality built into its legal structure.

The point about how taxes were *perceived* is of central importance to understanding why the English financial system proved such a success and why the French eventually failed. As James Riley has recently emphasized, the greatest problem facing the authorities in eighteenth-century France was the widely held belief that the tax system was both exceptionally punitive and singularly unjust. This perception was not just that of a supposedly overburdened peasantry but also of many high-ranking officials. Such a view does not accord with modern scholarship. Mathias and O'Brien, Michel Morineau and Riley himself, though they may differ on the precise pattern of fiscal imposition in France, do not paint a picture of a state crushed by the weight of taxes. On the contrary, they show the tax burden to be lighter than in Britain and, in Riley's case, argues that after the War of Austrian Succession, 'the long-run peacetime growth of revenues was suspended'.[97] Why, then, the hostility to taxes in France? The conventional answer to this question has been that the legal privilege of exemption from some taxes made the system inherently unjust. This unfairness was compounded by revenue farming which enabled financial middlemen to cream off enormous personal profits at the expense of the monarch and the public. Riley has challenged the veracity of these views, arguing that privilege was of diminishing importance in tax avoidance and that overhead on tax collection of *c*.13 per cent was little worse than in Britain.[98] Even the Farmers General, he argues, were not as corrupt or venal as has been supposed. But, as Riley's account makes clear, the revenue system contained two fatal flaws. First, both its operations and its privileges were highly conspicuous: the large army of *milice financière*, the enshrining of tax exemption in law, the conspicuous wealth of the Farmers. Secondly, though the system was highly visible, the public was vastly ignorant of its workings. All sorts of speculation about the tax system, including the most fantastic stories of corruption, were possible, indeed were encouraged by the fact that so little was known. The reform debate of 1763 was severely hampered by a lack of solid information about the true costs and overheads of the revenue system. This was not because the French monarchy was without any form of accounting. It was attributable both to the fact that the administration of a large proportion of the revenue was in private hands – financial middlemen and *traitants* were not about to reveal their profits – and to the absence of a public forum which could secure accountability.

The contrast with England is telling. Controversy over any tax measure in the British parliament was invariably accompanied by the presentation of accounts, reports and papers to the lower house. Gross and net produce, the costs of collection, the extent of drawbacks, the number of revenue officers employed – all of this information was available to the legislature. Many MPs, of course, paid little attention to the figures and fine print and even fewer probably knew how to interpret them. But such papers were accepted as reasonably accurate and as the basis on which policy should be made. The documents were public information produced by accountable government departments.

This was not true of materials on the French revenue which reached the public sphere. It is difficult to imagine an English minister encountering the difficulties of Jacques Necker, the reforming Director General of French finances. As part of his campaign against a financial system held in thrall by private interests, Necker published a national budget, his *Compte Rendu au Roi* in 1781. From the very first the veracity of his figures was questioned. His enemies stigmatized them as a spurious and self-justificatory account of French finance. The account may have been presented to the public but it was not a public account. Necker's project remained mired in the world of private financial interests from which it sought to escape. No matter that Robert Harris has shown that Necker's accounts were remarkably accurate.[99] It is the ease with which they could be doubted that is important.

The public exposure of state financial operation is not, of course, the only circumstance that explains financial success. The Dutch were able to borrow at lower rates of interest than the English – 2.5 or 3 per cent in the first half of the eighteenth century – despite the absence of public accounting. Indeed one scholar has argued that the veil of ignorance may have protected Dutch finance, for investors might have been shy of lending if they had known that over 70 per cent of tax revenues were needed to service the Dutch debt.[100] Public knowledge of a government's financial state was only beneficial if the information revealed was likely to inspire confidence.

But contemporaries were convinced that England's fiscal system was successful because it was visible. Public accounting and public knowledge, it was argued, created a climate of public confidence which produced willing investors and compliant taxpayers. After the Seven Years War this view became something of a shibboleth enshrined in the highly influential book of the international financier, Isaac de Pinto, whose *Traité de la Circulation et du Credit* was published in Amsterdam in 1771. De Pinto's views were taken seriously because he was known as an experienced and wealthy financial expert who had advised or invested in the French, English and Dutch national debts.

De Pinto's fiduciary analysis was shared by Necker. Necker's reform proposals and plans, as he acknowledged in the opening pages of his *Compte Rendu au Roi*, were all designed to develop French finance on what he took to be English lines: to create public confidence through the publication of national accounts, to ease the task of tax collection by ensuring taxpayers' consent, and to finance massive military effort by an orderly and regular system of long-term borrowing.[101]

Though Necker's reforms were only partially successful, one can sympathize with his analysis. At almost every level, the eighteenth-century English fiscal system worked with remarkable smoothness and very little friction. Its operations were fixed, orderly and routine. Year after year the parliamentary Committees of Ways and Means and of Supply prepared legislation which passed through the commons with little or no opposition. As Lyttleton put it, 'The Treasury and Parliament never depart.'[102] Fiscal legislation, indeed, had the lowest failure rate of all types of statute introduced into eighteenth-century parliaments. The record of successful parliamentary opposition to taxes after 1700 is a feeble one: the brief defeat of a leather tax in 1700, the overturning of Walpole's administrative reforms during the Excise Crisis of 1733, Pelham's loss of a sugar tax in 1744 and the refusal of the house to vote an extra shilling on the pound on the land tax in 1767. The defeat of four pieces of legislation in a period which saw hundreds of acts affecting public finance is clear evidence of the ease with which money bills could be implemented.

Parliamentary consent made public resistance to tax collection extremely difficult. Though there were occasional attacks on revenue officers these were usually carried out by professional smugglers rather than by outraged taxpayers. Most magistrates cooperated with government officials and helped them enforce the law. Officers who used their position to tyrannize the public were dismissed; revenue commissioners enjoined their employees to act with courtesy. As a result tax riots were much less frequent than in either France or Holland. Though extraction rates were high, the ground swell of grumbling and complaint was muted when compared with the voluble criticism, much of it from ministers themselves, voiced in France.

The importance of parliamentary consent in securing the effectiveness of English tax-gathering is underlined by the extent of tax resistance in those territories where the legitimacy of parliamentary jurisdiction was challenged. In North America in the 1760s the powers of the colonial legislatures were opposed to the authority of parliament. Not only were duties evaded but the very legitimacy of colonial taxation was questioned. Put another way, Massachusetts was to London as Britanny was to Paris. A local estate challenged the fiscal authority of the central power.

In Britain the most vehement opposition to taxes came from British subjects in Scotland. The riots against the Scottish malt tax in 1725 were the most violent of the century. Part of this resistance is doubtless attributable to Jacobite sentiment hostile to the Hanoverian regime. But the chief grounds on which taxes were opposed was that their imposition violated the terms of the 1707 Treaty of Union between England and Scotland. Not even a British parliament, it was maintained, could alter that agreement.

With the important exception of Scotland and the North American colonies, British taxes were collected with relative ease. The lack of locally entrenched representative institutions made resistance to the central government extremely difficult, while the presence of a centrally appointed administration made collection expeditious as well as discrete. It is difficult to resist Necker's conclusion that the English sheep were willing to be shorn, not because of a peculiar pusillanimity – that would have been entirely out of national character

– but because they regarded taxation as a legitimate aspect of parliamentary government.

The raising of loans, like the levying of taxes, was accomplished through the use of a well-tried and regular financial system. Here eighteenth-century English finance worked on a seventeenth-century Dutch model: it used a public bank to handle the loans, based the debt on long-term redeemable annuities, and spread the debt amongst a sustantial number of borrowers. The precise links between the English eighteenth-century financial revolution and the Dutch system of public funding which originated in the Habsburg Netherlands in the mid-sixteenth century have never been established.[103] But the similarities are so great, the obsession of English ministers with Dutch methods so well known, and the arrival of William III and his Dutch advisers so timely, that it is hard to believe that contemporaries were wrong when they described the new fiscal arrangements as 'Dutch finance'.

The role of the Bank of England and the close collaboration between the Treasury and leading London financiers meant that, even in years when credit was tight, the government had a system of raising funds. As in so many spheres of financial administration, these arrangements contrast with the expedients adopted by the French state. In the early eighteenth century partial repudiation of debts, reduction of interest rates on long-term obligations, the suspension of payments of short-term debts all undermined the credit of the French monarchy and raised the interest rates it had to pay on subsequent borrowing.[104] This rather dismal record during and after the War of Spanish Succession produced a much more conservative policy from the mid-century. The government was determined not only to show faith with its creditors but to reduce the principal of its debt by moving away from perpetual loans to fixed-term, self-amortizing borrowing. This laudable desire for financial reform proved disastrous. Fixed-term loans commanded higher rates of interest than perpetual securities. They therefore *raised* the annual cost of servicing the debt. In France they increased it disproportionately because of the excessively generous terms on which life annuities were offered. The effect on French finances, when combined with the heavy borrowing which characterized both the Seven Years and American Wars, was catastrophic. In 1753 servicing the French debt cost 30 per cent of ordinary revenue; by 1764 the comparable figure was 60 per cent.[105] French financial policy, in other words, moved in the opposite direction to that of Britain, which had adopted the Dutch pattern of funding by perpetual redeemable securities. As a result unit costs of servicing the English debt fell, while French costs rose. Subsequent French finance ministers persisted in a policy of raising most French credit through loans which had a fixed term at which the capital would be paid off. In consequence interest rates remained high, as did the proportion of revenue used to service the debt.

This is not to say that French public finance was an enduring failure during the last century of the *ancien régime*. On the contrary, given the structural obstacles that encumbered French public finance, it is remarkable that so much money was raised both through taxes and borrowing. Moreover, important improvements were made in the 1770s when Necker, pursuing what he described as 'the genius of good administration', namely 'prudence, order and good faith',[106] managed to bureaucratize parts of the fiscal apparatus.[107]

But the French never managed to solve the political problems associated with collecting taxes. For all Necker's efforts, they failed to break the hold of private interests on both taxes and borrowing, and they therefore failed to create a fiscal system which was public and could appear to be just. This may not have been an administrative disaster but it was a political catastrophe. When this failure was combined with serious policy errors over funding, it proved a fatal mixture.

III

THE PARADOXES OF
STATE POWER

Between 1688 and 1714 the British state underwent a radical transformation, acquiring all of the main features of a powerful fiscal–military state: high taxes, a growing and well-organized civil administration, a standing army and the determination to act as a major European power. Why did this happen? Why, after a long period of comparative international isolation during which England had been a minor military power, did Britain become a major military and diplomatic actor?

The tendency has been to regard this abrupt and radical change as an inevitable consequence of Britain's successful involvement in the protracted and expensive struggles against Louis XIV. As Charles Tilly's pithy dictum puts it, 'war made the state, and the state made war.'[1]

And there is certainly no lack of evidence for this interpretation. Seventy-five per cent or more of England's public expenditure in this period went on waging war, and an even higher percentage of tax revenue was spent on military operations and on servicing the debts incurred in wartime. As we have seen, the fiscal and military departments dwarfed the rest of the bureaucracy. Their chief task was not to serve the welfare of the nation but to provide the resources – the money, supplies and manpower – which were the desiderata of an effective military power.

Though there can be little doubt that war was *responsible* for the expansion of the state, it does not follow that war therefore *caused* the expansion of the state apparatus. We have to push the question one stage further and ask why it was that English policy changed so markedly in the late seventeenth century, embroiling in a major European conflict the nation that had previously avoided such terrible conflagrations as the Thirty Years War.

On several occasions during the course of the seventeenth century, the monarch or head of state had attempted to involve his English subjects in European hostilities. Almost invariably he had been restrained by the fiscal conservatism and parsimony of the House of Commons. England did not lack the capacity to become a major belligerent, but the executive was unable to overcome the fiscal constraints imposed by a legislature unwilling to provide the financial wherewithal for the country to become a great power. Occasionally, of course, the government could call on exceptional resources and circumvent parliamentary restraint but, as both Charles I and Cromwell discovered, such a policy was fraught with difficulty and, in the long term, bound to excite opposition. For much of the seventeenth century the commons successfully limited the government's freedom of movement by keeping a tight rein on the public purse.

After 1688, however, and despite the hostility shown both in and out of parliament towards increased government spending, the crown was able to raise both income and expenditure to unprecedented levels. This is all the more surprising in view of the political independence of the lower house. The commons was far from being the lackey of the administration and frequently overturned or rejected government proposals. What needs to be explained, then, is why the commons was willing both to countenance and to finance a major European war, to embark on a policy which, by the standards of the period, was almost as radical as the deposition of a king.

England's entry, through the eager offices of William of Orange, into the confederation of states determined to hold Louis XIV in check, dragged the nation into more than twenty years of continental warfare. At the outset few Englishmen realized the extent of their commitment, and most parliamentary politicians either wished or assumed that England's role as a European belligerent would be thankfully brief. Even fewer envisaged the transformation that the wars would wreak on the nation's institutions. Those who tried to predict the future were apt to imagine it as most unpalatable. The examples of a militarily beleaguered and highly taxed United Provinces or of a French state dominated by an autocratic monarch with an insatiable appetite for self-aggrandizement were dark auguries for Englishmen who wished for peace and plenty, liberty and the Protestant faith.

The inability of late Stuart politicians to predict the consequences of their nation's entry into war warns us against assuming that the institutional changes of the time were inevitable, a necessary consequence of England's becoming a belligerent power. We need to remember that the act of waging war did not inevitably lead to the development of new and more powerful state institutions. Indeed, in early modern Europe war often succeeded in diluting rather than concentrating state power. The absence of effective public institutions to manage the business of war prompted the growth of *private* military enterprise.[2] The recruitment of troops was handed over to military enterprisers and the collection of revenue assigned to private consortia of financiers. The ruler's grip on his subjects was weakened by venality, the financial burdens of war led to the abandonment of bureaucratic reform, the presence of hostilities on home territory produced administrative breakdown. Fiscal pressures also enhanced the powers of institutions such as parliaments and estates whose approval was necessary for the levying of taxes. So, though wars might provide opportunities for rulers to consolidate their power and assert themselves against their subjects, they might equally lead to a loss of control, to the growth of private interests which appropriated such public functions as recruitment and tax gathering.

The Nine Years War subjected the English state to all the stresses and strains that accompany involvement in a major war – fiscal crisis, financial scandal, mismanagement and corruption, the virtual collapse of parts of the administration. But what emerged was a *public* fiscal–military apparatus, remarkably untainted by private interests. This had not been an inevitable outcome. William's desperate need for cash led him to offer public offices to private financiers with no administrative experience,[3] and there was frequent discussion of a reversion to revenue farming.[4] The rapid, sprawling growth of administration and the remarkable growth in the amount of public moneys increased the temptation to defraud the public and enhanced the opportunity to do so. On occasion in the 1690s it looked as if the administrative system would break down and the money would run out. But, close as the English came to disaster, they succeeded in averting catastrophe. Moreover the lessons of the 1690s were learnt remarkably quickly. If the War of Spanish Succession produced a notable number of fortunes for soldiers, sailors, contractors and remittance men, it nevertheless saw both a significant reduction in the politicization of administration and in the habit of egregious peculation. The English state managed to avoid the sort of spoliation to which other regimes had so often fallen prey.

Why, in what is conventionally viewed as the most unstate-like of states, did the government manage both to cope with the pressures of war and to retain much of its integrity? Two circumstances were vital. First, William and his followers were the beneficiaries of the administrative reforms initiated by their predecessors. Thus, thanks to Charles and James, the revenue departments were sufficiently well rooted to avoid being swept away by the winds of war. Secondly, the commons restrained malfeasance and secured public accountability. The price that MPs exacted for supporting the war was the opportunity to subject its operations to unparalleled surveillance.[5] This did not prevent peculation and administrative corruption, but it certainly rendered the offences both more risky and more liable to detection. It checked abuse, even if it did not entirely eliminate it.

The commons was not only the watchdog of the state, but also the forum within which the controversial views surrounding the war were debated. The impact of foreign policy, the significance of war, the repercussions – fiscal, administrative and political – of the struggle against Louis XIV were all discussed with a passion that occasionally approached ferocity. These arguments about the war are of great importance, for they enable us to understand why the commons was prepared, however reluctantly, to support hostilities, and they go far to explain why the administrative and fiscal apparatus assumed the form it did.

Domestic Policy and Foreign Affairs

The overthrow, flight or 'abdication' of James II was a watershed in British history. Though there were obvious continuities between the English polity

ruled by the Catholic James and the realm governed by the Protestant William
and Mary, there were also significant differences. Nearly all political institutions and a good many of those who manned them survived into the new
reign, but the new world, though dotted with familiar landmarks – a powerful
monarch, a substantial army, a flourishing court and the consummately *poli-
tique* Earl of Sunderland – nevertheless contained much that was unfamiliar.

Nowhere was this more apparent than in that most jealously guarded of
royal prerogatives, the making of foreign policy.[6] After 1688 a royal policy
previously marked by acquisitive amity or sympathetic neutrality towards
France was replaced by one of active hostility. Despite the rise to power of
Louis xiv's France, Charles ii had shown remarkably little anxiety about his
overmighty Catholic neighbour. Indeed, Charles had a marked propensity to
make himself the client of the French king, and resisted the efforts of his
ministers, particularly those of Danby, to develop an anti-French Protestant
foreign policy. James ii, perhaps because of his preoccupation with domestic
affairs, remained equally unperturbed by French aggrandizement.

Such insouciance about the French, which many of Charles and James's
subjects did not share, did not survive the Glorious Revolution. William's
acquisition of the English crown was, as many Englishmen realized, no philan-
thropic act. It accorded with his determination to build a European alliance
which at best would destroy French hegemony in Europe and which at worst
would hold Louis xiv in check.

But the concerns of most Englishmen were far more parochial. They were
fighting neither for a Dutch king nor for a balance of power in Europe. They
cared little for either. They fought to preserve the revolution of 1688, to avert
the return of James ii, whom Louis supported, and to avoid the Catholicism
and executive intrusion that had been the hallmarks of his reign.

A great many politicians, especially the tories, were therefore concerned to
contain the scope of England's military involvement. They wanted to play a
subsidiary rather than a leading role in the continental war; they wanted a
'blue water' strategy which looked to the navy and to commercial and colonial
gains rather than towards the balance of power in Europe. During the war
itself they achieved only limited success. But by 1697, with universal war-
weariness and the nation in the throes of a major financial crisis, many MPs,
as William discovered to his disgust, were also eager to turn their backs on
the Continent and to revert to an isolationist foreign policy.

Between 1697 and 1701 it seemed as if the legislature would succeed in
expunging many of the effects of nearly a decade of war. The standing army
was decimated to a mere 7000 and the war leaders of the whig Junto impeached.
The 1701 Act of Settlement – more properly entitled, 'An Act for the further
limitation of the crown and the better securing the rights of the subject' –
introduced a variety of constraints on royal power. Clauses in the Act removed
placemen from the commons, made privy councillors more accountable to
parliament for their advice to the king, gave judges greater independence,

restricted the religion and movement of the monarch, and attempted to prevent his taking foreigners' advice. Many of these measures were aimed personally at William, whose proclivity for Dutch guards, Dutch advisers and European politicking was much disliked. But their effect was to limit the strength of the fiscal–military state as a whole.[7]

But William's opponents had not reckoned with the behaviour of Louis xiv. The French king's conduct in 1701, which included not only provocations over the Spanish Succession and in the Netherlands but the recognition of the Old Pretender and attacks on English trade, convinced all but the most diehard members of the peace party that war, if it were not inevitable, was probably imminent.[8] The dismantling of the English military machine was abruptly reversed. Paradoxically, Louis xiv was one of the greatest allies of those who argued for all-out war against France. He also bears some responsibility for the emergence of England as a fiscal–military power. If William, aided by James, pushed England into the military arena, it was the French king who kept her there.

In 1689, when England first entered the war against France, it was widely recognized that the domestic consequences of losing the war would have been catastrophic. If William had been defeated by James and Louis, if the campaign in Ireland had proved disastrous or Louis's descent on England successful, not only would the balance of power in Europe have been transfigured, so would the domestic polity, which would have had to stomach the return of a Catholic king. As Major Wildman reminded the commons in November 1689: 'We talk not here for the King, but for the Kingdom. I have heard a doctrine preached here, "Take Care we be not principals in the war against France": but against King James we are principals in that war to defend us from popery and slavery.'[9]

It was this link between the fate of English *domestic* political arrangements and the outcome of the struggle between Louis xiv and his enemies which distinguishes the Nine Years War from earlier European conflicts in which the English had engaged. Apart from the Elizabethan struggle with the Spanish, earlier wars had seemed more discretionary, a matter of choosing whether or not the island kingdom would venture forth to enter into a European conflict. But after 1688 the English were involved whether they liked it or not. Moreover, the stakes were exceptionally high. Not everyone might agree with William iii's characterization of the war as 'not so properly an act of choice as an inevitable necessity in our defence',[10] but it was widely understood that, whatever else it might be, the struggle with James and Louis was a war of English succession, fought to preserve a Protestant regime. Indeed the importance of this war aim is borne out by the first clause of the Treaty of Ryswick by which Louis recognized William as England's ruler.

The circumstances of the 1690s – the threat of foreign invasion, William and Mary's tenuous hold on the throne, the fear of domestic plots and insurrection, and the apprehensions about the fate of the Protestant religion both in

Britain and Europe – were a boon to those who had long advocated an anti-Catholic and anti-French foreign policy. William's whig supporters pressed home their advantage, portraying high taxes and an expensive war as a lesser evil than the potential loss of domestic and religious liberty. As the whig MP Hampden put it in a series of rhetorical questions,[11]

what will it avail to say that you are cozened, and, if you give more, you shall be cozened? But are you the better for saving your Money, if Ireland be lost, perhaps England too? Popery, French and Irish, to dwell among you, and govern you; and saving the Taxes will be cold comfort at last, to say 'I have saved £100 in taxes, and perhaps my estate will be sequestered, or worse: I must either renounce my religion or lose it.'

These words were, of course, the special pleading of an ardent supporter of William, the scion of a famous parliamentary family. They would doubtless have fallen on the deaf ears of Jacobites, Catholics and some of those politicians who dreaded the consequences of England's involvement in a European war. But the rhetoric of Hampden and his colleagues was not without effect. Defence of the new regime or, at least, a desire to avoid a return to the old, does seem to explain why many MPs who might otherwise have been unwilling to fight a war were prepared to support the struggle against France. For once arguments for war based on 'state necessity' seemed persuasive. As one commentator conceded,[12]

Our dear bought experience has taught us what Vast Taxes are absolutely necessary to maintain the armies and Fleet, which are requisite for our security; and for the defence of our religious and civil rights; and provided that we attain those ends, it will not be thought, at long run, we have bought them any too dear. In this case we may say, *diminium plus toto*. A wise and good man will rather chuse (if it come to that pass) to enjoy one half of his estate, with the liberty of his conscience and the preserve of his birthright, than to possess a double or treble proportion of his riches, whilst his mind must be enslaved to superstition, of knavish and interested priests, his innocent friends and countrymen sacrificed to the idol of arbitrary power (as we have seen lately practiced) and the title that is left him in his own possession and Liberty, only precarious and during pleasure.

The circumstances of the 1690s tipped the balance decisively towards those who were not only willing but eager to cut French military and maritime power down to size.

But critics of the war, even when they conceded its seeming inevitability, did not give up the struggle to contain what they regarded as its potentially damaging consequences. They had, however, to confront an irresoluble paradox. The Glorious Revolution was not only a Protestant but a 'country' revolution, concerned both to preserve the true faith as England's official religion and to reduce the powers of central government. But, in order to protect the revolution from its enemies, the powers of the state had perforce to grow as never before. Attempts to solve this contradiction lay at the heart of parliamentary politics of the period. The opponents of higher taxes, deficit financing, an expanding civil administration and a standing army fought bravely to hold big government in check. Yet, at bottom, they recognized that the fiscal–military state protected Englishmen's liberties as much as it threatened them. It was undesirable but necessary. This view, which was slowly and painfully accepted, explains why the focus of opposition to the fiscal–military state gradually shifted away from the attempt to secure its abolition to a policy of containment. For all their brave rhetoric, the opponents of big government knew that though they might win many battles, they could not and, in some cases, did not wish to win the war.

Nevertheless their resistance, as they themselves recognized,[13] was not in vain. If they did not stem the tide of government they were able to reduce its flow or ensure that it ran into what they saw as less harmful channels. The determination to secure accountable government, to root out peculation and graft, and to avoid the indiscriminate expansion of civilian and military offices produced a far more honest and proficient administration than would ever have emerged if such reformist initiatives had been entirely absent. The state apparatus that emerged from this conflict between the advocates of strong government and their opponents was never quite as either side wished or intended: it was never the leviathan that its opponents feared, but neither was it the toothless creature that its apologists apprehended.

The Struggle over Money

At the heart of the struggle over the character and scope of late Stuart government lay the battle over finance. Control over money was the commons' most powerful weapon, albeit one which had been used incompetently in the conflicts between the monarch and the lower house during the 1670s and 1680s. Yet even in this earlier period it had been recognized that, as one MP put it, "tis money that makes a Parliament considerable & nothing else'.[14] The Convention and the early parliaments of William and Mary were chastened bodies, determined to learn the lessons their predecessors had overlooked. If the last years of Charles II's reign had reminded them of the fragility of the power of the commons, the reign of James II had demonstrated that disastrous and divisive policies could easily be pursued by a monarch unconstrained by the need to consult 'the representative of the people'.

Post-Revolutionary politicians knew that they themselves were largely to blame for the follies and disasters that had· led to the invitation, signed by both whig and tory, beseeching William of Orange to rescue Englishmen and their liberties from the obduracy and autarchy of a Catholic king. Charles II at the Restoration and James at his succession had been treated with excessive trust. 'The heat of loyalty', remarked Sir Robert Howard, a former secretary to the Treasury, 'was carried on formerly to excess'.[15] Credulous royalism had led parliament to confer a generous financial settlement on both of Charles I's children; parliament itself had granted the monarch the wherewithal 'to govern by Arbitrary Power, and abolish Parliaments'.[16]

Nearly all MPs – including royal servants as well as back-benchers and radical whigs – were determined to avoid the errors of the past. They hardly needed to be reminded that 1688 gave them such an opportunity. When, in an oft-quoted remark, William Harbord, a West country MP, told the commons that 'You have an infallible security for the administration of government; all the revenue is in your hands, which fell with the last King, and you may keep that back,'[17] he was preaching to the converted. Though some, especially amongst William's most fervent admirers, thought it churlish to try to constrain the nation's saviour, many more agreed with William Garraway, the member for Arundel who remarked that, 'We have had such violation of our Liberties in the last reigns, that the Prince of Orange cannot take it ill, if we make conditions, to secure ourselves for the future.'[18]

The most obvious way to check the power of the crown was through the calling of frequent parliaments, and the way to secure frequent parliaments was to ensure the financial dependence of the monarch. The experiences of the previous reign provided ample information about what paths to avoid and what fiscal routes to follow. James had been financially independent for two reasons. First, parliament had granted him a competency for life, rather than for a limited number of years. Second, this competency took the form of the yield from certain duties. The royal revenue was made up of indirect taxes – customs and excises – on international trade and domestic commerce. Though the monarch could not change the rate of these taxes without the consent of parliament, the yield fluctuated according to the prosperity of the economy. The boom that took place for most of James's reign was therefore an important contributory factor to his fiscal independence.

James had capitalized on these advantages by launching a determined campaign for administrative improvement designed to maximize the returns of the revenues to which he was legally entitled, to reduce local resistance to taxes and to create an effective royal bureaucracy. Though the collection of all indirect taxes became more efficient, the greatest progress was made with the excise. Writing after the Revolution (and with an admittedly large axe to grind) Charles Davenant, the political arithmetician and former Excise commissioner, maintained that a large proportion of the increase in excise returns between 1683 and 1688 was the direct result of administrative reform.[19]

James's financial independence and the bureaucratic initiative, so redolent of French absolutism, which accompanied it were burnished on the political memory of William and Mary's early parliaments. They took no chances. Deep as they were in the Dutchman's debt, the commons would not grant him a competency for life. Though William and Mary enjoyed the hereditary excise during their reign, parliament would make up their ordinary income from customs revenues for a period of only four years. Moreover, the commons deliberately increased the crown's fiscal dependence by failing to provide William with extraordinary income to service his wartime borrowing, thereby forcing him to burden his ordinary revenue with debts. At the same time the commons fought back against the administrative initiative begun by James. The last two clauses of the bill of rights took up financial grievances against the hearth tax and the excise. William, no doubt hoping for a generous fiscal present in return, magnanimously abandoned the hearth tax. Though the measure was popular both in the commons and with the public at large, it failed to elicit the expected response. Instead the lower house proceeded, in the first excise Act after the Revolution, to remove a number of administrative innovations that James's excise commissioners had introduced, and to change the rules of evidence to favour those who disputed the duties.[20]

The overall effect of these measures was to end the possibility of financial independence for the crown. Not even in peacetime could the monarch use his ordinary revenue 'to live of his own'. In future he had perforce to turn to parliament if he were to remain solvent. The object of securing fiscal dependency was clear: to ensure the regular calling of parliament. This, in turn, would enable the lower house to scrutinize the actions of the executive and redress the grievances of their constituents. The debates of 1689 and 1690, as both Henry Horwitz and Clayton Roberts have shown, leave no doubt that the commons were determined to secure frequent parliaments by holding the power of the purse.[21]

The financial settlement hammered out in 1689 and 1690 meant that in future the ability of the king's ministers to secure parliamentary consent to additional revenues was to be of vital importance to the monarch. From the outset of William and Mary's reign, government ministers sought to initiate an ambitious plan to enable the crown not only to cover its usual expenses but also to wage war on a grand scale. There were two major components in this scheme: a direct tax, a subsidy or assessment equivalent to 2 shillings in the pound; and what was referred to as a 'general excise', a tax on the sale of staples. The latter tax would have meant a duty not only on drink but on foodstuffs and such basic items as clothing, leather goods, soap, candles and salt.

A subsidy was, of course, a time-honoured means of supplying the monarch with extraordinary revenue;[22] the proposal for a general excise was, however, a more recent and more controversial plan. The scheme may have been advocated because William, as a Dutchman, would have been familiar with the fiscal possibilities of a general excise. In the United Provinces in the late seventeenth century about half of the cost of most commodities was attributable to excise duties. But a general excise scheme was just as likely to be of English origin and to be based on the parliamentarian John Pym's excises which had been introduced in July 1643. These taxes had originally been laid on drink – beer, ale, cider and perry – but had spread so quickly that in little more than a year there were excises on soap, cloth, spirits, butcher's meat, salt, poultry, herring, alum, copperas, caps, hats, hops, saffron, silk, tin, iron and wood. The kinds of commodity chosen by the late seventeenth- and eighteenth-century proponents of excises as possible sources of revenue tended to be those which had also been included in Pym's list of excise imposts. To some extent, therefore, there was a (largely unsuccessful) attempt after the Glorious Revolution to revert to the fiscal policies of the parliamentarians during the Civil War.

The government's plan to secure a general excise began immediately after the Glorious Revolution. Late in 1689 a scheme for a general excise on staples failed in a parliamentary committee. In the following year there were many rumours of a plan to introduce a new general excise scheme, although none materialized. In 1691, Charles Davenant helped Sidney Godolphin draft another scheme. In the next two years excise schemes were debated in the commons, and in the spring of 1693 Sir Robert Howard, one of the Lords of the Treasury, worked up a new government proposal. In the following session the government, conscious of the fierce opposition its policy provoked, narrowed its objectives, moving for an excise solely on leather and on soap. For the next two years these proposals were the focus of a protracted battle about taxation in the commons.[23]

A general excise had obvious attractions for the king. Its ubiquity promised to yield large sums yet it was easy to collect. As Charles Davenant put it in his tract of 1695, *An Essay upon Ways and Means of Supplying War*,[24]

excises seem the most proper Ways and Means to support the government in a long war, because they would lie equally upon the whole, and produce great sums proportionable to the wants of the public. . . . That kind of revenue must needs be very great, where so large a part of the people are every minute paying something towards it; and very easy, when every one, in a manner, taxes himself, making consumption according to his will or ability.

Taxes on production or sales could be assessed less obtrusively and more accurately than duties on wealth or realty; their incidence was less visible than a poll tax, because they were levied not on the public at large but on producers and distributors who passed the costs on to consumers in the form of higher prices. They were also less subject to the fluctuations which plagued customs duties affected by the wartime disruption of trade. A general excise had a further attraction. Thanks to the reforms introduced by James II's commissioners, the Excise employed a body of royal administrators second to none. In short, excises offered the monarch and his ministers the tantalizing combination of administrative simplicity and high returns. They were also the only duties which looked as if they might provide a sufficiently broad tax base to reduce or even, perhaps, to remove the government's need to borrow money. The case for a general excise, it should be remembered, was the case for avoiding a burgeoning public debt.

But many MPs lacked the enthusiasm of the likes of Charles Davenant for such taxes. They feared that a general excise would allow the monarch to reacquire the fiscal independence of which he had been deprived by the revolutionary financial settlement. They were strongly averse to raising supply through taxes with a flexible or unpredictable yield or by imposts that required 'an army of officers'[25] to collect the revenue. Such duties raised the prospect, reminiscent of James II's reign, of a monarch able, through a combination of good fortune and administrative efficiency, to live off his ordinary revenues. Thus the debate about a general excise was seen by many MPs as part of the larger question of the financial independence of the crown.

The commons worried that a general excise would somehow build itself into the fiscal system and then prove difficult or impossible to dislodge. 'We would have taxes so laid', said one commentator, 'as when the necessity of taxing ceases, the taxes may cease with them'.[26] But, as the whig parliamentary diarist Narcissus Luttrell remarked, 'these excises . . . are not likely to be got of[f] again (as the land tax) when the occasion ceases, they take root by their many officers . . . and tho necessity raised them at first, they are apt to find occasion for their continuance'.[27]

The early and explicit advocacy of a general excise by the court affected all subsequent debates about excise taxes on specific commodities. A proposal to tax a single item – leather or salt, for instance – was immediately interpreted by many in the house as the thin edge of a thick fiscal wedge. Thus it was reported by Bonnet, the envoy of the court of Brandenburg, that during the debate in 1694 on a leather excise, 'quelques uns alléguant que leur condition alloit devenir pire que celle des Hollandois, chez qui rien n'exempt de taxe'.[28] Or, as Hampden put it somewhat more pungently, 'when the serpant gets his head into a hole, it is no hard matter for him to draw his whole body after it'.[29] Debates about individual taxes therefore assumed disproportionate importance for individual MPs. A single excise presaged a general one; a general excise promised fiscal independence to the crown; fiscal independence threatened the revolutionary settlement; excises therefore jeopardized the Glorious Revolution.

The land tax, on the other hand, offered no such threat. Voted annually, the tax was of a fixed term and, by the end of the Nine Years War, had a fixed yield of c. £500,000 for every shilling in the pound levied by the lower house. Controlled in the metropolis not by the crown but by the commons, the tax's administration in the field was in the hands of local dignitaries and not in the power of the royal bureaucracy. Land tax assessors, collectors and receivers were all private citizens rather than state employees. They were appointed by local commissioners and were not answerable to a central board or office in London.[30]

Some parliamentary commentators maintained that one of the land tax's most admirable features was that those who were responsible for its imposition were most hurt by it. This guaranteed that, once the tax was no longer essential, it would be sure of a prompt reduction or a swift repeal. In this respect, as in so many others, it differed from excises which 'do not immediately touch the members of parliament themselves, who are landed men, and therefore not so directly concerned to get them off'.[31] MPs opposed to excises were afraid of the insidious attraction they might hold for the landed classes.[32]

The commons' decided preference for the land tax – its willingness to fund most of the war effort between 1692 and 1713 by a tax which fell primarily on landed wealth – is therefore explained in a single word: control. The tax might fall heavily on the landed classes, but the commons knew that when the time came they could easily (or so they thought) throw off the burden. The tax created no class of insidious bureaucrat, no creatures of the crown ready to support monarchical power and to subvert elections. Though the land tax was in this period the strong arm of the fiscal state, its financial muscle was only exercised at the behest of the commons. It is this that explains why Paul Foley could report to his fellow 'country' MP Robert Harley in September 1692 that some MPs preferred to pay 6 shillings in the pound on the land tax rather than support a general excise.[33] The commons were determined not only to limit the monarch's ordinary revenue, but also to keep a tight rein on all extraordinary funding.

Criticism of a general excise was also fuelled by the view, expressed by many MPs, that excises were disproportionately harsh on the poor. Many critics recalled that the Restoration excise had been granted to Charles II to replace royal revenues lost because of the abolition of the Court of Wards. Wardship had penalized the rich; excises, it was argued, encumbered the middling sort and the poor: 'it is the generality of the Trading, Working, Industrious and Profitable Part of this Kingdom, that . . . bear the burden. . . . [It falls] upon the backs of the most Industrious part of the Common People.'[34] A general excise on drink, victuals and staples, it was maintained, would have been more discriminatory, making the poor

pay more than the wealthiest of their neighbours, suitable to what they have; for though a rich man spends more in exciseable things than a poor man doth, yet it is as much as he can do to provide the necessaries for his family out of which he pays his proportion.

Such critics saw through the 'voluntarist' arguments of Davenant and his colleagues, which claimed that the payment of excises was a matter of choice. They knew perfectly well that a tax on basic commodities left the poor with little or no choice but to pay. They also saw that such taxes consumed a much higher proportion of the poor subject's income.[35]

The defence of their humble constituents served MPs well when they returned to their localities. But their chief concern was undoubtedly the threat posed by the possibility of a monarch able to dispense with parliament. This apprehension, more than any other consideration, explains why MPs like Robert Harley were ready to 'pray God direct in the matter, & prevent a General Home Excise'.[36]

As it turned out, Harley's supplication was not in vain. Despite the frequency with which the Treasury introduced excise measures during the Nine Years War, the policy of securing a general excise enjoyed very little success. The overall fiscal plan of a general excise and a low land tax was never realized because the government never succeeded in passing a comprehensive excise bill. Repeated efforts secured the passage of only a small body of excise legislation: additional duties on beer, wine and spirits, the salt tax in 1694, the duties on glass, bottles and tobacco pipes of 1696 which proved a failure and were repealed three years later, the malt tax, which became an important feature of the standing revenue, and the leather tax passed in the same year, 1697, which provoked enormous hostility and which was not renewed after it had run its three-year term. The financial labours of an elephant produced a fiscal mouse.[37]

Why did the government's initiative prove such a failure? Why, at a time when the nation seemed in great peril, were ministers unable to secure the fiscal legislation they deemed necessary? We know why many MPs opposed excises, but this does not answer the question of why they enjoyed such success.

Part of the answer lies in the parlous state of political management for much of William's reign. In the years immediately after the Glorious Revolution, the unsuccessful conduct of the war, the administrative difficulties and malfeasance exposed during the rapid expansion of the executive, the political divisions within the king's administration, and the rank mediocrity of some of the crown's ministers – especially of those dealing with finance – meant that the commons lacked incisive leadership and informed guidance from the government front bench. In August 1692, when the privy councillor, the Earl of Rochester prepared a memorandum urging the king to make all speed with preparations for the next parliamentary session, he conceded somewhat disconsolately, 'It is perhaps too confident a thing for anyone to say that parliament will, or will not do anything, whatsoever that may be, proposed to them.' Lord Carmarthen, the president of the council, added an even more pessimistic and defeatist note to Rochester's original comment: 'Sir J. Lowther [a Lord of the Treasury] says nobody can know, one day, what the house of Commons would do the next, in which all agree with him.'[38] This confession reflects, in part, the difficulty of organizing the house in a period when political allegiances were rapidly changing. But it is also, as John Kenyon has pointed out,[39] an astonishing admission of political impotence. Not even the return of Sunderland – whose skills as a political manager were second to none – nor the emergence of the whig Junto as the dominant and most efficient group in the king's administration could establish a firm and lasting grip on the commons. Between 1694 and 1696 the ministers of the Junto managed to tighten their tenuous grasp, but by 1697 the commons had once again escaped their hold.

Only in the reign of Anne was the Treasury front bench able to assert its control over that most important of government concerns, the passage of financial legislation. If, under William, government fiscal policy was constantly thwarted, after 1702 it was almost never checked by parliamentary opposition. The triumph was reflected in parliamentary procedure. In 1706 a decision was made preventing any MP from introducing a money bill without the recommendation of the crown. This gave the Treasury a monopoly over fiscal legislation. In 1713 this ruling became part of the commons' standing orders.[40] By 1711 such occurrences as the temporary defeat of a leather tax by the group of high tory MPs, the October Club, were sufficiently rare to take most political commentators by surprise. [41] In the previous reign such events had been commonplace.

The failure of William's ministers to establish strict control of the legislature is largely attributable to the 'rage of party'. Ferocious party conflict was ubiquitous. Despite the efforts of such 'undertakers' as Sunderland, Shrewsbury and Godolphin, men who looked for a politics of moderation which would best serve the interests of the monarch and state, party warfare was not confined to the shires or the floor of the House of Commons but forced its way into government, racking successive ministries and rending the fabric of royal administration. As we saw in chapter 4 the 1690s witnessed repeated political purges of the revenue departments. The employment not only of humble field officers but also of commissioners and those involved in making policy was subject to the vagaries of party conflict. Again, it was not until Anne's reign that the ministers of the crown, most notably Godolphin, were able to temper party zeal by a concern for administrative probity and continuity.

The debilitating effects of party conflict on the formation of financial policy were obvious to contemporaries. in July 1696 when Charles Davenant was once again floating his favourite project for a series of new excises in his *Memoriall concering Creditt*, he blamed the failure of earlier schemes on lack of planning and on the absence of unanimity within the Treasury:[42]

Excises probably have hitherto miscarried in Parliament because they came crudely thither, and because such as offer'd them to the house, were not agreed among themselves, in what manner, and where they should be collected; what number of officers were needfull to ascertain the Duty, and what would be the yearly Produce of every Branch. Upon which Account (as men walk fearfully in the dark) so the parliament was afraid to touch upon Excises which were so ill understood, and had been so little digested

The political turbulence of the 1690s pushed the ship of state off course. It also meant that those other than royal officers had the chance to seize the helm. The weak grasp of the king's administration on fiscal policy meant that other groups in the commons were able not only to thwart official policy but to take the legislative initiative. Policy was not coolly formulated at Whitehall but hammered out in the heat of debates at Westminster. From the floor of the house opponents of the government offered fiscal counter-proposals to those of the king's ministers; often the commons preferred these measures to those put forward by the administration. Indeed many of the taxes introduced by the commons in the 1690s were schemes designed to pre-empt or replace government excise proposals. The poll taxes, the wine duty levied on retailers in 1693, the tax on births, marriages and deaths of 1695 and the proposed capitation of 1696 were all introduced as alternative measures to the dreaded excise.[43]

This independent initiative was often led by MPs who sat or who had sat on one of the successive Commissions of Public Accounts which the commons established after 1691 in order to scrutinize government revenue and expenditure. Important 'country' politicians of both whig and tory persuasion - men like William Clarges, Thomas Foley and Robert Harley – played the part of fiscal watchdogs, using the powers of the commission to requisition departmental accounts and to examine administrative expenditure. The commission was another instance of the commons' determination to set financial constraints on the crown and to ensure that the house exacted the right to detailed scrutiny of public moneys in return for its unprecedented grants of revenue. The commission was also the major source of fiscal ideas and financial information for those who wanted to cut government expenditure and pare government revenue to a bare minimum, 'endeavouring to be frugal by good management'.[44]

The Commissioners of Accounts have been condemned by some historians as meddlesome, factious and misinformed. But though the commissions formed in Anne's reign have been especially criticized, [45] most recent historians have argued that the commissions of the 1690s performed several valuable services. [46] First, as we have mentioned, their members were actively involved in policy making – formulating fiscal schemes and pressing them in parliamentary debate. Second, they were recognized by MPs, especially those of a 'country' persuasion, as an alternative source of financial expertise to the Treasury bench. The commissioners, after all, had examined government accounts in detail – that, indeed, was their chief responsibility – and they often produced figures and estimates that differed from those of the government. They gave back-benchers the confidence and resolve to question the crown's proposals and policy; they bolstered the commons' determination to secure fiscal accountability.

The commissioners also improved fiscal probity. This may seem an excessively credulous claim in view of the 1690s' reputation as a decade remarkable for financial scandal and egregious peculation in all branches of government. Even the commons itself was not untainted: in 1695 the Speaker, Sir John Trevor, was expelled for taking bribes from the East India Company to aid the passage of legislation in which they were an interested party. Such malfeasance was duplicated in many departments. Treasury officials took bribes, naval officers extorted protection money from merchant ships, contractors fiddled their books, victualling commissioners supplied inedible food and undrinkable beer, army officers pocketed their men's pay and tax officials engaged in fraud. No wonder that Robert Harley, always ready with a sententious phrase, could condemn William's reign as 'an age of fraud and corruption'.[47]

We should, however, put this indubitably reprehensible record in perspective. In William's reign the state apparatus and government spending grew as never before. Yet there was little planning or order to this growth, not the least because of the commons' unwillingness to admit that the war against the former King James and Louis XIV might be a long one. A confused administrative labyrinth took shape in which the nefarious peculator could easily hide. Government expansion meant expanded opportunities for fraud: more money to appropriate, more men with the chance to embezzle it.

But the standards of public misconduct, however deplorable, were no worse than most other European states and were certainly better than they had been in the early seventeenth century. The extent of our knowledge of 'corruption' in this period reflects the extent to which it was exposed by contemporaries determined to root out fraud. William's reign would appear to us as a far more virtuous age if it had not been for the assiduous investigations of such reformers as the Commissioners of Accounts. Their work meant that an aggrieved official or a virtuous administrator (quite often the former posing as the latter) could use the commissioners to air a complaint, secure redress or remove an evil.[48] The existence of the commissioners meant that government officials, however successful they were at obstructing the commission's work, had to proceed with greater probity and caution, for there was always the possibility that their colleagues might become their accusers. Sometimes such complaints were petty or spiteful, motivated by personal or party malice, but occasionally they led to the exposure of real abuses and their eventual reform.

The activities of the Commissions of Accounts and of their parliamentary supporters are symptomatic of two features of fiscal politics in the reign of William III. First, fiscal policy was the result of various pressures from many political groups, including those outside the administration. Throughout the Nine Years War it was never the monopoly of a single party or interest. In consequence the ship of state, though not rudderless, steered a zig-zag course dictated by the shifting aims of a changing crew. Second, the vagaries of fiscal policy were in large part the result of a clash between two conflicting priorities of the commons. On the one hand, they were determined to secure fiscal accountability; on the other, they were, for all their anxieties and misgivings, prepared to grant the crown unprecedented amounts of money.

In the struggle to constrain the revenue and to ensure parliamentary accountability the country politicians proved too successful for their own good. Though government fiscal policy was subject to unprecedented scrutiny throughout William's reign, and though, for most of the Nine Years War, the country opposition, both whig and tory, held the Treasury on a tight leash, the success of the crown's critics eventually redounded against them.

In their determination to prevent the crown from establishing a perdurable fiscal apparatus and a standing royal revenue of capacious proportions, the commons tried to restrict both the term of taxes and the extent of government long-term borrowing. Just as they feared duties and imposts which would be difficult to remove once hostilities ended, so they were reluctant to permit public borrowing which would require substantial taxes for many years to come to pay off the interest on long-term loans. They feared that the need to service a long-term debt would erode the distinction between the high taxes which were regrettably necessary in wartime and the low duties which thankfully typified periods of peace. Long-term borrowing, like its handmaiden long-term taxes, threatened the policy of containing the effects of war, a strategy which was dear to the hearts of so many parliamentarians.

The opponents of long-term borrowing were unable to prevent the practice in its entirety. In 1693, 1694 and 1697 the government resorted to long-term loans raised either through public lotteries or the sale of annuities. It also borrowed from the chartered companies, most notably from the Bank of England, which was established, after a bitter political battle, in 1694.[49]

The opponents of the Bank feared both its political ancestry – which was decidedly Dissenting and whig, not to say republican[50] – and its role as a link between an administration bent on prosecuting the war and a financial interest which stood to profit by an escalation of hostilities. Their response was to try to replace the Bank of England by a Land Bank, which they felt would be more representative of and more answerable to the parliamentary classes. This plan almost succeeded in 1696 but eventually foundered on the hostility of the court and on the Land Bank's inability to weather an escalating credit crisis.[51]

Though the Land Bank scheme failed, the opponents of long-term borrowing largely succeeded in their aim of keeping such loans to a minimum. As we have seen, long-term borrowing contributed less than 10 per cent to payments for the cost of the Nine Years War. Unlike all subsequent wars in the eighteenth century, current taxes and short-term borrowing provided the bulk of the funds.

Such a policy clearly served the ends of those who were suspicious of the executive and eager to retain as much parliamentary control of financial affairs as possible. It was also not an intrinsically unsound financial strategy, though it did place a tremendous burden on short-term borrowing. Its greatest weakness was its dependence on a wide variety of short-term fiscal expedients which had been introduced to avoid the general excise. Too many of these taxes suffered from one or both of two major difficulties. First, they failed to produce their estimated yield. Sometimes this was attributable to the impact of the very war the taxes were supposed to fund. Thus the shortfall on successive customs duties[52] was partly a result of the French privateers, operating from St Malo and Dunkirk, who so successfully managed to disrupt British overseas trade. Similarly, the excise commissioners blamed the inadequate returns of the additional beer excise on high prices, tight credit and a fall in demand which accompanied the war.[53]

But it was just as likely that a tax failed to produce an estimated yield because the original projections about its return were hopelessly misinformed or wildly optimistic. For all the claims of political arithmeticians, and for all the forecasts of projectors – whose schemes more often resembled the

prognostications of the soothsayer than the estimates of an economic analyst
– it was extremely difficult to produce accurate calculations about tax yield.
In some cases – such as the tax on marriages, births, burials, bachelors and
widows – the information on which an estimate could be based could only be
properly gathered once the tax had been levied. In others – like the excises
on salt, glass, stoneware, earthenware and tobacco pipes – it was hard to assess
the impact of the duty on the level of demand for the taxable item. Precise
estimates were also inhibited by the way in which tax policy was formulated.
The Treasury's lack of control, the eagerness of MPs to embrace taxes which
offered an alternative to the dreaded excise, the *ad hoc* character of so much
decision-making: these circumstances were not conducive to careful planning
and statistical precision, even if they had been possible.

Unreliable yields did not reassure public creditors, who knew that the
government relied on tax income to pay the interest on the loans they had
extended to the state. Davenant saw the situation quite clearly: 'nothing can
be so prejudicial to the public credit, as that taxes should not answer what
they are given for by parliament'.[54] As it became increasingly apparent that
so many tax funds were seriously deficient – to the tune of over £5 million
by 1697[55] – so government borrowing became more and more difficult. The
confidence of public creditors was also affected by the second characteristic
of these taxes, namely the short period for which they were voted. How was
the creditor to be paid once the tax had lapsed? Could he or she be sure that
future funds would be earmarked to service that part of the debt in which
they had invested?

By 1697 the proliferation of short-term borrowing – in the form of exchequer
tallies, departmental credit and the new exchequer bills – the accumulation of
tax deficiencies and the sharp deflation, largely attributable to the Recoinage
of 1696-7, were all contributing to a crisis of confidence in public credit. The
financial reconstruction that followed involved much that was anathema to
opponents of the executive: the extension of existing tax funds, the introduction of new levies and the reorganization of the debt – largely with the help
of that *bêtise* of tories and country MPs, the Bank of England – into what
was known as 'the First General Mortgage', a fund which effectively became
part of the long-term debt. Subsequent legislation extended the duties covering
these liabilities to the year 1720. In 1711 they were made perpetual.[56]

Though in the short run the proponents of fiscal conservatism had
triumphed, in the long term their success in holding down both borrowing
and taxes contributed to a fiscal crisis whose resolution guaranteed both permanent debts and perpetual taxes. By 1698 it had become clear that public
deficit finance was not an evanescent phenomenon but a long-term part of the
workings of the English state. Gradually the opponents of the financial revolution came to recognize that a reversion to earlier days was no longer possible.
It was now necessary to harness and tame the forces of public credit, not to
seek their abolition.

Political Parties, Country Ideology and the State

In my discussion so far I have tended to avoid those perennial questions about political structure and party allegiance which have dominated historical debate about the politics of late seventeenth and early eighteenth-century England. As we shall see, the question of whether the most appropriate configuration of politics was whig and tory or court and country is less relevant to our understanding of how the English state developed than might at first appear, though it is not totally without importance. Indeed, no study of the state under the late Stuarts can avoid considering the significance of what has variously been described as 'country ideology', 'the country persuasion' and 'the country interest' by which they refer to a political sensibility with a long and stout pedigree which jealously guarded rights and privileges – whether local, individual or parliamentary – was suspicious of executive power and committed to the notion of responsible government.[57] Almost no historian would deny that one or other of these terms aptly describes a vision of politics critical of big government which was espoused by a substantial number of politicians in this period.

Most of the scholarship which discusses what I will call 'country ideology' has addressed two distinct concerns. Students of political theory have examined the intellectual content and political pedigree of its claims. They see the history of country ideology as one chapter in the long history of the concept of political 'virtue', as part of a major intellectual saga beginning in classical antiquity and ending with industrial society.[58] Political historians, on the other hand, look at country ideology in a more immediate and less expansive context. They are concerned with country ideology as a *motive* for political conduct: did a specific politician or a particular political group advocate certain measures or behave in a certain way because they believed in country ideology, or was their political conduct determined by allegiance to either the whig or tory parties, or by simple greed for the rewards of high office? Much less attention has been paid to the *effects* of country ideology and to the impact of what most historians would characterize as country measures.

Yet the presence of country ideology as a credible prescriptive analysis of English political life and its importance as a means of legitimating opposition to government influenced not only the character of English political discourse but also the development of the state. This may seem a large claim when set against the usual perception that country ideology and its adherents failed to hold back government expansion. We need, however, to distinguish between their inability to stop the development of the state and the *effects* of their resistance on the form that government institutions came to assume.

What, then, was the substance of country ideology? Its favourite measures included the encouragement of parliamentary scrutiny of the executive, the enactment of legislation to secure regular and frequent parliaments, the passage of bills to reduce the number of placemen and the size of the standing army, and the implementation of social and moral reform. All of these proposals spoke to the fear that more government would produce worse government, especially when it threatened to remove the power of governing from those who governed best. What was feared, in other words, was a loss of authority on the part of the landed classes, who, by virtue of their proprietorship, were deemed to be the natural rulers of the nation.

They viewed the possibility that they might be replaced by a special category of governors whose chief stake in society was the power they derived from their office rather than from the ownership of property as inevitably corrupting and harmful to the polity. In this way country ideology was profoundly hostile to the very notion of 'the state'. It saw the emergence of a class of governors separate from civil society as a fundamental obstacle to good governance. To place power in the hands of the courtier, the office-holder and the professional soldier was to confer authority on those who knew their duties to their master, but probably lacked a proper understanding of their obligations to the nation. The development of government as a special interest could only have ill consequences: the enactment of bad and potentially arbitrary policies, the abuse of public trust for private gain and the suborning of men into serving wicked ministers or an ill-advised king. It was therefore the duty of all subjects, especially those in authority, to limit the power of such people: to curb the executive, to scrutinize its actions and to call them to account. Negative as this view may appear, it nevertheless, as Colin Brooks has emphasized,[59] was constructive as well as critical. Indeed, one of its most powerful tenets was the obligation it imposed on its adherents to participate in the business of governing.

Who held such views and advocated country measures? The short answer is that almost all English politicians, at one time or another, took up country positions or supported country legislation. In the 1670s and 1680s the proponents of country politics were usually whig; in the 1690s country politics were bipartisan, embraced by many from both parties; under Anne they were predominantly tory. Even members of the whig Junto, usually regarded as the most forceful advocates of strong government, were not immune from the country persuasion. In the 1690s they were advocates of one of the favourite country measures, triennial parliaments, while in Anne's reign they used the country tactic of demanding an inquiry into the conduct of the war to embarrass a predominantly tory administration.[60]

If country ideology attracted those of every political persuasion, it was also never the exclusive rhetoric of a particular social group. Its 'country' label notwithstanding, it was spoken not only by bucolic back-benchers from the shires but also by disgruntled placemen and courtiers, the holders of government stock, and the directors of the Bank of England and of the major trading companies.[61] Its precepts may have enshrined the ideal of a politician unencumbered by office, independent of the ministry, untainted by paper money and sustained by a landed estate of ample proportions, but such men had no monopoly on country politics.

The frequency with which the language of country ideology was deployed by politicians of all parties and the ease with which country politics could be used to attack the ministry of the day have led commentators to view professions of adherence to the country creed with considerable scepticism. As Francis Hare put it,

when men are out they have nothing to do but to act the patriot, to spy faults in those that are in, to make themselves popular by invectives against the ministry, or by self-denying motions [i.e. place bills], in order to be taken off by the prince, or to ingratiate themselves with the people.[62]

Modern historians have similarly viewed advocacy of a country creed as frequently self-serving or as a camouflage for other interests. Both David Hayton and Geoffrey Holmes have drawn our attention to many examples of the use of country arguments to achieve ends supposedly incompatible with country politics (usually the acquisition of government office), and of whig and tory politicians pursuing party goals through the advocacy of country positions.[63]

None of this is, of course, very surprising, nor should it be taken, as it sometimes is, as a sign of the weakness of country argument. Indeed, the evidence cited by most historians of party shows quite clearly that, whether or not whig and tory were the chief means of political organization in the period, country ideology was undoubtedly the predominant form of parliamentary discourse. It is tempting to say that country ideology was not the victim of manipulative politicians but that manipulative politicians were held in thrall by country ideology. The absence of a well-developed, coherent justification for legitimate political opposition to government (a problem compounded by the fact that administrations were rarely manned exclusively by either whigs or tories), meant that a country platform was virtually the only larger ideological context in which ministerial opponents could place their hostility to government policy. There were, of course, peculiarly whig and tory variants of country ideology, as well as some areas, such as religion, where its precepts did not apply. But, when it came to discussing war, foreign policy, money and the state, it was the *lingua franca*.

There were several consequences of this monopoly. Firstly, specific conflicts over policy tended to escalate into larger issues about the structure and nature of government. Just as each separate excise tax was easily construed as the first step towards a general excise, the fiscal independence of the crown, and the undermining of the revolutionary settlement, so each additional soldier, placeman, foreign subsidy and continental expedition was portrayed as pushing the nation down a slippery and ever-steepening slope towards ministerial autarchy. This, indeed, was the view that *had* to be argued by anyone hoping to oppose government policy successfully or who, at the very least, wished to be bought off by receiving a lucrative or powerful office. Party politics and political ambition fuelled the fires of country criticism. Politicians eager for power faced the constant problem that they had to adopt a rhetoric which threatened to undermine their authority once they had achieved high office, and which made them vulnerable to charges of apostasy and double-dealing if they entered government. In a highly contentious political environment, the prevalence of country discourse suffused politics with an anti-institutional bias which acted as a powerful counterweight to the growth of state power.

Second, the strength of the country persuasion meant that any expansion in the powers of government was subject to the strictest scrutiny. Given the inherent capacity of the state to grow and the undoubted opportunities for public servants to act corruptly, it was deemed essential to subject the workings of administration to what Robert Harley pithily summarized as 'cheque, inspection, control, supervision'.[64] The growth of the executive was therefore no formality but required rigorous justification. Almost any aspect of government was likely to fall under parliamentary scrutiny. It is not surprising, then, that as government grew it did not spawn many sinecures. Faced by a suspicious and prying House of Commons, ministers found it hard enough to achieve the administrative expansion they deemed necessary to the war effort without wasting their energies on the creation of useless offices.

A suspicious and sceptical attitude towards the conduct of government and its officials also helped those in government who were advocates of administrative reform. Government officials were, of course, never entirely happy about the parliamentary proclivity for prying into official business. But they were also not averse to using parliamentary pressure for their own reformist ends. As Brooks points out, the customs commissioners used the criticisms of the commissioners of accounts to increase their leverage over idle subordinates.[65] Similarly, William III drew on parliamentary criticism to reinforce his determination to clean up the workings of the revenue boards at the end of the Nine Years War. The impulse for what Harley called 'regulating, new moulding & refforming'[66] or what the post-master general described as 'punctuall Oeconomy'[67] was to be found not only on the benches of the House of Commons but in the offices at Whitehall. Indeed, the political 'managers' of late Stuart governments – Sunderland, Shrewsbury, Godolphin and Harley – shared the desire for honest and efficient government with many proponents of country ideology.

Finally, though country arguments were unable to stem the tide of administrative expansion, they played an important role in separating politics from administration. As we have seen, a series of measures – place acts – passed in both William and Anne's reigns led to the exclusion of a large number of government officials from many different departments. By the Hanoverian Succession only senior officials in the main departments of state remained in the commons, and many of them were required to seek re-election if they were already sitting in the house when they assumed office. These measures were, of course, intended to preserve the independence and integrity of the commons rather than to depoliticize public service, but their practical consequence was to create a class of office-holder whose tenure long exceeded that of the politicians it served.

We tend to forget just how successful place acts were in preventing the rising tide of office-holders from engulfing the commons. The number of placemen in the lower house grew remarkably little between 1688 and 1714 when viewed in the context of the overall growth in the number of state servants. In 1690 there were approximately 100 placemen in the lower house. A decade later they numbered between 120 and 130.[68] For most of Anne's reign the total hovered between 120 and 140.[69] In a period when the size of the bureaucracy doubled, its representation in the commons rose by a mere 40 per cent.

Why was country ideology able to exercise such an important influence in shaping both English political argument and the English state? Part of the answer lies, as I have already indicated, in the absence of any alternative political language with which to legitimate parliamentary opposition. Much of its effectiveness derives, however, from the context in which it was deployed. Unlike similar ideologies elsewhere in Europe, it occupied a position close to the heart of power. It was not the ideology of provincialism – the creed of a provincial assembly or estate – but a view of politics expressed both at Westminster and Whitehall.

After 1688 the commons was not only the watchdog of government but part of the government itself. The link which connected these two seemingly disparate not to say contradictory functions was the commons' control of finance. Public finance made the commons an essential actor in the performance of the fiscal–military state; it also enabled the lower house to take a greater part in government by scrutinizing and monitoring its processes. The commissioners of accounts, the call for the presentation of departmental papers on almost every subject to the commons, the contentious claim that the lower house should have a say in foreign policy – all of these attempts to secure government accountability and parliamentary direction were sustained by the commons' power of the purse.

Similarly the enactment of country measures depended on the commons' control of cash. A triennial bill only became law in 1694 because the monarch's need for money forced him into conceding the legislation. Clauses successfully excluding placemen from the commons were tacked onto money bills which the lords could only alter at their peril and which monarchs were, for obvious reasons, loath to veto. The peacetime standing army was decimated after the Nine Years War because the lower house was the true paymaster of the forces. Fiscal control put the bite into the bark of country politics.[70]

But the country persuasion was not always and invariably persuasive. Its effectiveness stemmed in part from its plausibility and applicability to current political circumstance. In the 1690s the country case could hardly have seemed more telling. The 1680s had seen a recrudescence of the power of central government which, with the possible exception of the 1650s, was without parallel in the seventeenth century. The 1690s threatened to continue the trend. In many respects William continued where James had been forced to leave off. The fabric of the state was there for all to see: the military hospital at Chelsea, new naval buildings at Greenwich, a huge ordnance depot at the Tower, a new palace at Hampton Court. William was no puppet but a military monarch who wished to rule with the full panoply of power.[71] The war looked as if it would enable him to do so. Similarly, in Anne's reign, the emergence of a new-found militarism, personified in the extraordinarily powerful figure of the Duke of Marlborough, reactivated fears of military government and political autocracy.

But if, throughout William and Anne's reigns, growth in the powers of government and the influence of those who led it seemed a self-evident problem, the capacity of those who feared these developments to affect policy also varied according to circumstance. Country ideology was a far more effective weapon to opponents of government at times of war-weariness and when it could be combined with such gut issues as English chauvinism. A perfunctory glance at the most outspoken and orotund examples of country rhetoric cited by historians quickly reveals how often these utterances date either from the years between 1697 and 1701, or from the final years of the War of Spanish Succession. The combination of a protracted war, high taxes, economic recession and a divided political nation fuelled sympathy for the country cause and also made it far more likely that either legislation or parliamentary inquiries critical of both the structure and personnel of government would result.

But the deployment of country ideology in this period gradually acquired a certain amount of inbuilt constraint. The factious use of country measures was usually recognized as such and, in consequence, usually lost support. MPs in 1708-9, for example, were able to distinguish between the politically tendentious calls for an inquiry into the conduct of Marlborough and the much more legitimate complaints about the management of the Admiralty. Even at the end of William's reign, which saw the most successful and sustained attack on the fiscal–military state by parliament, prudence tempered the assault. And, when the threat of war returned, so did the troops and the taxes.

Those who professed to fear the fiscal–military state gradually reached an accommodation with it. Placemen were excluded from the commons, but never in their entirety. The peacetime standing army was reduced but not abolished. The issue of public deficit spending became less and less the national debt itself and more and more a question of who should control it (whigs or tories; the Bank or the South Sea Company) and how to avoid its abuse by stock-jobbers.

The shift in sensibility is captured in the career of Robert Harley (whom I freely admit was neither a straightforward nor typical political figure). In the

1690s Harley was calling on God to stop a general excise. Between 1711 and 1714, the same man, now Earl of Oxford, presided over the greatest increase in excise taxes since the Glorious Revolution.[72] This is not, as the sententious might have it, a mere case of predictable political hypocrisy. It was simply the recognition that, if these things were to exist, it were better they were managed well than badly. Oxford's action was part of a major financial reconstruction designed to eliminate a substantial part of the short-term debt, to put the nation's finances on a firm footing and to transfer, via the South Sea Company, some of the state's fiscal power away from the Bank of England. It was also intended to relieve the landed classes from the onerous burden of the land tax, whose imposition had become an increasing source of complaint as the war dragged on. Harley's aim was to avoid what many regarded as the worst aspects of the fiscal–military state without inflicting lasting damage on its operations.

Historians often regard the opposition to an increase in the size of the armed forces, to an expanding bureaucracy and to high taxes under the later Stuarts as a singular instance of a hopeless and reactionary resistance to inevitable change, which was only able to flourish because of the factiousness of politicians. Typically, this view sees country ideology as the tool of the unscrupulous or the naive belief of the credulous and idealistic. It does not contemplate the possibility that country politics was supported on the pragmatic grounds that, even though its platform stood little chance of wholesale adoption, it preserved the nation from the worst excesses of the state. Yet this is precisely what it succeeded in doing. Nor does this view see the genuine dilemma posed by the larger context of politics after 1688. The wars against Louis xiv were fought for many reasons, but one of their most important aims was the creation or retention of a particular sort of Protestant polity. Yet, as we have seen, the cost of that defence was the creation of a state which threatened that vision of English society and politics. One of the major political concerns of the period was how to steer a safe course between preserving the regime and avoiding its excesses. On the whole, this difficult task was accomplished. Paradoxically, a strong parliament effectively resisting much that was proposed by government eventually produced a stronger state.

IV

In parts II and III we charted the contours and explained the emergence in late seventeenth-century England of a new kind of British state. Because her fiscal and military apparatus was organized anew and on an unprecedented scale, Britain was able to act as she had never done before: to become a major military power, to acquire an extensive empire and to assume a place in the front rank of European states. As we have seen, these developments were extremely controversial. On the floor of the House of Commons, in pamphlets and newspapers, and amongst the tables and benches of coffee houses and taverns, Englishmen debated the virtues and vices of different fiscal and foreign policies.

The controversy over the related questions of how the state should be structured and what powers it should exercise was fuelled by a widespread awareness that changes in the character of the state and its activities had affected Britons in every walk of life. But this perception was surrounded by controversy and confusion. Individuals readily identified *specific* instances in which the state touched their lives and impinged upon their interests. Genteel landed proprietors who experienced difficulties securing mortgages because of wartime state borrowing, younger sons who became professional soldiers or civilian functionaries, merchants whose cargoes were captured by enemy privateers, shopkeepers who sold less tea, tobacco and sugar because of wartime price rises, candlemakers forced to comply with the regulations of a new tax, farmers whose grain exports were disrupted in wartime, luxury goods artisans whose products flourished behind the barrier of wartime protection, seamen who were pressed into the senior service or the day labourer who found himself inveigled or coerced into the army: they all understood only too well how they were affected by the state. But when it came to assembling an aggregate balance sheet – assessing the incidence and effect of the tax system, as Joseph Massie attempted in 1756[1] – or measuring the costs and benefits of pursuing a particular military strategy, (a favourite exercise of pamphleteers at the end of the Seven Years War) the conclusions of eighteenth-century commentators were highly suppositious even when they were decked out with figures and facts.

The modern historian can sympathize with this proclivity for conjecture. It is extraordinarily difficult, even when examining modern societies, with their plethora of statistics, to assess the impact of war on economic development, and of state taxation, borrowing and spending on the economy as a whole.[2] In the following two chapters I do not propose to tackle such intractable problems. My object is not to consider the macro-economic question of the extent to which the state helped or hindered the long-term economic development of Britain. Rather, I want to examine the short-term impact of war on different sections of society and the immediate economic and social effect of changes in the configuration of state power. I am as much concerned with contemporary perceptions of the operations of government as I am with how we can now see that it acted. For the eventual purpose of this inquiry is to understand why and how members of civil society responded to the changes in the nature of the British state we investigated at the beginning of our discussion.

6

THE PARAMETERS OF WAR

In seeking to understand how eighteenth-century wars affected the British economy – and, indeed, how the British economy affected the state's capacity to wage war – we inevitably confront questions about the character of those wars and the distinctive nature of economic arrangements in Britain. We need, in other words, to understand the aims and policies that drove England into a period of almost continuous warfare with France as well as the course and outcome of those conflicts. We also have to engage – however unwillingly – in the complex debate about the evolution and character of the British economy in the Georgian era. For it was the interplay between the making of policy, the conduct of war and course of the economy which coloured contemporary understanding of what struggles with France meant.

It was a truth universally acknowledged in the era before Adam Smith that the government had both the right and obligation to regulate the economy for the public good. Such intervention was usually concerned to achieve one or more of three aims. First, the protection and enhancement of national wealth by securing what was termed 'a favourable balance of trade'. To this end, the government took measures to promote exports, to limit imports, especially of finished goods, and to encourage import-substitute manufactures. Second, the support of industries and activities that enhanced England's military power: the manufacture of iron, copper, brass and gunpowder, the provision of such naval stores as masts, tar and hemp, the building of a strong merchant marine and the 'nursing' of a substantial body of skilled seaman. Finally, the maintenance of good order and social harmony through the regulation of the market, the alleviation of poverty and the protection of employment.

The first two of these aims were those most directly connected with the diplomatic and military activities of the eighteenth-century state. Indeed, it is tempting to argue, in the manner first associated with Adam Smith, that the pursuit of a favourable balance of trade, together with the protection and encouragement of strategically important commerce and trade amounted to a 'mercantile system'. Such political and fiscal arrangements, it is maintained, underpinned a vigorous pursuit of competitive trading in international markets and justified the use of force in the acquisition of empire.

Seen in this context, the naval and commercial wars between the English and the Dutch (1652-4, 1665-7, 1672-4), together with the passage of the Navigation Acts (1651, 1660, 1662) were but the *mise en scène* in an unfolding drama of commercial competition and imperial expansion that halted only with the loss of the North American colonies a century later. According to Smith and others, this performance was orchestrated by a number of powerful commercial and mercantile interests, most notably chartered and regulated companies of merchants and investors, which manoeuvred government policy into serving their own ends.

This view has much to recommend it. Throughout the late seventeenth century and eighteenth century the debate about commercial policy and the role of the state was dominated by, though not exclusively confined to, 'mercantilist' assumptions. The importance of a national monopoly of the international carrying trade and of colonial markets, the self-evidence of the zero-sum struggle for world commerce, the strategic and economic need for substantial holdings of bullion, the importance of encouraging demographic growth and domestic industry – these were all the clichés of their day. How and whether these economic shibboleths should apply in particular cases was the subject of much debate, but only rarely were the precepts themselves subject to challenge.[1]

Moreover, the view that national policy was best served by an aggressively conducted 'blue water' strategy[2] was no longer confined to swashbuckling sailors of fortune, overseas investors eager for a quick return, merchant adventurers ambitious for new markets and Protestant zealots anxious to establish their own communities on some occidental hill. Under Charles II, as under the Commonwealth and Protectorate, 'blue water' strategy became official policy. Commercial wealth and naval power were seen as mutually sustaining. Flourishing trade fuelled the navy – providing funds in the form of customs revenues and manpower in the shape of able seamen, while an effective seaborne force was able not only to guard existing channels of trade but to open up new routes to commercial wealth.[3] Though this seventeenth-century version of blue water tactics did not, as yet, recognise the value of military operations in Europe to direct England's opponents away from moral warfare, in every other respect it exactly anticipated eighteenth-century strategy.

Enthusiasm for this policy spread far beyond the wharfs and counting houses of British ports. A blue water strategy made sense to almost all members of commercial society and to those, including many taxpayers and country gentlemen, who preferred their wars to be cost-effective if not downright cheap. And the policy had a political as well as economic dimension. For it had the additional advantage of avoiding any increase in the size of the army.

It therefore could not contribute, however obliquely, to the creation of a military force likely to threaten Englishmen's liberties.

The prevalence of blue water assumptions both amongst ministers and in the nation at large makes the use of power to secure profit unsurprising. The object of all three Anglo-Dutch Wars was to destroy Dutch trade and shipping. The first Dutch War was the direct consequence of the Rump's determination to enforce the Navigation Ordinance of 1651, whose chief provisions had been aimed at the Dutch. The Second Dutch War grew out of the Anglo-Dutch struggle for control of the West African slave trade. And if the Third War owed more to the geo-political intrigues that led to the Secret Treaty of Dover than to commercial policy *per se*, its avowed object was the control and restriction of Dutch shipping through the establishment of tolls on the Scheldt and the Maas.[4]

Power followed profit into the eighteenth century. The East India Company, the largest of the chartered companies, exercised an enduring influence on British politics. The South Sea Company's narrow-minded intransigence pushed Walpole into a colonial war with Spain in 1739, while William Pitt's rise to power at mid-century, together with his conduct of the Seven Years War, reflect the triumph both of mercantile interests in the City and of an ideology of aggressive commercial expansion.

This boldly drawn picture needs some qualification. Though economic debate and commercial policy were informed by a number of economic precepts, it is far from clear that these assumptions were peculiarly 'mercantilist'. Many of them antedated the commercial era they are supposed to characterize. Nor can these broad assumptions be elevated into a coherent philosophy which will *explain* government policy. Many of the features of the 'mercantilist state' – privileged trading companies and protectionist tariffs, for example – owed as much to the financial needs and fiscal requirements of governments as to any desire to create an aggressive commercial system.[5]

This is not, however, an argument for abandoning the term 'mercantilist'. It may lack much explanatory force, but it does provide a useful characterization of an era in which the relationship between state power and international trade was seen as a problem of exceptional importance, one which was normally formulated as a debate about the interventionist obligations of rulers rather than as a matter of free trade. Seen in this light mercantilism is not reducible to a coherent policy. But neither can it be dismissed as purely pragmatic. Rather its historically specific *assumptions* (some novel to the epoch, others not), together with the language in which they were expressed, both affected and gave meaning to the different and varied policies pursued by individual states.

The absence of a coherent mercantilist policy (as opposed to the prevalence of a mercantilist ideology) is in part explained by the absence of a coherent mercantile interest, capable of bringing uniform and sustained pressure to bear on those who made government policy. Warring commercial factions competed as much with one another as with their foreign rivals. Planters and merchants in the New World quarrelled over whether or not to expand or restrict the production of such commodities as tobacco and sugar. The chartered companies squabbled with interlopers in their trade, attempting to keep all rivals, including other chartered bodies, away from the markets they monopolized. Conflicting interests all sought to deploy the powers of the state for their own ends. Unanimity among the merchants was therefore rare, for government policies which favoured the interests of one mercantile body were likely to conflict with those of another. The mercantilist 'system' was therefore a loose and flexible structure whose configuration changed over time; it was the adaptable framework within which merchant groups competed with one another.

It was also difficult for even the most powerful mercantile groups to transmute their wishes into policy because they exercised no *direct* control over the actions of the state. The making of policy – especially foreign policy and military strategy – was not the perquisite of merchants but the prerogative of monarchs; its execution not the task of traders but of ministers. Keeping commercial objectives to the fore was therefore very much a matter of persuading monarchs and ministers of their continued importance. In the late seventeenth and early eighteenth centuries, however, British rulers had other matters on their mind. The rise of Louis xiv's France and the dynastic vagaries of the English succession turned policy-makers decisively towards Europe. The views of the scions of the Houses of Orange and Hanover were dominated both by a grand concern for the European balance of power and by a more parochial love of their native land, whether it were the polders of Holland or the turnip fields of Hanover. In these assumptions they were followed by Stanhope, Townshend and Carteret, the ministers who dominated foreign affairs in the first half of the century. Almost all members of the executive gave precedence to Europe before the rest of the world and placed power before profit. Trade and commerce, especially colonial trade and commerce, were of secondary importance.

The mercantile interest therefore had less effect on the day-to-day conduct of foreign policy than we might at first suppose. Indeed, men of commerce, especially those connected with the New World, constantly lamented that they were unable to secure a sympathetic hearing from the government during the heyday of the whig supremacy. This is not to say that the English government was unwilling to use diplomatic pressure for commercial ends. It did so frequently. In the late 1720s, for example, English diplomatic efforts succeeded in securing the suppression of the Ostend Company, an Austrian rival to the British East India Company for the trade of the Indies. Such limited action should not, however, be equated with the development of a foreign policy whose overall design was to improve Britain's commercial position.[6] Ministers preferred courts to counting houses, diplomacy to trade.

But no minister could entirely escape the pressures of blue water interests.

Every servant of the crown, even Carteret, knew full well that there were important political advantages to protecting or encouraging British commercial interests, just as he was aware of the liabilities incurred by antagonizing any powerful commercial group. For support of blue water policies and an unwavering attachment to the importance of trade were too strong an assumption, too deeply embedded in the national consciousness, to be either disregarded or dislodged.

The character of English politics ensured the survival of blue water policies in the age of the balance of power. Foreign policy might be the prerogative of the crown but it could not be isolated either from the concerns of the legislature or from public pressure exerted by interested parties. Parliament's power over the purse, the ability of individual members to call for diplomatic papers and the minister's need to command the confidence of the lower house all meant that in practice the royal prerogative, however proudly proclaimed, was hedged around by parliamentary constraint. Subsidy treaties had to be laid before the legislature. Cessation of territory, it was claimed, required parliamentary approval. Even if the crown and its ministers had no legal obligation to present a foreign policy measure to parliament, they were likely to do so on prudential grounds. A controversial policy could become acceptable only once it had been debated and approved in parliament. The support of the legislature in turn strengthened the hand of the ministry both at home and abroad.[7] Such endorsement, though it was usually secured, was no foregone conclusion. If policy was formulated and negotiated in private, it was also the subject of public scrutiny and debate.

Nevertheless a blue water policy was temporarily eclipsed under William III and during the War of Spanish Succession, when British troops were committed on the Continent in unprecedented numbers. The two great wars against Louis XIV were fought primarily in European theatres – the Low Countries, Spain, Italy and Southern Germany, the Mediterranean – and their two chief (and closely related) objects were the preservation of the Protestant Succession and the revolutionary settlement of 1688 together with the containment of a seemingly all-powerful French state. As we saw in Part III, it was the indivisibility of these aims which largely explains why the English became so thoroughly embroiled in the struggle over the European balance of power and why it was so difficult for them to extricate themselves from the bloody struggle on the Continent. The domestic price of French hegemony in Europe was simply too great for even the most isolationist of MPs. Hence their support, however reluctant, for the wars against Louis XIV.

But blue water aims and tactics re-emerged during the War of Spanish Succession as part of Britain's wartime agenda. After the Anglo-Dutch expedition to Iberia in 1704 the two original goals of protecting the succession and the balance of power were supplemented by a third aim, very much in keeping with the seventeenth-century blue water tradition, namely the securing of strategic gains to guard and nurture English commerce. England's growing ambitions during the War of Spanish Succession shows both the nation's burgeoning military confidence and the extent to which she was able to seize the initiative from France. They also indicate the perdurable appeal of policies which looked to the navy as the means and trade and commerce as the end of military strategy.

By the Treaty of Utrecht (1713) the English achieved their three main wartime objectives: the Protestant Succession and the revolutionary settlement, if not yet secure, had nevertheless been preserved; territorial concessions in Europe restricted the powers of France (as well, incidentally, as those of Austria); and the acquisition of Gibraltar, Minorca, Hudson's Bay, Newfoundland and Nova Scotia provided England with territories and bases that both protected her shipping and enhanced her naval power. In addition, the commercial concessions extracted from the Spanish – including the notorious contract granted to the South Sea Company to supply slaves for their Central and South American empire, the *assiento* – gave England what seemed an important advantage over her French and Dutch rivals in the New World.

The Treaty of Utrecht marked England's arrival as a major European power. But it in no way guaranteed that she would remain one. The triumph over France had only been accomplished at great cost. The subsidization of allied troops with its enormous foreign remittances; the raising of substantial English armies which drained native manpower; the quagmire of the inconclusive Iberian campaign, which swallowed men and money; and the extensive damage inflicted on the English merchant marine by enemy privateers had all taken their toll. It was by no means certain that England would make as quick a recovery as France, which had far greater resources at its disposal. The years after the peace of Utrecht were characterized by a new rivalry between the two major powers, a competition to see which could achieve the most rapid fiscal, military and diplomatic reconstruction.

Britain's greatest advantage over her French rival lay in her naval supremacy. The powerful French fleet, the legacy of the Colberts, *père et fils*, had been battered by the Anglo-Dutch fleet at La Hogue in 1692 and sapped of its remaining strength by a gradual withdrawal of royal funding. In wars that pitted France against the rest of Europe, Louis XIV preferred to see the nation's hard-pressed resources go to his armies rather than to a navy which had clearly been eclipsed by its foes. Britain's other great maritime rival, the financially beleaguered United Provinces, also reduced its naval expenditure, leaving the Royal Navy the lion's share of operations during the War of Spanish Succession. By 1714, only the Spanish navy posed a threat to British naval hegemony and this was abruptly ended when, in 1718, Admiral Byng destroyed the Spanish fleet off Cape Passaro.

But naval supremacy had yet to be transformed into commercial dominance. The avaricious schemes of merchants and traders to dismember the Spanish colonial empire were still far from realization. The Dutch still dominated the world carrying trade. Much was promised but little had yet been achieved.

Indeed, after twenty-five years of warfare, all of the great powers in western Europe were concerned to avoid policies which might lead to another major war. Both France and England were especially determined to secure peace. Not only were they war-weary and eager to replenish their depleted resources, but their ruling dynasties were also in jeopardy. In England George I faced a Jacobite threat that endured beyond the unsuccessful rebellion of 1715. In France the Orleanist succession, secured only in the frail body of the five-year-old Louis xv and by the regency of Philip, Duke of Orleans, was plagued by the rival claims of Philip v of Spain.

This dynastic insecurity goes a long way towards explaining the ostensibly anomalous *entente* between England and France which emerged in the aftermath of the Treaty of Utrecht. For more than fifteen years the English and French remained allies, seeking with some success to anchor the western European state system on the rock of the 1713 settlement. This did not prevent diplomatic and military conflict between individual European states. The period between 1713 and the war of Polish Succession (1733) was filled with minor confrontations – between Austria and Spain in the Mediterranean, Spain and England on the high seas, England and Russia in the Baltic, and Hanover and Austria and Austria and France in continental Europe. But these rivalries were not allowed to escalate into a major European conflict. This circumscription of hostilities is not attributable to a new-found irenicism in England and France. In the 1720s neither great power was ready to renew their conflict. And, if in the 1730s Walpole clung to his hopes for peace, the French, after they had brilliantly consolidated their diplomatic position in Europe, were ready to launch another major European war.

The French initiative put the British on the defensive. At a time when French power in Europe was palpably on the increase, Britain was diplomatically isolated. Moreover, French trade was booming at a time when trade was sluggish in England. French merchants took much of the entrepôt traffic in colonial commerce from the British, developing re-export markets in northern Europe. French sugar production, notably that of St Domingue, eclipsed that of the British islands, reducing profit margins as it forced European prices downwards.[8] Trade with Spain and its empire, whether legal or illicit, did not provide the expected compensation for French competition. The murmurs of complaint about Walpole's pusillanimous foreign policy by British merchants in the Caribbean, which reached a crescendo between 1737 and 1739, should be seen in this light. The belligerence of these years, which pushed Walpole into war in 1739, was the product not of commercial optimism but of a fear that other colonial powers were squeezing the English out of the trade and markets they so earnestly desired. Many critics of the Walpolean regime stigmatized its foreign policy as an abandonment of Britain's blue water tradition and a criminal neglect of British trade, in a campaign against the government that was well orchestrated and had powerful supporters. But its success cannot be attributed to organization alone; the appeal was a powerfully patriotic one, drawing on an analysis that commanded widespread approval.

The hostilities of 1739 were the beginning of the two mid-century wars which saw British military power reach its eighteenth-century zenith. Between the outbreak of the War of Jenkins's Ear and the signing of the Treaty of Paris in 1763, Britain not only managed to check French power in Europe but also became a great colonial and commercial power. As the conflict between the great powers spread – affecting not only Europe and the Caribbean but also North America, the East Indies, West Africa and even the Pacific Ocean – so Britain gradually gained the upper hand, eventually trouncing both France and Spain and acquiring substantial overseas territories.

Such an outcome was not inevitable. The early years of both the War of Jenkins's Ear and the Seven Years War were notable for their absence of military success, especially in the theatres beyond Europe. In 1739 the Spanish empire proved far more difficult to dismember than the British expected, and at the outset of the Seven Years War the French held the initiative in Canada, the West Indies and India.

Nor did colonial warfare supersede the European struggle as a priority for those who made British foreign policy. In both wars Britain was heavily involved in continental hostilities. Carteret's policy of the 1740s, which brought a sizable British army to Europe for the first time since the War of Spanish Succession, could hardly have been more continental in character. It was part of his grand but unsuccessful design to make Britain the arbiter of Europe. In the Seven Years War there was much less direct participation by British troops in continental hostilities. But, as in the earlier war, unprecedented subsidies were granted to England's allies.[9]

The policy of European involvement was regularly castigated as costly; it was also condemned as a 'Hanoverian' measure, giving higher priority to the protection of the monarch's 'country seat' in Hanover than to England's overall strategic interests. But the Duke of Newcastle, and even William Pitt, the architects of Britain's colonial triumph, recognized that a British commitment to continental involvement was essential if gains were to be made elsewhere. As Newcastle put it,

A naval force tho' carried never so high, unsupported with even the *appearance* of a force upon the Continent will be of little use. . . . France will outdo us at sea, when they have nothing to fear by land. . . . I have always maintained that our marine should protect our alliances upon the Continent; and they, by diverting the expense of France, enable us to maintain our superiority at sea.[10]

This policy was not, however, a rejection of the blue water tradition but, as Daniel Baugh has emphasized, its true consummation:

The characteristic strategy was to assume a basically defensive stance against the main force of the enemy and to rely on alliances, combined operations, and economic pressure to produce a satisfactory outcome. Pervading the whole approach was a sense of enduring struggle in which cost-effective strategy and an unflagging commercial and productive capacity eventually would see Britain through. There was no concept of knocking out France on land, or even permanently reducing it militarily, except perhaps by economic pressure.[11]

But, if Britain's success in the mid-century wars was in large part dependent on her continental subsidies and allies, it was victory beyond Europe that captured the popular imagination. The growth of colonial markets, most notably in North America, the timely publicity of such interested parties as the South Sea Company and the West Indian merchants, and the dramatic seizure of such strategically vital settlements at Louisbourg in 1745, Gorée in 1758, Quebec in 1759 and Martinique and Havana in 1762, fired an easily kindled enthusiasm for policies which apparently combined national aggrandizement with numerous opportunities for private profit.

The unprecedented scale of operations (together with their unprecedented cost) led the nation to expand its political horizons and to raise its expectations of the spoils of victory. The dreams of the early eighteenth century were made tangible by acquisitions in every non-European theatre. Britain came to think of herself as a world power. As the Duke of Newcastle put it, 'Ministers in this country, where every part of the World affects us, in some way or another, should consider the *whole Globe*.'[12]

The key to British success was her blue water policy: the retention of a European ally or allies to divert the resources of France towards an expensive European campaign, and the establishment of naval supremacy. The former was an unpopular tactic which occasionally almost foundered on the complexities of European diplomacy or the military weakness of France's foes. The latter was achieved only at the end of the War of Austrian Succession but dominated the Seven Years War. The British navy bottled up the French fleet and strangled French foreign trade, enabling Pitt to mount amphibious expeditions against enemy strongholds in the New World. The Seven Years War, with its stunning series of victories, was the first war during which British overseas trade expanded, rather than experiencing the short-term cutback normally associated with the wartime disruption of commerce. It marked the apogee of blue water strategy. When George III succeeded to the throne in 1760 there was no doubt that Britannia ruled the waves.

But the hubris of the Seven Years War had its nemesis in the American War of Independence. For, if the wars of the mid-eighteenth century demonstrated the full power and capacity of the British fiscal–military state, the American War revealed its limitations. After the Seven Years War all the major colonial powers – Spain, France and Britain in launched programmes of administrative and fiscal reform in their colonies. The notorious administrative reforms and taxes implemented by George Grenville in the Thirteen Colonies were paralleled by the centralizing measures of José de Galvez in New Spain, and the efforts of Choiseul to extract revenue from the prosperous French West Indies.[13] The aims of the metropolitan powers were in part strategic. They were eager to improve the defences of existing or newly acquired territories and to prepare for the reacquisition of those that had been lost. But the chief concern was fiscal. Colonial war was expensive. Britain's average annual expenditure during the Seven Years War was nearly three times greater than it had been during the War of Spanish Succession, and more than double the annual cost of the conflict between 1739 and 1748. The metropolitan government, convinced that domestic taxes could be raised no further and that the escalating debt was threatening to get out of control, sought financial help from the colonies it had so ably defended.

Britain's attempts to tax the American colonies in the 1760s revealed the limits of her fiscal power. As we have seen, the highly centralized character of the English state, the proficiency of her bureaucracy and the legitimacy accorded parliamentary statute meant that it was extremely difficult in England to offer overt resistance to taxes. None of these conditions, however, obtained in North America. The metropolitan power was far removed, colonial administration before Grenville had been notoriously lax and the colonial legislatures were a source of authority which competed with both king and parliament in London. The resistance the British government encountered in North America demonstrated an unpalatable truth that even the most powerful eighteenth-century state was forced to accept: the political cost of squeezing revenue out of a far-flung province was not worth the niggardly fiscal return. State power declined at the periphery. The failure to recognize this was an invitation to disaster.

The war which began between the metropolitan power and her North American colonies in 1775 was quite unlike any other eighteenth-century conflict in which Britain had engaged. First and foremost it was, in the eyes of many, an unnatural phenomenon, a fratricidal conflict. The consequences of this unusual and disturbing circumstance can be seen both in the conduct of the war in North America and in the politics of the mother country. British army commanders in North America were reluctant to wage an all-out war; senior naval officers like Admiral Keppel, who supported the opposition to Lord North's government, refused to serve in North America. At home, the war – though probably supported by a majority of citizens, especially after the entry of France and Spain on the American side – proved remarkably divisive. Proponents of the government's policies revived the ugly anti-republican rhetoric of the seventeenth century and attacked opponents as if they were the presbyters of old; pro-Americans raised money to succour American prisoners of war, displayed their sympathies by wearing colonial blue and buff or, in the case of the Duke of Richmond, by sailing their yacht with an American pennant through the ships of the British navy. Every eighteenth-century war provoked disagreement about its conduct, but no earlier conflict had divided the nation so fundamentally.

This was not the worst of it. The American War saw Britain diplomatically isolated as never before. The victories of the Seven Years War had left Britain without a European ally. Convinced by the success of Pitt and Newcastle that the enduring strength of Britain's empire depended upon the nation's ability to mobilize European allies against France, George III's ministers eagerly pursued alliances with several central and east European powers. But such negotiations came to naught. As the Partition of Poland showed, Prussia, Russia and Austria were more interested in central Europe than the Atlantic littoral, and each of these powers had their own reasons for wanting Britain cut down to size.

But the important change after 1763 was not so much England's diplomatic isolation as France's determination to pursue different tactics in the struggle against her greatest rival. The Seven Years War had made clear that the only way in which France would contain the growth of British power was to confront it directly: to channel French resources into a naval build-up and to avoid expensive military entanglements in central Europe. This was precisely the French policy of the 1760s and 1770s. Choiseul, Vergennes and Sartine pumped funds into shipbuilding and the naval infrastructure.[14] In 1778 the French uncharacteristically refused to intervene in the Bavarian Crisis which promised to escalate into a major European war. On this occasion, at least, the French were not to be diverted. British strategy remained the same; the French, however, had changed their tactics.

Diplomatic isolation, together with the French (and Spanish) determination to revenge their earlier defeat, placed Britain in a perilous situation. Not one continental power came to her aid. By 1780 she was at war with France, Spain and Holland, and beleaguered by the several neutral powers who resented her interference with their shipping. No continental war distracted Britain's foes. France and Spain were able to devote their unreserved attention to avenging the defeats of the Seven Years War. Lord Sandwich, First Lord of the Admiralty, in an often-quoted passage, summarized Britain's dilemma:

It will be asked why, when we have as great, if not a greater, force than ever we had, the enemy is superior to us. To this it is to be answered that England till this time was never engaged in a sea war with the House of Bourbon thoroughly united, their naval force unbroken, and having no other war or object to draw off their attention and resources. We unfortunately have an additional war on our hands which essentially drains our resources and employs a very considerable part of our army and navy: we have no friend or ally to assist us: on the contrary all those who ought to be our allies except Portugal act against us in supplying our enemies with the means of equipping their fleets.[15]

Britain in 1780 was rather like France in the War of Spanish Succession. She was perceived in Europe to be an overmighty power and was forced to fight in none-too-splendid isolation.

The American War had one other unique feature: it was fought with supply lines three thousand miles long. Weapons and ammunition were shipped across the Atlantic. So were almost all provisions: 'oats for the horses; salted beef and pork, butter, oatmeal, pease and flour for the men'.[16] The task was a formidable one. The force in North America was no temporary expedition –

even if it had been originally intended as one – and the opportunities to forage on the march, like any European force, were curtailed by an inhospitable climate and a hostile populace. As a result the British state confronted unprecedented logistical problems. As Mackesy reminds us, 'every year a third of a ton of food was needed for each man in America, besides the weight of the casks in which it was packed. Without reckoning packaging, 29,000 tons of provisions were shipped to the army all over the world in 1782.'[17]

Such logistical demands over such great distances could not be met for long by any eighteenth-century state. In 1776, and again in 1780, the problems of supply severely hampered the British military effort in North America. But we should not underestimate the extent to which the British government surmounted the difficulties of feeding and arming its troops. Despite the scepticism of foreign observers, who were sure that a transatlantic war could not be fought successfully, the British supplied their North American campaign for nearly six years. The British lost the war – an outcome Mackesy has persuasively argued was by no means inevitable[18] – not because of their inability to provision and supply, but because they lacked decisive strategic leadership and, above all, because their naval forces were overstretched, often outnumbered and unable to establish the hegemony they had enjoyed during the Seven Years War.

The American War, then, revealed the limits of Britain's military power. Though she might defeat a wealthier and more populous nation like France, when her enemy's resources were diverted into continental Europe, Britain's chances of victory over her traditional foe were slim when she lacked continental allies. Englishmen liked to think of the wars of this period as a grand struggle between the two great powers of England and France; other nations were seen as mere pawns in the game. Such a view both overestimated British military might and underestimated the vital importance of her allies. The blue water strategy needed a European war. As Paul Kennedy trenchantly reminds us, 'the hard fact remains that, of the seven Anglo-French wars which took place between 1689 and 1815, the only one which Britain lost was that in which no fighting took place in Europe'.[19] Contemporaries often spoke as if intervention in Europe and a blue water policy were antithetical strategies. But, as statesmen came to realize, involvement in Europe – provided it was of the right kind – was very much a part of blue water strategy. The persistent tension between the monarchical imperative to look to Europe and the desire for a war of commerce was therefore a valuable one. Provided neither concern was completely lost, and despite their mutual antagonism, they helped rather than hindered British military success.

The Economy

Eighteenth-century Englishmen were convinced that Britain's ability to win wars was in large part attributable to a thriving economy. They drew particular attention to the importance of trade and commerce in sustaining warfare just as they emphasized warfare which sustained trade. But the question arises of how justified such commentators were in their assumptions about the singular importance of commerce and in their implicit belief that the British economy, like the British political system, was significantly different from that of its French rival. The question becomes all the more pertinent if we are interested in understanding not only the effect of the economy on the state's capacity to wage war, but also the impact of the conduct of war on English society. Were there certain (unique) features of the economy which meant that the ebb and flow of war and peace had a singular effect on English men and women?

Few economies have been as intensively studied as that of eighteenth-century England. There are quantitative investigations of regional and national economic growth, debates about the causes, timing and existence of the 'industrial revolution', studies of particular industries and regions – especially of those characterized by rapid growth – assessments of the relative contribution of agriculture, industry and services to the economy and a plethora of surveys designed to reduce the vast body of monographic literature into a manageable corpus.[20] No other eighteenth-century European economy has received so much attention.

The reasons for this are obvious enough. No other European state assembled so much quantitative data about the nation's economic activities. Though the interpretation of this statistical data is fraught with difficulty,[21] it has provided historians with a unique opportunity to quantify and reconstruct a 'pre-industrial' economy. The attractions of such quantitative material have been enhanced by historians' knowledge of Britain's subsequent economic performance. Few scholars have avoided asking the question of how Britain achieved economic hegemony in the nineteenth century. And, in consequence, most have been as open as eighteenth-century commentators to conjecture about the peculiarities of British economic life in the Georgian era.

Rapid growth was for many years considered to be the chief distinction of the British economy in the eighteenth century. But recently Britain's economic development has been drawn to a new pattern, one which follows contours shaped by increasingly sophisticated quantitative analysis. Though we should be cautious about the weight we ascribe to these figures – relatively small changes in the statistical series, whose precision it is easy to question, would change the overall picture quite markedly – they suggest that Britain's economic growth in the eighteenth century was less sustained than might be supposed. Early eighteenth-century economic indicators have been revised upwards, later eighteenth-century economic indicators have been revised downwards. As a result the curve of economic growth has been flattened.[22] The picture that emerges is one of *gradual* improvement in real output during the course of the century (1700–1760 0.69 per cent per annum; 1760–1780 0.70; 1780–1801 1.32 according to Crafts).[23] The rapid and sustained acceleration in growth usually described as 'the industrial revolution' is now seen by many historians as a nineteenth-century phenomenon.

This more sober and less exhilarating interpretation of British economic growth in the eighteenth century has had two important consequences. First, it has led some historians to question the assumption that the British economy was self-evidently superior to that of its main rival, France.[24] Indeed the numbers aggregated by Rostow seem to indicate that between 1700 and 1780 total production in France rose at a slightly higher rate than in Britain and that both agricultural and industrial output grew more rapidly on the Continent than across the Channel.[25] Second, the apparent absence of a distinctive or radical change in the statistical aggregates has shifted historians' attention away from the question of growth and towards the issue of whether the English economy had other special features or qualities. If it were growing no faster than its greatest rival, was it perhaps structured and organized rather differently?

In recent examinations of the structure of the eighteenth-century English economy, three connected features stand out: the rapidity of urbanization from the mid-seventeenth century, the high proportion of the population engaged in non-agricultural employment and the growth in agricultural productivity which made these two developments possible.

In the late medieval and early modern periods England was not especially urbanized by European standards. The percentage of the population living in towns of more than 5000 was small and, apart from London, there was no city to rival the numerous towns in the Netherlands, France and Italy with populations of 20,000 or more. This picture began to change in the seventeenth century. Between 1670 and 1750 urban dwellers grew from 13.5 to 21.0 per cent of the total population. The urban population outside London grew even more rapidly from 4.0 to 9.5 per cent. In the eighteenth century not only did this urban expansion continue but the rank order of towns was radically transformed. The old regional centres, with the exception of Bristol, Newcastle and Norwich, were toppled from the top of the urban hierarchy by rapidly growing ports, manufacturing and dockyard towns such as Manchester, Liverpool, Birmingham, Leeds, Sheffield and Plymouth. By 1801, the date of the first national census, seventeen such provincial towns had populations between 20,000 and 90,000.[27]

Seen in a European context, this urban growth was remarkable. Wrigley has calculated that between 1600 and 1750 the number of English towns with populations between 5000 and 10,000 doubled, while in continental Europe the total of such towns actually fell. In the first half of the eighteenth century England was responsible for 57 per cent of all European urban growth; between 1750 and 1800 it accounted for 70 per cent. As Wrigley summarizes his conclusions, 'Over the full two hundred-year period [1600-1800] the urban percentage quadrupled in England, scarcely changed in the rest of northwestern Europe, and advanced rather modestly on the continent as a whole.

The English experience appears to be unique.'[28] England may not have been the most urban nation in Europe – the Dutch urban population peaked at nearly 40 per cent in 1700 – but it was the *most rapidly urbanizing*. Thus, while in France the percentage of urban dwellers grew from 9.1 to 11.1 per cent, a tiny increase of 2.0 per cent between 1500 and 1800, the comparable English figure rose from 5.5 per cent in 1520 to 27.5 per cent in 1801.[29] This occurred while the total English population was increasing at a faster rate than that of France and most other European countries. By 1800 the English population was more than three and a half times that of 1500; in the same period the French population failed even to double.[30]

A second feature of the English economy was the large proportion of the labour force engaged in non-agricultural employment. The sampling of parochial data, the reconstruction of village occupational structure and the refining of seventeenth- and eighteenth-century tables of social structure all indicate that in the early eighteenth century the number of English men and women employed in agriculture was little more than half and that by mid-century a majority of the English were engaged in non-agricultural work.[31] Even in the rural shires between a quarter and a third of the workforce laboured outside the agricultural sector.

Industry was by no means an exclusively urban phenomenon. Indeed during the eighteenth century rural areas saw some of the most remarkable industrial development. In the countryside of the West Midlands, the Lancashire and Yorkshire Pennines and the West Country, cottages and workshops produced textiles, metal-wares and leather goods. Both by European standards and when compared with other economies at similar stages of development eighteenth-century England had disproportionately large industrial, commercial and service sectors.[32]

This is not to belittle the importance of the agricultural sector. On the contrary, it is to point to its greatest achievement, namely its sustained growth in *efficiency* as well as output. Between 1670 and 1750 the number of people supported by each 100 members of the agricultural workforce rose by 32 per cent from 165 to 219.[33] These gains in productivity enabled the non-agricultural sector to grow at a time when the rural agricultural population was hardly growing at all. The achievement is all the more impressive in that it did not produce major price increases in foodstuffs before the 1760s and that it enabled England to be a net exporter of agricultural products during the first half of the eighteenth century. Commercialized agriculture – and very little agricultural output consisted of subsistence farming – was one of England's most efficient 'industries'.[34]

To summarize: eighteenth-century England was a rapidly urbanizing society with a large proportion of its workforce engaged in industry, commerce and the provision of services. Production, including agricultural output, was overwhelmingly for the market. Contemporaries described England as a 'commercial society' and foreign visitors repeatedly commented on the absence of a peasantry, the prevalence of agriculture for the market, the extent of services, the substantial size of the middle ranks of society and the business acumen of the commercial classes. Historians debate whether or not these features were new to the eighteenth century, but few deny their presence in Augustan England.

In Chapter 4, I emphasized the administrative and political advantages the English enjoyed over the French in the collection of revenue. The English were unencumbered by the two major obstacles to tax collecting in France: they did not have to support numerous venal office-holders and they were free of the administrative nightmare of tax-gathering in different autonomous jurisdictions. They also enjoyed the advantage of the legitimacy conferred on revenue gathering by the consent of parliament. All these factors made fiscal appropriation in England a much easier task than in France.

But there is a strong *prima facie* case that Britain's economy also helped. It is one of the clichés of the literature of taxation that, as Gabriel Ardant puts it, '*tax collection and assessment are indissolubly linked to an exchange economy*'.[35] All tax collectors face three major problems: those of measurement – assessing liability on the basis of wealth or output; of collection – persuading or coercing subjects and citizens to pay their taxes; and of remittance – getting money from the point of collection into the coffers of the state. All three are exceptionally difficult to accomplish not only in a poor economy but in one characterized by subsistence agriculture, by scattered, small-scale production, by local markets, poor communications and by exchange in kind rather than through cash or credit. Conversely, an economy with commercialized farming, concentrated or large-scale production, inter-regional and national markets and a well-developed monetary or credit system will be much easier to tax. The English economy resembled the second stereotype more closely than did the French.

If a more commercialized economy enhanced the state's capacity to raise revenue, it was also more vulnerable to the economic effects of war than a predominantly agrarian society with large areas of subsistence production. Greater economic interdependence meant that, when war helped or hindered one form of economic activity, its effects were also felt among a larger group who had economic links with those who were immediately affected.

In considering both the economy's effect on the state's war-making capacities and the consequences of war upon the economy we need a more refined and discriminating picture than that provided by an analysis based on occupational change and sectoral growth. We need, above all, to know about the character and extent of markets for individual products, services and labour – the nature and scope of the links forged between different regions and different sorts of economic activity. This, in turn, requires that we attend as much to networks of distribution, and to the services which eased the circulation of goods, as to the business of production itself. Unfortunately, as Julian Hoppit has recently pointed out,[36] we know much less about the quality of markets and the nature of distribution than we do about the more easily measured extent of agricultural and industrial production. As the OECD indicated in its recent survey of the service sectors of modern economies, it is exceptionally difficult to measure and evaluate the importance of an economy's tertiary sector. Quantification is inhibited by the difficulty in measuring the output of services. And it is also hard to assess the importance of activity in a sector treated as a residual part of the economy. Disparate services and occupations are lumped together – financiers next to street vendors – because they cannot be pigeon-holed elsewhere.

In short, evidence about markets and services is usually patchy, often not aggregated and always difficult to interpret. Nevertheless, there is sufficient cumulative data to assert with some confidence that between the late seventeenth and late eighteenth centuries the British economy saw national integration increase, more and more subjects become involved in long distance trade, including small producers and retailers, and inter-regional – indeed international – systems of credit develop. This is not to deny that many national markets – including that for labour – were, in the language of economists, 'imperfect'. Nor is it to overlook the importance of local markets for many goods and services. But the ledgers and inventories, business records and correspondence of so many eighteenth-century Englishmen repeatedly reveal economic horizons which extended beyond the parish, region and nation. Whether as producer, consumer, debtor or creditor, even the most humble of subjects became part of an economic order whose scope and complexity rendered it liable to fiscal measurement and vulnerable to wartime disruption.

Local and regional markets were linked together through steadily improving transport services which distributed goods by river, road and sea. Pedlars, badgers, carters and carriers, chapmen, innkeepers, sea and barge captains, factors, merchants and middlemen – all facilitated the national marketing of goods.[37] This, in turn, made possible the development of that regional specialization in both agriculture and industry which was such a marked feature of the eighteenth-century English economy. The maintenance of navigable waterways, the growth in the number of turnpike roads and the development after 1770 of a canal system all helped facilitate inter-regional trade.

Increased speed of service, a greater volume of traffic and the gradual elimination of seasonal fluctuations in road haulage were the most important improvements in transport. They appear to have had some effect on transport costs, though rather less than one might suppose. Land freight rates remained stable for much of the period; as prices rose after mid-century, so the real cost of transport fell.[38] The proliferation of transport services, together with the slow decline in real costs, indicates the extent of the demand for these services. Producers, wholesalers and retailers quickly absorbed the increased capacity of the transport system.

Improved transport changed both the scope and character of the retailing trade. The statistical evidence is patchy but revealing. The number of shops and shopkeepers increased; outlets were to be found in even the smallest hamlets and villages. T. S. Willan has shown that in the seventeenth century approximately 2600 shopkeepers from 822 different locations issued trade tokens, which were used as low-denomination copper currency.[39] This number of shopkeepers is clearly an underestimate, as not all would have been able to afford to have such tokens stamped and engraved. By the end of the century, when contemporaries were commenting on the increased number of shop-keepers, Gregory King estimated their total at 40,000. King's calculation, like his measurement of all those employed in trade and commerce, is extremely conservative. The full extent of King's error is revealed by the first systematic survey of shops in England and Wales carried out by the Excise Office in 1759.[40] On the basis of detailed returns sent by their officers in all of the excise collections in England and Wales, the commissioners informed the Treasury that there were 141,700 retail outlets in England and Wales, of which 21,603 were in the metropolis. This figure did not include stalls at fairs and on markets, wholesale warehouses or premises licensed as alehouses. Few shopkeepers owned more than one shop; many shops were staffed by more people than their proprietor. It seems reasonable to suppose that at least 150,000 English men and women were employed in shops. Retailing, even if it were combined with workshop production, was one of the nation's most common occupations.

Thanks to an efficient system of distribution numerous shops were able to carry goods produced both at home and abroad. The inventory of Henry Hancock, a Sheffield grocer, is typical of tradesmen of this period. He sold a rich assortment of foodstuffs and spices: sugar (of several varieties), rice, currants, raisins, treacle, prunes, vinegar, hops, pepper, aniseed, turmeric, liquorice, cinnamon, cena, fennel, nutmeg, cloves, and carroway seeds. He had 45 gallons of brandy and eight barrels of tobacco in his shop. He also stocked paper, twine, soap, books, starch, flower of sulphur, borax, red lead, verdigris, brimstone and parcels of nails.[41]

Shopkeepers could only maintain such a varied stock if they had access to a number of merchants and wholesalers. Abraham Dent, who kept a shop in Kirkby Lonsdale, some twenty-four miles north-east of Kendal in the county of Westmorland, purchased goods from 190 suppliers in fifty-one different locations. Even the agricultural produce he sold – flour and barley for instance – usually came from outside the county.[42] The shopkeeper linked the market town and local community to a network of markets that stretched beyond the nation's boundaries and across oceans and continents. Ranged on the shelves of the local shop were goods from the great cloth-making districts of England – Wiltshire and Gloucestershire, the West Riding of Yorkshire and East Anglia – from the metal-working towns of the West Midlands and South Yorkshire, from the metropolis, and from the Mediterranean, the Baltic, the East and West Indies and North America.

The provision of more retail outlets and an overall improvement in communications were only two, albeit important aspects of the growth of eighteenth-century Britain's economic infrastructure. Market towns and provincial centres provided a wide variety of services for the surrounding agricultural communities, the local craftsmen, and the traders and merchants who ebbed and flowed through the town. Communities erected exchanges and market halls, innkeepers built public rooms onto their hostelries, local engravers and printers produced advertisements and circulars, more and more lawyer's offered legal services, while local attorneys who matched up savers and borrowers performed those credit functions which, by the last quarter of the century, had been taken over by 120 country banks. Though the evidence is fragmentary and is often derived from the rather selective lists published in eighteenth-century trade directories, it nevertheless all points in one direction: to the growth of a tertiary and service sector which eased the path of local trade and led it into the broader thoroughfares of national and international commerce.

Even as the nation was knit together commercially, so more and more economic activity became linked to long-range, large-scale international markets. This development was particularly associated with the expansion of extra-European trade from the late seventeenth century onwards. The colonies were not Britain's most important trading region – as late as the 1770s Europe provided Britain with 47 per cent of her imports and 62 per cent of her exports[43] – but they were its fastest growing markets. They received disproportionate emphasis not only because of the swiftness of their expansion but also because they contributed to some of the most *visible* changes in British economic and social life. The emergence of tobacco, tea and sugar as staples in the domestic economy of all classes; the presence in London of prodigiously wealthy West Indian nabobs whose extravagance made them a byword for tastelessness; the rapid expansion of the cottage industries producing textiles in Yorkshire and metal goods in the West Midlands for transatlantic markets: all were tangible evidence of the colonial contribution to British prosperity.

The tentacular growth of world trade spawned merchant princes whose assets spread over four continents. The Scot Richard Oswald was typical of this new breed. Together with his compatriots Alexander Grant and John Sargent he presided over business interests in Europe, Africa, America and Asia. Oswald and his partners invested in Scottish industries – glass works, collieries and rope works – acted as government contractors in Germany during the Seven Years War, built a slave 'factory' at Bunce Island near the mouth of the Sierra Leone River in West Africa (complete, as David Hancock tells us, with its own golf course), owned plantations in the West Indies, speculated in land investment with the Ohio Company and in Nova Scotia and East Florida, and invested in the lucrative gin franchise in Bengal. No scheme better captures the extent of this international empire than Oswald's plan to import Chinese into western Scotland to remedy local depopulation.[44]

Few merchants had such extensive commercial interests. Oswald reached

the peak of eighteenth-century commerce, leaving many others to occupy a
more modest middle ground. But his career, which combined the ruthless
exploitation of colonial resources, skilled use of the monopolies of mercantilism, and dextrous tapping of the purchasing power of the state, exemplifies
the opportunities created both by interlocking international markets and by
the presence of the largest economic actor in eighteenth-century Britain,
namely the state.

Oswald's career is symptomatic of the substantial rewards that could be
derived from international trade rather than typical of those who engaged in
overseas commerce. The tangled skein of trans-oceanic trade caught more
small fry than big fish within its mesh. The product of the worsted weaver
working in his small cottage on the bleak moors above Heptonstall in the
West Riding of Yorkshire linked him to the New England fishermen who
wore his worsted cloth. These Yankee salts, in turn, sold their fish caught off
Newfoundland to the slave owners of the Caribbean islands and to the
merchants of southern Europe. The prosperity of coastal New England (in
part dependent upon a buoyant demand for fish in the West Indies and
southern Europe) and the political sensibilities of the colonists had a direct
effect on the fortunes of the weaving and spinning communities scattered over
the Yorkshire hills.

It was not only the substantial capitalist, the great trading companies and
substantial merchants who were affected by the course of international trade.
Small producers, the workers in cottage industry and comparatively humble
investors were drawn into trade networks that spanned the oceans. Such small
investors as shopkeepers were tempted to trade with the New World by the
lure of what were reputed to be vast profits. As Roger North commented, 'It
is remarkable that . . . all men that are dealers, even in the shop trades, launch
into adventures by sea, chiefly to the West India plantations and Spain. A
poor shopkeeper that sells candles will have a bale of stockings or a piece of
stuff for Nevis or Virginia.'[45]

One of the commonest bonds which linked men both within the domestic
economy and in the international market-place was that forged between
creditor and debtor. International bills of exchange settled the accounts of
Bristol merchants with traders in the Chesapeake; inland bills of exchange
passed between the provincial shopkeeper and the London wholesaler; small
masters, craftsmen and farmers raised money by signing short-term bonds or
mortgaging their property; local attornies encouraged widows to lend to those
in need of capital; shopkeepers allowed their customers to pay 'on tick';
tradesmen extended credit to one another; even labourers' pay was sometimes
given in the form of credit rather than cash.[46]

Credit was everywhere. Contemporaries estimated that two-thirds of all
transactions involved credit rather than cash.[47] Surviving inventories indicate
the importance of borrowing and lending. In a recent study of wealth in pre-
industrial Cumbria, 30 per cent of a sample of local yeomen had 50 per cent

or more of their assets out in credit.[48] At the other end of the country, in Petworth in Sussex, between a third and a half of local tradesmen 'were filling the useful function of bankers, tiding neighbours over bad crops and fires, enabling them to acquire their own houses or restock a farm'.[49] Such medium and long-term loans were paralleled by short-term credit which was the lubricant that smoothed most commercial transactions. As Peter Mathias reminds us, the circulating capital of most eighteenth-century businesses, which took the form of stock and trade debts, was usually four or five times greater than fixed assets.[50] Trade without credit was an impossibility.

The flexibility of Britain's credit markets was both their greatest asset and their greatest drawback. The ease with which money could be borrowed ensured that few savings lay idle and that the full financial resources of the economy were successfully deployed. Long-distance transactions were not encumbered by the expensive and dangerous task of physically moving large quantities of cash, and commerce was not constrained by the lack of specie which was such a marked feature of eighteenth-century Britain. The effects of irregular, unpredictable and varied returns on investment – the consequence of slow communications or long-distance transactions – were also mitigated by recourse to credit. Indeed, it is hard to imagine the sort of expansion that occurred in eighteenth-century markets without the development of a well-articulated system of private borrowing and lending.

But easy credit brought its problems. Though it was useful it was also dangerous, as likely to ruin as to benefit its user. Julian Hoppit has pithily characterized the hazards of credit as 'overtrading, synchronization and interdependency'.[51] Overtrading was the consequence of seeking too much credit – a risk made greater by the ease with which money could be borrowed and by the habit of using short-term credit instruments like bills of exchange to raise capital. Excessive debts made traders vulnerable in a credit crisis.

Overtrading was a feature of the credit system individual borrowers could chose to avoid. But synchronization and interdependency were the inevitable lot of anyone enmeshed in a credit network. They had to time disbursements and the calling in of debts to sustain their solvency, and their economic well-being was inextricably bound up with the prosperity of their creditors and debtors.

Eighteenth-century commentators were acutely aware of how sensitive and fickle credit could be. Charles Davenant wrote,

Of all beings that have existence only in the minds of men, nothing is more fantastical and nice than Credit; it is never to be forced; it hangs upon *opinion*; it depends upon our passions of hope and fear; it comes many times unsought for, and often goes away without reason; and when once lost, is hardly to be quite recovered.[52]

In short, credit was a matter of confidence and confidence was a matter of opinion.

The traders, craftsmen and shopkeepers who depended for their livelihood upon networks of borrowing and lending recognized the value of comporting themselves in ways which would 'raise their credit' and reduce the hazards of borrowing. As the shopkeepers' guide *The Tradesman's Director* put it,

Credit, that Jewel in Trade, that Flower that is so soon blighted, cannot be too tenderly nursed, or too earnest endeavours used to establish and cultivate it; and as the precious Possession so much depends upon the good will of others, the Conduct of a Shopkeeper, in his Neighbourhood and to his Fellow Tradesmen should be such as . . . by shewing an universal good will and Friendship, to attract their Respect and conciliate their Affections; for his good Name, in Numbers of Instances, will greatly depend on their Justice and Courtesy . . . But pray what does this *Credit*, or *Trust* arise from? Why from that *Credit* or *Reputation*, that the Tradesman has acquired by his Industry, Integrity, and the other good qualities we have been inculcating . . . It is punctuality in his Dealings, and his industrious Attendance on his Business, that will give him Credit with all that know him, and Riches will flow in upon every Side.[53]

But, though an individual could take steps to ensure his own credit, making borrowing easier and foreclosure less probable, the interlocking character of credit networks and the consequent interdependence of creditors made him likely to suffer for the economic misfortunes of others. As one eighteenth-century commentator remarked, men and women whose livelihood required that they extend credit 'are certainly in a constant hazardous Situation, and though perfectly circumspect and parsimonious themselves, as their Effects are in so many different Hands, may chance to be hurried in a Instant to the most distressful Ebb, by the failure of a Customer or Correspondent'.[54]

A shrewd trader could in theory reduce his risks by extending credit to only a few select customers. In practice, because of the shortage of specie and the extent of markets, this was not possible. As a result all creditors and debtors were susceptible to changes in business confidence. The elasticity of the money supply, a direct consequence of the flexibility of the credit system, exaggerated the booms and slumps to which the economy was prone. In good times credit was easy, lenders were eager to put their money to work, medium-term borrowing was easy and the number of bills of exchange multiplied as the volume of transactions increased. But a faltering of confidence, an alteration of 'the Opinion' on which credit depended, produced both a credit squeeze and a liquidity crisis. Merchants and tradesmen struggled to realize their assets – to switch from bills of exchange to specie and from trade credit to hard currency. Debts were called in at a time when it was hardest to pay.[55]

This pattern, with its conveniences and hazards, was a familiar one to eighteenth-century Englishmen. 'When [Credit] is in flourishing circumstances,' one of them wrote, 'a very little money circulates immense sums in Bills; but when a general distrust spreads amongst the dealers, it is quite the contrary; and there is not so much paid or circulated, as even the money itself would answer without bills.'[56]

As more and more people were enmeshed in the web of credit and as markets grew in tentacular fashion, linking British provinces both with one another and with distant climes, so Englishmen increasingly perceived themselves as individually more and more affected by the circumstances which influenced national business confidence. Though the economy was not yet fully integrated, and though there were still those who might be relatively immune from the changing fortunes of specific trades and markets, economic interdependence was such that seismic disturbance in one part of the economy frequently produced eruptions elsewhere.

This process of national integration – with its better communications, regional specialization and national markets – was sometimes a liability as well as a help to the trader. But it was of great use to the tax-collecting authorities. Customs and excise officers used the postal network to mail bills of exchange and forward their books and ledgers to the central offices in London. They relied on local middlemen and factors, chiefly engaged in agricultural processing, to act as remitters of tax moneys to the metropolis. For a fee these traders offered their private channels of credit as conduits for public funds. Thus, in the early eighteenth century, the Worcester excise remitter was a grazier, the Hereford remitter a maltster, the Kent remitter a timber merchant and the Suffolk remitter a cheesemonger.[57]

This list of remitters reminds us of the importance of commercialized agriculture in sustaining Britain's tax base. If excises were the largest category of tax in Georgian England, agricultural processing and its products were by far the most important source of revenue. Beer, malt and hops accounted for about 75 per cent of all excises; such products as soap, candles and leather made up much of the rest. The steady flow of indirect taxes into the Exchequer was achieved more through the labour of farmers and rural middlemen than by the endeavours of merchants who dominated overseas trade.

Both groups, while contributing to the state's fiscal power, had little doubt that state policy, especially the conduct of war, was one of the most important circumstances affecting both commercial confidence and the performance of the economy as a whole. As a result their perceptions of war were markedly economic in character. They judged martial strategy and military policy by the criteria of economic advancement and national prosperity. Waging war was, of course, about being a great power, but a great power of a particular sort. The object of national aggrandizement was not to reacquire the long-lost medieval empire on the Continent nor even to dominate Europe. It was to create a prosperous nation, a rich polity based on commerce. This was not the way in which some British monarchs viewed either war or foreign policy in this period. Their views were courtly and dynastic, in the French manner to which so many German princelings aspired. But the example to which most of the nation looked was the Dutch. In the seventeenth century that amphibious group of United Provinces had demonstrated conclusively that a small but rich country could be a great power.

If, in the larger realm of strategy, most subjects perceived commercial matters to be of vital importance, they also knew that the decision to wage war or sign a peace, like the success or failure of British arms, produced marked short-term fluctuations in the economy. War also affected prices and wages, benefited certain occupational groups and handicapped others. In addition it changed the nature of business risk, making enterprise both more hazardous and more profitable. It is to these risks, viewed in the light of what we know about the eighteenth-century economy, that we turn in the next chapter.

WAR AND TAXES

War and the Economy

One of the most conspicuous features of the eighteenth-century British economy was the irregularity of the fluctuations in its fortunes. No trend resembled the uniform pattern of the modern business cycle. Growth and decline were erratic and unpredictable, the product, as T. S. Ashton demonstrated in his classic study, of the success or failure of harvests, of financial crises and last, but by no means least, of the conduct of war.[1]

Though the first of these factors was in the hands of the gods, the last two were within the purview of the state. The possibility of war, the declaration of hostilities, the success or failure of Britain's redcoats and Jack Tars, the threat of foreign invasion and the prospect of peace all had economic and financial as well as military implications. This lesson was not lost on England's enemies. The main object of the various invasion schemes mooted by England's opponents was not the capture of territory but the creation of a financial panic which would bring the nation to its knees.[2]

No two eighteenth-century financial crises were exactly alike. Their character, causes and scope were all different. Julian Hoppit, in the most recent study of financial crises, has emphasised their heterogeneity.[3] Some, notably those of 1701, 1715, 1720, 1745 and 1761, he classifies as crises in public finance directly connected to the operations of the national debt. Others – in 1710, 1726, 1763 and 1778 – he views as crises which involved both public and private finance. The one in 1772 he attributes solely to a loss of confidence in private finance.

Yet this variety should not conceal the fact that, of all these crises, only one had no connection with the workings of the fiscal–military state, and only one other, that of 1720, was not in part attributable to military hostilities and the conditions of war.[4]

Similarly, nearly all of the slumps in foreign trade before the end of the American War were connected to the conduct of war. Only the recessions of 1766–70 and of 1722–3 occurred in peacetime. In 1702, 1705, 1719–21, 1726–8,

1739, 1744–5, and 1775–82 the disruption of communications, the conduct of naval warfare, and the predatory activities of enemy privateering led to a significant fall in foreign trade. In every war in this period, with the exception of the Seven Years War, hostilities produced a decline in the volume of the nation's trade. It was therefore quite often the case that war years were characterized by the double misfortune of simultaneous trade slumps and financial crises.

The most severe of these recessions were not confined either to the metropolis or to the leading figures in the financial and mercantile community. The squeeze of 1710–11, for example, affected trade throughout the kingdom. A commercial traveller in the north of England wrote, 'This is such a time as we never had before . . . I cannot see but other people are as hard sett to get money for their Masters notes as I am . . . I cannot take money from people whether they have it or noe.' Ten years later the South Sea Bubble had a similar effect. As one pamphleteer complained,

an universal Stop is put to that Credit which circulated our Commerce; and every Note and Bill, except those of the *Bank* [of England], and some few others, is now become as mere a piece of waste paper, as if a *Prayer* or a *Creed* was written on it instead of money . . . There is not a *Market Town* in England but has not felt it already, and will feel it yet more. The Inland-Trades are so far from taking the Bills they usually did, that they are frightened at the sight of a Bank Note.[5]

Such crises, it has recently been argued, were nevertheless limited in scope. To judge by the evidence of the commissions of bankruptcy, they produced fewer insolvencies than crises later in the century and were confined chiefly to the circles of high finance in the metropolis. Unlike crises after 1770, they involved few merchants and manufacturers and few men from the provinces. Julian Hoppit has explained this contrast by three features of the earlier crises: their restriction to the sphere of public finance; 'by the nature of the links between public and private finance which at that time were relatively weak and poorly developed; and finally by the lack of integration nationally, which largely insulated private finance from a crisis of confidence on a large scale'.[6] Though Hoppit is undoubtedly correct in emphasizing the greater integration of credit networks, largely through the agency of country banks, in the last quarter of the century, I am sceptical about his attempts to limit the scope of such crises as those of 1710-11 and 1720. The quantitative evidence supports his view but much of the qualitative evidence does not. Metropolitan and provincial credit markets may not have been directly linked but they were united by their loss of confidence in the credit mechanism. The actual structure of credit markets was less important than the widespread perception of a crisis fuelled by a well-developed press and the intense public interest in the South Sea affair.

If eighteenth-century commentators were aware that the conduct of war, foreign or Jacobite invasion or the (mis)management of the public debt were likely to provoke financial crisis, they were also of the view that both prices and wages tended to rise in wartime. This is hardly surprising. The rapid increase in the money supply, as the government issued large numbers of exchequer, victualling and navy bills to meet its current expenditures would, it is reasonable to assume, have pushed up costs. Indeed, Elizabeth Schumpeter, in her study of prices and public finance, reached precisely this conclusion, singling out the years 1695–7, 1709–11 and 1780–4 as those of increased prices 'when either the total unfunded debt [i.e. number of exchequer, victualling and navy bills] was large or when borrowing was relatively heavy in proportion to revenue raised by taxation'.[7] The cumulative effect of short-term borrowing was inflationary, becoming more and more visible towards the end of long and expensive wars.

This was not the only contribution wars made to higher prices. The cost of commodities also rose because of the new or increased taxes introduced to cover the prodigious expense of protracted warfare. The recently published industrial price index constructed by Patrick O'Brien enables us to chart the impact of new taxes on such commodities as salt and candles. During the 1690s, when duties were imposed on salt (1694) and then substantially increased (1698), the price of salt, an important staple for all classes, more than doubled. Walpole's repeal of the tax in 1730 – supported by many MPs on the grounds that it would provide relief for the poor – led to a two-thirds fall in price. The reintroduction of the duty two years later pushed the price back up to its former level. Thereafter (though with the exception of the year 1743) salt prices remained stable until Lord North once again raised the duty during the American War.[8] A similar correlation between the imposition of taxes and a rise in prices can be seen in the case of candles. The duties of 1710–11 imposed during the War of Spanish Succession produced a 20 per cent increase in candle prices.[9] In like manner, higher beer and malt duties during the Seven Years War led to a 26 per cent increase in the wholesale price of a barrel of beer.[10]

While taxes pushed up the prices of a select number of commodities subject to duties, war had the more general effect of raising the cost of carrying and distributing industrial goods and agricultural produce. In wartime, goods imported from overseas or domestic commodities, like coal, which were normally transported by coastal vessels, were vulnerable to destruction and capture by enemy naval ships or privateers. Even in peacetime ocean-going trade was a risky business, especially when conducted over long distances. Ships were wrecked in storms and hurricanes, seized by pirates or corsairs; foundered because of poor navigation or ill-repair; were abandoned by disgruntled crews or burned like tinder when they caught fire.[11] War with a sea-going enemy only compounded the risks.

These hazards encouraged multiple ownership of both ships and their cargoes, a strategy designed to spread the risks of loss among several small investors. It was quite usual to purchase a sixteenth, thirty-second or even a sixty-fourth of a vessel. All but the smallest ships were therefore owned by a consortium of proprietors: merchants, tradesmen, shipwrights and mariners as well as gentlemen and widows who all hoped to turn a profit with their modest investment. Similarly the cargoes themselves were very often provided by different shopkeepers, small masters and wholesalers.

The perilous nature of investment in overseas trade during wartime stimulated the growth of marine insurance to compensate for heavy losses. In the late seventeenth century the majority of trading vessels were uninsured. By the 1720s, in large part because of the risks associated with more than twenty years of warfare, marine insurance had come to be the norm. At the same time London had eclipsed Amsterdam as the centre of marine insurance in Europe. By mid-century there were nearly forty insurance brokers in London, underwriters in the major provincial cities and a body of insurance case law which had been formulated by Lord Mansfield in the court of King's Bench. Marine insurance in London centred on Lloyd's Coffee House in Lombard Street. There the proprietor produced his famous *Lloyd's List* with its comprehensive information of ship arrivals and departures.

In certain instances war impeded the growth of marine insurance. Some especially hazardous routes commanded such high premiums that they discouraged investors, while in others underwriters thought the risk too great to offer any policy at all. In 1707, for example, the Quaker shopkeeper William Stout commented on the impossibility of obtaining insurance for the Virginia trade. He himself failed to insure his part of a cargo bound for the West Indies because he believed it would have eliminated his profit. Such imprudence cost him dearly. The ship was captured by a privateer. Stout's investment was a total loss.

Stout's response to his misfortune reveals, however, that the risks associated with war were more likely to stimulate than restrict the practice of marine insurance. Stout was an exceptionally cautious and calculating man. When he next invested in cargoes during the War of Austrian Succession, he made sure that they had full and proper coverage.[12]

Marine insurance protected traders against total loss during a war. But the additional risks associated with hostilities could only be covered by higher premiums. In the irenic 1730s, for example, Portuguese wine shipped to Britain was insured at the rate of 30 shillings a ton. Two years after the outbreak of the War of Jenkins's Ear insurance costs had more than trebled.[13] These increased costs were not entirely absorbed by merchants, though they may well have reduced their profits. Part of the increase was passed onto the customer in the form of higher prices.

The costs of wartime foreign trade, whether in the northern seas or in the Caribbean,[14] were inflated not only by higher insurance premiums but also because wartime demand for skilled seamen raised their wages, and also because the use of wartime convoys increased the length of many voyages. So, though shipping freight rates fell during the course of the eighteenth century – Ralph Davis points out that the cost of shipping a ton of sugar across the Atlantic was a third lower in 1770 than in 1670[15] – in the short term war raised freight charges.

The impact of these additional costs on commodity prices can be seen most clearly in those trades most liable to disruption during war. The coastal coal route between the north-east of England and London was one of eighteenth-century Britain's busiest thoroughfares. It was also one of the most exposed. Colliers plying their trade in the North Sea were vulnerable to capture by French privateers, while the seamen in the coal trade, whose reputation as sailors was second to none, were the target of the navy's press gangs.[16] The effect on coal prices was dramatic: in 1740, for example, Newcastle coal purchased in the north-east was quoted at the same price as in 1739, but in London coal had risen, with the outbreak of war, from 28 shillings to 36 shillings a chaldron, an increase of nearly 30 per cent. The fuel that glowed in London hearths was consistently more expensive when the nation was at war.[17]

If seaborne distribution and coastal trading proved too hazardous in time of war, goods were transported over land. This was usually more expensive, especially if they were bulky. At the beginning of the War of Spanish Succession, William Stout commented that 'This warr put a stop again to comerce by sea betwixt this country [Lancashire] and London, so that we were obliged to have our goods by carts or waggons from London.'[18] The freight rates for this route were considerably higher than those for the coastal trade the war had disrupted.

The cumulative evidence, then, points strongly towards war as an important factor in inflating prices. This conclusion needs, however, to be placed in context. First, war appears to have had comparatively little impact on agricultural prices, which were chiefly affected by the wind, sun and rain, which determined the plenitude of the harvest. (It should be added that the years which saw the sharpest price rises were those, like 1740, in which war and dearth coincided.) Second, before the French Revolution war had little *long-term* effect on the prices of either agricultural or industrial goods. Indeed the chief feature of price series before the 1760s is their remarkable stability. It was only in the 1760s that the price of agricultural products turned upwards and only in the 1790s that industrial goods followed suit.[19]

Viewed through the telescope of the modern historian of economic development and placed in the context of the great inflation with which the eighteenth century ended, the short-term price fluctuations we have discussed seem very minor indeed. But long-term price data obscure the local impact of temporary price changes. There was no compensation for the London poor who paid more for their precious fuel in wartime winters, the ubiquitous beer drinker whose heavily taxed jug of ale rose in price by more than 16 per cent during the Seven Years War, or the smoker who paid more for his evening pipe of tobacco. It is possible that war brought long-term price benefits – that it induced merchants and traders to try to cut down their overhead costs and led to improvements in inland transport. (There is incontrovertible evidence, for example, that the size of ships' crews fell quite sharply during the course of the eighteenth century.)[20] But the immediate effect on the consumer was to raise his weekly expenses.

The precise impact of these price rises on the standard of living is extremely difficult to calculate and depends, of course, on the pattern of wartime wages as well as that of other wartime costs. Eighteenth-century wars certainly affected the labour market. The military demand for troops and auxiliary personnel acted as a sponge, mopping up much unemployment and under-employment amongst the labouring poor.[21] This no doubt pleased the magistrate and the overseer of the poor, for it meant that more of the population were gainfully employed, either in a military or civilian capacity. Family income may therefore have been larger because more family members were at work. There is, however, little evidence to suggest that wartime pressure raised wages in the labour market as a whole. And many of the labouring poor were resistant to the notion that service in the armed forces was of any real benefit to them (except when volunteering secured exemption from a conviction for felony), rather than a help to the nation.

But certain employments directly connected to the conduct of war derived considerable benefits from the wartime activities of the fiscal-military state. The wages of seamen and naval dockyard workers, for example, rose during hostilities; lay-offs and reduced wages came with peace. Dockyard towns like Portsmouth thrived in wartime and were no friends of peace. As Edward Gibbon remarked in 1762, 'This day the SUSPENSION OF ARMS was solemnly declared at Portsmouth and Gosport, to the great regret of their inhabitants, who find their account much better in War.'[22]

Certain trades and industries were highly sensitive to the effects of armed conflict. A. H. John has argued that the domestic iron, copper and brass industries were all stimulated both by the wartime demand for ordnance and armoury and by the higher price of imported raw metals. Domestic output increased and technical innovations such as the reverberatory furnace and the production of coke pig iron were introduced, achieving greater efficiency and reduced costs.[23]

Luxury goods industries, which before the late seventeenth century lay in the long shadow of their French competitors, also flourished in time of war. Successive embargoes and high duties on French goods provided a defensive barrier behind which the fledgling British industries were able to grow. Between 1688 and 1714 the British glass, paper, silk, cutlery, watch and toy industries were able not only to improve the quality of their work (much aided, it should be added, by refugee Huguenot craftsmen from France) but also to capture a sizable portion of the domestic luxury goods market. The eighteenth-century wars with France succeeded not only in limiting French strategic influence but also in helping to develop distinctive English craftsman-ship in the world of high fashion.

The impact of war on two other major industries, shipbuilding and shipping, was altogether more ambiguous. Civilian shipbuilding, as well as work in the royal dockyards which built the biggest ships of the line, was certainly stimulated by the wartime demand for more naval power. In the first two years of the War of Jenkins's Ear, for instance, the navy contracted with civilian shipyards for twenty-six vessels with between twenty-four and fifty guns each.[24] During this war nearly all naval frigates and sloops as well as a number of ships with fifty or sixty guns were built in private yards. While the larger first three rates of naval vessel were constructed at the naval dockyards at Portsmouth, Deptford and Chatham, swifter and less cumbersome ships were built in the merchant yards of the north-east of England. Civilian shipbuilders continued to produce many of the navy's smaller craft. By the end of the Seven Years War even the North American shipbuilding industry was employed in building British naval vessels.[25]

But while shipbuilding burgeoned, shipping itself suffered during almost every major conflict. Each naval war was fought at two strategic levels. In the first instance there was the struggle between the grand fleets, which produced those infrequent, sanguinary and spectacular battles so lovingly depicted in all their graphic gore by British seascape painters. In addition, a more prosaic and profitable skirmishing war aimed to disrupt and destroy the enemy's commerce. This conflict was fought by naval sloops and cruisers, by government-sanctioned privateers and by the larger armed vessels of the merchant marine. The British navy reigned supreme in the former type of warfare during every contest before the American War. The great ships of the line were also able to make an important contribution by blockading enemy fleets and thereby depriving their opponents' merchant marine of naval protection, a task they performed in exemplary fashion during the Seven Years War. But naval hegemony did not prevent enemy action from taking a very heavy toll on British merchant shipping. Indeed, it may have contributed to the losses in the merchant marine because Britain's opponents, mindful of the strength of her great fleets, sought to avoid major battles and directed their efforts towards inflicting damage on more vulnerable civilian ships.

The merchant marine suffered especially badly in the wars against Louis XIV. Between 1688 and 1697 Britain lost 4000 merchant vessels to the enemy. During the first five years of the Nine Years War, the French captured and destroyed over 200 ships amounting to over 21,000 tons of shipping from the single port of Bristol.[26] The enemy's success continued into the next century. In the War of Spanish Succession 3250 merchant ships were captured by England's foes.[27] No individual incident exceeded the disaster of 1693, when the entire Smyrna fleet, despite the presence of an accompanying naval escort, was taken by the French fleet. But throughout the period the French successfully harassed and sank British ships, making overseas trade a particularly hazardous enterprise.

When the Smyrna fleet was captured by the French navy, it constituted the most successful single action of their *guerre de course*, in which naval vessels and privateers together devoted their attentions to destroying British commerce. But the privateers from St. Malo, Dunkirk and numerous other channel ports, not the French navy, inflicted the greatest overall damage. This was the heroic age of French privateering, in which the bravura and bravery of Jean Bart and the Chevalier de Forbin feature so prominently. Privateers from the single port of St. Malo captured over 2000 British vessels between 1688 and 1713.[28] Though English privateers and naval cruisers exacted retribution to the tune of over £440,000 in prizes during the Nine Years War and over £1 million in the War of Spanish Succession,[29] the French seemed to have the better of the battle against seaborne trade.

The mid-century wars saw the balance of the conflict over merchant shipping tip in Britain's favour. Losses during the war of Austrian Succession were again heavy – 3238 ships in all – but there was ample compensation in the 3434 enemy vessels which were captured or sunk.[30] Yet this success was modest when compared to the triumph of the Seven Years War, when British naval power reached its apogee: very few ships were lost and no fewer than 1165 French merchant ships were taken as prizes.[31] The commercial war had been decisively won.

But Britain was unable to repeat her success during the American War. Diplomatic isolation, the action of the combined Spanish and French navies – the latter refurbished and refinanced – together with the success of predatory privateers on both sides of the Atlantic took their toll on the British merchant marine and contributed to a major recession in trade. During the six years of conflict 3386 vessels were taken by the enemy.[32]

Not every vessel that was captured was lost to the British merchant marine. Many vessels were ransomed and only their most valuable (and portable) cargo removed. Though this was preferable to appropriation of the ship, it still inflicted serious financial losses on those who had invested in a voyage. And, because any individual vessel was owned by a substantial number of investors, shipping losses were widely felt.

The risks faced by the owners of ships and cargoes in wartime epitomize the effect armed conflict had on many forms of enterprise in the eighteenth century. War upped the stakes: risks were higher but so were profits. Getting a cargo to Jamaica was more hazardous than in peacetime, but if the ship were able to avoid capture its owners stood to make a fatter profit. During wars sailors might be pressed into the navy or killed by an enemy privateer, but if they survived in the merchant service they were far better rewarded than in peacetime. The soldier and sailor hazarded their lives, but the prospects of promotion were greatly enhanced by wartime casualties. For the privateer or naval rating there was always the chance – remote but often conjured in the imagination – of windfall riches in the form of prize money. Few sailors ever became as rich as Admiral Anson whose share of the prize money from Cape Ortegal in 1747, when over £300,000 of French specie was captured, was nearly £63,000. But many captains and admirals made enough to purchase a country seat.[33] And even humbler men, like John Booth of Lancaster, a merchant seaman impressed into the navy who rose to be a mate, gained enough prize money to buy a small estate.[34] As Sir John Barnard, a persistent supporter of a blue-water, expansionist foreign policy put it, 'War is the harvest of a sailor, in which he is to store provisions for the winter of old age.'[35]

Barnard's use of a comfortable image derived from husbandry fails to convey any sense of the hazards and dangers faced during eighteenth-century wars by numerous civilians as well as by those who found themselves in the front line. In the best of circumstances eighteenth-century economic life was still remarkably capricious and unpredictable. War, the main business of the state, only compounded the problem. It fuelled financial crises, increasing the volatility of credit. It precipitated slumps in foreign trade, pushed up prices, favoured some sectors of the economy while penalizing others and affected a diverse range of occupations and employments. The knock-on effects of strategic and diplomatic developments were felt through large parts of the economy, which, by the standards of the day, was highly commercialized. Moreover, in a society which, compared with most other European countries, was exceptionally well-informed about political, diplomatic and military developments, it was *presumed* that state policy had an important bearing on the lives of English subjects.

The Fiscal—Military State and Society

Three consequences of the growth of the fiscal-military state were of particular concern to contemporaries. First, they worried about the damage inflicted by the fiscal–military state on the 'landed interest'. This was not a new-found sensitivity about the plight of the agricultural labourer but a fear that changes in the nature of government and the character of wealth had undermined the power of those substantial landed proprietors who, by virtue of their extensive acres, were regarded as the 'natural' rulers of society. Second, the emergence of a 'financial interest', whose wealth was derived from dealings with government – as investors, contractors and remitters – and held in the form of stocks and government securities, was viewed not only as a threat to the landed classes but as creating a lobby with a vested interest in keeping the nation at war. And finally there was general speculation on the incidence and deleterious effect of taxation on all sections of society as well as upon the economy as a whole.

No group complained more vociferously about their plight during the wars against Louis xiv than the landowners. Indeed, the very idea of a landed interest – a novel conception because the landed classes had not before had to define themselves against any other segment of society – was born out of the adversities suffered during the Nine Years War and the War of Spanish Succession. Their grievances are well summarized by that self-appointed apologist, Henry St. John, Viscount Bolingbroke:[36]

We have now been twenty years engaged in the two most expensive wars that Europe ever saw. The whole burthen of this charge has lain upon the landed interest during the whole time. The men of estates have, generally speaking, neither served in the fleets nor armies, nor meddled in the public funds & management of the treasure.

A new interest has been created out of their fortunes, & a sort of property wch was not known twenty years ago is now encreased to almost equal to the terra firma of our island. The consequence of all this is that the landed men are become poor & dispirited. They either abandon all thoughts of the publick, turn arrant farmers & improve the estates they have left; or else they seek to repair their shattered fortunes by listing at Court, or under the heads of Partys. In the mean while those men are become their masters, who formerly would with joy have been their servants.

Bolingbroke's statement, as Geoffrey Holmes has pointed out, is characteristically overdrawn and hyperbolic. But such views were widespread during the reigns of the last two Stuarts. It became a political cliché that landowners were punitively taxed, found it difficult to borrow in wartime, enjoyed little of the spoils of war and had their economic and political pre-eminence challenged by wealthy financiers.

Such complaints are not difficult to explain when we consider the enormous increase in taxation after 1688. As we saw in Part I, the overall tax burden in England more than doubled after the Glorious Revolution. And the bulk of that increase, at least until the end of the War of Spanish Succession, was borne by means of the land tax.

After 1688, then, the *apparent* tax liability of the landed interest rose both absolutely and in comparison with the fiscal obligations which seemed to fall on other social groups. This sense of injustice was further reinforced by the often-repeated belief that all taxes, including those on commodities, eventually fell upon land,[37] and by the failure to tax offices and other forms of movable property. Land, it was asserted, was getting a raw deal.

Critics of this view might well, of course, have pointed out that the land's fiscal liability was very much a self-inflicted wound. Parliament's decision to rely on a land tax was, as we have seen, a political manoeuvre intended to ensure that it controlled both the levying and collection of the bulk of public revenue. But, though the tactic was recognized as politically prudent, this did not prevent the land tax from becoming increasingly unpopular. Towards the end of the War of Spanish Succession, when harvests were poor and both rents and land prices fell, the steady murmur of resentment reached an unprecedented peak. As Humphrey Prideaux wrote to John Ellis from Norfolk in 1708, 'All that I can tell you from hence is, that rent comes heavyer from the tenants; and when the land lord receives nothing, how can he pay anything? . . . I am afraid we will not be able to find the funds for another year.'[38] Growing opposition to the land tax was undoubtedly an important factor in smoothing the Earl of Oxford's move away from the land tax and towards indirect taxation in the final years of Anne's reign. The costs of keeping a tight rein on the fiscal system came to be perceived as simply too great.[39]

This impression of the landed interest's uniform misfortune at the hands of the tax gatherer, a picture graphically painted by pamphleteers and politicians opposed to the war with France, needs to be refined. There were considerable regional differences, which were widely recognized at the time, in the effect of the land tax. Indeed, apart from its high rates, this 'inequality' was the chief source of criticism of the tax.[40] It was notorious that landowners in the less prosperous regions, notably in the north and north-west of England, paid a far smaller proportion of their rental in tax than landowners in the south. In 1708-10, for instance, the Duke of Kingston was paying 17 per cent on the rental of his estates in the south-east. In Cumberland and Westmorland the northern magnate, Sir James Lowther, paid at the rate of 4 per cent,[41] while in Yorkshire the rate seems to have varied between 10 and 15 per cent.[42]

Many of the problems associated with the inequitable distribution of the land tax were attributable to the adoption or retention of regional practices of tax assessment which perpetuated inequalities favouring the outlying regions. Though this diminished local opposition to collection, it meant that parts of the West Country, Wales and the north-west were much less heavily taxed than the south-east. This, in turn, ensured that a number of MPs would always be determined to oppose revaluation. Successive governments were therefore understandably reluctant to embark on the difficult and potentially unpopular task of a major land tax reassessment.[43]

If war raised the land tax it also helped to diminish the capacity of the landed classes to borrow money. Eighteenth-century mortgages, including those on landed property, were far more flexible than they are today. Either party to the mortgage could withdraw at six months' notice, or could insist on a change in the rate of interest as a condition of continuing the loan.[44] Private rates of interest were controlled by law, with a limit of 6 per cent before 1714 and 5 per cent thereafter, but in the sphere of public borrowing the state was able to offer what rate it saw fit.

In wartime, when it was possible to obtain a high and secure return in the public funds, savings were often diverted away from private credit markets and into loans to the state. The private borrower suffered not from exorbitant rises in the rate of interest, for these were illegal, but in a squeezing of funds.[45] The wartime experience of the erstwhile borrower is illustrated by a letter of 1759 from Hoare's, a bank heavily involved in the mortgage market, to one of their customers:

At present we do not advance Money to anyone on any security. . . . The uncommon supply of millions and millions granted and now raised [to pay for the Seven Years War] obliges all of our Profession to be prepared for the Payments [to customers moving their money from the bank into government stock] coming on, so that instead of lending out money, we have called it in on this occasion.[46]

If obtaining or renewing a mortgage was more difficult in wartime, fore-closure of an existing mortgage or loan was also more probable. The lenience shown to borrowers in peacetime was not carried over into the periods of financial stringency associated with war. In 1695, for instance, there were two hundred court actions for ending mortgages.[47] Contemporaries commented on the way bankers and lawyers who had lent to the landed classes were obtaining estates by default. The acquisition of the estate of Osterley Park by the tory banker Sir Francis Child was not the only instance of a phenomenon which was much resented by the landed gentry.[48]

War was therefore believed to squeeze the landowning classes by putting them under pressure from two directions. Higher wartime taxes probably raised their costs, making it more likely they would want or need to borrow additional capital. But, at the same time, government borrowing both contracted the amount of existing private credit and made new loans harder to obtain. At no time did this egregious misfortune seem more obvious than during the war of Spanish Succession.

The effects of higher taxation and restricted credit on individual landed proprietors depended, of course, on a variety of other circumstances. Whereas later Stuart politicians were concerned to convey the impression of a united landed interest, bound together by mutual suffering, modern historians have drawn our attention to the many differences among the landed classes. Vari-ations in tax incidence, the size of estates, the types of farming and regional topography, as well as in access to either metropolitan or provincial credit markets meant that the impact of the fiscal-military state was never uniform. Prior indebtedness, the profligacy of a single proprietor or demographic bad luck also took their toll on family fortunes. Nevertheless one has to agree with Holmes's conclusion that, if the position of the landed interest under William III looks less bleak in the light of modern scholarship, its misfortunes at the end of Anne's reign are hard to deny.[49]

But equally it is noticeable how quickly assertions of the identity of the 'landed interest' began to decline after the Peace of Utrecht.[50] Though many of the objects of landowners' wrath, including high taxes, the national debt and stock-jobbers, were as much vilified as ever, such criticism was less likely to be imputed solely to a 'landed interest'. The view that the landed classes should be accorded any special privilege also came under attack.[51] By the 1730s, the claim of Walpole and his supporters to represent the landed interest was criticized not on the grounds that it was untrue, but because it was felt that politicians should only take the part of the *national* interest.[52] The public good was more important than any specific interest, landed or otherwise.[53] By mid-century commentators like Josiah Tucker challenged the idea that landowners had a separate identity, arguing that they were deeply implicated in commercial society: 'those *supposed* Distinctions of *Landed* Interest and *Trading* Interest', he complained. 'are the most *idle* and *silly*, as well as *false* and *injurious*, that ever *divided* Mankind'.[54]

These arguments were intended, of course, not to *describe* the changing position of the landed classes but as *normative* statements designed to support a particular political or economic view. They do, however, point to a number of changes in the relationship between landed proprietors and the state. As we saw in Chapter 4, after 1714 the land contributed a diminishing proportion of total tax revenue. Moreover, the use throughout the eighteenth century of the land evaluation made in 1692 to determine land tax liability had the effect of taxing a diminishing proportion of most proprietors' wealth. When rents began to rise after 1750, the government was unable to tap landowners' new-found prosperity. This, in turn, meant that areas of improved husbandry gained even greater advantages over those which stagnated or declined. The greater their success the smaller the proportion of profits which went in taxes. Adherence to the 1692 assessment, then, meant both that the incidence of the land tax declined over the course of the century and that the most successful agriculturalists derived disproportionate benefits from this fall in taxes. Indeed, we can say with Adam Smith and Arthur Young that the form the land tax assumed was no disincentive to agricultural improvement;[55] it may even have encouraged innovation.

At first sight, therefore, the financial contribution of the landed classes to the fiscal–military state fell during the course of the century. Such a conclusion assumes, of course, that the economic and legal incidence of the tax both fell on the landowner. This was not necessarily so. Just as assessment varied regionally, so did conventions about who should pay. In the north-west it was assumed that landlords paid, though many, such as the Viscount Lonsdale, succeeded in transferring the obligation to their tenants.[56] It seems likely that, as landowners gradually came to understand how the land tax worked, and as their position *vis-à-vis* their tenants improved, so they passed on the costs of the tax.[57] This conclusion is reinforced by one recent study based on contemporary wage and price data which suggests that the true burden of the land tax may have been borne not by landlords but by farmers and their labourers.[58]

The cumulative evidence therefore points towards a decline in the contribution of landowners to land tax revenues. It is possible, of course, to argue that excise taxes, which, as we have seen, replaced the land tax as the chief source of revenue, also burdened the landed classes. They were imposed, after all, on such agricultural staples as malt and hops and on such products of agriculture as beer, spirits, leather, soap and candles. But by the mid-eighteenth century it was the predominant view that consumers as a whole – including, it had to be conceded, some very big spenders whose income derived from land – were bearing the brunt of indirect taxes in the form of both customs and excises. As Patrick O'Brien has recently reminded us, we have to be exceptionally cautious about any conclusions we might draw about the economic incidence of taxation in eighteenth-century England.[59] Nevertheless his rigorous 'speculations', as he calls them, corroborate the view that the landed classes enjoyed a real reduction in their fiscal burden.

During the course of the eighteenth century the disadvantageous effects of war on the landed classes therefore seem to have diminished. Taxes were lower. Rates of interest, even for public securities, gradually fell. Moreover, as Habbakuk has shown, ways were found to protect landowners from the credit squeezes associated with war. Courts were increasingly reluctant to foreclose on mortgaged land. New forms of borrowing, notably annuities on the life of the seller, circumvented the constraints of the usury laws.[60] The burden of war on the landed classes was not again to be so onerous until the French revolutionary wars.

The expansion of the state apparatus and the growth in state activity conferred advantages as well as obligations upon the aristocracy and gentry. The emergence of a new type of wealth in the form of public funds and securities meant that landowners were able to diversify their sources of income by buying into the ever-growing issues of government stock. This new option was adopted only gradually. In the early years of the national debt, during the wars against Louis XIV, provincial gentry were reluctant to invest in what they saw as a risky enterprise based on a fictitous form of wealth. The speculative mania of 1720, culminating in the collapse of the South Sea Bubble, lured many an *ingénue* into the stock market, but these inexperienced investors, many of whom were landed gentry, were those who suffered most severely when the bottom fell out of the market. Like John Liddell-Bright of Carbrook in Yorkshire, who was desperate to revive his flagging landed fortune, these provincial proprietors were ignorant of public finance but eager to make a quick killing. When the South Sea Bubble burst they were among the most vociferous advocates of public retribution against the South Sea Company and its accomplices.

The shock of 1720 temporarily retarded but failed to prevent the growth of gentry stock-holding. Indeed, by encouraging the government to broaden the base of stock-holding and thereby loosening the grip of the big financial companies on the debt, Walpole's financial reconstruction after the Bubble aided the provincial and rural investor. As we saw in Part I, by the 1760s there were over 60,000 holders of public funds. Landowners who were not also office-holders may not have owned a large percentage of the total debt – their individual holdings were not that large – but by mid-century provincial gentry were using the funds as a safeguard for savings and as a means of providing for younger sons or (less usually) for younger daughters. The trend in stock-holding is epitomized by the ownership in securities amongst MPs. By the 1740s there were more opposition MPs than government supporters with money in the public funds.[61]

The growth in the number of state offices open to the landed classes also helped compensate for high taxes. As a political memorandum of the 1730s sardonically put it: "'Tis the land tax makes them all want places.'[62] The long-standing provision for younger sons through appointment to a clerical living was now supplemented by a commission in the standing army or navy, or by an appointment to government office. As we have seen, the army, navy and central bureaucracy all expanded in this period. By 1714 there were *c.* 4000 commissioned officers in the army and about 1000 in the navy. Holmes estimates that by 1725 there were 2700 posts in the central offices of government in London; by 1760, there were said to be over 16,000 civilian administrators overall.

These posts provided a competence, sometimes a comfortable and prosperous way of living, but rarely a fortune. Only a few offices, like the Paymaster of the Forces, enabled their incumbents to reap massive rewards. It is noticeable that there are no eighteenth-century mansions equivalent to the sixteenth and seventeenth-century 'prodigy houses' built with money earned and peculated from public office. The spoils to be gained by public service were distributed more evenly and the opportunities for private appropriation, as opposed to legitimate public reward, were constrained (though not eliminated) by the prospect of parliamentary exposure. Great fortunes were rarely made. Nevertheless the proportion of landed families whose members held offices in national government grew. The full extent of this involvement is revealed by Stone's figures for the percentage of owners of landed estates with family ties to either office or a profession. By the eighteenth century over 40 per cent of proprietors in Hertfordshire, over 50 per cent in Northumberland and more than 60 per cent in Northamptonshire had such links.[63] The fiscal–military state certainly offered good enough opportunities to enable office-holders, both civilian and military, to build on a comfortable if not a massive scale.

Access to the perquisites of office was, of course, dependent upon political patronage and personal connection. After the Hanoverian Succession and under the whig supremacy many tories were proscribed from office, and they only gradually returned as the political atmosphere thawed in the 1740s and 1750s. The precise extent of this proscription has never been measured with any precision, and I suspect that its impact on the national administrative class (as opposed to the appointment of local JPs) has been exaggerated. By 1714 there were already administrative dynasties of both tory and whig origin which continued to thrive after George I's accession. Departmental tradition and internal promotion protected administrators, as opposed to those who were purely political appointees. Sinecures as well as 'political' offices were kept in whig hands, but the world of lower and middle rank officials had a rationale of its own.

The growth in the number of genteel national office-holders in the eighteenth century had two important social consequences. It increased the number of

gentry who were absent from their country estates and it helped erect a more
sharply defined social distinction between the gentry and their social inferiors.
The landed classes still married the *female* offspring of rich merchants and
prosperous tradesmen. But, whereas seventeenth-century gentlemen's sons
went into trade and were apprenticed in the City, this practice declined in
favour of a career in the army or navy or as a minor functionary. This helped
perpetuate a distinction between those who worked for the public good or as
public servants and those who worked for private gain or profit. The obligation
to fulfil public duties was viewed as an essential component of gentility.
Office-holding was therefore compatible with the gentlemanly ideal in a way
that trade, business and finance were not. It is no coincidence that, in a period
when office-holding became a vital support for those who were genteel but
disadvantaged either by birth (because they were a younger son) or by poverty,
the snobbery towards 'trade' grew apace. By the late eighteenth century the
landed classes had fully developed that exquisite condescension towards trade
which was hardly present a hundred years before.[64]

Landowners and proprietors showed themselves to be remarkably adroit at
adapting to the changes created by the growth of the fiscal–military state.
Their early hostility gradually gave way to a series of accommodations which,
at worst, limited the adverse effects on their social position and which, at best,
gained them certain advantages. Bolingbroke's view that the members of the
landed interest did not share in the spoils of the fiscal–military state is
nonsense. Naval and army officers as well as senior civil administrators were
all drawn predominantly from the landed classes and, if few financiers could
boast such origins, many landed proprietors were lured into speculation or
investment in the Funds.

The Financial Interest

If the landed classes' gains from the growth of the state were not immediately
obvious, being concealed by their frequent protestations of economic and
political misfortune, 'the financial interest' was both one of the most
conspicuous and immediate beneficiaries of the changes in government. Its
success excited much resentment. Perhaps the single most frequently made
complaint about the expansion of the eighteenth-century fiscal–military state
was that it had created a 'financial interest', a consortium of bankers, 'monied
men', investors, speculators and stock-jobbers who lived parasitically off the
state's need to borrow money to fund its wars. According to their critics,
financiers were responsible for a multitude of sins. They were commonly
viewed as part of a whig plot to tie the public to the new regime of 1688 and
as the true power behind ministry and monarch. Their activities, it was
claimed, hurt the land by reducing the value of real property and by restricting
the landed gentleman's borrowing power. Trade was equally their victim,
deprived of capital invested in the public funds and made less competitive by

the higher prices which were the result of commodity taxes imposed to service the debt. But, above all, the 'financial interest' was accused of making private fortunes at the nation's expense by lending the state their own and other people's money, by covert dealings to manipulate the price of government stock and by the overt espousal of a belligerent and bellicose – and therefore expensive – foreign policy.[65] As one pamphleteer put it, a financier 'can come into a *New War*, or any other Scheme for our Destruction, for War is his Harvest, and the Plunder of his Country the Crop he would be reaping'.[66]

Though such men provoked unprecedented hostility, the connection between the state and private financiers was not a new one. In the early seventeenth century moneyed men and goldsmiths such as Philip Burlamachi and Sir Paul Pinder had advanced large sums to the first two Stuarts. During the Interregnum and under Charles II financially powerful figures like Alderman Edward Backwell and Sir Thomas Vyner had performed a variety of financial services for the Council of State and the restored king, acting as loan agents, bullion merchants and remitters to creditors abroad. By the 1670s, goldsmith bankers like Backwell and Vyner – who together were owed £645,000 by Charles II – were assigning the interest on the royal debt to their creditors, thereby involving their depositors in what we might call the precursor of the national debt.[67]

Such seventeenth-century bankers had a way of worming themselves into the fabric of the state. In order to recoup their loans, or at least to protect their interest, they combined lending to the monarch with tax farming, the operation of monopolies granted by royal fiat, or the tenure of offices in the fiscal apparatus. All of these provided financiers with privileged access to royal income which thereby acted as collateral for the king's loans. This meant that it was difficult to identify clearly a 'financial interest' when the government's creditors were neither state fish nor society fowl.

But after the Glorious Revolution, though financiers retained close links with government, they were recognizably separate from it, acting as middlemen and brokers between the state and the public. The incorporation of the Bank of England in 1694 and its gradual assumption of the management of the long-term national debt together with the chartering of the new East India Company and the South Sea Company, marked the corporate embodiment of the financial interest.

The new financiers were overwhelmingly whig in politics and disproportionately Dissenting in religion.[68] Even the South Sea Company, established as a counterweight to the whig Bank, had a very large whig membership.[69] Such predilections gave some credence to the critics who saw the financial interest as the proprietors of the new regime. But much of this comment was, of course, *parti pris*. Indeed many opponents of the new financial institutions were not country gentlemen but tory scriveners, goldsmiths and money lenders whose business was threatened by the emergence of new forms of investment.[70]

They were likely to express one of the commonest fears about the 'financial revolution', namely that it was proving too great a success.[71]

Jealous critics of the financial interest were right to envy its good fortune. The new institutions and the individual financiers, merchants and stock-brokers who comprised their membership performed two extremely lucrative services for the state. They acted as undertakers or underwriters of government issues of stock – linking the state and large numbers of individual investors – and they negotiated contracts for the payment and provisioning of British troops in the nation's colonies and battle stations. These two functions were intimately connected: the list of major subscribers to almost every large issue of eighteenth-century government securities included many government contractors, and most government contractors were involved in helping float loans. Thus of the twenty-two undertakers of the £8 million government loan of 1759, seven men, who subscribed nearly £3 million, were also government contractors.[72] Of a total of forty-six contractors employed by the government during the American War, fourteen had partnerships with banking firms, and therefore indirect links with government stock, and thirteen with no such financial connections nevertheless subscribed nearly £350,000 to the public funds.[73]

The combination of public debt management and government contracting is not a surprising one. The most lucrative contracts were for the supply and remittance of money either to garrisons such as Gibraltar or to pay troops in Europe or America, services that the big merchant and banking houses which underwrote government loans were best equipped to provide. Contractors also needed access to a substantial amount of credit, both because of the scale of their operations and because of the time it took to realize a profit.

Underwriting government loans or managing government contracts was a lucrative business. Profits ranged from the comfortable £1,200 per annum made by Edward Lewis between 1764 and 1782 for operating a packet boat service to the British West Indies, to the astonishing sum, somewhere between a quarter and three-quarters of a million pounds, made between 1741 and 1751 by John Gore, the Hamburg merchant and South Sea Company director.[74] This fortune came from his charges for remitting money for the government to Holland, Germany, Austria and Piedmont. Norman Baker, in his study of contractors during the American War, calculates they could expect a return of between 15 and 20 per cent on their outlay until 1780, and 10 per cent under more stringent auditing thereafter.[75]

Not surprisingly, many members of the 'financial interest' became very rich. When George Amyard, who had been banker for the government's diplomatic service and had also held contracts to remit money and supply grain to Germany during the Seven Years War, died at the youthful age of forty-six, he was said to have 'left clear £160,000 in sterling'.[76] Sampson Gideon, the most important underwriter of government loans in the mid-eighteenth century, left a fortune of £580,000 at his death in 1762, while Samuel Fludyer, a cloth merchant who held victualling and remittance contracts in North America during the Seven Years War, was reputedly worth £900,000 at his death.[77] Only a handful of eighteenth-century businessmen and merchants – in trades like mining and brewing – left comparable fortunes. As Grassby has pointed out, the greatest wealth was to be made in government finance.[78]

The typical eighteenth-century loan manager and contractor was a man with good banking and mercantile connections. He might, like Sir Gilbert Heathcote, Sir Theodore Janssen, Sir William Scawen and Samuel Fludyer, be a director of the Bank of England. And, if not connected with the Bank, he would probably, like the American War contractors Richard Atkinson and George Wombwell, be a director of the East India Company.

Political connections were equally important. Prior to the younger Pitt's reforms in the 1780s, contracts were dispensed through government patronage and were not subject to competitive bidding. A seat in the commons combined with support for government in the lower house was one way to obtain a chunk of a government loan or secure a lucrative provisioning contract. Chauncy Townsend was brutally frank about why he entered parliament: 'half Gibraltar was my object'.[79] Not every contractor was lobby fodder for the government but the political behaviour of most contractors and financiers was obviously designed not to bite the hand that fed them. And this, of course, led their critics to see them as not only rich sharks but venal toadies.

Economic resentment and political hostility towards the financial interest was combined with social antipathy, religious hostility and chauvinism. Many members of the financial interest either inherited wealth, came from established mercantile dynasties or had made fortunes in commerce or trade. They were not actually parvenus or men who had previously lacked substance; nor, once they invested in public finance, did they abandon other branches of business. A financier like Samuel Fludyer, for instance, was the son of a substantial clothier. Others, especially those, like Thomas Walpole, who had gentry backgrounds, married into public finance. But there were a small number of financiers who were self-made men of obscure and socially dubious background. The presence of such parvenus, as well as a leavening of monied men of Dutch, French Protestant and Jewish extraction, excited both snobbery and xenophobia. This was compounded by a religious antipathy towards leading corporate financiers who tended to be both whigs and dissenters. What especially galled critics of the financial interest was the way in which its leading figures were willing and able to flout the convention that money gained from finance should be sunk into land. As Holmes puts it, 'To many in the landed interest it seemed monstrous that Londoners whose new riches were giving them access to political influence should evade both the heavy taxation and social responsibilities which an extensive landed estate incurred.'[80]

But, once the agitation in the aftermath of the South Sea Bubble had subsided, criticism of the financial interest rarely achieved its earlier levels of Swiftian vituperation. The rhetoric was wheeled out and dusted off during the

Excise Crisis of 1733, whenever a bill against stock-jobbing was brought before the commons, and during debates in 1737 and the 1750s over lowering the rate of interest. But it lacked its old venom and was more concerned with *abuses* of the system of public credit than with the inherent illegitimacy of public deficit spending.

Politicians and pamphleteers began to defend public finance and to laud its virtues. During the wars with Louis xiv it had been argued that the debt created a safe repository for wealth. As one pamphleteer put it,[81]

The Effect of the Taxes, is to Produce a New and very considerable Estate to the People. I mean the Publick Funds: These afford a much larger Interest for Money, and much better Security for Principal, than formerly could be had. . . . In this Article the People gain about Four Hundred Thousand Pounds *per annum*, for so much the interest amounts to; and is apparently an Additional Estate given to Industrious Men.

But this had not entailed the conclusion drawn by some commmentators in mid-century that 'The *Debts* of the *Public* are part of the *Constitution*, inter-woven with all kinds of *Property*, and . . . cannot be separated, without *subverting the Constitution*.'[82] Such views were not confined to financiers and large holders of public stock. Even back-bench MPs defended the debt.[83]

But the greatest eulogies to public credit came in the aftermath of the unprecedented expense and extraordinary victories of the Seven Years War. Thomas Mortimer, the translator of Isaac de Pinto's laudatory account of English public finance, *Traité de la Circulation et du Crédit*, as well as the author of the best-selling *Every Man his Own Broker*, praised public credit as 'a National good . . . a masterpiece of human policy' and a 'bulwark of the state'.[84] He also maintained that the funds helped prevent arbitrary power. No monarch would act capriciously because none could afford to forfeit the public confidence on which the funds relied. These may have been minority views, but their assertion reflected a new-found confidence among the defenders of the national debt.

Support for the debt paralleled its gradual penetration into society at large. As the number of fundholders increased, so antipathy to public credit diminished. The financiers and contractors who attracted antipathy towards the debt, though they were the most conspicuous beneficiaries of the 'financial revolution', had become only the most visible tip of a growing fiscal iceberg. As tories, country gentlemen and provincials invested in the funds, so they, in their minor way, became part of the financial interest. Antagonism between the great financiers and the public could easily revive, as it did at the end of the American War, but, on the whole, commentators came to accept the value of one of the fiscal–military state's most successful devices.

Taxes, Merchants, Middlemen and Consumers

The funds that fed the financial interest were derived from indirect taxes in the form of customs and excise. These, at least in the first instance, were of more concern to merchants and traders than to the landed classes whose protests against the land tax and public credit were sometimes in danger of drowning out the complaints of their commercial brethren. The land tax may have borne a larger proportion of the tax burden during the wars against Louis XIV but the incremental effect of more and more indirect taxes was to confound the free workings of commerce. From 1688 the fiscal requirements of government created an exceptionally complicated tangle of rules and regulations whose difficulties were to perplex both traders and legislators for a century to come.

Before the Glorious Revolution the fiscal demands of the state had comparatively little effect on overseas and inland trade. Customs duties, with the exception of the lowly taxed exported woollens and the highly taxed imported wines and spirits, were levied at the comparatively low rate of 5 per cent on a commodity's official value, while the domestic excise was confined to the brewing industry. But after 1688 the web of regulation became both more extensive and more tangled.

In the case of the customs, additional duties were imposed on imported manufactured goods, raw materials and food stuffs; the overall customs rate rose to 15 per cent by 1704–5. Subsequent wars produced further increases. At the end of the War of Austrian Succession a further 5 per cent duty was added; in 1759 another 5 per cent, raising the rate to 25 per cent.[85]

Each new duty not only raised costs but complicated regulations. Because each new indirect tax was assigned to a specific fund or loan, its return had to be recorded in a distinct account. A new impost added to an already labyrinthine system of computation and bookkeeping. As the third report of 1784 into frauds in the revenue put it, customs regulations had become 'a Cloud of complicated Materials, and abstruse Science'.[86] New duties required rules and standards to ensure that the tax was levied fairly. The importer and exporter had not only to pay the tax but to conform to a complex system of regulation. As Elizabeth Hoon, the historian of the eighteenth-century customs, puts it,

there were dozens of laws regulating imports and exports that had to do with the condition of the commodity, the size of the cask or hogshead in which it was imported, the tonnage of the ships which could bring it, allowances of draft (the deduction made for the turn of the scales), tare (the batement permitted for the weight of the outside packing that contained goods) and damage.[87]

In addition the importers of most commodities which paid duty on arrival in England could claim a 'drawback' if the goods were re-exported.

It is calculated that by 1760 there were eight hundred separate Acts of parliament affecting customs duties. It was no wonder that the *Universal Dictionary of Trade and Commerce* should complain that

we may see, what a maze our merchants must be in about them [customs duties], when they come to their computation. If likewise we consider the many exceptions, and exceptions from exceptions; the many regulations, and regulations of regulations, for collecting those customs, we must conclude it no easy matter for any merchant in this country to be master of this branch of his business, if he be what we call a general merchant.[88]

The effect of customs tariffs and regulations was fourfold. In the first instance, it involved the merchant in complex dealings with the customs house. Papers had to be filled out and filed, goods to be cleared by customs officers. The long room of the London customs house was constantly crowded with clerks, brokers, merchants and revenue officers; merchants shoved and elbowed their way past one another or slyly offered clerks extra fees and bribes to clear their goods before their rivals. When the Maryland tobacco merchant Joshua Johnson arrived in London in 1771 to act for his firm of Wallace, Davidson and Johnson, he was shocked by the commercial manners of the metropolis – 'I found there was a necessity to push my way through the crowd' – and intimidated by the bustle of the long room – 'the plagued Customs House frightens me'.[89] Like most merchants he was obliged to employ a broker who charged him fees for transacting his customs business, though when he was better acquainted with the port he was able to employ a (less expensive) clerk for customs work.[90]

Mercantile entanglement in customs regulations also meant that merchants had to include duties in their calculations of profit and loss. This was a complex issue. Those who purchased taxed goods they planned to export or re-export had to decide whether to pay the so-called 'long' or internal price, or to take the 'short' or external price. The long price included taxes and therefore required that the purchaser obtain the bounty or drawback from the customs when the goods left the country. The short price was lower, but meant that the seller rather than the purchaser might take advantage of the customs rebates. The price differences had to be balanced against the inconvenience and delay of dealing with government officials.

Importers had to make similarly tricky calculations. When an importer's goods had been assessed at the customs wharf he entered a bond to pay the duty in a certain period of time, usually within eighteen months. Early payment was handsomely rewarded by the revenue with a 7 per cent discount. This was above the prevailing legal rate of private interest and meant, as Jacob Price has pointed out, that it paid businessmen to borrow privately in order to pay off their debt to the state.[91] If the duty on imported goods was raised, the merchant also had to calculate how much he would, in turn, raise his prices. Obviously he wanted to pass on the increased cost to the customer, but he also had to be wary of raising the price so much as to reduce aggregate demand.

The payment of customs duties also tied up merchant capital. Thus in 1774 Joshua Johnson complained to his partners that, 'I am plagued for money; at this time we have £1,350-odd pounds (sic) locked up in the Customs House [in claims for drawbacks and bounties] and cannot touch a farthing of it.'[92] As Sir Thomas Robinson remarked in a Commons debate in 1733, a high tariff 'obliges the Merchant to keep a double stock in ready money'; it also 'confines that Trade to a very narrow circle of dealers'.[93] Brougham put it more trenchantly in the early nineteenth century: 'Taxes have the obvious effect of excluding small capitals from trade'.[94] As the fiscal burden grew, so the capital requirements of the new merchant were greater, which, in turn, made access to a trade that much more difficult. Indeed, by the late eighteenth century there were many examples of traders in taxed commodities seeking to manipulate fiscal regulation to prevent potential rivals from entering business.[95]

The final and most notorious effect of rising tariffs was to encourage traders to smuggle. Contemporary commentators saw the incentive to smuggle as twofold. It was obviously profitable to avoid duties on those commodities which were taxed at very high rates – between 65 and 119 per cent in the case of tea.[96] But smuggling also avoided the delays and compliance costs of which 'fair traders' complained. As one pamphleteer put it in 1751, 'Every such difficulty and Necessity, every Expence, every Delay, every Vexation, is an additional Duty upon fair Trade, and a premium upon smuggling, repaying and balancing the hazard, by Advancing the Price of Things.'[97]

The scope and extent of smuggling is a matter of controversy.[98] What can be said with some certainty is that it was largely confined to a few commodities: luxuries like silk, lace and French spirits which were of high value and comparatively portable; tea, whose price was kept artificially high by the East India Company monopoly; and tobacco, where the duties were evaded not by specialized smugglers, but by 'legitimate' merchants in the trade.

During the course of the century traders in smuggled goods were increasingly distinguished from those who were known as 'fair traders'. William Stout's comment in the 1750s held true for the rest of the century:

It was not accounted as a crime to bribe the officers of the customs, or defraud the King of his customs [in the late seventeenth century] . . . But now the customs is more narrowly inspected, nor is there now much attempt made by any merchants of reputation and good conscience'.[99]

Towards the end of the century more and more merchants were willing to help fight against the illicit trader. They collaborated with revenue officers and formed associations to prosecute smugglers.[100] Yet their success was only limited. In the 1770s and 1780s smuggling firms used larger, swifter vessels, carried more and more weapons and were as willing to use violence as the notorious Sussex smugglers of the 1730s. In short, though the pattern of smuggling may have changed, it remained a serious problem for the fair trader and for government throughout this period.[101]

The growth of customs duties during and after the wars with Louis XIV was paralleled by the proliferation of excise regulation. In addition to the excises on drink, taxes were imposed on salt (1695), malt (1697), candles (1710), leather, hops (1711), paper, printed goods and printed silks, soap, starch, and gold and silver wire (1712), silver plate (1719), and from mid-century on a variety of luxury items, including coaches, carriages, male servants, and race-horses.[102] At the same time the duties on that staple of excise revenue, English beer and porter, were raised each year from 1689 to 1693 and in 1710, 1761, 1779, 1781 and 1782.

The new legislation was accompanied by a body of rules and regulations even more complex and intrusive than those which governed the customs. It was not only excisable goods that were regulated but the manner and way they were produced and marketed. Thus all producers had to register their premises with the nearest excise office; they were also required to register their business equipment and the tools of their trade, all of which were officially marked and labelled by excise officers. Any change in production or alteration of the premises had also to be recorded at the excise office. Most traders had to make either six-weekly (in the provinces) or monthly (London) returns of the goods they produced, and to pay the duty within six or four weeks of entry. Failure to do so made traders liable to a double duty. Notice when production would begin was often required, and the hours when excisable commodities could be produced or sold were also often stipulated. Products such as starch and soap had to be produced in standard sizes. Producers and retailers were required to admit excisemen at any time, to open any boxes and chests the officers requested to see, and to help them in their duties. It was a universal requirement that proper weights and measures be provided for the use of the excisemen though at the expense of the trader.

The case of candlemaking conveys the full extent of excise intrusion upon traders. Any person making candles was 'not to set up, alter or use any melting house, or place for melting or keeping candles, or materials, or use vessel for melting without notice' to the excise office. By the statute 11 George 1 c. 30 failure to enter 'each place, mold and utensil' at the office incurred a fine of £100 for each place or item not recorded. Returns of production had to state weight, number, size and quantity produced. Candles could only be manufactured at fixed hours and after due notice to the excise office. Registered candles could not be mixed with unentered ones, cracked or soiled candles had to be destroyed by the excise officer. Candles could only be sold legally at a fair, in a public shop or in a market. If they were shipped, they had to be marked in such a way as to indicate quality, quantity, weight, by whom they were sold and where they were consigned; failure to comply with these regulations resulted in confiscation. In sum, the premises on which a candle-maker worked, the tools that he used, the time that he worked, the way in which he transported and sold his goods – all of these were supervised by the excise branch of the revenue service.[103] It was difficult to evade these regulations. For chandlers, like soapmakers, could not legally ply their trade without first being inspected by the officer who kept their vats, moulds and utensils under lock and key.[104]

Such detailed surveillance explains why the producers of excisable goods were so much more concerned than overseas merchants with the issue of intrusion upon their privacy. As one anti-excise polemicist put it in 1733, traders

can never properly call either their Time or their Goods their own, being always exposed to the Molestation of those petty Tyrants, to the neglect and interruption of their business.

Besides, they are not able to dispose of their goods, even after they have paid all the Duties for them, without a Permit from one of those officers; and the Traders are put to the Trouble of keeping an exact Account of what they buy and to whom they sell; by which they expose the Circumstances, Mystery and course of their Business, and lay it open not only to the Officers of Excise, but to every Man.

Emphasis was, of course, on the financial costs of complying with excise regulations: the need of most London brewers to employ watchmen to admit excisemen who could enter premises at any time of day or night; the way in which capital was tied up in bonds for the payment of duty rather than being employed 'to great advantage'.[105] But these 'clogs on trade', which the excisable traders shared with the merchant paying customs duties, were compounded by the feeling that the exciseman was a viper in the bosom, a state creature capable not only of extorting taxes but also of undermining the family by molesting traders' wives and seducing traders' daughters.[106]

As the tariff barriers and walls of regulation grew, so they provoked both more resentment and more public debate. Under both Walpole and Pelham critics pointed to what they saw as the system's fundamental flaw: that the structure and organization of indirect taxes undermined England's international competitiveness by raising the price of English commodities. Elaborate regulations, they claimed, raised the cost of commercial transactions. Or, as the parliamentary opposition put it in 1735,[107]

our cause has suffered more by the Domestick Improvements made by our Neighbours, during the last long Tranquility in Europe, than it has done by any other means; except the heavy Duties we have laid upon ourselves, and the great Trouble and many Fees and Perquisities we have subjected our Merchants to, both in importing and exporting their goods & Merchandize: These Inconveniences will in time most certainly ruin every Branch of our Trade, if we do not take care to remove them speedily.

To compound the problem, taxes on basic goods raised the price of English labour, thereby adding to the cost of manufactures. In Sir John Barnard's words,[108]

Taxes upon Coals, Candles, Soap, Leather, and such other Taxes as now lie heavy upon the poor Labourers and Manufacturers, and thereby enhance their Wages in every part of the Kingdom, but especially in the City of *London*; by which the prime cost of all our Manufactures is so much enhanced, that it is impossible for our

Merchants to sell them in foreign markets so cheap, as Manufactures of the same kind and goodness are sold by the Merchants, even of those Countries, where the interest of money is as high as it is in this.

Seen from this point of view both customs and excises were sapping the nation's commercial and industrial strength.

This analysis was widely accepted and prompted a number of policies and recommendations for reform. Between the Peace of Utrecht and the Seven Years War there were several proposals for a major reorganization of the tax system, with a view to cutting indirect taxes. But this involved raising or restructuring the land tax or the introduction of some other direct tax, such as one upon houses. This type of reform, whose most eloquent advocate was Sir Matthew Decker, a member of the East India Company, was to be accompanied by a reduction and simplification of customs duties in the hope both of stimulating trade and eliminating smuggling.[109]

Such plans were usually though not invariably linked to schemes to reform excise taxes. These aimed to reduce excise taxes on the poor.[110] The motives behind this policy appear to have been both mixed and contradictory. On the one hand, it was a cliché, briefly but ineffectively challenged by the pugnacious West Country clothier, William Temple, that taxes on items of everyday use were passed on to employers in the form of higher wages.[111] The poor, in other words, did not suffer the burden of the tax, which fell on the merchants, manufacturers and landowners for whom they worked. On the other hand, many legislators expressed sympathy for the poor and hostility to their being taxed, presumably on the grounds that they did in fact bear the brunt of the duties. As Wyndham put it, 'by taking from the rich, we only diminish their luxury, but by squeezing from the Poor, we increase their misery'.[112] This latter view considered the contribution of the poor to be excessive and therefore to violate the general dictum that subjects should contribute to the state in proportion to their means.

Such views had comparatively little effect on legislation. Walpole introduced a number of reforms in the Customs service, eliminating duties on the export of manufactured goods, reducing some import duties, as well as tightening up revenue policing. Pelham and the younger Pitt both cut duties on certain items to reduce smuggling, but they did not achieve a significant reduction in overall rates. Throughout the eighteenth century ministers were aware of the argument that lower rates might eventually produce higher revenues, but they were too timorous to put the idea to the test.

The aim of reducing excises on those items which were deemed among the essentials of the poor, such as salt, candles, beer, cider, soap, starch, leather and malt, also failed to produce any substantive reform. Pelham, North and the younger Pitt all tried to levy excises on such luxuries as carriages, coaches and male servants. But such duties were not a success. They were costly to administer and they failed to yield the substantial sums obtained by levying taxes on basic goods and staples. The pious aspirations expressed by legislators concerned to relieve the poor were not translated into statute. Taxes on basics remained. In some cases, notably beer and malt, the rates of duty rose even higher. Excises might have pinched more cruelly: there was no tax on clothing, nor on basic foodstuffs apart from salt, and cheap candles and cheap soap paid duties at a lower rate. But the conclusion seems inescapable that excises hit the pockets of most consumers rather than just the purses of the prosperous.

As many commentators have pointed out,[113] the options of eighteenth-century fiscal legislators were severely limited as long as they refused to countenance a properly policed tax on wealth. Yet the only changes in this direction prior to the younger Pitt's triple assessment and income tax were the excises on luxuries, and the graded taxes, first introduced by Pelham, on windows. These were but a feeble step towards direct taxation, and stumbled against the implacable opposition to the sort of scrutiny that a tax on income would necessarily entail. Customs revenues were limited by the nation's mercantile needs and by the regrettable incentive to smuggle caused by higher rates of duty. It was therefore excises *faute de mieux*.

This meant that consumers bore the brunt of the burden just as traders had to cope with the administrative inconvenience. And, unlike their social superiors, there were fewer compensations in the form of government places and the chance to invest in the Funds. Many of middling sort, it is true, occupied the lower echelons of administration, working as tidewaiters, excisemen and clerks. Equally, there were plenty of state creditors from the middle ranks of society. And, at a more prosperous level, local merchants could make the sort of profits from revenue remitting which enabled them to start up as bankers. Such opportunities were not to be sneezed at, but they were open to only a very small proportion of the middling and lower sort.

The effect of the fiscal–military state on the domestic economy and social order was a persistent source of debate throughout the eighteenth century. There were, as we have seen, a number of ways in which different groups of people could adjust to or take advantage of the changes brought about by changes in the character of the state. But the most direct way in which the public could respond to these developments was by seeking to affect or shape the policies of government. If government were to be more and more active and legislation more intrusive, then it was clearly of value to those affected by statutory regulation and fiscal imposition to intervene in the making of policy. Such involvement could not be achieved directly. It required subtle intervention, the application of pressure both on the legislature and the ministers who headed government departments. It entailed careful preparation, the mounting of a case, the employment of the arts of persuasion. And this, in turn, embroiled both officials and interested parties in a debate about the compatibility of private interests with the public good.

V

THE POLITICS OF INFORMATION:
Public Knowledge and Private Interest

The earliest forms of organized government depended for their foundation upon the discovery of writing. The ability to transcribe, to create an enduring and verifiable record, the power to enumerate and make lists were necessary conditions of the first administrations that flowered in the valley of the Euphrates. The power of governments has been and always will be in large part dependent upon their capacity to order and manipulate different sorts of information. A growth in state power is usually accompanied – either as cause or effect – by changes in either the extent or the nature of a government's hold on social knowledge.

In this respect the important changes in English government that occurred in the late seventeenth and early eighteenth centuries were no exception. Administrative developments also entailed radical changes in the scope, organization and management of public information. This was nowhere more apparent than in the departments of central government – the Treasury, the fiscal boards, the Admiralty and Navy Boards, the offices of the Secretaries of State and the Board of Trade – whose assumption of new and more extensive administrative responsibilities was accompanied by a growing appetite for data and information.[1]

To be more effective government required greater knowledge; skilled government needed more detailed and precise information. The first and most marked impression conveyed by the official papers of the main government departments of the period is their sheer volume. The boxes of treasury memoranda, the in and out letter-books of the customs commissioners, the minutes and accounts of the Excise, the petitions to the Admiralty, the muster-books of the Navy Board, the volumes of state papers and the colonial reports of the Board of Trade all bear witness to the cumulative industry of a clerical staff unaided by the typewriter and the copying machine.

Such large bodies of information were of little use unless they were accessible: available to the relevant officials and organized in such a manner as to yield the requisite data. As we saw in Chapter 3, in the late seventeenth and early eighteenth centuries the papers of government employees gradually came to be regarded as departmental or official documents rather than the private property of office-holders. Papers were arranged in series, copied or filed according to established office convention, bound and indexed, so that departmental officials had ready access to the information they contained. The information itself was often organized in statistical, tabular or mathematical form: lists of ships entering and leaving ports; tables of prices; accounts, broken down by commodity and region, of tax returns; aggregates of military manpower and occupational data.

This information was not, of course, assembled out of curiosity and inquisitiveness. It was gathered with a number of particular ends in mind. In the first instance the state required information to implement policy. If Britain were to play a major part on the grand stage of European strategy, information about the diplomatic and military plans of her rivals was needed. If a new duty was required to fund another government loan, some knowledge or informed prediction about its return was necessary. Hence the growth of a diplomatic and spy network which covered much of Europe. Hence also the occasional surveys, carried out by revenue departments, of economic activity which might provide a fruitful source of revenue.

Information was also needed to ensure that government policy proved effective. Was a tax producing its expected yield? Had high duties succeeded in their goal of excluding the goods of foreign competitors? How effective was the campaign against smuggling? Such inquiries led senior officials to accumulate information not only about the activities of the state's subjects but also about the actions of its employees. For the success of a policy depended as much on its implementation as its conception. How it was carried out by government employees – whether they worked conscientiously or were indolent, venal and negligent – was a vital matter in gauging the success of such government operations as tax gathering. Hence the need to monitor minor functionaries and officers in the field.

It is no surprise that the most effective example of this practice was the administration of the Excise. Like all financial departments of the period, the Excise Commission was heavily dependent upon regular financial accounts to monitor its revenue-gathering operations. But, as we have seen, it also used an elaborate scheme of diary and record-keeping to scrutinize the actions of its workforce, a system that depended for its effectiveness on the examination of several different records of the same event. Not only were officers required to record their working day, including precise details of any measurements they undertook, but these facts and figures had to correlate with independent accounts drawn up by excise supervisors. The diaries and accounts which survive reveal a record-keeping system of great complexity and singular detail.[2]

Most of the information gathered by departments was not intended, at least in the first instance, for public consumption. Its invariable object was to help departmental officials, though it was sometimes used by officials in other government departments and, with increasing frequency, by parliament itself. However, if information gathered by government officials was to be more widely disseminated, it had to overcome two major obstacles – the reluctance of officials to release their jealously guarded ledgers and letter-books, and the intractability of the information itself, which was often organized in ways which made it extremely difficult to use for purposes other than those for which it was originally intended.

The pressures to disseminate such information were nevertheless sufficient to overcome the recalcitrance of bureaucrats and the opacity of their records. At least four different constituencies pressed for greater access to the figures and memoranda produced by departments of state. First, ministers of the crown wanted to be able to draw on all of the various resources of the different departments in order to exercise firm control over government policy. Second, parliament, both as a policy-maker and as the body dedicated to securing a responsible executive, was eager for access to government documents and statistics. Third, a number of occupational groups and special interests directly affected by state policies were also eager to learn the grounds on which such decisions were made. Finally, the general public had a substantial appetite for the sorts of information that only the very considerable resources of the state could provide.

The growing desire to acquire knowledge of the government's actions, to prize out of the corridors of power information about activities within them, can be seen as an obvious response to the growth in state activity which was such a prominent (and worrying) feature of the English polity after 1688. But one must place the extensive interest in state bookkeeping and in the quantitative data the government accumulated so rapidly in a larger context. Both the state's concern with enumeration and public inquisitiveness about its results stemmed from a larger interest in the power of arithmetical and mathematical techniques to render the political and social world more intelligible, and therefore more open to control. In short, the increased demand for knowledge was fuelled by changes in ways of understanding and classifying the world.

The most conspicuous manifestation of this new view of social knowledge in the late seventeenth century was the advocacy of what William Petty first called 'political arithmetic'. This early version of political science believed that the application of 'the Terms of *Number, Weight,* or *Measure*' to the resources of a state provided the means by which to understand them. The use of 'the ordinary Rules of Arithmetick' entailed 'a sort of Demonstration . . . where the perplexed and intricate ways of the world are explain'd by a very mean peice (sic) of Science'.[3] As the mathematical popularizer John Arbuthnot put it,

Arithmetic is not only the great instrument of private commerce, but by it are (or ought to be) kept the public accounts of a nation. . . . Those that would judge or reason truly about the state of any nation must go that way to work, subjecting particulars to calculation. This is the true political knowledge.[4]

The science of political arithmetic promised much more that it could deliver. The paucity of rigorously gathered quantitative data and insufficient discrimination in the choice of statistics meant that the plethora of numbers which populated the works of political arithmeticians concealed their suppositious nature and frequent inaccuracy. Particularity was confused with the truth. Nevertheless it seemed as if the enumeration of a series of observable facts would finally provide exact answers to those long-standing questions about the comparative resources of England and her rivals. The terms of trade, the amplitude of national wealth and the extent of population all seemed close to quantitative resolution. The early practitioners of political arithmetic were bold (not to say foolhardy) in their attempts at comparative numerical analysis. But their claims, and their insistence on the importance of numbers, helped stimulate demand both within and outside government for more quantitative data presented in accessible form.

If the ability to use arithmetic was deemed to be necessary to understand politics, then the qualities of a good ruler or able minister had to be redefined. Statesmanship and good government were no longer merely a matter of moral virtue and political courage. They also required technical knowledge and expertise, especially skill in the science of number. Political arithmeticians such as William Petty, Gregory King and Charles Davenant urged the importance of a ruler's ability to make fine calculations about the state's resources. Only then could state power be properly deployed. For Davenant the great statesman was the leader who had, in his words, 'a computing head'. 'The abilities of any minister have always consisted chiefly in this computing faculty,' he remarked, adding 'nor can the affairs of war and peace be well managed without reasoning by figures upon things.'[5]

Once the link between the making of policy and the ability to enumerate had been forged, the demand for more statistics grew apace. Prevailing assumptions about the connection between profit and power, between a flourishing polity and a strong state, meant that if a government were to evaluate its performance against that of its principal rivals it needed quantitative information not only about its own operations, but about economic activity in the nation at large. Above all the government wanted to know about trade, for the balance of trade was seen as one of the chief indicators of England's success or failure as a commercial power.

It is therefore not surprising that the first government department devoted exclusively to the compilation of statistics was the office of the Inspector-General of Imports and Exports established in 1696. The task of the Inspector-General was to produce annual abstracts of imports and exports from the customs records in order to reconstruct England's balance of trade.[6] The project frightened the French into establishing a similar office in 1713, but, like so many quantitative schemes of the period, its grand aspirations were only partially fulfilled. The accuracy of the annual reports was brought into question by the inability of the customs commissioners to estimate the extent of contraband and smuggling, while their effective use was hampered by the difficulty of measuring the value rather than the volume of trade over a period of time.

Other, even more ambitious schemes never reached fruition. One early eighteenth-century projector proposed a scheme for an advisory council to the First Lord of the Treasury. It was to have consisted of a board of five men, with a secretary and a clerk. Their task would have been to assemble detailed information on trade and navigation, the operation of public revenue collection, the availability of supplies for war, and the state of the market in public funds.[7] The proposal underscores the enthusiasm of early eighteenth-century officials for information gathering. On the other hand, its failure to be implemented reminds us that the romance of officialdom with the world of number was not always as fruitful as might at first appear.

Nevertheless the expansion of the state played an important part in stimulating the desire to learn the skills of number and calculation. The government, chiefly in its fiscal capacity, was the most important single body collecting quantitative information. It sponsored special instruction in applied mathematics at the Christ's Hospital school in London. Several of the early political arithmeticians held government posts, drew their information from government records, or produced new series of data in their capacity as public servants. During the Interregnum William Petty worked as Surveyor of Ireland. Charles Davenant was one of the excise commissioners responsible in the 1680s for the introduction of the so-called 'Method' into excise assessment and collection. He went on, after a period of political disfavour, to become Inspector-General of Imports and Exports in 1702. At a humbler level, minor government officials were enthusiastic proponents of the science of number. They published works on mathematics, surveying and accounting, wrote essays on probability, placed mathematical conundrums in newspapers and offered personal instruction in arithmetic and bookkeeping. The eponymous hero of Henry Mackenzie's sentimental novel, *The Man of Feeling* (1771), was not the first or only British youth to acquire his numerical skills at the hand of the village excise officer.[8]

The desire to be numerate was, in turn, stimulated by a growing number of opportunities for employment in government. The most rapidly expanding areas of state employment were the fiscal departments which required arithmetical skills of their employees. (Indeed, excise employees had to learn both algebra and calculus.) When John Jackson published his *Mathematical Lectures* in 1719 one of his chief arguments in favour of his little book was 'The necessity that Gentlemen are under, that would be Considerable in the Art of War or any great Employment . . . which cannot well subsist without a considerable knowledge in the *Mathematics*.'[9] It was not only the counting house but the departments of state which required numeracy; it was not just the shopkeeper but the gentleman in office who needed to know how to reason 'by figures upon things'.

Thus did the policies and organization of the state stimulate fact gathering and calculation in late seventeenth and early eighteenth-century England. But they were not the sole sources of these activities whose development frequently depended upon the interplay between the government and interested parties in civil society. Nowhere can this be seen more clearly than in parliament. The eighteenth-century House of Commons occupied a paradoxical position in government: on the one hand, the frequency of its meetings and the volume of its business made it very much a part of the governing process; on the other, it retained its ancient role as 'the grand inquest of the nation' whose task was to check abuses in government and look to the grievances of the constituents its members represented. In either case MPs, acting both collectively and individually, needed adequate and accurate information to ensure just and honest government.

When dealing with those matters of state administered by the chief government offices, MPs were entitled to call for papers and accounts prepared in the relevant department. Even routine legislation – annual bills of supply for example – produced a sizeable body of accompanying documentation, either presented to the house by the Treasury or called for by its opponents. When controversial measures were introduced, the steady flow of paper quickly became a flood. During the Excise Crisis of 1733, for example, the government either chose or was forced to disgorge a prodigious amount of data. The size and cost of the revenue departments; import and export figures on such commodities as tobacco, tea, coffee, cocoa, wine, spirits and sugar; the yield of duties over the preceding seven years; the number of seizures of contraband and the frequency of revenue fraud over the previous decade; all of these papers and accounts were deemed necessary to ensure the proper deliberations of the house on Walpole's revenue scheme.[10]

At such times government departments were apt to complain that their clerical staff were unable to cope with the legislature's calls for information. Such protestations can be attributed to the time-honoured tactic of administrative prevarication, employed in the hope that the curious and the critical will eventually be bored into surrender. But they were not entirely implausible, especially when it is remembered that departmental information was not only sought to judge government policy, but also to cast light on such matters as the fortunes of a particular industry or the fate of a particular trade.

The information culled or extracted from the departments of state was by no means the only data presented to parliament. As Joanna Innes has pointed out,[11] many MPs, especially those interested in such questions as poor law, penal and criminal law reform, went to great lengths to provide the house with valuable information about matters we would today describe as domestic or social policy. Drawing on the expertise of fellow MPs, many of whom were experienced in law and local government, and, later in the century, on information solicited from JPs and local officials outside the house, reformers such as Thomas Gilbert bolstered their case for legislative improvement with a battery of facts and figures.

Such tactics were employed not only by those who professed the public good, but also by those who represented special interests. Lobbyists, as we shall see in the second section of this chapter, were concerned both to provide parliament with information and statistics and to obtain knowledge of the actions of the state, by using the commons' right to call for papers and accounts.

During the course of the eighteenth century lobbyists' access to such information progressively improved. In the early years of the century few government papers or committee reports presented to the commons were subsequently printed. Neither the *Journals* nor the debates were publicly available, except for the occasional newspaper report of the lower house's deliberations. The only regular printed source of parliamentary information was the *Votes and Proceedings* which were published from the 1680s onwards. The *Votes* were chiefly intended for MPs, each of whom received a free copy. But for most of the century the number of printed copies of the *Votes* exceeded the number of MPs. Some of these were sent to government departments, but many more were sold commercially. At least one MP believed the *Votes* to have a national circulation. The parliamentary diarist William Cocks remarked that when the lords criticized the commons in 1701 'the print of our Votes . . . will reflect upon us to the people all over the Kingdom'.[12] By the 1730s over 1000 copies of the *Votes* were sold daily to the general public.[13]

The *Votes* provided a minimum of information for those outside parliament. Their skeletal account of proceedings informed the reader of the presentation of petitions, the formation of committees and the passage of motions and bills. But they included remarkably little detail of the substance of parliamentary deliberations. Their greatest deficiency, from the lobbyist's point of view, was their failure to reproduce important accounts and papers. In the 1740s, however, the commons voted to have their *Journals*, previously available only in manuscript, put into print. By the late 1760s, a complete set of back numbers of the *Journals* had been published, and current *Journals* began to appear shortly after parliamentary sessions ended. Unlike the *Votes*, the *Journals* contained many (though by no means all) parliamentary reports and papers. These were supplemented after 1767 by the publication of a separate series of collected parliamentary committee reports which appeared while the house was in session. The availability of these official documents, when combined with the increasing frequency (and accuracy) of published parliamentary debates, meant that in the second half of the century interested bodies outside the legislature had far greater access to parliamentary information than ever before.[14]

Even those members of the public who were not directly affected by a matter on which the state produced facts and figures showed considerable interest in government materials that were printed or published. This curiosity has to be understood in the context of a prevailing desire to acquire what contemporaries described as 'useful knowledge', knowledge applicable to everyday life and reducible, through the science of number, to a series of figures or tables. This knowledge was not confined to information either produced by or descriptive of government activity. It included not only state statistics but information about the population, the economy and society at large.

The demand for such information was not simply a function of its usefulness. 'Useful knowledge' was a type, a category of knowledge, not necessarily of immediate value to those who acquired it, but having the potential to be deployed usefully. A table of currency exchange rates or a set of foreign trade figures might not be 'useful' to a country gentleman but he would recognize them as 'useful knowledge'. Indeed the libraries of many eighteenth-century gentlemen were filled with compendia of information such as Postlethwayt's *Universal Dictionary of Trade and Commerce*, or comparable volumes produced by Richard Rolt and Thomas Mortimer.[15] Such works were important not as practical guides but as constructs, ways of ordering knowledge which provided their reader with a means of viewing and analysing the world.

This is not to deny that many works of 'useful knowledge' were purchased and used because they provided practical information, guidance and instruction. Books of tables and ready reckoners designed to speed calculations and ensure precision fall into this category. So do the growing number of 'how to' books which provided instruction in a trade or calling, together with information about the complex legal requirements traders had to follow if they were not to fall foul of an increasingly regulatory state. These volumes told shopkeepers how to fill out the vouchers they needed if they bought and sold excisable goods; they informed overseas merchants of the complex rates and labyrinthine regulations of the customs service, and they epitomized the growing body of statute law which regulated such different matters as the size of cartwheels and of bars of soap, or the length of tallow candles.

But even these works should be viewed as more than practical documents. *The General Shop Book or Tradesman's Universal Director*, published in 1756 seems, at first sight, to be 'a most useful and necessary Companion to lie on the Counter of every shopkeeper, whether wholesale or retail, in Town or Country'. But the contents of its title page reveal it not just as a guide but as a portrait of commerce which places the small shopkeeper within a much larger context:

Comprehending and Explaining the domestic and foreign trade of Great Britain and the Plantations, whether carried on by companies or private persons; and the several trades and professions exercised at home; the various commodities and manufactures exported and imported to and from the different countries of the World; the Course of Exchange, the Ballance of Trade, the Business of the Custom house and Waterside, invoices, entries, insurances, bottomtree, coins, weights, measures, etc. Likewise the distance of all market towns in England, from London, their fairs and Markets. The Inns where the Carriers and Coaches put up, and the days they come in and go out. With maps of the Roads, a Plan of London, a Chart of the Seacoast, and many other useful particulars.

A shopkeeper was likely to derive as much satisfaction from learning how he fitted into a larger world whose boundaries and territories were defined by numbers and tables as from using the discrete pieces of information *The General Shop Book* offered him.

Interest in 'useful knowledge', then, cannot simply be attributed either to changes in the role of the state, or, indeed, to changes in the nature of the economy. They played their part. But at bottom the emphasis on 'useful knowledge' constituted a change in perception, the growth of a new vision of state and society.

That view, as we have seen, depended upon a faith in the powers of number. Mathematics and arithmetic were seen not merely as discrete forms of intellectual endeavour but also as an exemplary mode of reasoning applicable to the analysis and understanding of all sorts of human endeavour. Popularizers of mathematics like John Arbuthnot believed that only the comparative youth of the subject inhibited its universal application.[16] Other commentators emphasized that calculation, even when it was not directly applicable to the subject at hand, was invaluable because of the mental training it provided. It was the paradigmatic case of sound reasoning. The author of *The Accomplished Merchant* (1740) urged the aspiring trader to devote himself to the study of figures because it infused

the Habit of just Reasoning, Reflection and Observation . . . And as the Studies we recommend abound with Truths the most certain, so every other Species of Knowledge, either of a Mercantile, or *any other Nature* [my italics], may receive Aid from them. Probabilities of every Kind, more or less remote from Certainty, will sooner be discovered by as Mind a little season'd to Truth and undeniable Reasoning. There is a general Congruity and Affinity in all just Reasoning; and this Habit happily acquired in one thing, will be easily transferr'd to any other.[17]

The object of applying mathematical science to 'useful knowledge' was to make *accurate* decisions, to reduce the elements of chance and caprice in what was perceived to be an unpredictable world. The risks and dangers associated with 'Meer *Hazard* and *Chance*' were contrasted with the security conferred by reason and computation.[18] The high standing of all forms of calculation, especially mathematical calculation, stemmed therefore from their power in the eyes of eighteenth-century observers to produce precision, certainty and security out of seeming chaos and disorder.

This faith, stretched to a point of extreme credulity, can be seen in the proliferation of life insurance schemes in the early eighteenth century. These projects purported to draw upon recently invented *mathematical* probability theory,[19] and upon life tables drawn up by such political arithmeticians as Sir John Graunt and William Halley. They were given such reassuring names as the Safe Society, the Secure Society, the United Society and the Unquestionable Society. Their claims were an extravagant tribute to the power fashionably attributed to mathematics. As one later insurance society put it, 'these assurances are grounded upon the expectancy of the continuance of life, which, although the lives of men, separately taken, are uncertain, yet in a number of lives is reduced to certainty; the length of some abundantly compensating for the shortness of others'.[20] The principle was all well and good but the practice, as was so often true with statistical projects in this period, was found wanting. Many of the schemes were scams for raising money; even the more reputable lacked a proper mathematical basis for their calculations and, as a result, soon went out of business. But the enthusiastic custom they were able to command attests to a touching faith in the ability of mathematics to bring the world to order.

The use of mathematical techniques such as probability theory was supposed to make 'useful knowledge' generally or universally applicable. Indeed, 'useful knowledge' was quite often also described as 'universal knowledge'. This description had another connotation besides that of being general or extending to all. Universal also meant, to cite Johnson's *Dictionary*, 'not particular' or 'comprising all particulars'. In this sense universal knowledge was not only comprehensive but impartial. It was these connotations that were exploited in eighteenth-century pamphlet and periodical titles, with such names as the *Universal Intelligencer*, the *Universal Register* and the *Universal Magazine*.

If knowledge was to be universal, it had perforce to be public, and so it was often described: people spoke of 'public knowledge', 'public information' and 'public intelligence' and newspapers were given titles like the *Public Ledger* and the *Public Advertiser*. Of course 'public' can be taken to mean simply 'having to do with public affairs or matters of state'. But the term 'public knowledge' was also understood to mean information that was unconcealed, generally known and in open view.

It does not follow, however, that such information was universally available, just as it was far from the case that the universal science of mathematics was universally comprehended, or that different traders had equal access to commercial information. Rather, the proliferation of such terms as 'public knowledge' and 'public information' reflects a widely held desire to push out into the open – into the public sphere – knowledge and information previously arcane, obscure or private. In short, the claim that a specific item of information was *public* knowledge was more often normative than descriptive. Paradoxically, of course, the call to make certain sorts of knowledge 'public' often came from extremely partial special interest groups. Though they couched their claim in the language of universality, they often sought 'public' knowledge in order to enjoy private advantage. Such, as we shall see, was the politics of information in eighteenth-century England.

Lobbies and the State

'The lobby' was not an invention of the era after the Glorious Revolution. Bodies concerned to affect government policy through the skilled practice of the politics of information had existed earlier in the seventeenth century. But after 1688 they grew in number, adopted more sophisticated tactics and devoted more and more attention to parliament rather than to other parts of government.

These developments were in large part a response to the political changes that emanated from the Glorious Revolution. After 1688 England had a standing parliament which, thanks to the strict financial settlement negotiated with the crown, met every year and not, as had previously been the case, at the whim of the monarch.

The permanence of parliament, the greater length of its sessions, and its much increased legislative activity (by the 1760s passing as many as 200 bills a session), made it a far more important policy-making body than it had been before 1688. This is not to deny the importance of the departments of state as bodies which formulated and implemented policy. Though lobbyists paid more attention to parliament, they knew full well that it would have hindered their cause if they had thereby neglected to solicit the ministers and function-aries of Whitehall. But after 1688 pressure groups frequently combined their intrigues behind the closed doors of government offices with the exploitation of the more open forum of the lower house. There, with the help of sympathetic members, they could air their views publicly and solicit the support of disin-terested parties.

By the reign of George III there were a great many of these lobbies and interest groups: religious associations such as the Quaker London Meeting for Sufferings and the nonconformist Protestant Dissenting Deputies, which represented Presbyterians, Independents and Baptists; trade associations such as the Society of West India Merchants or the Virginia Merchants who met at the Virginia Coffee House; colonial lobbies spearheaded by their parliamentary agents in London; an Irish lobby organized by the agent of the Lord Lieutenant; local English lobbies often organized around guilds and trading groups such as the Bristol Merchant Adventurers; and industrial and manufac-turing lobbies, like the Midland Association of Ironmasters or the West Riding Committee of Worsted Manufacturers, originally led by London city companies but eventually organized from the provinces by businessmen like Samuel Garbett who inspired the General Chamber of Manufacturers founded in 1785.

Many of these lobbies either extended or depended upon long-standing corporate institutions – guilds and liveried companies, for instance – while others were newly congealed around a specific interest. The object of these associations was to represent and to act on behalf of a particular or special interest. Much of the lobbyists' time was spent monitoring the formulation of policy and the passage of parliamentary legislation. It was essential to ensure that no measure which affected a body like the Virginia Merchants or the Distillers' Company was passed without a scrupulous examination of its contents and a careful consideration of its implications. The purpose of this scrutiny was to enable a lobby to intervene promptly if it thought a measure conflicted with its interests. Intervention could come at almost any stage, and might even take the form of proposing a policy *de novo*. This could only be achieved, however, with the cooperation and support of the relevant government department. The Anglo-Russian commercial treaty of 1734, for example, was initiated and planned by the Russia Company. But its completion was the product of a fruitful cooperation between the Company and the Board of Trade.[21]

Government officials in many departments – this was especially true of the Board of Trade – recognized that special interest groups were useful because they were often better informed than the servants of the crown about distant colonies and the arcana of different branches of commerce.[22] Merchants were often the first to hear of foreign news, even in advance of the government. In 1784, for instance, businessmen in Birmingham knew of Joseph II's ban on British goods long before this information reached the Treasury. Ministers only learnt of the embargo after they received a warning memorandum from the Manchester Chamber of Trade.[23]

Ministers therefore encouraged lobbyists to provide them with information, a request which provided pressure groups with the opportunity to help shape policy in a subtle and discreet way. As Alison Gilbert Olson has pointed out, the strength of a group like the Virginia merchants' lobby lay not in 'direct political influence but [in] their possession of information about conditions in Virginia and the state of the tobacco trade, information otherwise unavailable to statesmen who needed it'.[24]

Recognizing the power that knowledge conferred, some groups tried to restrict government access to information. One way in which manufacturers could resist the introduction of a tax on a commodity they produced was to withhold details of its production processes. This would make it extremely difficult to ascertain the best way to levy a tax and very hard to calculate the potential yield. In the 1690s the leather trades used such tactics to obstruct a proposed leather duty. And when, in 1697, a London leather dealer helped the excise service design a new tax, he was blackballed by his fellow tradesmen and driven out of business.[25] Information, whether hoarded or spent, was part of the currency in which lobbies traded.

Lobbyists had a narrow path to tread. On the one hand they wished to exercise as much influence as possible; on the other, an excessively hectoring or obtrusive lobby, one which threatened to *dictate* policy rather than provide informed advice, was likely to stiffen a minister's resistance to a proposal. Even the younger Pitt who, like Henry Pelham before him, showed an unusual degree of solicitude for commercial opinion, would not bow to the collective pressure of the General Chamber of Manufacturers. He was glad 'to collect, from all parts of the kingdom, a just representation of the interests of all the various branches of trade and manufacture'[26] but he would not, as the association's founder Samuel Garbett hoped, allow the chamber to contribute actively to the formulation of policy.

In these circumstances lobbyists had to adopt discreet and subtle tactics. But they also needed to develop organizations that could work effectively within the constraints imposed upon them. They had to observe a degree of political decorum, accepting the punctilio of government departments and honouring the conventions of parliamentary procedure. The most effective lobbies operated on at least two fronts. They closeted themselves with ministers and they opened up debate in parliament, using the time-honoured tactic of the petition, a formal request, presented by a member, for redress of grievances.

Some groups were able to mount extensive petitioning campaigns. The leather trades, for example, presented over 150 petitions from over 100 different locations between 1697 and 1699 in their two-year-long campaign to have the leather duties repealed (see Figure 8.1).[27] The scope of this campaign, which successfully prevented the renewal of the tax in 1699, certainly belies the often-held assumption that it was not until the 1780s that nationally coordinated lobbying was possible. In fact, throughout the eighteenth century there were many cases of inter-regional cooperation in the submission of petitions. The wording, for example, of the tanners' petitions of 1717 from London, Chester, Gloucester, Exeter, Worcester and Shrewsbury is so close as to reveal a common hand. The same can be said of the glass manufacturers' petitions of 1760 and of the provincial brewers' petitions of 1767. The geographical extent of such petitioning is not at all surprising. The levying of indirect taxes, which imposed *nationally* uniform rates on commodities, encouraged the emergence of organizations which transcended local and regional boundaries.

The object of petitioning was to secure access to the parliamentary forum. This not only meant the presentation and possible reading of the petition but the vital establishment of a committee to consider its contents. This, in turn, entailed the examination of witnesses and the presentation of expert and interested testimony. Lobbyists and their allies could then appear before the House of Commons and present their case in person. Petitioning, then, was the key to the house.

It did not, however, invariably unlock the door. Petitions had to be presented by members of the commons and, though some MPs like Sir John Barnard felt obliged to present a constituent's petition regardless of its contents, there were others who would not present or who would obstruct the presentation of petitions of which they disapproved.[28] Even if a petition were presented, it might be rendered nugatory by a motion of the house to let it lie upon the table, which effectively killed it. Members were

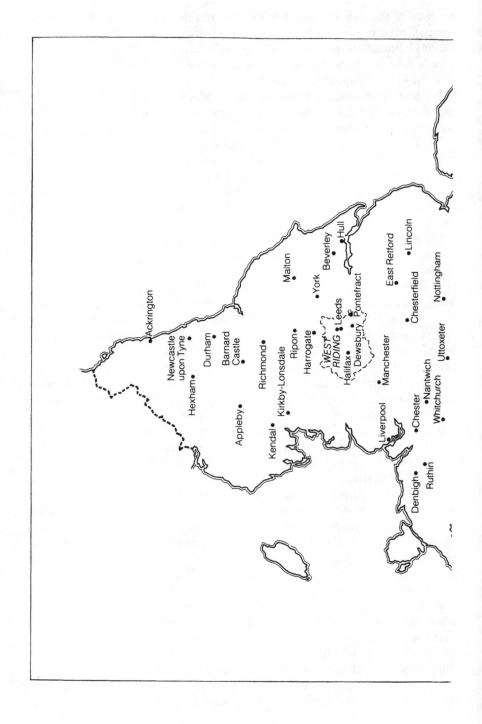

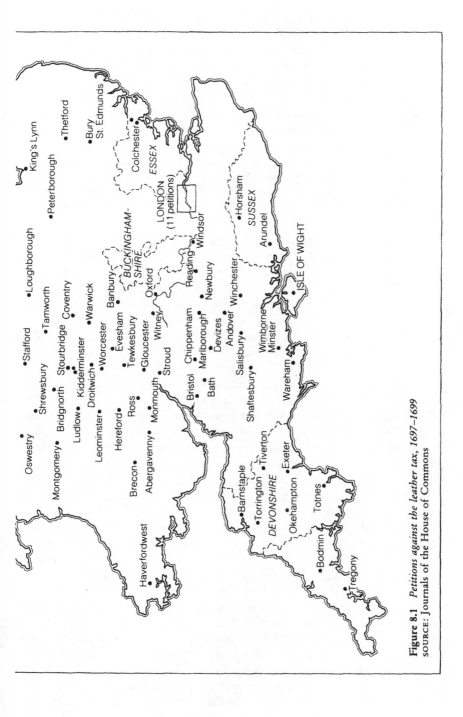

Figure 8.1 *Petitions against the leather tax, 1697–1699*
SOURCE: Journals of the House of Commons

not even allowed to peruse its contents privately; it could be brought out of obscurity only on the approval of a motion made by an MP.

Lobbies were also constrained from presenting petitions against taxes. Though in all other cases petitions against a measure were received by the house *before* its final passage through parliament, tax proposals – measures which, by the first decade of the eighteenth century, were a monopoly of the Treasury – could be petitioned against only *after* their enactment. As Arthur Onslow, Speaker of the House of Commons between 1728 and 1761, put it,

> where petitions are offered against laying a new duty, the House would not receive them, the House being the most competent judges of what was for the advantage of the nation, which they represent. But against duties already laid the petitions are always received, because the particular people who suffer under that experiment are most capable of informing the House of the grievance which is felt in consequence of the duty.[29]

This convention was challenged in the year of the Excise Crisis, in 1736 over the Gin Act and again during the Stamp Act Crisis in 1765, but it was not overthrown. MPs recognized that the protracted annual task of providing ways and means to fund the state might never be completed if every anti-tax petition were heard. This procedural convention explains why opponents of fiscal measures placed such importance on learning about plans for new taxes before they reached the lower house. They wanted to be able to nip such measures in the bud by lobbying the relevant government department and by presenting 'memorials' to the Treasury.[30] It also explains why opposition to fiscal measures like the 1733 excise bill took the form of instructions to MPs rather than petitions to the House of Commons.[31]

The presentation of a petition was therefore no simple matter. It required the good offices of a sympathetic MP and enough support in the house to ensure that it was not tabled. Once it had been read and a committee, normally chaired by the MP who had presented the petition, had been formed, it had to be vigorously supported, perhaps defended from hostile forces, if it were to lead, by circuitous parliamentary procedure, to a new measure on the statute book. Parliamentary lobbyists, then, had to begin soliciting support even before their petition was presented, and might have to continue to do so throughout the remainder of the session. If a lobbying campaign were delayed or tied up in committee, it might well have to be renewed in the following year. Thus it took all of two years for the London goldsmiths to secure the passage of a new plate bill to control the quality of silver plate in 1739.

Lobbying on this scale was not only time-consuming but expensive. It also required careful organization if it were to succeed. The London goldsmiths spent over £500 to ensure the passage of the 1739 Act.[32] In that same year the curriers spent over £2100 to obtain a statute, vehemently opposed by the cordwainers, which allowed curriers to cut leather into small pieces.[33] Such great expense was unusual but not unique. London Distillers' spent almost £1000 in their fruitless opposition to the Gin Acts of the 1730s,[34] while the Committee of North American Merchants disbursed over £1500 in their altogether more successful opposition to the Stamp Act.[35]

Measures like the Stamp Act or those which favoured one branch of a trade over another were, of course, controversial and therefore likely to involve interested parties in considerable expense. But even an uncontentious piece of legislation was quite costly. The 1731/2 Report of the Select Committee on Commons Fees remarked 'that extravagant payments for Bills which pass in Parliament to Counsel, Solicitors, and other persons without doors is equal to the charge of the fees, which in a single bill which passes without opposition amounts to about £60'.[36] A minimum overall cost of £120 was no small expense, and meant that a lobby would not sponsor legislation lightly.

One means by which a lobby's expenses could be defrayed was through a subscription. Throughout the seventeenth and eighteenth centuries lobbies raised money in this way. In 1694, for example, playing card manufacturers levied a subscription of 10 shillings a master and 2 shillings per journeyman to defray the expenses in seeking repeal of the tax on cards.[37] Three years later London brewers raised a comparable levy of 5 shillings per public house to pay for the costs of repealing the duty on London coals.[38] They were repeating a tactic they had used to oppose the double excise of 1692.[39] The Gold and Silver Wire Drawers Company required each member of their court of assistants to subscribe two guineas towards the cost of passing an Act of Parliament in 1702 and eleven years later used the same stratagem in their opposition to the new excise on wire.[40] Tanners raised money nationally in 1717 to prevent the export of bark used in the tanning of hide to Ireland.[41] Subscriptions such as these continued throughout the eighteenth century. In 1737–8 both the cordwainers and curriers raised money nationally, and in the 1760s the Society of West India Merchants funded its parliamentary efforts through a charge on trade from the Caribbean islands.[42]

How was the subscription money spent? Apart from the payment of parliamentary fees – a requirement not only for those who were promoting a bill but also for any lobby which wanted copies of parliamentary documents – lobby funds were first and foremost employed to pay the expenses of members of the group who personally attended the house, the government departments and individual MPs. They were also used to retain a solicitor-agent and an 'indoor official' who offered the specialized services – legal counsel and parliamentary information – without which a lobby stood little chance of success. Subscription moneys also covered the printing costs incurred in producing lobby propaganda.

The essence of lobbying was attendance at the House of Commons in person. Jonathan Swift described to Stella how in 1711 he and a number of Irish friends 'went to the lobby of the House of Commons, to solicit our friends' and 'to engage the members I am acquainted with in our interest' to defeat a proposed increase in the import duty on Irish yarn.[43] Interested parties were likely, when they heard of proposed legislation, to act promptly in lobbying the house. In 1710, for example, the Company of Playing Card Makers, having heard at one of their meetings about a bill 'for the better preventing Excessive and Immoderate Gaming', immediately marched down 'to the Parlt House to solicite the Company Business'.[44] The practice was soon well established. During the Excise Crisis of 1733 Sir John Bernard, admittedly a great friend of trade lobbyists, asserted without contradiction by his fellow members that

> it is certain that any Set of Gentlemen or Merchants may lawfully desire their Friends, they may even write Letters, and they may send those Letters by whom they please, to desire the Merchants of Figure and Character to come down to the Court of Requests and to our Lobby, in order to solicite their Friends and Acquaintance against any Scheme or Project, which they may think prejudicial to them.[45]

But an intimidating mob at the doors of the house, like the 'Thousands of Shoemakers, Curriers, Cobblers, etc.' who demonstrated against the drawbacks on exported hides in 1714 so that, as one member put it, 'when wee have cum from the House they have stood in such a long Rank that wee have in a manner Run the Gauntlett through them'[46], was never accorded the same recognition and respect. On the contrary, such pressure was counterproductive: when Walpole was mobbed in the Court of Requests after he had withdrawn his excise bill of 1733, the house unanimously condemned the action of the crowd.[47]

Most lobbies recognized that large-scale demonstrations were not the means to achieve their ends. It was far better to employ a small body of well-informed and well-organized lobbyists – men like Stephen Monteage, who, in acting for the York Buildings' Company, the subject of a select committee in 1733, attended both the commons and the lords on no fewer than sixty-five days.[48] Provincial and colonial lobbies, whose distance from parliament made it difficult for them to solicit MPs personally, either sent individuals to London or hired agents to represent them in the metropolis. Thus, in the years 1711 to 1714, the Chester tanners sent one of the city's aldermen to lobby in London, the Scottish saltpan masters on the Firth of Forth retained a London agent from 1739 onwards, and both the American and West Indian colonies used parliamentary agents, some of whom were themselves MPs.

Many trade and commercial lobbies, especially those based in the metropolis, solved the problem of organization by forming a small committee made up of the most reputable and influential members of their calling. In 1738, for instance, the London goldsmiths established a committee 'of six or seven gentlemen, who have the best acquaintance with the Members of the House of Parliament'.[49] Though these bodies were usually established with a particular legislative agenda in mind, some committees remained active for years at a time. A trade that was the frequent object of parliamentary legislation was likely to need a standing committee to guard its interests in parliament. Thus the London Distillers Company, engaged in an occupation that attracted the attentions of both the taxman and the moral reformer, established parliamentary committees to monitor the commons' proceedings in 1689–90, 1695–8, 1701–4, 1711–14, 1717–18, 1720, 1722, 1724–39, 1743, 1745–7 and 1751.[50]

Such committees – and most eighteenth-century London city companies employed them during the course of the century – met regularly in one the coffee houses or taverns in the Palace Yard, just outside the commons. At Alice's Coffee House, Hell Coffee House and at Waghorne's in New Palace Yard, the committees plotted and intrigued.[51] Here they coached witnesses before they appeared before the house or a select committee, treated both officials of the commons and MPs to food and drink and met with the most important figure in the eighteenth-century lobby, the solicitor-agent.

The solicitor-agent was a lawyer who specialized in handling parliamentary business. His task was twofold: to draft any legislation the lobby required and, in cooperation with a committee or agent, to orchestrate the tactical pressures necessary to push the legislation through both the commons and the lords.

Thanks to the work of Sheila Lambert, we have long known about the work of one of the most important of these men, Robert Harper, who drew up no fewer than 613 bills between 1717 and 1767. In the 1740s Harper was drafting sixteen to twenty bills for each parliamentary session. Between 1732 and 1762, Dr Lambert tells us, Harper drafted 458 or 37 per cent of the private acts that received the royal assent.[52] Harper specialized in estate and enclosure bills and held a virtual monopoly of the field. But he had many colleagues who did the rather different work of representing industrial and commercial interests.

It is clear from the accounts of printers who prepared the drafts of parliamentary bills that by the 1770s there were a number of solicitors who specialized in securing the passage of turnpike and navigation bills.[53] No doubt the very sharp increase in the number of turnpike bills during the 1760s created a demand for the sort of expertise that the solicitor-agent could offer. But even before the accession of George III lobbies could turn to a number of such men. I have identified sixteen lawyers who were active as agents for industrial and commercial interests between the Glorious Revolution and the end of the Seven Years War.[54]

The tasks these men performed are exemplified by the itemized bill that John Barrett, solicitor-agent for the gold and silver wire drawers, submitted to the company in the spring of 1698. In a proposed law to prohibit the importation of bonelace, the wire drawers wanted a clause inserted that would also bar gold and silver thread imports. They wanted, in other words, to continue to enjoy protection from French competition, even after the resumption of trade with France after the Peace of Ryswick. To achieve that end they hired Barrett and one other solicitor, a Mr Morton. Barrett charged £33 (quite a modest fee) for his services. In return for this payment he drafted a new version of the bill, met with the two MPs who had promised to sponsor it, organized a petition in its favour, drew up a breviat of the bill, solicited MPs to attend select committee meetings – he was given a coach for six days to speed his task – and attended the House of Lords for four days to help the bill's passage.[55]

Undoubtedly the most important task of a solicitor agent like John Barrett was to ensure the continued attention of MPs on the lobby's proposal. Interest and support had to be sustained if the bill were to stay alive, for most bills were not killed by the quick thrust of a hostile vote but slowly asphyxiated in the committee rooms in which they were allowed to languish.

The ease or difficulty of the solicitor-agent's task depended on the clout and connections enjoyed by a lobby, and on the willingness of lobbyists to exploit them. Did members of the lobby have friends in high places? The support of powerful MPs, especially those in high office, was of incalculable benefit. The wire drawers, for instance, sought out the aid of Sir Henry Hobart, not only because they knew he wished to protect the textile trade of his Norfolk constituents but because, as a recently appointed customs commissioner, he was in a position to do so. Lord Egmont, a leading light in the Irish Lobby, went straight to the top in 1731, when he solicited the support of Sir Robert Walpole for the removal of duties on the importation of Irish yarn.[56] In the 1770s and 1780s both Matthew Boulton and Samuel Garbett relied heavily on a network of genteel and aristocratic connections to support their lobbying efforts. In 1773 Boulton promoted a bill to have an assay office established in Birmingham. His prospects were undoubtedly enhanced when, as he wrote to his partner, 'Lord Derby took me about with him yesterday in his Chariot to several ministerial Members pressing them to serve us.'[57]

The solicitor-agent and the lobby he represented often employed parliamentary officials to monitor legislation and to help draft bills. These were clerks of the commons who, by virtue of their responsibilities, had unparalleled knowledge of parliamentary procedure and unrivalled access to parliamentary information. Thus John Hookes, a clerk without doors, acted for the wire drawers in 1698, Edward Stables, clerk assistant, was employed by the brewers to draft a clause in the 1725-6 victuallers' bill, and Culverwell Needler, clerk assistant, was consulted by the wire drawers in 1701-2.

Some of these clerks were kept on retainer. The Protestant Dissenting Deputies paid Robert Yeates, the clerk of engrossments, a regular fee of ten guineas a year to watch over their interests in parliament.[58] Lucas Kenn, who served as a clerk on several select committees, including the 1730 Select Committee on the State of the Gaols,[59] was paid six guineas a year by the London Distillers' Company. In 1744, however, he was fired for an offence which indicates what lobbyists expected of their employees in the house. Kenn was dismissed because 'he hath been guilty of a great neglect in not giving timely notice to the Company of a Clause added in an Act of Parliament passed this Session to the great prejudice of the trade.' He was replaced by Newdigate Poyntz, another clerk, who had the additional advantage of being the relative of one of the most prominent members of the Distillers' Company, Robert Poyntz.

As Sheila Lambert has emphasized, such contacts within the house were invaluable to any lobby:

No outside agent could have done what Edward Barwell, committee clerk, was able to do for a client in 1774: he promised to give the client warning when a petition in which he was interested was to be presented to the House; he was able not only to do this, but to give his client a copy of it before it was presented, so that he might prepare his opposition.[60]

Clerks were not the only parliamentary officials to benefit from the activities of the numerous lobbies. The doorkeepers of the house were often paid gratuities for distributing lobby propaganda. This usually took the form of a brief document – probably a single sheet, certainly no more than a few pages – which contained the phrase 'The Case of' or 'Reasons for' in its title. A tip of 5 shillings, such as that paid by the cordwainers to the commons' doorkeeper in 1711 for distributing copies of their 'Reasons', ensured that all MPs entering the house would have a copy pressed into their hands. Bored or inattentive during a debate, they could peruse a pithy document which amounted to a short written brief on behalf of the lobby. Some MPs considered these papers sufficiently important to have them forwarded to them if, for any reason, they were absent from the house.[61]

Such 'Cases' were also circulated among government officials and potential supporters of influence before the lobbyists' business came before the house. For example, Lord Egmont, known to be an active back-bencher with a special interest in trade, was visited in February 1731 by the agent for Barbados, who informed him of the case drawn up on behalf of the island's merchant community. 'He read to me their printed case, which he had given to Mr Walpole and the Speaker, and was now going to give to Sir Robert, but refused to let me have one as yet.'[62] Egmont would almost certainly have obtained a copy a few days later, when the West Indian merchants' business came up in parliamentary debate.

Distributing copies of a case was a tactic widely used by special interest groups in the late seventeenth and early eighteenth centuries. In 1710, for example, cases were presented to MPs by representatives of the following bodies: attorneys, booksellers and printers, the exporters of herrings and of beef and pork from Scotland, the japanners of England, paper merchants, stationers and playing card makers, tobacco merchants, wax chandlers, the warreners of England, the inhabitants of Rotherhithe, charity school children, and the planters and inhabitants of Nevis and St Christopher.

The costs of this propaganda, especially when compared with the other expenses of organizing a lobby, were extremely low. Apart from the 5 shillings payment to the doorkeeper, a *douceur* which was often supplemented by a certain number of free meals at Waghorne's, the only additional expense was the modest cost of printing a run of the cases. In the parliamentary session of 1711-12 the curriers had 700 copies of their 'Reasons' in favour of a drawback on curried leather printed at a cost of £1 8s od.[63] This cost approximately the same as having a lobbyist personally attend at parliament for a single day.

Despite their low cost and the ease with which they could be distributed, fewer cases were printed by lobbies during the course of the century.[64] The gradual demise of these single sheets is partly explained by the desire of those petitioning parliament for a more extended format in which to state their views. Special interest groups continued to circulate propaganda among MPs, but more and more often it took the form of a pamphlet. Thus a committee of the London Distillers' Company drafted and had printed *Some Observations on the present State of the British Distillery* which they presented to the lords of the Treasury, the excise commissioners and MPs in the spring of 1737.[65]

The eclipse of 'the Case' is also attributable to a change in the tactics of many special interest groups. From the 1730s, largely, as we shall see, because of the Excise Crisis of 1733, lobbies extended the ambit of their appeal beyond the Court of Requests, the Palace of Westminster and the offices of government. They addressed not only 'the Grand Inquest of the Nation', as the commons was called, but the public itself. It is revealing to contrast the campaign of 1697-9 to repeal the leather tax with that against the excise bill of 1733. The former, despite the extraordinarily impressive number of petitions it was able to muster, produced almost no propaganda apart from a few 'Cases' and the petitions themselves. But the much briefer campaign against Walpole's excise scheme of 1733 was marked by a remarkable effusion of printed matter – prints, handbills, pamphlets, sermons and sheets of statistics[66] – almost all of which was directed not just at MPs but at the public at large. There had been the occasional attempt to make such an appeal earlier. In 1705, for instance, shopkeepers had appealed in the *Post Boy* for support for their bill against hawkers, and in 1709 one of the parties in the controversy over the Weaver navigation bill had published a pamphlet in favour of legislation.[67] But such tactics were not used systematically until the 1730s.

Special interests were quick to occupy this new terrain. In 1743-4, for example, the West India merchants opposing Henry Pelham's proposed increase in the sugar duty deliberately emulated the publicity-seeking tactics of 1733. Such an appeal to the public was intended to complement rather than to replace the wooing of government officials and MPs. Overt solicitation of public support worked in tandem with discreet pressure exerted in the corridors of power. The West India men first presented their 'Case' to Prime Minister Henry Pelham. But this did not prevent them broadening their appeal:

The printed case has been sent to the respective house of every Member of Parliament in Town. The Agents, Planters and Merchants, have also agreed and divided themselves into several small parties to attend upon the several Members, and many of them have already been addressed on the Subject and every one of them will be solicited personally, before the Bill comes into the House. All people that have any Interest with such as have influence with Members are also Courted, and People in general seem to think as we do, in opposition to the Bill. Copies of the case have also been dispersed to the several sea ports of the Kingdom, besides publishing it in the *Evening Post*, and nothing shall be wanted to make the clamour popular, and if possible to get this d—d Bill as much abhored as the Excise Scheme.[68]

By the second half of the eighteenth century groups seeking the passage of new Acts of Parliament, even those of a local character such as turnpike and canal bills, routinely presented their case in the columns of the local and national press. Thus, when the Trent and Mersey Canal bill was first mooted in 1765, one of its most ardent supporters, Josiah Wedgwood, urged that its proponents place two letters a week in the metropolitan *St James's Chronicle* as well as writing letters to newspapers in Liverpool, Manchester, Derby, Nottingham and Birmingham.[69]

Such tactics were only possible because of England's flourishing provincial press. Without an effective and widely ramified system of news distribution, the appeal of special interests would have been confined to Westminster or, at best, to the metropolis. But as the fund of provincial news grew, so more and more lobbyists invested their hopes in the use of the press, and so more and more readers were brought into the competitive market-place of social interests.

It has been suggested that lobbyists' appeals to the public were regarded by many MPs as improper violations of the political convention that parliament alone could determine what was for the public good.[70] But it is perhaps more illuminating to recognize that the emergence of special interest groups willing to lay their case before the public was in part a *consequence* of parliament's claim to be the sole body to adjudicate what was *pro bono publico*. When lobbies failed in parliament they transferred their appeal to a more public court. They also changed the character of this appeal – the nature of their arguments – to excite the sympathy and win the support of a much broader audience.

Late seventeenth and early eighteenth-century interest groups used three sorts of argument to combat legislation they abhorred. The first and least effective narrowly addressed the particular concerns of the trade or occupation opposing a bill. They pointed to how a particular measure – the imposition of a customs or excise duty, for example – would probably lead to a price rise in the product they manufactured, to falls in production, and increased unemployment. In addition, lobbyists commonly argued that industrial and commercial regulation exacted what today would be called compliance costs. Conformity to rules and regulations wasted valuable time and might require additional employees, the need to pay duties in cash placed a strain on traders' liquidity, and the presence of taxes increased their capital requirement.

The second type of argument against legislation was a pragmatic one – that the proposed measure was unworkable. In the case of taxes it was often argued that a new impost would provide an exiguous yield and incur administrative and regulative costs which would make the duty more trouble than it was worth. Thus in 1711 the tory government dropped a proposed tax on London bricks and tiles when the brickmakers were able to produce statistics that showed that the overhead of tax collection would almost equal the potential yield.[71]

The third characteristic argument is what we may term quasi-mercantilist. Measures were typically attacked on the grounds that they adversely affected the balance of trade, harmed the British colonies and plantations, or had a deleterious effect on Britain's premier export industry in textiles.

These arguments required statistical backing, because government departments were usually in a position to produce figures to challenge or corroborate a special interest's interpretation of their position. No group wished to suffer the embarrassment of the Sugar Islands lobby, whose claim in 1774 that the duty on coffee had led to a fall in sales was refuted by government figures showing a steady expansion in coffee consumption.[72] Lobbies therefore concocted their own statistics. When, for example, the wire drawers sought the repeal of the gold and silver wire duty in 1712, they bolstered their case by producing figures to show the increased costs of poor relief in those London parishes where wire drawing was the chief occupation.[73] In 1738, when ironmasters in the Midlands complained of a depression in their trade, they presented a parliamentary committee with figures on the number of iron forges, both past and present; with information from customs records; and with poor law data designed to reveal the plight of workers in industrial parishes dependent upon the iron trade.[74] Poor rates seem to have been a particularly popular source of information. They were also used by the watchmakers of Clerkenwell to oppose the younger Pitt's tax on timepieces and watches.[75]

As these examples make clear, special interest groups and lobbies were heavily dependent upon information gathered by both local and national government. They needed access to official records if they were to make an effective and convincing case. Lobbies therefore went regularly to government departments seeking information. In 1714, for instance, the Chester tanners paid 13s 8d in fees and expenses to have copies made of the Liverpool customs port book to help their defence of the drawback on exported hides.[76] Twenty years later London shoemakers asked to examine the excise commissioners' books in order to prove the hardship they claimed to be suffering.[77]

The ways in which lobbyists obtained information from the departments of state changed during the eighteenth century. As we have seen, in the late seventeenth century lobbyists did not enjoy extensive access to government information through the good offices of parliament. The absence of printed reports and debates meant that, even if papers were called for by the lower house, such information was not broadly available. The formal procedures to secure information had not yet been harnessed to the lobbyists' purposes.

This did not mean that special interest groups were entirely without information. Indeed it was probably easier to obtain government information through unofficial and informal channels at the beginning of this period than it was to become later. It was also less difficult to obtain information by approaching government departments directly rather than through parliament. This was largely attributable to the character of the administrative departments in the late seventeenth century. Government was more 'permeable', the line between state and society less clearly drawn. Compared with the mid-eighteenth century turnover of administrative personnel was rapid. Many of these office-holders took their books and figures with them when they left their posts. Disgruntled and politically alienated officials were only too willing to pass on information to interested parties, especially those opposed to the current administration. At the same time administrative and fiscal schemes were put before government by 'projectors' who enjoyed no official government standing. There was much less sense of departmental loyalty and of belonging to an administrative class. The bureaucracy had yet to acquire the institutional definition and administrative formality characteristic of the mid-century years when the whig party dominated judgement. This meant that on the whole government departments were sympathetic to the needs of the different lobbies and responsive to their requests just as they were attentive to projects and schemes that did not originate within the bureaucracy itself. Information was quite widely circulated among interested parties but it was not yet publicly available.

Gradually government became less porous. Departmental loyalty became stronger as officials moved less and less frequently between different government offices. Dynasties of bureaucrats emerged. Though the Treasury was still inundated with 'projects', they were mostly pet schemes of officials in other departments. The different boards and commissions became reluctant to divulge information; they showed a tendency to refuse access to their accounts and figures. It became harder for lobbyists to go to a department directly to extract the material they wanted, though this was not a consistent trend. Government offices under Henry Pelham were notably more open than under Sir Robert Walpole. In the 1760s and 1770s departments began to display the inflexibility and institutional rigidity associated with the most sclerotic of administrations. But, in the aftermath of the American War, and at the behest of the younger Pitt, government offices were again more amenable to outsiders, both in responding to interest groups and in providing information.

But an important countervailing trend overcame any restrictions on access to government information. As insider dealings with the departments became more difficult, so the use of parliament to obtain government information became more common. Though private negotiation never entirely ceased and private interest remained invaluable, the focus of lobbyists and special interests shifted not to parliament itself but to a broader public beyond Westminster. Ironically, then, administrative enclosure led to an opening up of debate.

Lobbyists responded by transforming their arguments to give them a broader appeal. The economic arguments so characteristic of special interests were opened up to elaborate a general picture of the economy, or, at the very least, to consider the impact of one special interest upon the polity as a whole. Opponents of the proposed additional sugar duty of 1744, for instance, argued that the tax, in the first instance, would be detrimental to the business of the sugar refiners. But this, they maintained, was just the beginning:[78]

The *Sugar-Refiners* are a numerous and useful Body of People, who employ a great number of hired Servants in the *Manufacture*; furnish employment and subsistence to many other *tradesmen* and *manufacturers*, such as *Black-smiths, Founders, Copper-smiths, Plumbers, Bricklayers, Masons, Potters, Carpenters, Coopers, Backmakers*, and many other tradesmen; and they already contribute greatly to the *publick Revenue*, by a large consumption of *Coals* and *Candles*, *Paper* and other *taxed* Commodities; and if they and their families are ruined, or are obliged to quit their manufacture, great numbers of people, depending on them, must suffer with them, and the *Publick revenue* be greatly diminished.

Arguments of this sort attempted to reconcile the private interest of the lobby with a more broadly defined concern for the public good. They sought to demonstrate that the aims of sectional economic interests were compatible with the notion of '*salus populi*'. In so doing, they conceded what was generally recognized by all eighteenth-century political commentators, namely that private interests were perforce subordinate to the public good. 'Private interests', wrote one commentator, inscribing what was a political shibboleth, 'cannot stand where the public good of the nation is concerned'[79] or, as the *Political Register* trenchantly put it, 'private considerations cede to those of the state'.[80]

The implications of this view for any definition of the ambit of state power were far-reaching. Those who determined what was *pro bono publico* had enormous powers. As one pamphleteer put it,[81]

In the plague, it is lawful to confine a few within a certain district, though it be almost certain death, rather than hazard the infection's being spread through the whole country: And in a fire tis never disputed whether a few houses should not be blown up, to prevent the flames spreading through the whole town. And all this for the best reasons in the world, viz, that properties and even lives of the few must be sacrificed to the health, utility, safety and welfare of the whole community.

The good of the whole, it was generally agreed, lay in the hands of the legislature: 'the LEGISLATURE of every Country are the best Judges, what is, or what is not for the Benefit of the Whole'.[82] And it therefore followed, as one pamphlet defending a special interest was forced to concede, that 'Every impartial man must . . . allow that it would be just in a legislature to destroy the trade, wealth and industry of any one set of men in the kingdom for the public advantage'.[83] Here we see elaborated a fully fledged notion of parliamentary sovereignty; indeed, we might almost call it parliamentary absolutism. It is also a view that recognizes that the sovereign body represents what we might characterize as an overriding interest, the interest of the state.

How were special interests to contend with the full ideological force of government? In what ways could they defend what were palpably sectional interests? And how, indeed, could they persuade disinterested parties to support them? To whom could they appeal in the face of a hostile or unsympathetic legislature? The answer to these questions emerged in the 1720s and 1730s and can first be found fully answered during the Excise Crisis of 1733.

The debate of that year was public as well as parliamentary. A plethora of printed material was distributed not only in Westminster but throughout the country. The arguments marshalled in these printed polemics were not the narrowly economical case that had been deployed thirty-five years earlier against the leather tax. Though opponents of Walpole's excise scheme were led by sectional interests in the tobacco and wine trades, as Jacob Price has shown,[84] they argued not that they were defending the economic interests of these groups, but that they were protecting the political interests of every British subject. The excise scheme was abhorrent, it was said, because it deprived Englishmen of their liberties, not because it cut into merchants' profits. The issue, in other words, had been universalized. It was no longer a matter of a contest between the government and sectional interests adjudicated by the legislature; it had been recast as a struggle between the state and its subjects judged by the general public. This interpretation of the crisis of 1733 was a partial one and failed to command universal acceptance. But it provided the most important precedent and the most useful exemplar for subsequent campaigns against state intrusion.

Immediately after the Glorious Revolution those worried by the expansion of the state apparatus were chiefly concerned with the threat this posed to the *corporate* liberty of parliament. The burning question was whether or not a burgeoning executive would enable the monarch to dispense with 'the representative of the people'. This anxiety overshadowed (though it certainly did not entirely obscure) concern for the liberties of individual subjects. But by the mid-eighteenth century it had become clear not only that parliament had been preserved but that it claimed (and sometimes enjoyed) unprecedented powers. The increased emphasis on the rights of individual subjects was a natural concomitant of the legislature's claim to absolute authority. As the legislature came to look more and more like a part of the state apparatus and less and less like the representative of the people (a function it nevertheless succeeded in retaining), so political debate expanded into the public sphere. This trend, always encouraged by some members of the legislature and made possible by a national infrastructure of print, was exploited by those interest groups the state itself had largely brought into being.

I do not mean by this that the occupations of West India merchants, wire drawers or tanners were defined by their contact with the state. But the dealings of such people with the state defined them as *interests*. Trades and corporate bodies hedged around with legislation – protective, regulatory or fiscal – were the first to mobilize lobbies and conduct parliamentary campaigns. As Adam Smith pointed out, 'the clamour and sophistry of merchants and manufacturers' were effective because they had a 'superior knowledge of their own interest' to most other men.[85] They learned this lesson in their dealings with the state. In this way, government intervention helped create new social forms in civil society.

By the 1780s relations between special interest groups and government departments were radically different from those in the first quarter of the eighteenth century. Whereas in the earlier period lobbies had often opposed government measures at their inception, by the time of the American War they were urging departments into greater legislative activity. Once special interest groups were enmeshed in the legislative fabric of the state, they came to realize the many advantages that could be gained by legislative manipulations. The history of much of the lobbying after the mid-eighteenth century is best characterized as a struggle between competing interests (some within the same trade) to acquire economic advantage through the manipulation of government regulation and parliamentary statute.

Not all lobbies, as American historians have been quick to point out, enjoyed equal advantages. It is my impression – though it is only an impression – that, after a period under Henry Pelham when government departments were generally accessible, a distinction emerged between those groups which had effective purchase on government and those which did not. Some of the richer traders and merchants of the larger houses, whose wealth, influence and substantial contributions to government revenue were considered to entitle them to privileged treatment, were cosily intimate with the departments of state; others were kept out in the cold.

Those who were welcomed in the corridors of power took full advantage of their position. In the 1770s, for example, candlemakers, soapmakers, starchmakers, tea sellers and silk manufacturers all approached revenue commissioners with requests for tougher laws and more detailed regulation of their trades. They wanted to use fiscal legislation to limit business competition (a tactic which, of course, much exercised Adam Smith) and to discipline and police their employees. Traders in the 1730s had described the excise commissioners as harpies and blood-suckers. By the end of the American War revenue officers had been transmogrified into the 'Protectors of the fair Trader'.[86]

The most active proponents of government intervention became the powerful traders rather than the officials themselves. Officers of state opposed demands for tougher laws because they viewed such measures as 'extremely oppressive'.[87] Concerned more with administrative probity and retrenchment than with the traders' desire to corner markets and control their employees, they sought to restrain the worst excesses of the powerful lobbyists. They did not, however, prevent such groups from enjoying great advantages over their rivals because of their access to the corridors of power.

This might seem to vindicate Adam Smith's view that state policy had become the tool of the mercantile interest. But such an interpretation would be too simple. The history of eighteenth-century commercial lobbying amply demonstrates that, despite the use of such terms as 'trading' or 'commercial' or 'mercantile interest', trading and industrial groups were as much divided, one against another, as they were from the 'landed' or 'financial' interest. Curriers and cordwainers, both in the leather trade, fought one another over the incidence of the leather tax and over the right to monopolize certain industrial processes. Provincial and metropolitan soap manufacturers quarrelled over the question of how often to pay the soap duty, a seemingly trivial but in fact important issue, given the very different capital and credit requirements in town and country. Dealing with the state became one important way in which specifically defined groups sought to gain advantage over their rivals. There was, as the collapse of the General Chamber of Manufactures revealed, no homogeneous business interest. There were commercial and industrial interests whose very variety owed much to the government's imposition of a complex system of regulation. The state's intrusion upon civil society created sophisticated 'interests' whose political conduct was, in turn, informed by the open and accountable political system in which they operated.

CONCLUSION

The emergence of a peculiarly British version of the fiscal–military state, complete with large armies and navies, industrious administrators, high taxes and huge debts, was not the inevitable result of the nation's entry into European war but the unintended consequence of the political crisis which racked the British state after the Glorious Revolution of 1688. Though not inevitable, these changes in government were enduring. The overweening power of the Treasury, a highly centralized financial system, a standing parliament, heavy taxation, an administrative class of gifted amateurs lacking training in the science of government but with a strong sense of public duty, government deficits and a thriving market in public securities: all these features of modern British politics began under the later Stuarts and Hanoverians. They had a profound effect on the subsequent history of the British state, enabling it to arbitrate the balance of power in Europe, to acquire its first empire and, when that was lost, to build another.

The fiscal–military state affected society as well as government. It helped create a financial community – what today is called 'the City' – whose influence on politics and the economy was immediately controversial and remains so today. The eighteenth-century speculator had all the opportunities – legitimate or otherwise – available to the modern 'market-maker': the easy raising of capital for public or private funds; the simple, reliable and swift purchase and sale of stocks, shares and securities; dealing in futures and on the margin; insider trading; the creation of paper companies; and the covert manipulation of stock. Only the technology to speed these transactions was missing.

The growth in government and the rise of 'high finance' were the two changes which excited most comment and criticism but they were far from being the only effects on society. A volatile economy was made even more unstable by the fluctuating fortunes of war; taxes were paid by all subjects, regardless of rank. Landed gentry, farmers, shopkeepers and traders, labourers in husbandry and industry, merchants and manufacturers: all, in their different ways, were touched by the activities of the fiscal–military state. So much so, indeed, that some of them began to analyse their society in a way that placed conflict between economic and occupational interests to the fore; others formed associations or less formal bodies with the aim of influencing the state's policies to their own advantage. Such special interests quickly developed sophisticated techniques to put pressure on the legislature and departments of government.

These interests struggled to understand, subjugate or exploit the fiscal–military juggernaut that emerged, through the collision of conflicting forces, after 1688. They tried to do so by one of two, somewhat contradictory, processes: on the one hand, by circumscribing the state's power; on the other, by colonizing the state in order to gain control of its resources. Understanding the tension between these two aims lies at the heart of eighteenth-century British history.

NOTES

Introduction

1 Throughout this book I define the term 'state' as a territorially and jurisdictionally defined political entity in which public authority is distinguished from (though not unconnected to) private power, and which is manned by officials whose primary (though not sole) allegiance is to a set of political institutions under a single, i.e. sovereign and final, authority.

2 Michael Mann, 'The autonomous power of the state: its origins, mechanisms and results', in John A. Hall (ed.), *States in History* (Oxford, 1986), p. 114. Mann is also distinguishing between those powers over civil society which are rarely invoked but underpin the power of the state and those powers that are routinely exercized.

3 The transition from an English to a British state is discussed in Chapter 1.

I

Chapter 1: Before the Revolution

1 I owe this point to Lawrence Stone.

2 Alexis de Tocqueville, *Journeys to England and Ireland*, trans. George Lawrence and K. P. Meyer, (ed.) K. P. Meyer (New York, 1968), p. 75

3 For summaries of these developments see Joseph R. Strayer, *On the Mediaeval Origins of the Modern State* (Princeton, 1970), pp. 35–49; Keith Thomas, 'Great Britain', in Raymond Grew (ed.), *Crises and Political Development* (Princeton, 1978), pp. 47–8.

4 Bryce Lyon and Adrian Verhulst, *Mediaeval Finance: A Comparison of North-western Europe* (Brugge, 1967), p. 81; G. L. Harriss, *King, Parliament and Finance in Mediaeval England to 1369* (Oxford, 1975), ch. 1.

5 A. R. Myers, 'The English Parliament and French Estates General in the Middle Ages', *Studies Presented to the International Commission for the History of Representative and Parliamentary Institutions*, vol. 24 (1961), p. 143.

6 A point made with characteristic force by G. O. Sayles in *The King's Parliament in England* (London, 1975), ch. 7.

7 Strayer, *Mediaeval Origins*, p. 53.

8 For the problems associated with the idea of a military revolution and a good summary of the literature see Geoffrey Parker, 'The "Military Revolution", 1560–1660 – a Myth?', *Journal of Modern History*, vol. 48 (1976), pp. 195–214.

9 Figures *ibid.*, p. 206; Geoffrey Parker, 'Warfare', *New Cambridge Modern History* (Cambridge, 1979), vol. 13, p. 205.

10 See Lawrence Stone, *The Crisis of the Aristocracy, 1558–1641* (Oxford, 1965), ch. v 'Power', for these developments.

11 *Ibid.*, p. 266.

12 Sir Lewis Namier, *England in the Age of the American Revolution*, 2nd edn. (London, 1961), p. 7.

13 A point made with some force by Perry Anderson in *Lineages of the Absolutist State* (London, 1979), pp. 117–18.

14 My thinking on these matters has been much influenced by the comments and criticisms of Daniel Baugh. His views on this subject are to be found in an unpublished paper delivered at the Davis Center for Historical Studies at Princeton University and will be fully developed in his forthcoming book.

15 Kenneth Andrews, *Elizabethan Privateering: English Privateering during the Spanish War 1585–1603* (Cambridge, 1964), pp. 5, 10.

16 Kenneth Andrews, *Trade, Plunder and Settlement: Maritime Enterprise and the Genesis of the British Empire, 1480–1630* (Cambridge, 1984), pp. 358–63.

17 Paul Kennedy, *The Rise and Fall of British Naval Mastery* (London, 1976), pp. 53, 66.

18 Michael Duffy, 'The foundations of British naval power', in *The Military Revolution and the State, 1500–1800*, (ed.) Michael Duffy (Exeter Studies in History, no. 1, Exeter, 1980), pp. 52–3.

19 Wallace MacCaffrey, 'Place and patronage in Elizabethan politics', *Elizabethan Government and Society. Essays Presented to Sir John Neale*, ed. S. T. Bindoff, J. Hurstfield and C. H. Williams (London, 1961), p. 108; Penry Williams, *The Tudor Regime* (Oxford, 1979), p. 107; Gerald Aylmer, *The King's Servants: The Civil Service of Charles I, 1625–1642* (London, 1961), p. 440.

20 For a general assessment of this phenomenon see K. W. Swart, *The Sale of Offices in the Seventeenth Century* (The Hague, 1949).

21 *Ibid.*, pp. 8–13; Raymond Mousnier, *The Institutions of the Ancien Regime* (Chicago, 1984), vol. 2, p. 230.

22 Roland Mousnier, *La Venalité des offices sous Henry IV and Louis XIII* (Rouen, 1946), pp. 391–4; Richard Bonney, *The King's Debts: Finance and Politics in France, 1589–1661* (Oxford, 1981), p. 313.

23 Mousnier, *Venalité des offices*, p. 393.

24 *Ibid.*, p. 397–8.

25 Penry Williams, *The Tudor Regime*, p. 91.

26 *Ibid.*, pp. 85–107; Joel Hurstfield, *Freedom, Corruption and Government in Elizabethan England* (London, 1973), pp. 312–18.

27 W. Holdsworth, *History of the English Law* (17 vols., London, 1956–72), vol. 1, p. 260.

28 Stone, *Crisis of the Aristocracy*, pp. 70–127.

29 Hurstfield, *Freedom, Corruption and Government*, p. 312.

30 S. Scott, *History of Joint Stock Companies* (3 vols., Cambridge, 1910–12), vol. 1, pp. 222–3.

31 Gerald Aylmer, *The King's Servants*, pp. 239–40.

32 Stone, *Crisis of the Aristocracy*, p. 127.

33 Aylmer, *The King's Servants*, p. 246.

34 *Ibid.*, p. 249.

35 For this scheme see Stone, *Crisis of the Aristocracy*, pp. 117–18; Aylmer, *The King's Servants*, pp. 234–5.

36 Aylmer, *The King's Servants*, p. 230.

37 This seems to be Stone's view in *Crisis of the Aristocracy*, p. 119.

38 Swart, *The Sale of Offices*, p. 116.

39 John Elliott, *Richelieu and Olivares* (Cambridge, 1984), p. 85.

40 Conrad Russell, 'Monarchies, wars and estates in England, France and Spain *c.* 1580–1640', *Legislative Studies Quarterly*, vol. 7, no. 2 (1982), p. 215.

41 J. U. Nef, *Industry and Government in France and England 1540–1640* (American Philosophical Society, Philadelphia, 1940), pp. 126–9.

42 Stone, *Crisis of the Aristocracy*, p. 503

43 C. G. A. Clay, *Economic Expansion and Social Change: England 1500–1700* (2 vols., Cambridge, 1984), vol. 2, p. 253.

44 John, Earl of Stair, *State of the Public Debts*, (6th edn., London, n.d.), p. 28.

45 For a sober assessment of the economic costs of the Dutch War of Liberation (1568–1648) for all the combatants see Geoffrey Parker, 'War and Economic Change: The Economic Costs of the Dutch Revolt', in J. Winter (ed.), *War and Economic Development: Essays in Memory of David Joslin* (Cambridge, 1975), pp. 49–71.

46 Richard Bonney, *The King's Debts*, p. 281n.

47 Edmund Burke, *Speeches* (4 vols., London, 1816), vol. 2, p. 6.

48 Richard Chandler, *The History and Proceedings of the House of Commons* (14 vols., 1742–4), vol. 9, p. 44.

II

Introduction

1 See Howard Tomlinson, 'The Ordnance Office and the King's forts, 1660–1714', *Architectural History*, vol. 16 (1973), pp. 5–25 for surveys in the late seventeenth century revealing the dreadful state of English defences, forts and garrisons.

Chapter 2: Patterns of Military Effort

1 Alan J. Guy, *Oeconomy and Discipline: Officership and Administration in the British Army, 1714–63* (Manchester, 1985), p. 10.

2 These figures are from *British Parliamentary Papers*, vol. 35 (1868–9), pp. 697–700. They differ slightly from those based on Postlethwayt and used by Peter Dickson in *Finance and Government under Maria Theresia, 1740–1780* (2 vols., Oxford, 1987), vol. 2, pp. 158–60.

3 J. R. Western, *The English Militia in the Eighteenth Century: The Story of a Political Issue, 1660–1802* (London, 1965), *passim*.

4 Edward Gibbon, *Memoirs of My Life*, ed. Georges A. Bernard (London, 1960), p. 117.

5 See ch. 6 below.

6 Sidney Pollard, 'Fixed capital in the Industrial Revolution in Britain', *Journal of Economic History*, vol. 24, no. 3 (1964), p. 301.

7 Peter Mathias, 'Capital, credit and enterprise in the Industrial Revolution', *The Transformation of England* (London, 1979), p. 96.

8 John Ehrman, *The Navy in the War of William III* (Cambridge, 1953), p. 36.

9 Michael Duffy (ed.), 'The Foundations of British naval power', *The Military Revolution and the State, 1500–1800* (Exeter Studies in History, no. 1, Exeter, 1980), p. 62.

10 Daniel Baugh, *British Naval Administration in the Age of Walpole* (Princeton, 1965), p. 246.

11 National income figures taken from Peter Mathias, 'Taxation and industrialisation in England, 1700–1870', *The Transformation of England*, p. 118.

12 D. T. Jenkins, *The West Riding Wool Textile Industry 1770–1835: A Study in Fixed Capital Formation* (Edington, Wilts, 1975), p. 151.

13 Jacob M. Price, *Capital and Credit in British Overseas Trade: The View from the Chesapeake, 1700–1776* (Cambridge, Mass., 1980), pp. 25, 27, 29, 39.

14 Phillip MacDougall, *Royal Dockyards* (Newton Abbot, 1982), p. 66

15 *Ibid.*, p. 95.

16 Duffy, 'Foundations of British naval power', p. 58.

17 *Ibid.*, p. 59.

18 Cf. John Ehrman's and Donald Coleman's remarks about the late seventeenth century: 'the navy in 1688 was the most comprehensive and in some respects the largest industry in the country' and 'posed a need for large scale establishments and heavy capital expenditure such as was demanded by few forms of private enterprise in that age' (Ehrman, *The Navy in the War of William III*, p. 174; Donald Coleman, 'Naval dockyards under the Later Stuarts', *Ec.H.R.*, 2nd series, vol. 6 (1953), p. 139).

19 Martin van Crefeld, *Supplying War: Logistics from Wallerstein to Patton* (Cambridge, 1977), p. 37.

20 *Ibid.*, pp. 5, 31–2.

21 I am grateful to my colleague David Sacks for this analogy.

22 Baugh, *British Naval Administration*, p. 386.

23 N. A. M. Rodger, *The Wooden World: An Anatomy of the Georgian Navy* (London, 1986), p. 86.

24 BL Portland Loan 29/292.

25 Rodger, *Wooden World*, p. 84. I have converted cwt to lb on the assumption that most readers will be more familiar with the latter measure.

26 Cf. for a later period A. H. John, 'Farming in wartime: 1793–1815', in E. L. Jones and G. E. Mingay (eds.), *Land, Labour and Capital* (London, 1967), p. 28 for the effect of government food purchases in 1813. I owe this reference to Peter Dickson.

27 The price index is from Schumpeter, 'English prices and public finance, 1660–1822', *Review of Economic Statistics*, vol. 20 (1938), pp. 21–35. When we allow for inflation we can see that the Seven Years War was the most expensive of the conflicts we are considering.

28 E. A. Wrigley and R. S. Schofield, *The Population History of England, 1541–1871* (Cambridge, 1981), table A.3.1.

29 André Corvisier, *Armies and Societies in Europe, 1494–1789*, trans. Abigail T. Siddall (Bloomington, Indiana, 1979), p. 112; John Childs, *Armies and Warfare in Europe 1648–1789* (Manchester, 1982), p. 180.

30 Dickson, *Finance and Government under Maria Theresia*, vol. 1, p. 136.

31 For examples of such lists see Corvisier, *Armies and Societies*, p. 113; Childs, *Armies and Warfare*, p. 42; Geoffrey Parker, 'Warfare', *New Cambridge Modern History* (Cambridge, 1979), vol. 13, p. 205.

32 Corvisier, *Armies and Societies*, p. 114.

33 Childs, *Armies and Warfare*, pp. 47–8.

34 *Ibid.*, pp. 51–2.

35 Corvisier, *Armies and Societies*, p. 113

36 This and the following figures were drawn up by Robert Harley, then Chancellor of the Exchequer. (BL Portland Loan 29/45SF/44/218.)

37 Corvisier, *Armies and Societies*, p. 82.

38 *Ibid.*, p. 197.

39 Manfred Schlenke, *England und der Friderizianische Preussen, 1740–1763* (Munich, 1963), pp. 270–3.

40 Campbell Dalrymple, *A Military Essay* (London, 1761), p. 154.

41 For a useful summary of army structure and organization see Guy, *Oeconomy and Discipline*, pp. 19–32.

42 J. M. Hayes, 'The social and professional background of British army officers, 1714–63' (unpublished M.A. thesis, University of London, 1956), p. 70.

43 But see pp. 57-8.

44 Quoted in Sir Lewis Namier and John Brooke, *The History of Parliament: The House of Commons 1754–1790* (3 vols., HMSO, 1964), vol. III, p. 182.

45 Hayes, 'British army officers', p. 71.

46 Guy, *Oeconomy and Discipline*, p. 22.

47 Rupert C. Jarvis, 'The public monies', in *Collected Jacobite Papers* (2 vols., Manchester, 1971–2), vol. 1, pp. 175–97.

48 For the material on which this paragraph is based see Childs, *Armies and Warfare*, pp. 150–72.

49 Tony Hayter, *The Army and the Crowd in Eighteenth-Century England* (London, 1978), p. 94; J. A. Houlding, *Fit for Service: The Training of the British Army, 1715–1795* (Oxford, 1981), pp. 9–11.

50 *The Military Guide for Young Officers by Thomas Simes Esq.* (London, 1772), p. 382.

51 Except briefly between 1717 and 1721. See Charles M. Clode, *The Administration of Justice under Military and Martial Law* (London, 1872), pp. 53–4.

52 Charles M. Clode, *The Military Forces of the Crown: Their Administration and Government* (2 vols., London, 1869), vol. 2, p. 167–8.

53 Quoted *ibid.*, vol. 2, p. 223.

54 Quoted in Houlding, *Fit for Service*, p. 39n.

55 Jarvis, 'Transport', *Collected Jacobite Papers*, vol. 1, pp. 48–74.

56 Clode, *Forces of the Crown*, vol. 1, p. 232.

57 *Ibid.*, vol. 2, p. 5.

58 The exception was in the years 1697–1735 (Clode, *Forces of the Crown*, vol. 2, p. 7).

59 *An Extract of J. Nelson's Journal, being an Account of God's Dealing with his soul, from his youth to the forty second year of his age* (Newcastle, 1770), pp. 80 ff.

60 For material for this paragraph see Arthur N. Gilbert, 'Army impressment during the War of Spanish Succession', *Historian*, vol. 38, no. 4 (1976), pp. 689–708; Clode, *Forces of the Crown*, vol. 2, pp.

61 *Boswell's Life of Johnson*, (ed.) G. B. Hill and revised by L. F. Powell (6 vols., Oxford, 1934–50), vol. 2, p. 438.

62 Rodger, *Wooden World*, pp. 153–5.

63 A. N. Newman (ed.), 'Parliamentary diary of Sir Edward Knatchbull', *Camden Society*, 3rd series, vol. 94 (1963), p. 31.

64 *HMC Egmont Diary*, vol. 1, p. 11.

65 Richard Chandler, *The History and Proceedings of the House of Commons* (14 vols., 1742–4) vol. 9, p. 241.

66 Houlding, *Fit for Service*, pp. 82–4.

67 *Ibid.*, p. 82.

68 E.g. PRO Customs 48/12 f.156; 48/15 f.47; 48/18 ff. 181–2.

69 Hayter, *The Army and the Crowd*, pp. 155, 158; Houlding, *Fit for Service*, pp. 67–70, 73.

70 Hayter, *The Army and the Crowd*, p. 176.

71 Not all of these were killed by troops. Some died in the buildings that were burnt and destroyed.

72 Quoted in E. P. Thompson, 'The moral economy of the English crowd', *Past and Present*, vol. 50 (1971), p. 121.

73 Houlding, *Fit for Service*, p. 74.

74 *Ibid.*, p. 34.

75 Nicholas Rogers, 'Jacobite riots in early Hanoverian England', in Eveline Cruickshanks (ed.), *Ideology and Conspiracy: Aspects of Jacobitism, 1689–1759* (Edinburgh, 1982), pp. 70–88.

76 This was much more the predominant concern from the end of the Seven Years War.

77 This is especially clear from the published trials of smugglers. See, for example, *The Trials of the Smugglers and other prisoners at the assizes held at East Grinstead, March, 1748–9* (London, 1749), pp. 3–4; *The whole proceedings on the Special Commission . . . for the County of Sussex* (London, 1749), p. 14.

78 Cal Winslow, 'Sussex smugglers', in Douglas Hay, Peter Linebaugh and Edward Thompson (eds.), *Albion's Fatal Tree* (London, 1975), pp. 119–66; Collier Papers, Customs and Excise Library, Kings Beam House, no foliation.

79 See note 75 and Nicholas Rogers, 'Popular protest in early Hanoverian London', *Past and Present*, vol. 89 (1978), pp. 70–100; Eveline Cruickshanks and Howard Erskine Hill, 'The Waltham Black Act and Jacobitism', *Journal of British Studies*, vol. 24, no. 3 (1985), pp. 358–65.

80 *Parliamentary History*, vol. 9, p. 1311.

81 BL Add. Mss 35876 f. 381.

82 Personal communication, Daniel Baugh.

83 Hayes, 'Army Officers', pp. 99–100.

84 *Taxes Not Grievous and therefore not a Reason for an Unsafe Peace* (London, 1712), p. 15.

85 Hayes, 'Army Officers', Appendix 1; Houlding, *Fit for Service*, pp. 109–10, 115–16.

86 Hayes, 'Army Officers', pp. 81–2, 98.

87 André Corvisier, *Armies and Societies*, pp. 106–9; William Doyle, *The Old European Order 1660–1800* (Oxford, 1978), pp. 244, 247.

88 Childs, *Armies and Warfare*, pp. 92–8; Houlding, *Fit for Service*, pp. 115–16.

89 Guy, *Oeconomy and Discipline*, p. 1.

90 *Ibid.*, p. 165.

91 *Ibid.*, p. 163.

92 Baugh, *British Naval Administration*, pp. 93–102; Daniel Baugh, 'Naval administration 1715–1750', *Publications of the Naval Records Society*, vol. 120 (1977), pp. 35–6.

93 Michael Lewis, *A Social History of the British Navy, 1792–1815* (London, 1960), p. 36.

94 In using the term 'blue water' policy I follow the definition offered by Daniel Baugh:

blue water warfare was a form of technically advanced warfare emphasizing economic pressure. The military weight of the Continental powers was to be opposed by naval skills, superiority of equipment, and abundance of money and resources, as well as access to resources. All of these were chiefly derived from domestic industry and seaborne commerce. (Daniel Baugh, 'British Stategy during the First World War in the context of four centuries: blue water versus continental commitment', in Daniel M. Masterson (ed.), *Naval History: The Sixth Symposium of the US Naval Academy* (Wilmington, Delaware, 1987), pp. 87–8)

As Baugh emphasizes, this strategy does not preclude the use of alliances and subsidies to fight in Europe. But it does assume that European hostilities will primarily be conducted by the troops of allies rather than by the British army.

95 For this incident and the extreme resentment it provoked among the British officer corps see Richmond's letters to Newcastle, 24 June/5 May, 29 June/10 July 1743 printed in Timothy J. McCann (ed.), 'The correspondence of the Dukes of Richmond and Newcastle 1724–1750', *Sussex Record Society*, vol. 73 (1982–3), pp. 101–4.

96 Robert D. Horn, *Marlborough: A Survey of Panegyrics, Satires, and Biographical Writings, 1688–1788* (New York, 1975), *passim;* David Foxon lists over 200 verses on the subject of the Duke of Marlborough, as well as 68 on naval affairs and 75 on the Treaty of Utrecht (David Foxon, *English Verse, 1701–1750* (2 vols., Cambridge, 1975), *passim*).

97 Corvisier, *Armies and Societies*, p. 92.

98 Hubert C. Johnson, *Frederick the Great and His Officials* (New Haven, 1975), p. 57.

99 Gordon Craig, *The Politics of the Prussian Army, 1640–1945* (Oxford, 1955), pp. 9–10.

100 Johnson, *Frederick the Great*, pp. 256–7.

101 *Ibid.*, p. 274.

102 Corvisier, *Armies and Societies*, p. 82.

103 Alexis de Tocqueville, *On the State of Society in France before the Revolution of 1789*, trans. Henry Reeve (2nd edn, London, 1873), p. 121.

104 See, for example, the interesting correspondence between Henry Pelham and the Duke of Newcastle about a Yorkshire turnpike riot of 1753 cited by E. P. Thompson in 'Patrician society, plebeian culture', *Journal of Social History*, vol. 7, no. 4 (1974), p. 405:

> This affair seems to me of such consequence that I am persuaded nothing can entirely get the better of it but the first persons of the county taking an active part in defence of the laws; for if these people [the rioters] see themselves only overpowered by troops, and not convinced that their behaviour is repugnant to the sense of the first people of this county, when the troops are gone, hostilitys will return.

Chapter 3: Civil Administration

1 John Lord Sheffield, *Observations on the Commerce of the American States* (London, 1784), p. 238. Cf. *Considerations upon the Reduction of the Land Tax* (London, 1749), p. 64.

2 Gerald Aylmer, *The State's Servants* (London, 1961), p. 169.

3 J. R. Western, *Monarchy and Revolution: The English State in the 1680's* (London, 1972), esp. ch. 4.

4 Geoffrey Holmes, *Augustan England: Professions, State and Society, 1680–1730* (London, 1982), esp. chs. 8, 9; J. H. Plumb, *The Growth of Political Stability, 1675–1725* (London, 1967), pp. 11–14, 98–128.

5 Holmes, *Augustan England*, pp. 244, 255.

6 Peter Mathias, 'The social structure in the eighteenth century: a calculation by Joseph Massie', *Ec.H.R.*, 2nd ser., vol. 10 (1957–8), pp. 42–3.

7 John Beattie, *The English Court in the Reign of George I* (Cambridge, 1967), pp. 18–19.

8 For the sources for this data see foot of Table 3.2.

9 I am aware that this figure is considerably smaller than that of 14,000 given by John Binney and cited by Peter Dickson (Peter Dickson, *The Financial Revolution in England* (London, 1967), p. 217). This discrepancy may, in part, be explained by the fact that my figures are confined to the English revenue boards and by my exclusion of part-time revenue employees. I am, however, sceptical about Binney's figure.

10 Quoted in John W. Wilkes, *A Whig in Power: The Political Career of Henry Pelham* (Northwestern University Press, 1964), p. 105.

11 E. E. Hoon, *The Organization of the English Customs System, 1696–1786* (New York, 1958), pp. 164–5.

12 Customs 48/17 f. 191.

13 For a female example see the case of Charlotte Forman BL Add. Mss. 30869 f. 165; 30870 ff. 51, 68, 82, 99, 117, 179, 216, 238, 241.

14 'Report on the state of the excise office', PRO Customs 48/16 ff. 435–8.

15 PRO T44/15.

16 Gerald Aylmer, 'From office-holding to Civil Service: the genesis of modern bureaucracy', *Transactions of the Royal Historical Society*, 5th series, vol. 30 (1980), p. 96.

17 Quoted in W. R. Ward, 'Some eighteenth-century civil servants: the English revenue commissioners, 1749–98', *EHR* vol. 70 (1955), p. 50. Cf. p. 42.

18 Forty-three of 165 offices to be exact (*Sixth Report from the Select Committee on Finance: The Stamp Office* (1797), Appendix K).

19 Aylmer, 'Office-holding to Civil Service', p. 106.

20 Hoon, *Customs*, p. 131.

21 John Norris, *Shelburne and Reform* (London, 1963), p. 213.

22 *Sixth Report of the Commissioners for Examining, Taking and Stating the Public Accounts* (London, 1782), Appendix 36.

23 J. C. Sainty, 'The tenure of Offices in the Exchequer', *EHR* vol. 316 (1965), p. 470. For contemporary comment on this see Cambridge University Library, Add. Mss 6851 ff. 89–90.

24 Anon to Robert Harley, n.d., BL Portland Loan 29/283.

25 J. C. Sainty, *Treasury Officials 1660–1870* (Athlone Press, 1972), p. 7.

26 W. J. Smith (ed.), *The Grenville Papers* (4 vols., London, 1852–3), II, pp. 113–14.

27 John Cary, *An Essay on the State of England* (Bristol, 1695), p. 176.

28 John Beckett, 'Local custom and the "new taxation" in the seventeenth and eighteenth centuries: the example of Cumberland', *Northern History*, vol. 12 (1976), p. 107.

29 Norris, *Shelburne and Reform*, p. 195.

30 The twelve are: Treasury, Secretaries of State, lower Exchequer, Customs, Excise, Stamps, Post Office, Admiralty, Navy, Dockyards, Victualling and Paymaster of the Forces. Figures calculated from *Sixth Report of the Commissioners for Examining, Taking and Stating the Public Accounts, passim; Reports of the Commissioners for Enquiring into Fees in the Public Offices* (10 reports, 1786–88), published in *Parliamentary Papers*, vol. 7 (1806).

31 Calculated from Michel Morineau, 'Budgets d'état', *Revue Historique*, vol. 536 (1980), pp. 314–15.

32 See the balanced discussion of Pepys's views on such matters in Robert Latham and William Matthews (eds.), *The Diary of Samuel Pepys* (11 vols., London, 1970–83), vol. 1, p. ccxxiv.

33 See, for example, the letters from the Foley family about excise appointments even at a time when they were seeking the tax's abolition (BL Portland Loan 29/136).

34 BL Portland Loan 29/286 no. 65. These figures are incorrectly bound in a volume of customs material.

35 Holmes, *Augustan England*, pp. 242–3.

36 Calculated from Customs 47/77–85.

37 PRO Customs 47/83 ff. 110–12; Customs 47/84 f. 96.

38 PRO Customs 47/81 f. 22.

39 Hughes, *Studies in Administration and Finance*, pp. 275–6.

40 BL Add. Mss 38335 f. 47; cf. *ibid.*, ff. 51, 56.

41 *Ibid.*, f. 51; Louis Namier, *England in the Age of the American Revolution* (2nd edn, London, 1963), pp. 408–9, 411.

42 Hughes, *Studies in Administration and Finance*, pp. 273, 275–6.

43 'Fifth Report . . . on Fees, Gratuities, etc.', *Parliamentary Papers*, vol. 7 (1806), p. 184, Appendices 14–16, 18–20, 22–7.

44 Cambridge University Library, Cholmondley (Houghton) Mss 42/77; *Gentleman's Magazine*, vol. 24 (1754), p. 48.

45 'Third Report . . . on Fees, Gratuities, etc.', *Parliamentary Papers*, vol. 7 (1806), pp. 108, 111–12; 'Fifth Report . . . on Fees, Gratuities, etc.', vol. 7, pp. 209, 218, 220.

46 Holmes, *Augustan England*, pp. 249–251, 259–60.

47 Ryley to Lord Oxford, 13 November [1713], BL Portland Loan 29/283.

48 *Journals of the House of Commons*, vol. 43 (1787–8), pp. 562, 600.

49 Holmes, *Augustan England*, p. 260; R. E. C. Waters, *Genealogical Memoirs of the Extinct Family of Chichester of Chicheley* (2 vols., London, 1878), vol. 1, pp. 173–81.

50 Betty Kemp, *King and Commons, 1660–1832* (London, 1968), pp. 54–66; Geoffrey Holmes, 'The attack on the influence of the Crown, 1702–1716', *BIHR*, vol. 39 (1966), pp. 47–68.

51 Kemp, *King and Commons*, p. 95.

52 Charles Davenant, 'Discourses on the Public Revenues, and on the Trade of England, in Two Parts [1698]', *The Political and Commercial Works of that Celebrated Writer, Charles Davenant . . . collected and revised by Sir Charles Whitworth* (5 vols., London, 1771), vol. 1, p. 181.

53 Holmes, *Augustan England*, p. 256.

54 Hughes, *Studies in Administration and Finance*, p. 218; PRO Customs 48/16 ff. 301–2 for a counting house clerk receiving 16 shillings a week. But South Sea Company clerks – probably men at the top of the clerical ladder – were paid £40–£80 per annum, senior clerks received £100 or more. (Private communication from Peter Dickson.)

55 Holmes, *Augustan England*, p. 251.

56 Colin Brooks, 'Public finance and political stability: the administration of the land tax, 1688–1720', *Historical Journal*, vol. 17, no. (1974), p. 299.

57 E.g. Customs 48/15 ff. 242–3; *Calendar of Treasury Books* vol. 22, p. 211; Customs 47/272 f. 24; 47/274 f. 12.

58 J. C. Sainty, *Officeholders in Modern Britain*: vol. 1, *Treasury Officials, 1660–1900* (London, 1972), p. 6.

59 *Officeholders in Modern Britain: vol. 7, Navy Board Officials, 1660–1832*, compiled by J. M. Collinge (University of London, Institute of Historical Research, 1978), p. 8.

60 Collinge, *Navy Board Officials*, p. 92; *Officeholders in Modern Britain: vol. 4, Admiralty Officials, 1660–1870*, compiled by J. C. Sainty (London, 1975), p. 116.

61 Sir Lewis Namier and John Brooke, *The History of Parliament: The House of Commons 1754–1790* (3 vols., HMSO, 1964), vol. 2, pp. 220–2.

62 *First Report of the Commissioners on Public Accounts* (November, 1780), p. 21.

63 Calculated from Collinge, *Navy Board Officials*, passim.

64 Holmes, *Augustan England*, p. 250.

65 *Ibid.*, p. 249.

66 Thomas Hall, for example, served as an excise commissioner between 1691 and 1694, and with the Customs in Queen Anne's reign. Henry Ashurst and Edward Clarke served both as excise and hackney coach commissioners, while four of the first salt tax commissioners had earlier served in the Excise. Information on commissioners is derived from the lists in Robert Beatson, *A Political Index to the Histories of Great Britain & Ireland*, 3rd edn (3 vols., London, 1806), vol. 2, pp. 363–86.

67 Gertrude Ann Jacobsen, *William Blathwayt. A late seventeenth-century English Administrator* (New Haven, 1932), p. 403; John Ehrman, *The Navy in the War of William III* (Cambridge, 1953), pp. 284–5.

68 Holmes, 'Gregory King and the social structure of pre-industrial England', *Transactions of the Royal Historical Society*, 5th series, vol. 27 (1977), pp. 58–62.

69 Customs 47/24 ff. 12–13.

70 Ehrman, *The Navy in the War of William III*, pp. 556–7.

71 G. F. James, 'The Admiralty Establishment of 1759', *BIHR*, vol. 16 (1938–9), p. 27.

72 Jacobsen, *William Blathwayt*, p. 420.

73 R. D. Merriman, 'The Sergison Papers', *Naval Records Society*, vol. 89 (1949), p. 3.

74 Quoted in John L. Bullion, *A Great and Necessary Measure: George Grenville and the Genesis of the Stamp Act, 1763–1765* (Columbia, Mo., 1982), p. 59.

75 PRO Customs 48/11 ff. 330–1. For a similar hostility to technical innovation in salt production see Hughes, *Studies in Administration and Finance*, pp. 429–31.

76 Hughes, *Studies in Administration and Finance*, p. 209.

77 As far as I can see Henry Pelham was more successful than any other minister before the younger Pitt in reducing the size of the fiscal bureaucracy and in reducing the national debt. His importance does not, however, seem to have been recognized, no doubt in part because he never left a cache of papers comparable to those which survive Harley, Walpole, Newcastle and the younger Pitt.

78 See, for example, Add. Mss38344 ff. 140, 213–16, 223–4; Bullion, *A Great and Necessary Measure*, p. 39.

79 *Parliamentary Register*, vol. 17 (1780), p. 133.

80 L. Cross, *Eighteenth-Century Documents Relating to the Royal Forests, the Sheriffs and Smuggling* (New York, 1928), p. 293.

81 Norris, *Shelburne and Reform*, p. 213,; John Ehrman, *The Younger Pitt: The Years of Acclaim* (London, 1969), pp. 314–16.

82 This was not always true. Sometimes departments were allowed to take on additional clerks at especially busy times.

83 Ehrman, *The Younger Pitt*, p. 290.

Chapter 4: Money, Money, Money

1 P. G. M. Dickson, *The Financial Revolution in England: A Study of the Development of Public Credit, 1688–1756* (London, 1967), p. 10.

2 For the political context that surrounded this problem see ch. 5.

3 *The Political and Commercial Works of that Celebrated Writer, Charles Davenant ... collected and revised by Sir Charles Whitworth* (5 vols., London, 1771), vol. 1, p. 156.

4 G. M. Dickson and John Sperling, 'War finance, 1689–1714', *The New Cambridge Modern History*: vol. 6, *The Rise of Great Britain and Russia, 1688–1715/25*, ed. J. S. Bromley (Cambridge, 1971), p. 313.

5 Peter Dickson and John Sperling, 'Finance', *New Cambridge Modern History*, vol. 6, p. 285.

6 Michel Morineau, 'Les budgets d'état et gestion des finances royales en France aux dix-huitième siècle', *Revue Historique*, vol. 536 (1980), p. 320.

7 Peter Mathias, 'Taxation and industrialisation in Britain, 1700–1870', *The Transformation of England* (London, 1979), table 6.1; Patrick O'Brien, 'The political economy of British taxation, 1660–1815', unpublished paper to appear in *Ec. H.R.*, Table 2. I am grateful to Patrick O'Brien for showing me this paper prior to its publication.

8 Peter Mathias and Patrick O'Brien, 'Taxation in England and France, 1715–1810. A comparison of the social and economic incidence of taxes collected for the central governments', *Journal of European Economic History*, vol. 5 (1976), table 6.

9 *Ibid.*, Table 4.

10 Richard Chandler, *The History and Proceedings of the House of Commons* (14 vols. 1742–4), vol. 7, p. 313.

11 See Henry Roseveare, *The Treasury, 1660–1870: The Foundations of Control* (London, 1973), p. 262; S. B. Baxter, *The Development of the Treasury, 1660–1702* (London, 1957), p. 262.

12 There is a useful summary of these and other developments in Howard Tomlinson, 'Financial and administrative developments in England, 1660–1688', *The Restored Monarchy, 1660–1688*, ed. J. R. Jones (London, 1979), pp. 95–105.

13 For farming in this period see Christopher Clay, *Public Finance and Private Wealth: The Career of Sir Stephen Fox, 1627–1716* (Oxford, 1978), esp. pp. 41–2, 94; E. Hughes, *Studies in Administration and Finance, 1558–1825*, (Manchester, 1934) pp. 126–7; C. D. Chandaman, *The English Public Revenue, 1660–1688* (Oxford, 1975), esp. p. 70.

14 For a useful summary of the arguments in favour of farming see Charles P. Kindleberger, *A Financial History of Europe* (London, 1984), p. 161.

15 Davenant, *Works*, vol. 1, pp. 210–11.

16 Chandaman, *The English Public Revenue*, p. 254.

17 Hughes, *Studies in Administration and Finance*, pp. 159–60; Chandaman, *The English Public Revenue*, pp. 34–5, 74, 251; Baxter, *Development of the Treasury*, pp. 91–3.

18 Introduction of 'the method' and its associated reforms can be followed in BL Harleian Mss 4077, 5120.

19 Cf. Chandaman, The *English Public Revenue*, pp. 275–6.

20 *Ibid.*, pp. 142–3, 195: John Beckett, 'Land tax or excise: the levying of taxation in seventeenth and eighteenth century England', *EHR*, vol. 100 (1985), pp. 285–7.

21 O'Brien, 'British taxation', pp. 10–12.

22 For the economic implications of this see pp. 201–3.

23 For land tax administration see Colin Brooks, 'Public finance and political stability: the administration of the land tax, 1688–1720', *Historical Journal*, vol. 17, no. 2 (1974), pp. 281–300.

24 HMC *15.VI Carlisle Mss*, p. 103. The opposition conceded the point. See the remarks of Sir John Barnard in Chandler, *Debates*, vol. 7, p. 336.

25 John Owens, *Plain Papers relating to the Excise Branch of the Inland Revenue Department from 1821 to 1878: A History of the Excise* (Linlithgow, 1879), pp. 9–10; *Fifth Report from the Select Committee on Public Finance* (1797), p. 4; John Torrance, 'Social class and bureaucratic innovation, 1780–1787', *Past and Present*, vol. 78 (1978), pp. 58–64.

26 'Memoirs of the birth, education, life and death of Mr John Cannon', Somerset RO DD/SAS C/1193 4, ff. 59–65.

27 Thomas Clio Rickman, *Life of Thomas Paine* (London, 1819), p. 36.

28 W. Hersee, *The Spirit of the General Letters and Orders Issued by the Honourable Board of Excise from 1700 to 1827* (London, 1829), p. 136.

29 BL Harleian Mss 5120 ff. 47v-48, 55.

30 Charles Leadbetter, *The Royal Gauger; or Gauging made perfectly easy*, 7th edn (London, 1776), pp. 241–2; Owens, *Plain Papers*, pp. 252–7. For complaints about the number of books officers had to carry see Cambridge University Library, Cholmondley (H) Mss P27/32.

31 Diary of George Cowperthwaite, BL Lansdowne Mss 910 *Passim*.

32 [Thomas Paine], *The Case of the Officers of Excise* ([London, 1772?]), p. 8.

33 Owens, *Plain Papers*, p. 214.

34 [R. E.], *Choice Chips of Revenue Lore, being papers relating to the establishment of the Excise, Excise Duties, Salaries, Superannuation &c from 1660 to 1876* (Portsmouth, 1877), p. 141; Hersee, *The Spirit of the General Letters*, pp. 434–5.

35 *Choice Chips*, pp. 17, 19.

36 PRO Customs 48/12 ff. 101, 187–8, 379.

37 For an earlier organized attempt to secure a salary increase see PRO Customs 47/21 f. 46.

38 Miscellaneous Papers, Customs and Excise Library, King's Beam House, no pagination.

39 PRO Customs 48 f. 47.

40 Hersee, *Spirit of the General Letters, passim*; Owens, *Plain Papers*, p. 293; *Instructions for the Gaugers of the Excise in the Country* (London, 1725), pp. 8–9, 13–14.

41 Hersee, *Spirit of the General Letters*, p. 218.

42 Cannon, 'Memoirs', ff. 84–5.

43 See, typically, Cowperthwaite's conduct BL Lansdowne Mss 910 f. 46.

44 Cannon, 'Memoirs', f. 58.

45 Hersee, *Spirit of the General Letters*, pp. 61–3.

46 Owens, *Plain Papers*, p. 125; 'Excise Establishment, 1763', BL Add. Mss 10404 ff. 3–4.

47 Chatham Papers PRO 30/8/290 f. 71.

48 BL Lansdowne Mss 910 ff. 109–10.

49 *Ibid.*, ff. 74, 87.

50 *Choice Chips*, p. 56.

51 *Ibid.*, p. 70.

52 *Calendar of Treasury Books*, vol. 24 (1698–9), p. 253.

53 *Choice Chips*, p. 62; PRO Customs 48/18 ff. 51–3, 147, 158–63, 246.

54 PRO Chatham Mss 30/8/290 f. 71.

55 BL Add Mss 29458 ff. 16–18; PRO Customs 48/12 ff. 62–3. In the 1760s, when the cider tax was in force, the numbers policed were even greater. They were given as 103,000 cider producers and 134,000 other premises (BL Add Mss 35879 ff. 348, 353).

56 For a fuller discussion see ch. 7.

57 K. H. Hawkins and C. L. Pass, *The Brewing Industry: A Study in Industrial Organization and Public Policy* (London, 1979), p. 82.

58 Ezekiel Polsted, *The Excise Man, showing the Excellency of his Profession* (London, 1697), p. 45.

59 Quoted in Peter Mathias, *The Brewing Industry in England, 1700–1800* (Cambridge, 1959), p. 35.

60 Richard Burn, *The Justice of the Peace and Parish Officer* 15th edn, (4 vols., London, 1785), vol. 2, pp. 22 *seq.*

61 PRO Chatham Mss. 30/8/290 f.65.

62 Dickson, *The Financial Revolution*, p. 10.

63 Morineau, 'Budgets de l'état'. p. 326.

64 E. L. Hargreaves, *The National Debt* (London, 1930), p. 65.

65 Peter Dickson, *The Financial Revolution*, pp. 64–75. Some of these funds were originally for short-term obligations which were subsequently made permanent.

66 This was not lost on government ministers when they wanted to defend a particular tax. George Grenville, in response to a powerful and well-organized lobby against the cider tax of 1763, pointed out that repeal was only possible if an alternative source of revenue could be found to fund the £3.5 million in annuities and lotteries underwritten by the cider tax. He professed himself willing to repeal the tax if a substitute was available, but he placed the onus of finding a surrogate tax firmly on the shoulders of the lobbyists. (See 'Harris Diary', History of Parliament transcripts.)

67 I am aware that short-term and unfunded, like long-term and funded, are not entirely interchangeable terms, but they are sufficiently close to make the general trend clear.

68 Dickson, *Financial Revolution*, p. 457

69 *Ibid.*, table 7, p. 80.

70 Charles Davenant, 'Discourses on the Public Revenues, and on the Trade of England, in Two Parts [1698]', *The Political and Commercial Works of that Celebrated Writer, Charles Davenant . . . Collected and revised by Sir Charles Whitworth* (5 vols., London, 1771), vol. 1, p. 172; Panshanger Mss, Herts RO D/EP F898 ff. 5–6.

71 Hargreaves, *The National Debt*, p. 53n.

72 Dickson, *Financial Revolution*, p. 210.

73 Hargreaves, *The National Debt*, p. 64.

74 Dickson, *Financial Revolution*, p. 87.

75 *Ibid.*, p. 214; Hargreaves, *The National Debt*, p. 52.

76 Dickson, *Financial Revolution*, p. 239.

77 Hargreaves, *The National Debt*, p. 65.

78 *Ibid.*, pp. 63–4.

79 Dickson, *Financial Revolution*, p. 139

80 *Ibid.*, p. 134.

81 *Ibid.*, p. 198.

82 *Ibid.*, p. 198.

83 Morineau, 'Budgets d'état', p. 314.

84 Johnson, *Frederick the Great and His Officials* (London, 1975), pp. 15–16, 287–8.

85 See Reinhold Koser, 'Die Preussischen Finanzen von 1763 bis 1786', *Forschlungen zur Brandenburgischen und Preussischen Geschichte* (1903), pp. 101–2. I owe this reference to Peter Dickson.

86 Marjolein 't Hart, 'State and bureaucracy in the Dutch republic', unpublished paper, May 1986, p. 4.

87 Earl Robisheaux, 'The "private army" of the tax farms: the men and their origins', *Histoire Sociale*, vol. 12 (1973), pp. 256, 263.

88 George T. Matthews, *The Royal General Farms in Eighteenth Century France* (New York, 1958), pp. 110, 207.

89 A. L. Cross, *Eighteenth-century Documents Relating to the Royal Forests, the Sheriffs and Smuggling* (New York, 1928), p. 266.

90 Paine, *The Case of the Officers of Excise*, p.6; PRO Customs 47/104 ff. 50–1.

91 Marjolein 't Hart, 'Taxation and the formation of the Dutch State in the seventeenth century', unpublished paper, Vlaams-Nederlanse Sociologendagen Historisch-Sociologisch Onderzoek, 4 April 1986, pp. 3–4.
92 John Bosher, 'French administration and public finance in their European setting', *New Cambridge Modern History* vol. 8, pp. 586–7.
93 C. B. A. Behrens, *Society, Government and Enlightenment: The Experiences of Eighteenth-Century France and Prussia* (New York, 1985), p. 80; Johnson, *Frederick the Great*, p. 41.
94 Roland Mousnier, *The Institutions of France under the Absolute Monarchy, 1598–1789*, trans. Arthur Goldhammer (2 vols., Chicago, 1979–80), vol. 2, p. 636.
95 J. Aalbers, 'Holland's financial problems (1713–1733) and the wars against Louis xiv', in A. C. Duke and C. A. Tamse (eds.), *Britain and the Netherlands* (The Hague, 1977), vol. 6, pp. 85–6.
96 *Ibid.*, pp. 88–9.
97 James C. Riley, *The Seven Years War and the Old Regime in France: The Financial and Economic Toll* (Princeton, 1986), p. 162.
98 *Ibid.*, pp. 55, 61.
99 Robert D. Harris, *Necker: Reform Statesman of the Ancien Regime* (Berkeley, 1979), esp. pp. 217–35.
100 James C. Riley, *International Government Finance and the Amsterdam Capital Market, 1740–1815* (Cambridge, 1980), pp. 72–3 and notes.
101 Harris, *Necker*, esp. pp. 56, 87–8, 96, 121.
102 B. L. Add. Mss 33001 f. 176.
103 For the origins of the Dutch system see James D. Tracy, *A Financial Revolution in the Habsburg Netherlands* Renten *and* Renteniers *in the County of Holland* (Berkeley, 1985), *passim.*
104 Riley, *International Finance*, pp. 174–5 and notes.
105 Riley, *The Seven Years War* p. 231.
106 Quoted in Harris, *Necker*, p. 121.
107 See John Bosher, *French Finances, 1770–1795: From Business to Bureaucracy* (Cambridge, 1970), esp. pp. 142–65.

III

Chapter 5: The Paradoxes of State Power
1 Charles Tilly (ed.), *The Formation of Nation States in Western Europe* (Princeton, 1975), p. 42.
2 These views have been put particularly trenchantly by Tom Ertman in an unpublished paper, 'War and statebuilding in early modern Europe' (Harvard University, 1987).
3 Edward Hughes, *Studies in Administration and Finance*, p. 164; Charles Davenant, 'Discourses on the Public Revenues, and on the Trade of England, in Two Parts [1698]', *The Political and Commercial Works of that Celebrated Writer, Charles Davenant . . . collected and revised by Sir Charles Whitworth* (5 vols., London, 1771), vol. 1, pp. 182–98; *Calendar of State Papers Domestic* (1694–5), p. 181; BL Add. Mss 33038 f. 58; *Calendar of Treasury Books (CTB)*, vol. 9, part 2 (1689–90), pp. 366, 369.
4 For these proposals, notably those that led to the offering of the excise for farming in 1700 see PRO T1/58 item 37; T1/69 item 15; T1/71 item 62; T48/88 ff. 235–8; BL Portland Loan 29/278, 29/283; *CTB*, vol. 15, pp. 76–8, 87, 91, 94; *Historical Manuscripts Commission: Le Fleming*, p. 354; James Lowther

to Sir John Lowther, 2, 19 March, 3, 20 April, 1, 4 June 1700, Cumbria RO Lonsdale Mss LW2/D 34.

5   Henry Horwitz, *Parliament, Policy and Politics in the Reign of William III* (Manchester, 1977) pp. 87–8.

6   G. C. Gibbs, 'The revolution in foreign policy', in Geoffrey Holmes (ed.), *Britain after the Glorious Revolution* (London, 1969), pp. 59–79.

7   These developments are best followed in Henry Horwitz, *Parliament, Policy and Politics*, pp. 222 ff.

8   *Ibid.*, p. 296.

9   *Parliamentary History*, vol. 5, p. 409.

10 *Commons Journals*, vol. 10, p. 104.

11 *Parliamentary History*, vol. 5, p. 567.

12 *Ibid.*, vol. 5, Appendix 6, p. liv; cf. *Taxes no Charge: In A Letter from a Gentleman to a Person of Quality* (London, 1690), A2v.

13 See the remarks of James Stanhope quoted by Geoffrey Holmes in his *British Politics in the Age of Anne*, revised edn (London, 1987), p. 123.

14 Anchitell Grey, *Debates of the House of Commons, from the year 1667 to the year 1694* (10 vols., London, 1769), vol. 4, p. 115.

15 *Ibid.*, vol. 9, p. 125.

16 *Parliamentary History*, vol. 5, pp. lviii–ix.

17 Grey, *Debates*, vol. 9, p. 36.

18 *Ibid.*, vol. 9, p. 30.

19 Davenant, 'Discourses on the Public Revenues', pp. 176–80.

20 Henry Horwitz (ed.), *The Parliamentary Diary of Narcissus Luttrell* (Oxford, 1972), p. 78; PRO Treasury 48/88 ff. 243–5, 'Some observations on the rise and fall of the revenue of Excise'.

21 Henry Horwitz, *Parliamentary, Policy and Politics*, pp. 86–8; Clayton Roberts, 'The constitutional significance of the financial settlement of 1690', *Historical Journal*, vol. 20, no. 1 (1977), pp. 59–76.

22 John Beckett, 'Land tax or excise: the levying of taxation in seventeenth- and eighteenth-century England', *English Historical Review*, vol. 100 (April 1985), p. 286.

23 *Ibid.*, p. 300; Grey, *Debates*, vol. 9, p. 32; vol. 10, pp. 36–7, 341–3; Foley to Harley, 17 Sept. 1692, BL Portland Loan 29/135; Sunderland to Portland, 3 May 1693, Nottingham University Library, Portland Mss PwF 1212; Horwitz, *Luttrell Diary*, pp. 138, 311; *Calendar of State Papers Domestic* (1690–1), pp. 132, 465; (1691–2), pp. 352–3.

24 Davenant, *Works*, vol. 1, p. 62.

25 History of Parliament Transcripts, House of Lords RO, House of Commons Library Ms. 12 f. 106; [Sir Richard Temple], *An Essay uopn Taxes, calculated for the present Juncture of Affairs in England* (London, 1693), p. 12.

26 *Parliamentary History*, vol. 5, p. lxiv.

27 All Souls Mss 167, f. 37v.

28 Quoted in Leopold von Ranke, *A History of England, particularly in the seventeenth century* (6 vols., London, 1875), vol. 6, p. 240.

29 *Parliamentary History*, vol. 5, p. lxiv.

30 Colin Brooks, 'Public finance and political stability: the administration of the land tax, 1688–1720', *Historical Journal*, vol. 17, no. 2 (1974), pp. 281–300.

31 *Parliamentary History*, vol. 5, p. lx.

32 But see the alternative view that all taxes eventually fell on land discussed by William Kennedy, *English Taxation, 1640–1799* (London, 1913), pp. 80–1 and John Beckett in his 'Land tax or excise', p. 304.

33 Paul Foley to Robert Harley, 17 Sept. 1692, BL Portland Loan 29/135.
34 *Reasons most humbly submitted to the wisdom of Parliament for taking off the present duty of Excise upon Beer and Ale, and laying the Duty upon the Original Malt* (London, 1695), pp. 4, 16–18.
35 John Cary, *An Essay on the State of England* (Bristol, 1695), p. 174.
36 Robert to Sir Edward Harley, 5 Jan. 1691–2, BL Portland Loan 29/79.
37 My emphasis here differs from that of John Beckett who points to the growth in indirect taxes during the Nine Years War. (Beckett, 'Land Tax or Excise', pp. 298–9.) But many of these were customs and stamp duties, not excises, and apart from the higher duties on drink, the salt tax and the malt duty introduced at the end of the war, the new excises did not yield substantial amounts of revenue. Moreover as Figure 4.3 shows, the growth in the excise bureaucracy was neglible under William but nearly doubled under Anne.
38 *Calendar of State Papers Domestic* (1691–2), p. 410.
39 John Kenyon, 'Lord Sunderland and the king's administration', *EHR*, vol. 71, (1956), p. 581–2.
40 Peter Thomas, *The House of Commons in the Eighteenth Century* (Oxford, 1971), pp. 69, 72.
41 *The Wentworth Papers 1705–1739*, (ed.) J. J. Cartwright (London, 1883), p. 189; Kaye Parliamentary Diary, History of Parliament Trust, transcript.
42 A. P. Usher (ed.), *Two Manuscripts by Charles Davenant* (Baltimore, 1942), p. 101.
43 Colin Brooks, 'Projecting, political arithmetic and the act of 1695', EHR, vol. 97 (1982), p. 47.
44 *HMC Portland* III, p. 481.
45 Geoffrey Holmes, *British Politics in the Age of Anne* (revised edn, London, 1987), pp. 137–41.
46 J. A. Downie, 'The Commission of Public Accounts and the formation of the Country Party', *EHR*, vol. 91 (1976), pp. 33–51; A. MacInnes, *Robert Harley, Puritan Politician* (London, 1970), p. 42; Colin Brooks, 'The country persuasion and political responsibility in England in the 1690s', *Parliament, Estates and Representation*, vol. 4 (1984), pp. 142–3, 145–6.
47 *HMC Portland* III, p. 596.
48 See, for example, the action of a revenue officer against the Norfolk collector, Samuel Dashwood, in 1695. ('Treasury and Excise, 1689–1700', Customs and Excise Library, King's Beam House, ff. 126–8.')
49 Peter Dickson, *The Financial Revolution in England* (London, 1976), pp. 48–9, 52–7.
50 G. S. de Krey, *A Fractured Society: The Politics of London in the First Age of Party, 1688–1715* (Oxford, 1985), p. 109.
51 Rubini, 'The battle of the banks', *EHR*, vol. 85 (1970), pp. 693–714.
52 The relevant acts are 2 W. & M. c.4; 4 W. & M. c.5; 6 & 7 W. & M. c.1; 7 & 8 W. & M. c.10.
53 Excise Commissioners to Treasury, 1 Nov. 1692, PRO Treasury 48/88; Excise Commissioners to Treasury, 23 May 1695, PRO Customs 48/6 f. 26.
54 Davenant, *Works*, vol. 1, p. 139.
55 Dickson, *Financial Revolution*, p. 354.
56 *Ibid.*, pp. 353–5 for details of this episode.
57 Cf. Brooks, 'The country persuasion', pp. 141–2.
58 The classic work is J. G. A. Pocock, *The Machiavellian Moment* (Princeton, 1975), *passim*.
59 Brooks, 'The country persuasion', p. 146.

60 Holmes, *British Politics in the Age of Anne*, pp. xl–xli; David Hayton, 'The "country" interest and the party system, 1689–c.1720', in C. Jones (ed.), *Party and Management in Parliament, 1660–1784* (Leicester, 1984), pp. 45–9, 54–5.

61 Hayton, 'The "country" interest', pp. 42–3, 51–2.

62 Quoted in David Hayton, 'The "country" interest', p. 49.

63 *Ibid.*, pp. 50–2, 64; Holmes, *British Politics in the Age of Anne*, pp. 120, 138–41.

64 BL Portland Loan 29/45/44.

65 Brooks, 'The country persuasion', p. 144.

66 BL Portland Loan 29/288.

67 BL Portland Loan 29/136.

68 Horwitz, *Parliament, Policy and Politics*, Appendix D.

69 Holmes, *British Politics in the Age of Anne*, pp. 354, 364.

70 Horwitz, *Parliament, Policy and Politics*, pp. 311, 313–15.

71 Steven Baxter, 'The age of personal monarchy in England', *Eighteenth Century Studies Presented to Arthur M. Wilson*, (ed.) Peter Gay (Hanover, New Hampshire, 1972), pp. 3–11.

72 See p. 214.

IV

Introduction

1 [Joseph Massie], *Calculations of Taxes for a Family of Each Rank, Degree or Class: For One Year* (London, 1756), *passim.*

2 But see Peter Mathias, *The Transformation of England: Essays in the Economic and Social History of England in the Eighteenth Century* (London, 1979), ch. 6; Peter Mathias and Patrick O'Brien, 'Taxation in England and France', *Journal of European Economic History*, vol. 5 (1976), pp. 601–50; A. H. John, 'War and the English economy, 1700–1763', *Ec.H.R.*, series 2, vol. 7, no. 3 (1955), pp. 329–44.

Chapter 6: The Parameters of War

1 For an interesting and important discussion of these questions and of the debate about the role of the state and the possibility of free trade see Joyce Appleby, *Economic Thought and Ideology in Seventeenth-Century England* (Princeton, 1978), *passim.*

2 For the term 'blue water' policy see chapter 2 footnote 94.

3 Baugh, 'British strategy', pp. 90–1.

4 J. R. Jones, *Britain and the World, 1649–1815* (London, 1980), pp. 51–112.

5 See especially Donald Coleman, 'Mercantilism revisited', *Historical Journal*, vol. 23 (1980), pp. 774–85.

6 Jeremy Black, *British Foreign Policy in the Age of Walpole* (Edinburgh, 1985), p. 99.

7 G. C. Gibbs, 'Laying treaties before Parliament in the eighteenth century', in Ragnhild Hatton and M. S. Anderson (ed.), *Studies in Diplomatic History*, (Longmans 1970), pp. 116–37; Black, *British Foreign Policy*, pp. 75–89.

8 F. Crouzet, 'England and France in the eighteenth century: a comparative analysis of two economic growths', in Peter Mathias (ed.), *Causes of the Industrial Revolution in England* (London, 1967), pp. 146–8.

9 See p. 32.

10 Quoted in D. B. Horn, 'The cabinet controversy on subsidy treaties in time of peace, 1749–50', *EHR* vol. 26 (1930), p. 464.

11 Baugh, 'British Strategy', pp. 90–1.

12 Quoted in Richard Middleton, *Bells of Victory* (Cambridge, 1986), p. 77.

13 J. H. Parry, *Trade and Dominion: The European Overseas Empires in the Eighteenth Century* (New York, 1971), pp. 133–6.

14 Jonathan R. Dull, *The French Navy and American Independence* (Princeton, 1975), pp. 11, 49–60.

15 Piers Mackesy, *The War for America, 1775–1783* (Cambridge, Mass., 1965), p. 451.

16 *Ibid.*, p. 66.

17 *Ibid.*, p. 66.

18 *Ibid.*, pp. 510–16.

19 Paul Kennedy, *The Rise and Fall of British Naval Mastery* (London, 1976), p. 116.

20 It need hardly be added that very little of this literature makes mention of the fact that England was at war for much of this period.

21 See for example the discussion of trade figures in G. N. Clark, *Guide to English Commercial Statistics, 1696–1782* (London, 1938), esp. introduction.

22 N. F. C. Crafts, 'Economic growth in the eighteenth century: a re-examination of Deane and Cole's estimates', *Ec.H.R.*, 2nd series, vol. 29 xxix (1976), pp. 226–35; N. F. C. Crafts, 'British economic growth, 1700–1831: a review of the evidence' (working paper, Nov. 1982); C. K. Harley, 'British industrialization before 1841: evidence of slower growth during the industrial revolution', *Journal of Economic History*, vol. 42 (1982), pp. 267–90; Peter H. Lindert, 'Remodelling British economic history: a review article', *Journal of Economic History*, vol. 43 (1983), pp. 988–90.

23 Crafts, *British Economic Growth during the Industrial Revolution* (Oxford, 1985), p. 15.

24 N. F. R. Crafts, 'Industrial revolution in England and France: some thoughts on the question, "Why was England first" ', *Ec.H.R.*, vol. 30 (1977), pp. 438–9.

25 Cited in *ibid.*, p. 439.

26 Anthony Wrigley, 'Urban growth and agricultural change: England and the Continent in the early modern period', in Robert I. Rotberg and Theodore K. Rabb (eds.), *Population and Economy: Population and History from the Traditional to the Modern World* (Cambridge, 1986), p. 128. Much of what follows is based on Wrigley's important article, which depends, in turn, upon the findings of Jan de Vries in *European Urbanization, 1500–1800* (London, 1984), *passim*.

27 Wrigley, 'Urban growth and agricultural change', pp. 126, 130.

28 *Ibid.*, p. 148; cf. pp. 150–1.

29 *Ibid.*, pp. 140, 154, 158.

30 Figures from de Vries, *European Urbanization*, table 3.6.

31 Peter H. Lindert, 'English occupations, 1670–1811', *Journal of Economic History*, vol. 40 (1980), pp. 701–7; G. S. Holmes, 'Gregory King and the social structure of pre-industrial England', *TRHS*, 5th series, vol. 27 (1977), pp. 55–6; Peter H. Lindert and Jeffrey G. Williamson, 'Revising England's social tables, 1688–1812', *Explorations in Economic History*, vol. 19 (1982), pp. 385–408; Lindert and Williamson, 'Reinterpreting Britain's social tables', *Explorations in Economic History*, vol. 20 (1983), pp. 94–109; Wrigley, 'Urban growth and agricultural change', pp. 135–42; N. F. R. Crafts, *British Economic Growth*, pp. 13–16.

32 Crafts, *British Economic Growth*, pp. 48–69, esp. 67–8.

33 R. V. Jackson, 'Growth and deceleration in English agriculture, 1660–1790', *Ec.H.R.*, 2nd series, vol. 38, no. 3 (1985), pp. 333–51; Wrigley, 'Urban growth and agricultural change', p. 140; R. B. Outhwaite, 'English agricultural efficiency

from the mid-seventeenth century: causes and costs', *Historical Journal*, vol. 30, no. 1 (1987), pp. 202–3.

34 For the probable causes of these developments see E. L. Jones, 'Agriculture, 1700–80', in Roderick Floud and Donald McCloskey (eds.), *The Economic History of Britain since 1700* (2 vols., Cambridge, 1981), vol. 1, pp. 66–86.

35 Gabriel Ardant, 'Financial policy and economic infrastructure of modern states and nations', in Charles Tilly (ed.), *The Formation of National States in Western Europe* (Princeton, 1975), p. 166.

36 See the comments of Julian Hoppit, 'Understanding the industrial revolution', *Historical Journal*, vol.30, no. 1 (1987), p. 218.

37 The best study of this phenomenon is still R. B. Westerfield, *Middlemen in English Business, Particularly between 1660–1760* (reprint, Newton Abbot, 1968).

38 Eric Pawson, *Transport and Economy: The Turnpike Roads of Eighteenth-Century Britain* (London, 1977), pp. 296–7.

39 T. S. Willan, *The Inland Trade: Studies in English Internal Trade in the Sixteenth and Seventeenth Centuries* (Manchester, 1976), pp. 87–8.

40 Excise Commissioners to Treasury, 6 April 1759, PRO Customs 48/16 ff. 19–20.

41 David Hey, *Packmen, Carriers and the Packhorse Roads: Trade and Communications in North Derbyshire and South Yorkshire* (Leicester, 1980), pp. 192–3.

42 T. S. Willan, *An Eighteenth-Century Shopkeeper: Abraham Dent of Kirkby Stephen* (Manchester, 1970), pp. 28–30.

43 Roderick Floud and Donald McCloskey (eds.), *The Economic History of Britain since 1700: vol. 1, 1700–1860* (Cambridge, 1981).

44 David Hancock, Harvard University, Ph.D. in progress.

45 J. D. Marshall (ed.), 'The autobiography of William Stout', *Chetham Society*, 3rd series, vol. 14 (1967), p. 29.

46 For a fuller discussion of these phenomena see my 'Credit, clubs and independence', in Neil McKendrick, John Brewer and J. H. Plumb, *The Birth of a Consumer Society: The Commercialization of Eighteenth-Century England* (London, 1982), pp. 203–10; Julian Hoppit, 'The use and abuse of credit in eighteenth-century England', in Neil McKendrick and R. B. Outhwaite (eds.), *Business Life and Public Policy: Essays in Honour of D. C. Coleman* (Cambridge, 1986), pp. 64–78.

47 *Considerations on the Present State of the Nation, as to Public Credit, Stocks, the Landed and Trading Interests &c.* (London, 1720), pp. 19–20; *The Tradesman's Director, or the London and Country Shopkeeper's Useful Companion* (London, 1756), p. 10.

48 J. D. Marshall, 'Agrarian wealth and social structure in pre-industrial Cumbria', *Ec.H.R.*, 2nd series, vol. 33 (1980), p. 510.

49 G. H. Kenyon, 'Petworth Town and Trades, 1610–1760', *Sussex Arch. Colls.*, vol. 96 (1958), p. 82.

50 Mathias, *Transformation of England*, p. 94.

51 Hoppit, 'The use and abuse of credit',p. 66.

52 Charles Davenant, *The Political and Commercial Works of that Celebrated Writer Charles Davenant . . . collected and revised by Sir Charles Whitworth* (5 vols., London, 1771), vol. 1, p. 151.

53 *The Tradesman's Director*, pp. 8–10.

54 *Ibid.*, pp. 12–13.

55 See the excellent general discussion in T. S. Ashton, *Economic Fluctuations in England, 1700–1800* (Oxford, 1959), pp. 106–111.

56 *Considerations on the Present State of the Nation*, pp. 17–18.

57 *Calendar of Treasury Books, (CTB)* vol. 17 (1702), p. 163; *CTB*, vol. 17 (1703), p. 170; PRO Customs 48/12 f. 331; Customs 48/18 ff. 218–20; cf. L. S. Pressnell, 'Public monies and the development of English banking', *Ec.H.R.*, 2nd series, vol. 5 (1952–3), pp. 382–3, 390.

Chapter 7: War and Taxes

1 T. S. Ashton, *Economic Fluctuations in England, 1700–1800* (Oxford, 1959), *passim*.
2 Richard Pares, 'America versus continental warfare, 1739–63', *EHR*, vol. 51 (1936), p. 44.
3 Julian Hoppit, 'Financial crises in eighteenth-century England', *EcHR.*, 2nd series, vol. 29 1 (1986) pp. 39–58.
4 *Ibid.*, pp. 40–1, 45.
5 *Considerations on the Present State of the Nation as to Public Credit, Stocks, the Landed and Trading Interests &c* (London, 1720), pp. 17, 19. Cf. J. D. Marshall (ed.), 'The autobiography of William Stout', *Chetham Society*, 3rd series, vol. 14 (1967), pp. 44, 183.
6 Hoppit, 'Financial Crisis', p. 45.
7 Elizabeth Schumpeter, 'English prices and public finance, 1660–1822', *Review of Economic Statistics*, vol. 20 (1938), p. 26.
8 Patrick O'Brien, 'Agriculture and the home market for English industry, 1660–1820', *EHR*, vol. 100 (1985), pp. 793–5.
9 *Ibid.*, p. 793.
10 Peter Mathias, *The Brewing Industry in England, 1700–1830* (Cambridge, 1959), p. 360.
11 Ralph Davis, *The Rise of the English Shipping Industry in the Seventeenth and Eighteenth Centuries* (London, 1962), p. 87.
12 Ralph Davis, *The Rise of English Shipping*, pp. 87–8, 318–19; Richard Pares, *War and Trade in the West Indies, 1739–63* (Oxford, 1936), pp. 470, 495–6; A. H. John, 'The London Assurance Company and the marine insurance market of eighteenth-century London', *Economica*, vol. 25 (1958), pp. 126–9, 137–8; Patrick Crowhurst, *The Defence of British Trade, 1688–1815* (Folkestone, 1977), pp. 87–8, 95–6.
13 H. E. S. Fisher, *The Portugal Trade: A study in Anglo-Portuguese Commerce, 1700–1770* (Oxford, 1959), *passim*. For examples of other rate increases see Davis, *The Rise of English Shipping*, pp. 318–19.
14 H. S. K. Kent, *War and Trade in the Northern Seas* (Cambridge, 1973), p. 72; Pares, *War and Trade in the West Indies*, p. 500.
15 Davis, *The Rise of English Shipping*, p. 198.
16 T. S. Ashton and Joseph Sykes, *The Coal Industry of the Eighteenth Century*, 2nd edn (Manchester, 1964), pp. 200–1.
17 O'Brien, 'Agriculture and the Home Market', pp. 793–5; Ashton and Sykes, *The Coal Industry*, appendix F.
18 Marshall, 'The Autobiography of William Stout', p. 138.
19 These are my readings of Patrick O'Brien's series in 'Agriculture and the home market', pp. 787–99.
20 Davis, *The Rise of British Shipping*, pp. 72–3.
21 Douglas Hay, 'War, dearth and theft in the eighteenth century: the record of the English courts', *Past and Present*, vol. 95 (1982), p. 141.
22 *Gibbon's Journal*, ed. D. M. Low (London, 1929), 4 Dec. 1762. I owe this reference to Marcia Wagner Levinson.

23 A. H. John, 'War and the English economy, 1700–1763', *EcHR.*, 2nd series, vol. 7 (1955), pp. 330–3.

24 Daniel Baugh, *British Naval Administration in the Age of Walpole* (Princeton, 1965), p. 254.

25 For the importance of the north-eastern and American dockyards see Davis, *The Rise of British Shipping*, pp. 62–70.

26 BL Portland Loan 29/287.

27 Paul Kennedy, *The Rise and Fall of British Naval Mastery* (London, 1983), pp. 79, 85.

28 Crowhurst, *The Defence of British Trade*, pp. 18–19.

29 G. N. Clark, *The Dutch Alliance and the war against French Trade, 1688–1697* (Manchester, 1923), p. 61; G. N. Clark, 'War Trade and Trade War, 1701–1713', *EcHR.*, vol. 1 (1927–8), p. 266. More work needs to be done on English privateering.

30 Kennedy, *British Naval Mastery*, p. 93.

31 Larry Neal, 'Interpreting power and profit in economic history: a case study of the Seven Years War', *Journal of Economic History*, vol. 37 (1977), p. 28.

32 Davis, *The Rise of English Shipping*, p. 318.

33 Lawrence and Jeanne Stone, *An Open Elite?: England, 1540–1880* (Oxford, 1984) p. 199.

34 Marshall, 'The autobiography of William Stout', pp. 164–5.

35 Richard Chandler, *The History and Proceedings of the House of Commons* (14 vols., 1742–4).

36 Quoted in G. Holmes, *British Politics in the Age of Anne*, revised edn (London, 1987), p. 177.

37 W. Kennedy, *English Taxation, 1640–1799* (London, 1913), p. 80 and note; *Parliamentary History*, vol. 5, p. lxii.

38 M. Thompson (ed.), 'Letters of Humphrey Prideaux, sometime Dean of Norwich to John Ellis, sometime Under-Secretary of State, 1674–1722', *Camden Society*, new series, vol. 15 (1875), p. 199.

39 Hence the willingness of some pamphleteers in the country interest to support a general excise as an alternative to high land taxes, a position diametrically opposed to that of most country politicians in the 1690s (e.g. *The State and Condition of our Taxes Considered: or a Proposal for a Tax upon Funds, by a Freeholder* (London, 1714), p. 16).

40 E.g. *Some Considerations upon Taxes, and upon the Debts of the Nation. By the author of a Scheme for establishing a militia of 1700 Volunteers* (Eton, n.d.), p. 3; *A Letter from a Freeholder on the late Reduction of the Land Tax to one shilling in the Pound By a Member of the House of Commons* (London, 1732), pp. 7, 44–5; *A Letter to a Member of Parliament: shewing the justice of a more equal and impartial Assessment on Land* (London, 1717), *passim*; *An Essay on the Inequality of our Present Taxes, particularly the Land Tax* (London, 1746), *passim*; *Thoughts on the Pernicious Consequences of Borrowing Money* (London, 1756), p. 6.

41 R. A. C. Parker, 'Direct taxation on the Coke estates in the eighteenth century', *EHR*, vol. 71 (1956), pp. 247–8.

42 Holmes, *British Politics in the Age of Anne*, p. lvii.

43 *Ibid.*, p. lvii.

44 T. S. Ashton, *An Economic History of England: the Eighteenth Century* (London, 1955), p. 27.

45 Sir John Habakkuk, 'The rise and fall of English landed families, 1600–1800: I', *TRHS*, 5th series, vol. 29 (1979) pp. 202–3.

46 Quoted in David Joslin, 'London Bankers in Wartime, 1739–84', in L. S. Pressnell (ed.), *Studies in the Industrial Revolution*, (London, 1960), p. 168.

47 Sir John Habakkuk, 'The rise and fall of English landed families, 1600–1800: II', TRHS, 5th series, vol. 30 (1980), p. 210.

48 *Ibid.*, p. 216.

49 Holmes, *British Politics in the Age of Anne*, lv-lxi for an excellent summary of this material.

50 In making this claim I am, of course, drawing a distinction between the 'landed interest', employed as an economic category and the 'country interest', used as a political term.

51 Cf. *Considerations upon a Reduction of the Land Tax* (London, 1749), pp. 26–7.

52 For Walpole's claim see *Letter to a Freeholder* pp. 4–5.

53 Chandler, *History* vol. 7, pp. 289–92.

54 [Josiah Tucker], *A Brief Essay on the Advantages and Disadvantages which respectively attend France and Great Britain, with regard to Trade*, 2nd edn (London, 1750), p. xi.

55 See Kennedy, *English Taxation, 1640–1799*, pp. 127–8.

56 John Beckett, 'Local land tax administration', in M. Turner and D. Mills (eds.), *Land and Property: The English Land Tax, 1692–1832* (Gloucester, 1986), p. 166.

57 Holmes implies this in *British Politics in the Age of Anne*, p. lvii.

58 Jonathan Leape, unpublished paper, Harvard University.

59 O'Brien, 'The political economy of British taxation', *Ec.H.R.*, forthcoming.

60 Habakkuk, 'The rise and fall of English landed families: II', pp. 219–21.

61 N. C. Hunt, 'A consideration of the relationship between some religious and economic organizations and government, especially from 1730 to 1742' (Ph. D. thesis, Cambridge University, 1951), p. 314.

62 Quoted in E. Hughes, *Studies in Administration and Finance', 1558–1825* (Manchester, 1934) p. 301.

63 Lawrence and Jeanne Stone, *An Open Elite?* pp. 226–7.

64 For an interesting discussion of this question see Neil McKendrick, 'Gentlemen and players revisited: the gentlemanly ideal, the business ideal and the professional ideal in English literary culture', in *Business Life and Public Policy*, Neil McKendrick and R. B. Outhwaite (eds.) (Cambridge, 1986), pp. 98–136, esp. pp. 110–12.

65 For these criticisms see Peter Dickson, *The Financial Revolution in England* (London, 1967), pp. 17–32. For comments on the limited efficacy of many of these criticisms see the summary in Holmes, *British Politics in the Age of Anne*, pp. xlvii–liii.

66 *The State and Condition of our Taxes*, pp. 35–6.

67 R. D. Richards, *The Early History of Banking in England* (London, 1929), pp. 74–8.

68 De Krey, *A Fractured Society: The Politics of London in the First Age of Party, 1688–1715* (Oxford, 1985), pp. 106–112, 131–2.

69 *Ibid.*, pp. 238–43.

70 *Ibid.*, pp. 156.

71 See, for example [James Drake], *An Essay concerning the Necessity of Equal Taxes* (London, 1702), *passim*.

72 Lewis Namier, *The Structure of Politics at the Accession of George III*, 2nd edn (London, 1965), p. 55.

73 Norman Baker, *Government and Contractors: The British Treasury and War Supplies, 1775–1783* (London, 1971), pp. 225–7.

74 Namier, *Structure of Politics*, p. 47, n. 1; Sir Lewis Namier and John Brooke, *The History of Parliament: The House of Commons, 1754–1790* (3 vols., HMSO, 1964), vol. 3, p. 40.

75 Baker, *Government and Contractors*, p. 247.

76 Quoted in Namier and Brooke, *History of Parliament*, vol. 2, p. 21.

77 *Ibid.*, vol. 2, p. 444.

78 Richard Grassby, 'Merchant fortunes', *Past and Present*, vol. 46 (1970), p. 100.

79 Quoted in Namier, *The Structure of Politics*, p. 50.

80 Holmes, *British Politics in the Age of Anne*, p. li.

81 *Taxes Not Grievous, And therefore not a Reason for an Unsafe Peace* (London, 1712), pp. 16–18, 20.

82 *An Essay upon Publick Credit, in a Letter to a Friend Occasioned by the Fall in Stocks* (London, 1748), p. 5.

83 See, for example, the speech of Danvers in *HMC Egmont Diary*, vol. 1, p. 64.

84 Thomas Mortimer, *The Elements of Commerce, Politics and Finances, In three Treatises on these important Subjects. Designed as a Supplement to the Education of British Youth, after they quit the public Universities or private Academies* (London, 1772), pp. 365, 378, 381.

85 Ralph Davis, 'The rise of protection in England, 1689–1786', *Ec.H.R.*, 2nd series, vol. 19 (1966), pp. 308–13.

86 *Third Report from the Committee, appointed to enquire into the illicit practices used in defrauding the revenue*, 23 March 1784, pp. 16–17.

87 Elizabeth Hoon, *The Organization of the English Customs System, 1696–1786* (Newton Abbot, 1968), p. 33.

88 M. Postlethwaite, *Universal Dictionary of Trade and Commerce*, 4th edn (2 vols., London, 1774), entry 'Customs'.

89 Jacob M. Price (ed.), *Joshua Johnson's Letterbook, 1771–1773: Letters from a Merchant in London to his Partners in Maryland* (London Record Society, vol. 15, 1979), pp. 2, 4.

90 *Ibid.*, pp. xxiii, 2, 43.

91 Jacob M. Price, *Credit and Capital in British Overseas Trade: The View from the Chesapeake, 1700–1776* (Harvard, 1980), pp. 62, 100.

92 Price, *Joshua Johnson's Letterbook*, p. 134.

93 Chandler, *History*, vol. 7, p. 360.

94 Quoted in Edward Hughes, *Studies in Administration and Finance, 1558–1825, with Special Reference to the History of Salt Taxation in England* (Manchester, 1934), p. 359.

95 See Chapter 8.

96 W. A. Cole, 'Trends in eighteenth-century smuggling', *Ec.H.R.*, vol. 10, no. 3 (1958), p. 399.

97 *Further Considerations upon a Reduction of the Land Tax* (1751), p. 11.

98 Cole, 'Trends in eighteenth-century smuggling', pp. 395–409; W. A. Cole, 'The arithmetic of eighteenth-century smuggling', *Ec.H.R.*, vol. 28, no. 1 (1975), pp. 44–9; Hoh-cheung and Lorna H. Mui, 'Trends in eighteenth-century smuggling reconsidered', *Ec.H.R.*, vol. 28 (1975), pp. 28–43.

99 Marshall, 'The autobiography of William Stout', p. 147.

100 See PRO Customs 48/20 f. 123.

101 Although, as I emphasized in Chapter 4, the revenue officers were *not* overly worried about loss of revenue through smuggling. Their concern was with the safety of their officers. The government worried about public order, and the Treasury about possible loss of income, but the revenue commissioners looked on smuggling as the inevitable cost of high duties. (See *First Report from the*

Committee appointed to enquire into the illicit practices used in defrauding the revenue (1783), p. 8; Robert Nash, 'The English and Scottish tobacco trades in the seventeenth and eighteenth centuries: legal and illegal trade', *Ec.H.R.*, vol. 35, no. 3 (1982), pp. 371–2.)

102 The relevant statutes are 20 G.2 c.10; 16 G.3 c.34; 17 G.3 c.39; 24 G.3 c.31.
103 This account is reconstructed from Richard Burn, *The Justice of the Peace and the Parish Officer*, 15th edn (4 vols., London, 1785), vol. 2, pp. 52–6; *Instructions for Officers concerned in Ascertaining the Duties on Candles in the Country* (London, 1774), passim.
104 Joseph Pacey, *Reminiscences of a Gauger: Imperial Taxation, Past and Present, Compared* (Newark, 1873), p. 56; *Instructions to Officers*, p. 5.
105 PRO Customs 103/1, Page versus Moxon and Barnes, 13 Feb. 1778, f. 24; Caleb Danvers, *The Second Part of an Argument against Excises; in answer to the objections of several writers* (London, 1733), p. 19.
106 Such claims may seem a trifle sensational, but there is ample evidence that the exciseman's reputation as a roué and philanderer was justified. (See e.g., John Cannon, *Diary*, ff. 63, 68, 150; BL Harleian Mss 4077 f. 50v; PRO Customs 47/24 f. 21; 47/982 f. 29; 47/83 f.93; 47/152 f. 27; 48/13 ff. 81–2 for the sexual activities of excisemen.)
107 Chandler, *History*, vol. 9, p. 58.
108 *Ibid.*, pp. 396–7.
109 Kennedy, *English Taxation, 1640–1799*, pp. 114, 123–4, 132–3.
110 The elder Pitt on the other hand wanted to raise a general excise in order to create a huge free-trade zone.
111 *Ibid.*, pp. 113–21.
112 Chandler, *History*, vol. 7, p. 229.
113 Most recently Patrick O'Brien in his 'Political economy of taxation in England' (*Ec.H.R.*, Forthcoming).

V

Chapter 8: The Politics of Information

1 The following discussion owes much to an unpublished paper by Joanna Innes, 'The collection and use of information by government, circa 1690–1800'. I am grateful to her for allowing me to see this important essay.
2 See pp. 109–10.
3 *The Economic Writings of Sir William Petty, together with the Observations on the Bills of Mortality more probably by Captain John Graunt*, (ed.) Charles Henry Hull (2 vols., New York, 1963), vol. 1, pp. 239, 244.
4 Quoted in Patricia Kline Cohen, *A Calculating People* (Chicago, 1982), pp. 28–9.
5 Charles Davenant, *The Political and Commercial Works of that Celebrated Writer, Charles Davenant . . . collected and revised by Sir Charles Whitworth* (5 vols., London, 1771), vol. 1, pp. 131, 135.
6 G. N. Clark, *A Guide to English Commercial Statistics* (London, 1938), pp. 1–42.
7 B. L. Portland Loan 29/408 item 46.
8 J. Clarke, *The Housekeepers and Clarks Assistant* (London, 1783); Thomas Lydal, *Vulgar and Decimal Arithmetic Demonstrated* (London, 1710); Thomas Lydal, *A New Interest Pocket-Book* (London, 1710); Thomas Chaloner, *The Merriest Poet in Christendom; or Chaloner's Miscellany, being a salve for every sore* (London, 1731), pp. 92–3.
9 John Jackson, *Mathematical Lectures, Being the First and Second That were read to the Mathematical Society at Manchester* (Manchester, 1719).

10 Lists of these materials are in Sheila Lambert (ed.), *Sessions Papers of the Eigh-teenth-Century House of Commons* (145 vols., Wilmington, Delaware, 1975), vol. 1, pp. 67–71.

11 Joanna Innes, 'Collection and use of information by government and others, 1688–1800', unpublished paper.

12 Transcript of the Cocks Parliamentary Diary f. 68. History of Parliament Trust.

13 For the votes see Lambert, *Sessions papers of the Eighteenth-Century House of Commons*, vol. 1, pp. 15–16 and her article.

14 *Ibid.*, vol. 1, pp. 15–16.

15 M. Postlethwayt, *Universal Dictionary of Trade and Commerce* (2 vols., London, 1774); Richard Rolt, *A New Dictionary of Trade and Commerce, compiled from the information of the most eminent merchants, and from the works of the best writers on commercial subjects, in all languages* (London, 1756); Thomas Mortimer, *The Elements of Commerce, Politics and Finance, in three treatises on those important subjects. Designed as a supplement to the education of British youth, after they quit the public universities or private academies* (London, 1772).

16 E. G. R. Taylor, *The Mathematical Practitioners of Tudor and Stuart England* (Cambridge, 1968), pp. 145–6.

17 *The Accomplished Merchant, by a Merchant of London* (London [1740]), p. 12.

18 *Ibid.*, p. 14.

19 For which see Ian Hacking, *The Emergence of Probability* (London, 1975), and Daniel Garber and Sandy Zabell, 'On the emergence of probability', *Archive for History of Exact Sciences* vol. 21 (1979), pp. 33–53.

20 *A Short Account of the Society for Equitable Assurances on the Lives and Survivor-ships, established by deed, inrolled in his Majesty's Court of King's Bench at Westminster* (London, 1776), p. 3.

21 N. C. Hunt, 'A consideration of the relationship between some religious and economic organizations and the government, especially from 1730 to 1742' (unpub. Cambridge Ph.D. thesis, 1951), p. 280.

22 A point first made by Charles Wilson, 'Government policy and private interest in modern English history', *Economic History and the Historian: Collected Essays* (London, n.d.), p. 143.

23 John Money, *Experience and Identity: Birmingham and the West Midlands, 1760–1800* (Manchester, 1977), p. 33.

24 Alison G. Olson, 'The Virginia Merchants of London: a study in eighteenth-century interest-group politics', *William and Mary Quarterly*, vol. 40 (1983), p. 374.

25 PRO customs 48/7 f. 12.

26 J. M. Norris, 'Samuel Garbett and the early development of industrial lobbying in Great Britain', *Economic History Review*, 2nd series, vol. 10 (1958), p. 459.

27 L. A. Clarkson, 'The leather crafts in Tudor and Stuart England', *Agriculture History Review*, vol. 14 (1966), p. 27.

28 P. D. G. Thomas, *The House of Commons in the Eighteenth Century* (Oxford, 1971), pp. 17–19.

29 A. N. Newman (ed.), 'Parliamentary diary of Sir Edward Knatchbull', *Camden Society*, 3rd series, vol. 94 (1965), p. 145.

30 I owe this point to Vivien Dietz.

31 I owe this point to Joanna Innes. Fifty-four constituencies sent instructions to their MPs to vote against Walpole's Excise Bill in the early months of 1733. (Paul Langford, *The Excise Crisis: Society and Politics in the Age of Walpole* (Oxford, 1975), pp. 47, 172.)

32 Sir W. S. Prideaux, *Memorials of the Goldsmiths Company, being gleanings from*

their Records between the Years 1335 and 1815 (2 vols., privately printed, 1890), vol. 2, p. 231.

33 Edward Mayer, *The Curriers of the City of London* (privately printed, 1968), pp. 128–9.

34 Calculated from Distillers Journal, 1720–56, Guildhall Library, London Mss 6207/1A and Distillers Accounts, Guildhall Mss 6203/1.

35 Olson, 'Parliament, the London lobbies, and provincial interests in England and America', *Historical Reflections*, vol. 6 (1979), p. 369.

36 Quoted in Orlo Cyprian Williams, *The Clerical Organization of the House of Commons 1661–1850* (Oxford, 1954), p. 307. This figure is born out by the advice that James Watt received in 1775, when he was informed by friends that an act to extend his steam engine patent would cost £110. The actual cost was £119 8s. 4d. (Eric Robinson, 'Matthew Boulton and the art of parliamentary lobbying', *Historical Journal*, vol. 7, no. 2 (1964), p. 214).

37 Playing Card Makers. Court Minutes, vol. 2 (1674–1726), London Guildhall Mss. 5963 f. 104 v.

38 Brewers Company, Minutes 1691–1707, London Guildhall Mss 5445/24.

39 Brewers Company Minutes Book, 1691–1707, London Guildhall Mss 5445/24.

40 Gold and Silver Wire Drawers Company Minutes, London Guildhall Mss 2451/ 1 f. 308.; Horace Stewart, *History of the Worshipful Company of Gold and Silver Wiredrawers* (privately printed, 1891), p. 65.

41 R. C. Gwilliam, 'The Chester tanners and parliament, 1711–1717', *Journal of the Chester and North Wales Architectural, Archaeological and Historical Society*, vol. 44 (1757), p. 48. I owe this reference to Joanna Innes.

42 Lillian M. Penson, 'The London West India interest in the eighteenth century', *EHR*, vol. 36 (1921), pp. 383–4.

43 Quoted in Francis G. James, 'The Irish lobby in the early eighteenth century', *EHR*, vol. 81 (1966), pp. 543, 549.

44 Minutes of the Court of Company of Playing Card Makers, vol. 2 (1674–1726), London Guildhall Mss 5963.

45 Chandler, *History*, vol. 7, p. 352.

46 Peter Shakerley, MP for Chester quoted in Gwilliam, 'The Chester tanners and parliament', p. 46.

47 J. H. Plumb, *Sir Robert Walpole: The King's Minister* (London, 1960), pp. 270–1.

48 The Diary of Stephen Monteage, London Guildhall Mss 205/1 ff. 31–140.

49 Prideaux, *Memorials of the Goldsmiths Company*, pp. 224–5.

50 Guildhall Mss 6203/1, 6203/2, 6207/1, 6207/1A, 6208/4.

51 Bryant Lillywhite, *London Coffee Houses* (London, 1963), nos. 23, 558, 1480.

52 Sheila Lambert, *Bills and Acts: Legislative Procedure in Eighteenth-Century England* (Cambridge, 1971), pp. 7, 10.

53 D. L. Rydz, *The Parliamentary Agents, A History* (London, Royal Historical Society, 1979), p.31.

54 Material on these men is derived from the City company accounts in the Guildhall Library.

55 Accounts of the Gold and Silver Wire Drawers Company, Guildhall Mss 2452/1.

56 James, 'The Irish lobby in the early eighteenth century', pp. 554–5.

57 Quoted in Robinson, 'Boulton and the art of parliamentary lobbying', p. 219.

58 Lambert, *Bills and Acts*, p. 45.

59 Williams, *Clerical Organization*, pp. 133, 140.

60 Lambert, *Bills and Acts*, p. 50.

61 See, for example, James Lowther to Sir John Lowther, 1 Jan. 1701/2, Lowther Mss LW2/D34.

62 *Egmont Diary*, vol. 1, p. 149.

63 Curriers Company Accounts, London Guildhall Mss 14346 vol. 3, f. 404.

64 I draw this conclusion from an examination of the Eighteenth-Century Short Title Catalogue.

65 Distillers Journal, 1730–1756, London Guildhall Mss 6207/1A.

66 E. R. Turner, 'The excise scheme of 1733', *EHR*, vol.42 (1927), pp. 56–7 lists some of the major works.

67 *Post-man*, 2, 9, 30 Oct; 4, 17 Nov; 15 Dec. 1705. I owe this reference to Lee Davison; Hughes, *Studies in Administration and Finance*, p. 258.

68 Letterbook of Messrs Lascelles and Maxwell, 17 Jan. 1743–4, pp. 82–3 quoted in Lilian Penson, 'The London West India interest in the eighteenth century', *EHR*, vol.36 (1921), p. 380.

69 Money, *Experience and Identity*, p. 25.

70 Olson, 'Parliament, the London lobbies', *Historical Reflections*, vol. 6 (1979), p. 377.

71 *A Just and Exact Account taken out of the Books of several Brickmakers, Lime-burners, Tilemakers, Slaters, Masons and Paviours, of the Goods made, or brought in by them, within the weekly Bills of Mortality, or within Ten Miles of same, in the year 1711, in relation to the intended Duties on Bricks, Lime, Tiles, &c. humbly offer'd to the Consideration of this Hon. House* (Goldsmiths Library, Broadsides no. 1664).

72 PRO Customs 48/18 ff. 458–9.

73 *The Case of the Parish of St. Giles Cripplegate, before the Act for laying a Duty on Gilt and Silver Wire* (London), [1712?].

74 Innes, 'The Collection and use of information by government', p. 19.

75 Vivien Dietz, 'Direct taxation in England in the eighteenth century' (Harvard undergraduate thesis, 1985).

76 Gwilliam, 'Chester Tanners and Parliament', p. 46.

77 *Calendar of Treasury Papers 1731–4*, p. 564.

78 *Reasons against laying an Additional Duty on Muscovada Sugar, and more particularly against levying it by an Excise on Refined Sugar* [London, 1743–4].

79 Quoted in Hughes, *Studies in Administration and Finance*, p. 227.

80 *Political Register*, vol.4 (1772), p. 163.

81 *Distilled Spiritous Liquors the Bane of the Nation* (London, 1736), pp. iv–v.

82 Ibid., p. vi.

83 *An Impartial Enquiry into the present State of the British Distillery* (London, 1736), p. 2.

84 Jacob Price, 'The excise crisis of 1733', in Steven Baxter (ed.) *England's Rise to Greatness, 1688–1763* (Los Angeles, 1983), pp. 257–321.

85 Adam Smith, *An Inquiry into the Nature and Causes of The Wealth of Nations*, (ed.) Edwin Cannan (2 vols. in 1, Chicago, 1976), vol.1, pp. 143, 278.

86 PRO Customs 48/18 f. 236.

87 PRO Customs 48/19 ff. 174–8.

Index